DEDICATION

This book is affectionately dedicated to my parents, Jack and Marion, whose support of my eclectic interests from an early age resulted in a life-long fascination with the world.

Afoot and Afield in Los Angeles County

Jerry Schad

Photos and Maps by the Author

Wilderness Press
Berkeley

ACKNOWLEDGEMENTS

Many people have offered their time, talents, and knowledge during the various phases of producing this book. I would like to thank Ralph and Beth Davis, John Elwin, Ellen Feeney, Mike Fry, Rosalind Gold, Jerry Herring, Dan McNeill, Jane Rauch, Nick Soroka, Pamela Stricker, Gene and Emily Troxell, Charles Wilken, and my wife, René, for sharing adventures with me on the trail, and for helping with transportation during the past two years. Several people associated with local parks and preserves, and Angeles National Forest have been of assistance too, among them Margie Behm, Donald Gilliland, Gerald Reponen, and Larry Walters. Cathey Byrd designed the symbols that appear at the top of every trip description. Tom Winnett of Wilderness Press, in his usual meticulous way, superbly edited the text. I would also like to thank Tom for his sound advice and guidance during this and previous "Afoot and Afield" projects. Final appreciation goes to my wife, René, for patience and encouragement during a period in which I seemed to be either somewhere in the mountains above L.A., or behind a closed door toiling in front of my computer.

Jerry Schad
El Cajon, California
November 1990

Design by Thomas Winnett

Library of Congress Card Catalog Number 91-12466
International Standard Book Number 0-89997-102-4

Manufactured in the United States of America

Published by Wilderness Press
2440 Bancroft Way
Berkeley, CA 94704
(510) 843-8080

Write for free catalog

Library of Congress Cataloging-in-Publication Data

Schad, Jerry.
    Afoot and afield in Los Angeles County / Jerry Schad. -- 1st ed.
        p.   cm.
    Includes bibliographical references and index.
    ISBN 0-89997-102-4
    1. Hiking--California--Los Angeles County--Guide-books. 2. Los Angeles County (Calif.)--Description and travel--Guide-books.
    I. Title.
    GV199.42.C22L647 1991
    917.94'93--dc20   91-12466
                                                          CIP

PREFACE

Pummelled by great heavings of the earth's crust, desiccated by drought, torn by flood, tortured by fire, and pestered by the threat of human intervention, L.A.'s wild spaces are nonetheless not the wastelands they may appear to be when viewed through a brown veil of smog. In fact, if you take the time to venture almost anywhere beyond the sprawling metropolitan borders, you'll discover Nature is not only alive out there, it's often triumphant.

While doing field research for this book I've clambered over sandstone boulders the size of trucks, cooled off in the spray of frothing waterfalls, and trekked down a "wild and scenic" river. In the high country of the San Gabriel Mountains, I stood in stunned silence as a herd of two dozen bighorn sheep scooted across a rocky pass just below me. From a chaparral-clad slope above Glendale, I witnessed the strange juxtaposition of a deer's silhouette against the Oz-like towers of downtown L.A.

With friends I've admired sea stars in crystalline tidepools on the Malibu coast, scuffed through powdery snow in the San Gabriels, and inhaled the nectar-rich air of the Mojave Desert in bloom. From the Angeles Crest we've spotted white sails in Santa Monica Bay, and watched the sun sink toward a blue horizon dimpled by four offshore islands. Alone at dawn on the mile-high rim of the L.A. Basin, I've watched the glare of a million lights succumb to the pink twilight.

In all my field trips for this book (totalling more than 1000 miles of walking), never have I needed to venture more than 20 air-miles from the fringe of Los Angeles or its populous satellite cities. Yet once on the trail, I've seldom felt the weight of the teeming millions all around me; indeed in a few places I've walked all day without seeing another person.

Amazingly enough, only on a couple of occasions did I have to put up with the noxious clouds of smog trapped low over the city or borne into the backcountry by the winds. A careful reading of weather conditions and judicious and timely choices among the many possible places to visit in the county often yielded for me the special treat of pristine air and hundred-mile vistas.

This wide-ranging guidebook covers an equally wide-ranging county—a kingdom in itself with elements of coast, foothill, mountain, and desert rolled into a 4083-square-mile space. Remove the urbanized coastal plain and the semi-developed western Mojave from the county's area and you're still left with nearly 2000 square miles of wild or lightly developed land.

Most of L.A. County's publicly accessible open spaces lie north and west of the heavily populated coastal plain. Angeles National Forest, encompassing most of the San Gabriel Mountains, sprawls across 652,000 acres (1019 square miles), about one-quarter of the county's land area. In spite of Southern California's dry climate, the Angeles Forest supports about 240 miles of perennial streams and in some areas a forest cover resembling parts of the high Sierra Nevada. About 600 miles of trail (including a segment of the Pacific Crest National Scenic Trail) connect high and low points within the Forest and link together such disparate locations as the L.A. Basin and the Mojave Desert.

Tucked into the southwestern corner of the county and spilling over into Ventura County are the Santa Monica Mountains. This coastal range includes a patchwork of private and public lands, the latter under the jurisdiction of the National Park Service (Santa Monica Mountains National Recreation Area) and various state and local agencies. The pace of park-land acquisition in the Santa Monicas has quickened in recent years, and the trail network is rapidly expanding.

Close to the heart of the county's urban core are scattered islands of open space—the Santa Susana and Verdugo Mountains bordering the San Fernando Valley, the Puente Hills in the San Gabriel Valley and, of course, venerable Griffith Park.

Rounding out the list of better places to explore in the county are some more-or-less natural stretches of Pacific coastline, the rim of the western Mojave Desert, and Santa Catalina Island—most of which is managed for recreation by the L.A. County Parks Department.

Despite extensive coverage in this book of all the areas mentioned above, I will refer you to additional sources for more information on specific areas: John Robinson's classic *Trails of the Angeles* in many respects complements my coverage of the San Gabriel Mountains. *The Pacific Crest Trail, Vol. 1: California* (Schaffer, Schifrin, Winnett, Jenkins) contains a complete log and maps of the trail's route through the San Gabriel Mountains. Dennis Gagnon's *Hike Los Angeles, Vol. 1 and 2* includes hikes in and around the L.A. Basin. Milt McAuley's *Hiking Trails of the Santa Monica Mountains* is a good resource for that area. My two earlier volumes, *Afoot and Afield in San Diego County* and *Afoot and Afield in Orange County,* cover regions which are not within the scope of this book, but still within a short drive of Los Angeles. More reading resources can be found in Appendix 2 of this book.

Every trip in this book was hiked by me at least once during the period 1988–90, and every effort has been made to ensure that the information herein is current as of the day of publication. Road access and trailheads do change, however. New acreage is being acquired for public use, and the 1990s will doubtless see the construction of many new trails. Updates and new editions of this book are planned for the future. You can keep me apprised of recent developments and/or changes by writing me in care of Wilderness Press, 2440 Bancroft Way, Berkeley, CA 94704. Your comments will be appreciated.

Contents

Introduction

Coastline

Basin and Foothills

Santa Monica Mountains

Angeles Forest

Santa Catalina Island

Appendices

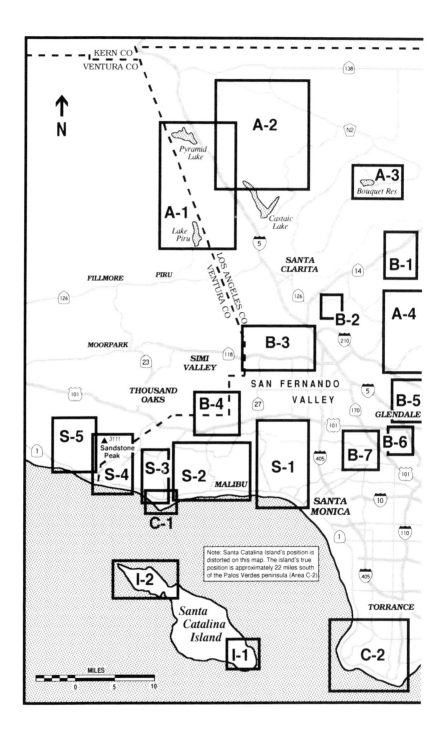

N

KERN CO
VENTURA CO

A-2

A-3
Bouquet Res

Pyramid
Lake

A-1

Castaic
Lake

Lake
Piru

5

SANTA
CLARITA

B-1

FILLMORE   PIRU

LOS ANGELES CO
VENTURA CO

126

126

B-2

A-4

MOORPARK

210

SIMI
VALLEY

118

B-3

23

101

THOUSAND
OAKS

SAN FERNANDO
VALLEY

27

B-4

5

170

B-5

GLENDALE

101

1

S-5

▲3111
Sandstone
Peak

S-4

S-3

S-2

MALIBU

S-1

405

B-7

B-6

101

10

SANTA
MONICA

C-1

1

110

405

Note: Santa Catalina Island's position is
distorted on this map. The island's true
position is approximately 22 miles south
of the Palos Verdes peninsula (Area C-2)

I-2

TORRANCE

Santa
Catalina
Island

I-1

C-2

MILES

0   5   10

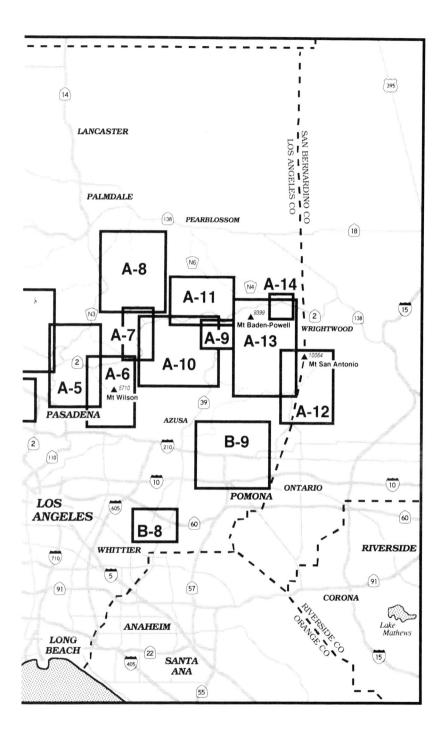

Author in the field

INTRODUCING LOS ANGELES COUNTY

Los Angeles County sits astride one of the earth's most significant structural features—the San Andreas Fault. For more than 10 million years, earth movements along the San Andreas and neighboring faults have shaped the dramatic geology and topography evident throughout the region today. The very complexity of the shape of the land has in turn spawned a variety of localized climates. The varied climates, along with the diverse topography and geology, have resulted in a remarkably diverse array of plant and animal life.

Exploring all this wonderful variety right in L.A.'s back yard is not hard to do. Conveniently enough, many of the best hiking opportunities start right on the edge of town—right off the freeway. Other trailheads can be quickly reached by way of lesser roads such as Pacific Coast Highway, Mulholland Highway, and Angeles Crest Highway. Fewer than a dozen of the hikes described in this book involve any kind of dirt-road driving to reach, and every trip (except for those on Santa Catalina Island) lies within 90 minutes drive of downtown L.A.—assuming light traffic.

In the next few pages of this book, we'll examine Los Angeles County's several climates, its spectacular geology, and its native plants and animals. In the short sections that follow, you'll find some important notes about safety and appropriate behavior on the trail; some useful tips on how to use this book effectively; and finally some helpful advice on how to choose and time your visits so as to avoid smog, excessive heat, and other discomforts that can detract from an otherwise pleasant outing. After perusing that material, you can dig into the heart of this book—descriptions of 175 hiking routes from the coast to the mountains, from sea level to 10,000 feet. Happy reading—and happy hiking!

Land of Many Climates

A fairly accurate and succinct summary of Los Angeles County's climate might take the form of just two phrases: "warm and sunny," and "winter-wet, summer-dry." In the world-wide range of climates, this pattern is called a Mediterranean-type climate, typical of less than 3 percent of the world's landmass.

Actually, a lot of variation exists, a fact readily apparent to anyone traveling almost any direction through the county. Inland, away from the moderating influence of the ocean, temperatures usually climb higher in the day and usually drop lower at night. Also, higher elevations mean cooler temperatures and more rainfall. Since both of these influences are at work in the L.A. area, it's helpful to picture the county as divided into several climate zones, each zone characterized by particular combination of weather characteristics. Informally, let's divide the county into five climate zones: coastal, inland valley, transitional, mountain, and high desert.

The coastal (or "maritime fringe") zone extends only a few miles inland across the coastal slopes of the Santa Monica Mountains, but about 15 miles across the flat, central urban basin of Los Angeles. Moist air from over the cool Pacific waters sweeps into this zone with some regularity during the daytime hours, while at night the "marine layer" often turns into fog or low overcast. Average Fahrenheit temperatures range from the 60s/40s (daily high/low) in winter, to the 70s/60s in summer. Rainfall averages about 12–15 inches annually, except in the Santa Monicas. The higher profile of this coastal range snags extra moisture from rain-bearing winter storms, yielding an extra 10–15 inches.

The inland valley zone encompasses such corners of urban L.A. as the San Gabriel and San Fernando valleys, plus the north slope of the Santa Monica Mountains and the lower foothills of the San Gabriel Mountains. This area, only partly under the influence of moderating sea breezes, experiences more extreme temperatures, both daily and seasonally: typically 60s/30s in winter and 90s/50s in summer. Precipitation averages about 15 inches annually, somewhat more in the foothills.

Higher lands even more removed from coastal influences are classified as having either transitional or mountain climates. Both these zones are found in interior mountain ranges and are characterized by somewhat lower average temperatures. The subtle difference between the two involves rainfall. Annual rainfall in the semi-arid transition zone, which encompasses the northwest corner of Angeles National Forest (the Saugus Ranger District) and the desert-facing slopes of the San Gabriel Mountains, is typically about 15–20 inches. The mountain climate zone, including most of the "Front Range" of the San Gabriels (facing the San Gabriel Valley) and the higher country along Angeles Crest High-

way, receives upwards of 30 inches—enough to support large areas of coniferous and broadleaf forest. Mt. Wilson, in the Front Range, for example, gets about 35 inches of precipitation, including about four feet of snow, annually. Average temperatures there range from 50s/30s in winter to 80s/50s in summer. Mt. Wilson's hilltop position spares it from the effects of cold-air drainage at night; so the day-night thermometer change is rather small. Not so for the canyon bottoms, especially in winter, when temperatures can plummet more than 40°F as the sun sinks out of sight.

In the "High Country" of the San Gabriel Mountains, enough snow falls and remains on the ground during the winter to permit skiing for about four months a year in a few areas. Several small but thriving winter-sports facilities exist here. Still higher, Mt. San Antonio (10,064') lies very near timberline, where the climate verges on alpine.

North of the San Gabriels, 50 or more miles inland, lies the county's driest climate zone, the high desert, which encompasses the westernmost Mojave Desert—the Antelope Valley. This area is almost completely cut off from the moderating influence of the ocean, and it experiences a relatively extreme "continental" type of climate. Temperatures typically range from 50s/20s in winter to 90s/60s in summer. The coastal mountains serve as a barrier to rain-bearing clouds moving inland, so annual precipitation amounts to only about 7 inches—somewhat more at the western tip of the valley near Interstate 5, and somewhat less at the county's northeast corner near Edwards Air Force Base.

The above "average" statistics tell only part of the story. Hot spells, for example, descend upon the county with some regularity, especially in the fall when searing Santa Ana winds come roaring down through the mountain passes toward the coast. This condition occurs when dry air moves southwest from a high-pressure area in the interior U.S. out toward southern

California. Flowing across low gaps in the mountains (notably Cajon Pass on the east flank of the San Gabriels, and Soledad Pass south of Palmdale), this air sometimes reaches the coastline or even Santa Catalina Island. As the air moves downward, it compresses and warms about 5°F for every 1000 feet of descent. At Malibu or Santa Monica, daytime highs can soar to 90–100°, rivaling the hottest temperatures recorded nationwide that day. High in the mountains, Santa Anas are much cooler, but they can assume gale and even hurricane force. Mt. Wilson has experienced more than a hour of steady winds in the 80–90-mile-per-hour range.

Santa Ana winds spread wildfires easily. Early Santa Anas (October and November) often coincide with the tail end of months of summer drought. Most wildfires in L.A. County are quickly controlled, but the combination of hot winds, dry chaparral and flammable hillside homes has set the stage time and time again for disasters of monstrous magnitude.

In a similar way, the generally bland average statistics for rainfall fail to reveal the normal situation—which is, metaphorically, feast or famine. A string of drought years can be followed by one or two very wet ones. In wet years much of the moisture received comes in the form of rather short but intense winter storms. A case in point is a monumental downpour recorded in January 1942 at Hoegee's Camp in the Front Range of the San Gabriels: more than 26 inches of rain fell in a 24-hour period. On another occasion in the San Gabriels, a rain gauge collected one inch in one minute. When dumped on steep slopes denuded of vegetation after a fire, such intense rainfall sends "debris flows"—torrents of water, rocks and soil with a consistency of wet aggregate cement—down through the canyons.

Despite Nature's occasional temper tantrums, more than nine times out of ten your outings in Los Angeles County are likely to coincide with dry weather and tempera-tures in a moderate register—for at least part of the day. Few other areas around the country, and probably no other great city in the world, can offer such good odds.

Reading the Rocks

A good way to approach the subject of L.A. County's geology is to think about the *geomorphology,* or shape and structure, of the landscape. Of California's many geomorphic provinces, the County claims parts of three: the Los Angeles Basin, the Transverse Ranges, and the Mojave Desert. The bulk of the county's urban area dominates the Basin province, while the mostly undeveloped San Gabriel Mountains and semi-developed Santa Monica Mountains (the two containing the majority of the hikes written up in this guide) belong to the Transverse Ranges. Since only a few of the trips in this guide border on, and none actually touch, the Mojave Desert, it will not be discussed in any detail here.

The Los Angeles Basin province extends from the base of the San Gabriel and Santa Monica Mountains in the north to the Santa Ana Mountains and San Joaquin Hills of

Jeffrey pines on Pacifico Mountain

Orange County on the south. It's a huge, deeply folded basin filled to a depth of up to 6 miles by some volcanic material and land-deposited sediments, but mostly by sediments of marine origin—sand and mud deposited on the ocean bottom from 80 million years ago to as recently as 1 million years ago.

Then, after uplift during the past 1–2 million years, the surface of the basin accumulated a layer of terrestrial sediment shed from the surrounding hills and mountains. The basin, in fact, would still be filling with sediment today were it not for the installation of flood-control barriers in the mountains, dams to catch debris at the

mouths of the canyons, and more than 2000 miles of storm drains and concrete-lined flood channels that carry flood waters to the sea. (Amazingly, some of the sediment cleaned out from behind the flood-control dams is trucked back up into the mountains; there's no room for it down in the city!)

The Transverse Ranges province encompasses in Los Angeles County the Santa Monica and San Gabriel mountains, plus the mini-ranges of Liebre Mountain, Sawmill Mountain, and Sierra Pelona lying northwest of the San Gabriels. Outside L.A. County, the province takes in part of the coastal mountains of Santa Barbara and

Major mountains, basins, streams and faults in Los Angeles County

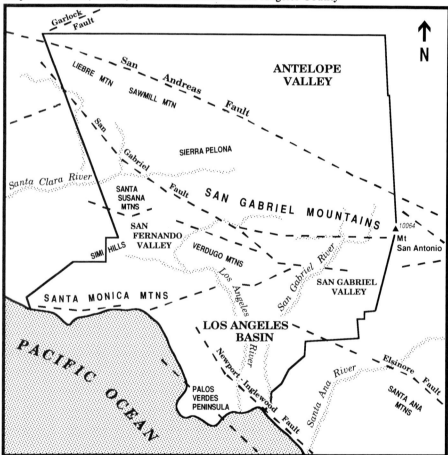

Ventura County, and the San Bernardino and Little San Bernardino mountains. As indicated by the name "Transverse," these east-west trending mountains stand crosswise to the usual northwest-southeast grain of California's other major mountain groups—Coast Ranges, Sierra Nevada, and Peninsular Ranges. This "kink" in the alignment of California's mountains is mirrored by a similar east-west jog in the San Andreas Fault, which defines the north edge of the San Gabriel Mountains.

The San Andreas Fault, of course, represents the boundary between two of the earth's major tectonic plates—the largely oceanic Pacific Plate and the largely continental North American Plate. For at least 10 million years, lands on the west side of the boundary have been sliding (often lurching) northwest relative to lands on the east side. Currently the average rate of movement is about 2 inches per year—enough, if it continues, to put Los Angeles abreast of San Francisco about 10 million years from now. A growing body of evidence now suggests that the movements along the San Andreas Fault do not simply involve one plate slipping past another; they also produce compression, which accelerates and possibly controls the process of mountain building along the central and southern California coast. In the area of the kink, centered on the San Gabriel Mountains, the compression forces are greatest. In this view, the San Gabriels are being squeezed horizontally about a tenth of an inch each year, and being thrust upward much more rapidly than that. At the same time, the Los Angeles Basin, which is underlain by folded and crumpled structures under its blanket of sediment, may be losing an average of ¼ acre per year due to compression.

The kink in the San Andreas Fault, and therefore in the alignment of the coastal mountains, might be explained by the fact that the part of the North American Plate over Nevada and Utah is stretching and spreading outward because it is thin and is closer to the earth's mantle there. The western Mojave Desert, which rides on the western edge of the North American Plate, may be jamming against the plate boundary, producing the kink.

Regardless of what has pushed them to their present heights, the mountains of the Transverse Range are relatively young as upthrust units—only a few million years old. This is not true of the ages of most of the rocks that compose them. The oldest rock found exposed in the Santa Monica Mountains—Santa Monica Slate—checks out at about 150 million years. Some rocks in the San Gabriels are representative of the oldest found on the Pacific Coast—over 600 million years of age.

The geologic history of the San Gabriels, which have been called the most complicated mountain range in North America, may never be fully deciphered. As one expert put it, "The San Gabes look like a flake kicked around on plate boundaries for hundreds of millions of years."

Caught in the tectonic frenzy of the moment, San Gabriel Mountains are surging upward as fast as any mountain range on earth, They are also disintegrating at a spectacular rate. Although they consist mainly of durable granitic rocks, much like those in the sturdy Sierra Nevada, the San Gabriel rocks have been through a tectonic meat grinder. Like mountains made of soft material, the tops of the San Gabriels are rounded. But the slopes are often appallingly steep and unstable. An average of 7 tons of material disappears from each acre of the front face each year, most of the coming to rest behind debris barriers and dams below. As you hike through the San Gabriel Mountains, and also the Santa Monicas (which to a lesser degree suffer erosion problems), the ultimate futility of dam-building, road-building, even trail-building in many places will become readily apparent. Like sand-castles waiting for the next ocean tide, the manmade improvements and even the natural vegetation clinging to mountain slopes wait for advancing tides of fire, flood, and earthquake to sweep them away.

Native Gardens

As mentioned earlier, Los Angeles County's varied climate, topography and geology have set the stage for a remarkable diversity of plants. There's a second reason too: Los Angeles County, and coastal Southern California for that matter, lies between two major groups of flora: a southern group represented by drought-tolerant plants characteristic of northern Mexico, and a northern group represented by moisture-loving plants typical of the Sierra Nevada and California's north coastal ranges. As the climate fluctuated, seesawing from cool and wet to warm and dry over the past million years or so, species from both groups invaded the present-day county borders. Once established, many of these species remained in protected niches even as the climate turned unfavorable for them. Some survived unchanged; others evolved into unique forms. Some are present today only in very specific habitats.

Several common, widely distributed trees—digger pine, limber pine, bigleaf maple, valley oak, and California buck-eye—reach their southernmost limits on the Pacific coast in or near Los Angeles County. California walnut and bigcone Douglas-fir, the former a foothill-dwelling tree and the latter an inhabitant of the higher mountains, have more restricted ranges centered approximately on the L.A. Basin. The Joshua tree, the trademark of the Mojave Desert, reaches its westernmost limit near Interstate 5 in northern L.A. County, and is widely distributed in the Antelope Valley and along the northern base of the San Gabriels.

The bulk of Los Angeles County's undeveloped and naturally vegetated land can be grouped into several general classes, which botanists often call plant communities or plant associations. In a broader sense, these are biological communities, because they include animals as well as plants. Several of the major plant communities in the county are briefly described, in the order you would encounter them on a journey from the coast, up into the San Gabriel High Country, and then down to the desert.

The sage-scrub (or coastal sage-scrub) community lies mostly below 2000 feet elevation, on south-facing slopes in the Santa Monica Mountains, the Simi Hills, the Santa Susana Mountains, and on some of the lower, hotter slopes of the San Gabriel Mountains. The dominant plants are small shrubs, typically California sagebrush, black sage, white sage, and California buckwheat. Two larger shrubs often present are laurel sumac and lemonade berry, which like poison oak are members of the sumac family. In some areas along the coast, prickly-pear cactus thrives within this community. Interspersed among the somewhat pliable and loosely distributed shrubs is a variety of grasses and wildflowers, green and colorful during the rainy season, but dry and withered during the summer and early fall drought. Much of the sage-scrub vegetation is "summer-deciduous"—dormant and dead-looking during the warmer half of the year, lush green and aromatic during the cool, wet half.

The *chaparral* community is commonly found between 1000 and 5000 feet elevation just about anywhere there's a slope that hasn't burned recently. Were it not for roads, firebreaks, and other interruptions, the chaparral would run in wide unbroken swaths along the flanks of most of the county's mountains. At low elevations, chaparral (which requires more moisture than sage-scrub) tends to stick to slopes protected from the full glare of the sun. At higher elevations, which get more rainfall, chaparral takes over the south slopes, while oaks and conifers thrive on slopes receiving less sun. The dominant chaparral plants include chamise, scrub oak, manzanita, toyon, mountain mahogany, and various forms of ceanothus ("wild lilac"). Yuccas, known for their spectacular candle-shaped blooms, often frequent the chaparral zones. The chaparral plants are tough and intricately branched, evergreen shrubs with deep root systems that help the plants survive during the long, hot summers. Chaparral is sometimes referred to as "elfin forest"—a good description of a mature stand. Without benefit of a trail, travel through mature chaparral, which is often 15 feet high and incredibly dense all the way up from the ground, is almost impossible.

The *coniferous forest,* which has two phases in Los Angeles County, takes over roughly above 4000 feet elevation, at least in areas with sufficient rainfall. The "yellow-pine" phase includes conifers such as bigcone Douglas-fir, ponderosa pine, Jeffrey pine, sugar pine, incense cedar, and white fir, and forms tall, open forest. These species are often intermixed with live oaks, California bay (bay laurel), and scattered chaparral shrubs such as manzanita and mountain mahogany. Higher than about 8000 feet, in the "lodgepole-pine" phase, lodgepole pine, white fir, and limber pine are the indicator trees. These trees, somewhat shorter and more weather-beaten than those below, exist in small, sometimes dense

stands, interspersed with such shrubs as chinquapin, snowbrush, and manzanita.

Pinyon-juniper woodland is found in narrow zones bordering the Antelope Valley and along the semi-arid Soledad Canyon area southwest of Palmdale, elevation roughly 3000–5000 feet. Here are found a couple of rather stunted conifers—the one-leaved pinyon pine and the California juniper. Usually these trees do not predominate, but are mixed with typical chaparral shrubs.

Joshua tree woodland, found in scattered locales along the north base of the San Gabriel Mountains, and more abundantly on rocky hills poking up from the Antelope Valley floor, is dominated by an outsized member of the yucca family—the Joshua tree. (L.A. County's best spot to view them is Saddleback Butte State Park east of Lancaster—not covered in this guidebook.)

Aside from this coast-to-desert cross-section of plant communities, there are others of more restricted range:

Bigcone Douglas-fir forest, San Gabriel Mountains

Joshua trees on Antelope Valley rim

Southern oak woodland, widely distributed in coastal and inland valleys and on some of the mountains near Antelope Valley's western tip, consists of dense to open groves of live oak, valley oak (near the coast), black oak (near the desert), and California walnut trees. Scattered conifers such as Coulter pine, digger pine, and bigcone Douglas-fir intermix with the oaks in some areas.

Riparian (streamside) *woodland,* one of the rarest (in terms of the land it covers) communities, thrives at lower and mid-elevations where water is always present on or close to the surface. Massive live oaks, sycamores, alders, bigleaf maples and cottonwoods, and a screen of water-hugging willows are the hallmarks of riparian woodland. Not only is this kind of environment essential for the continued survival of many kinds of birds, animals and fish, it is also very appealing to the senses. Riparian woodland is somewhat reminiscent of Eastern forests, with a palpable sense of dampness year round. Much of this habitat in

Southern California has been destroyed or is threatened by continued unbanization and attendant development of water resources or flood-control measures.

Other communities found in snippets along the coast or far afield in the Mojave Desert are *rocky shore, coastal strand, coastal salt marsh, freshwater marsh, grassland, sagebrush scrub, creosote-bush scrub,* and *alkali sink.* In many places in the foothills and mountains of the county you will also find planted trees introduced from other parts of the world. Eucalyptus, pepper, and other exotic trees are often on the sites of many old ranches, while many roadsides, especially in the Angeles National Forest, have been planted with drought-resistant cypress trees and non-native pines. Some of the non-urbanized areas of the county are natural grasslands given over to agriculture and grazing. In areas characterized by heavy grazing, one finds grassy flats and bald slopes—sometimes called *potreros* (pastures)—supporting mostly non-native vegetation like wild oats, filaree, fennel, mustard, and thistle.

Early-to-mid spring is the best time to appreciate the cornucopia of Los Angeles County's plant life. Many of the showiest species—spring wildflowers, for example—brighten the sage-scrub and chaparral zones at that time, and other plants exhibit fresh new growth. Peak periods for wildflowers vary according to elevation, slope, and proximity to coastal fogs. Generally, April is the best month.

One of the county's best wildflower spots (not covered in the trip descriptions that follow) is the Antelope Valley California Poppy Reserve, a small state park west of Lancaster. Parched and uninspiring 10 or 11 months of the year, it comes alive (most years) with carpets of orange poppies around April. These desert-dwelling members of a species that is more at home in the valleys and hills of central California evidently invaded the Antelope Valley through low-elevation passes to the west.

Creatures Great and Small

One's first sighting of a mountain lion, a bighorn sheep, an eagle, or any other seldom-seen form of wildlife is always a memorable experience, Because of the diversity and generally broad extent of its habitats, and the inaccessibility of many of its wilderness areas, Los Angeles County plays host to a healthy population of indigenous creatures. If you're willing to stretch your legs a bit and spend some time in areas favored by wild animals, you'll eventually be rewarded with some kind of close visual contact.

The most numerous large creature in the county is the mule deer, with a population of a least several thousand. Deer are abundant in areas of mixed forest and scattered chaparral up in the higher mountains, and also close to the coast in the Santa Monica Mountains. Deer like to have a protective screen of vegetation near them at all times, and a good supply of succulent leaves to munch on, so you won't often see them in wide-open spaces.

The mountain lion, once hunted to near-extinction in California, has made a substantial comeback. In Los Angeles an estimated 15 lions roam the San Gabriel Mountains, and a few more have been spotted in the Santa Monica Mountains. They're secretive, but wide-ranging creatures, so you're much more likely to spot the tracks of this cat than meet one face to face. Much more common is the bobcat, often seen scampering through the canyons of the Santa Monicas.

A few black bears (some of them "problem bears" deported from Yosemite) inhabit the deeper canyons of the San Gabriels; you're likely to come upon their scat if you spend much time in the more remote spots.

Coyotes are universally abundant, adapting to just about any habitat (except the urban core) with ease. At the foot of the mountains, where the urban-wildland interface is often a matter of a backyard fence or the curb of a cul-de-sac, coyotes make regular forays into the suburbs to snatch small pets or obtain water and food left unattended.

The county's most interesting (and surprisingly abundant) large mammal is the bighorn sheep. Some 700 of these agile animals maintain a tough existence on the steep slopes and rocky crags of the San Gabriel Mountains. Unlike mule deer, the bighorn prefer lightly vegetated, rugged terrain, on which they are capable of escaping almost any predator. They also shun contact with humans, although its not unusual to spot them quite near such popular High Country summits as Mts. Williamson and Baden-Powell. The sheep are superbly adapted to surviving on meager supplies of water and coarse vegetation, conditions that characterize the San Gabriel and Sheep Mountain wilderness areas, which were set aside partly for their benefit.

The county's mammals also include gray fox, raccoon, and various rabbits, squirrels, woodrats, and mice. Amphibians include tree frogs, salamanders, and pond turtles. Many streams supporting populations of rainbow trout exist in the San Gabriels. Some are artificially stocked to meet the demand of fishermen; others are natural fisheries where catch-and-release is the only method allowed. The tiny, unarmored three-spine stickleback, an endangered species, inhabits streams in Soledad and Bouquet canyons.

Among the commonly seen reptiles are rattlesnakes, which we will discuss in the next section.

Bird life is varied in the county, not only because of the coast-to-desert range of habitats, but also because the county lies along the Pacific Flyway route of spring-fall migration and also serves some overwintering birds.

Los Angeles County is also an ancestral home of several other creatures symbolic of wild America. California condors, having recently been removed from their last stronghold in Ventura County for breeding purposes, were commonly seen over the San Gabriel and Santa Monica Mountains at the turn of the century. It is expected they will be reintroduced to the Sespe country of Los Padres National Forest, and possibly to parts of the Saugus District of Angeles National Forest, sometime in the early 90s. Suitable habitat for the peregrine falcon exists in the Angeles Forest, and nesting pairs will probably be reintroduced there as well.

Hunted and trapped with vigor until about a century ago, grizzly bears were once the terror of the San Gabriel Mountains. (Thankfully for hikers, they won't return.) Also gone are the pronghorn antelope that once wintered in the Antelope Valley. Unaccustomed to barriers in their natural open habitat, the pronghorn would not cross or jump over even the most trivial obstacles. Fences and railroads built across Mojave Desert migration routes sealed their fate— death by starvation.

Health, Safety and Courtesy

Good preparation is always important for any kind of recreational pursuit, and hiking Southern California's backcountry is no exception. Although most of our local environments are usually not hostile or dangerous to life and limb, there are several pitfalls to be aware of.

Preparation and Equipment

An obvious safety requirement is being in good health. Some degree of physical conditioning is always desirable, even for those trips in this book designated as easy or moderate (rated ★ and ★★ in difficulty). The more challenging trips (rated ★★★, ★★★★ and ★★★★★) require increasing amounts of stamina and technical expertise. Fast walking, running, bicycling, swimming, aerobic dancing, and similar kinds of exercise that develop both the leg muscles and the aerobic capacity of the whole body are recommended as preparatory exercise.

For long trips over rough trails or cross-country terrain (there are several of these in this book) there is no really adequate way to prepare other than practicing the activity itself. Start with easy- or moderate-length cross-country trips first to accustom the leg muscles to the peculiar stresses involved in "boulder-hopping" or "non-technical climbing" (scrambling over steep terrain), and to acquire a good sense of balance. As we note later, sturdy hiking boots are recommended for such travel, primarily from a safety standpoint.

Several of the hiking trips in this book reach elevations of 7000 feet or more—altitudes at which sea-level folks may notice a big difference in their rate of breathing and their energy. A few hours or a day spent at altitude before exercising will help almost anyone acclimate, but that's often impractical for short day trips. Still, you might consider spending a night at Buckhorn Campground (6450′) or Crystal Lake Campground (5800′) before taking a hike along the Angeles Crest, or at Manker Flats Campground (6000′) before tackling Old Baldy. Altitude sickness strikes some victims at elevations as low as 8000 feet. If you become dizzy or nauseous, or suffer from congested lungs or a severe headache, the antidote may be as simple as descending one or two thousand feet.

An important aspect of preparation is the choice of equipment and supplies. The essentials you should carry with you at all times in the remote areas are the things that would allow you to survive, in a reasonably comfortable manner, one or two unscheduled nights out. It's important to note that no one ever plans these nights! No one plans to get lost, injured, stuck, or pinned down by the weather. Always do a "what if" analysis for a worst-case scenario, and plan accordingly. These essential items are your safety net; keep them with you on day hikes, and take them with you in a small day pack if you leave your backpack and camping equipment behind at a campsite.

Chief among the essential items is *warm clothing*. Inland Los Angeles County is characterized by wide swings in day and night temperatures. In mountain canyons and valleys, a midday temperature in the 70s or 80s can be followed by a subfreezing night. Carry light, inner layers of clothing consisting of polypropylene or wool (best for cool or cold weather), or cotton (fine for warm or hot weather, but very poor for cold and damp weather). Include a thicker, insulating layer of polyester "pile" or "fleece," wool, or down to put on whenever needed, especially when you are not moving around and generating heat. Add to this a cap, gloves, and a water-proof or water-resistant shell (a large plastic trash bag will do in a pinch)—and you'll be quite prepared for all but the most severe weather experienced in Southern California.

In hot, sunny weather, sun-shielding clothing is another "essential." This would normally include a sun hat and a light-colored, long-sleeve top.

Water and *food* are next in importance. Most streams and even some springs in the mountains have been shown to contain unacceptably high levels of bacteria or other contaminants. Even though most of the remote watersheds are probably pristine, it's wise to treat by filtering or chemical methods any water obtained outside of developed camp or picnic sites. Unless the day is very warm or your trip is a long one, it's usually easiest to carry (preferably in sturdy plastic bottles) all the water you'll need. Don't underestimate your water needs: during a full day's hike in 80° temperatures you may require as much as a gallon of water. Food is necessary to stave off the feeling of hunger and keep energy stores up, but it is not nearly as critical as water is in emergency situations in which water is needed to prevent dehydration.

Down the list further, but still "essential" for backcountry hikes, are a *map* and *compass, flashlight, fire-starting devices* (examples: water-proof matches or lighter, and candle), and *first-aid kit.*

Items not always essential, but potentially very useful and convenient, are sunglasses, pocket knife, whistle (or other signalling device), sunscreen, and toilet paper. (Note: sunglasses are an essential item for travel over snow.)

The essential items mentioned above should be carried by every member of a hiking party, because individuals or splinter groups may end up separating from the party for one reason or another. If you plan to hike solo in the backcountry, being well-equipped is very important. If you hike alone, be sure to check in with a park ranger or leave your itinerary with a responsible person. In that way, if you do get stuck, help will probably come to the right place—eventually.

Taking children on hiking outings involves a special kind of responsibility. "Project Hug-a-Tree" can provide you with information about training and outfitting a child to cope with the possibility of getting lost in the wilderness (send a self-addressed, stamped envelope to 6465 Lance Way, San Diego, CA 92120).

Special Hazards

Other than getting lost or pinned down by a sudden storm, the four most common hazards found in the L.A. County backcountry are steep, unstable terrain; icy terrain; rattlesnakes; and poison oak. Exploring some parts of the San Gabriel Mountains—even by way of the trails—involves travel over structurally weak rock on steep slopes. The erosive effects of flowing water, of wedging by roots and by ice, and of brush fires tend to pulverize such rock even further. Slips on such terrain usually lead to sliding down a hillside some distance. If you explore cross-country, always be on the lookout for dangerous run-outs, such as cliffs, below you. The side-walls of many canyons in the San Gabriels may look like nice places to practice rock-climbing moves, but this misconception has contributed to many deaths over the years.

Statistically, mishaps associated with snow and ice have caused the greatest number of fatalities in the San Gabriel Mountains. This is not because the San Gabriels are somehow inherently more dangerous than other ranges. Rather, it is because inexperienced lowlanders, never picturing their backyard mountains as true wilderness areas, are attracted here by the novelty of snow and the easy access by way of snow-plowed highways. Icy chutes and slopes capable of avalanching can easily trap such visitors unaware. Winter travel in the more gentle areas of the high country can be accomplished on snowshoes or skis; but the steeper slopes require technical skills and equipment such as ice axe and crampons, just as in any other high mountain range.

Rattlesnakes are fairly common in most parts of Los Angeles County below about 7000 feet. Seldom seen in either cold or very hot weather, they favor temperatures in the 75–90° range—mostly spring through fall in the lower areas, and summer in the higher mountains. Most rattlesnakes are as interested in avoiding contact with you as you are with them. The more hazardous areas include rocky canyon bottoms with running streams. Watch carefully where you put your feet, and especially your hands, during the warmer months. In brushy or rocky areas where sight distance is short, try to make your presence known from afar. Tread with heavy footfalls, or use a stick to bang against rocks or bushes. Rattlesnakes will pick up the vibrations through their skin and will usually buzz (unmistakably) before you get too close for comfort.

Poison oak grows profusely along many of the county's canyons below 5000 feet. It is often found on the banks of streamcourses in the form of a bush or vine, where it prefers semi-shady habitats. Quite often, it's seen beside or encroaching on well-used trails. Learn to recognize its distinctive three-leaved structure, and avoid touching it with skin or clothing. Since poison oak loses its leaves during the winter months (and sometimes during summer and fall drought), but still retains some of the toxic oil in its stems, it can be extra hazardous at that time because it is harder to identify and avoid. Mid-weight pants, like blue jeans, and a long-sleeve shirt will serve as a fair barrier against the toxic oil of the poison oak plant. Do, of course, remove these clothes as soon as the hike is over, and make sure they are washed carefully afterward.

Here are a few more tips:

Ticks can sometimes be a scourge of overgrown trails in the sage-scrub and chaparral country, particularly during the first warm spells of the year, when they climb to the tips of shrub branches and lie in wait for warm-blooded hosts. Ticks are especially abundant along trails used by cattle, deer, or coyotes. If you can't avoid brushing against vegetation along the trail, be sure to check yourself for ticks frequently. Upon finding a host, a tick will usually crawl upward in search of a protected spot, where it will try to attach itself. If you can be aware of the slightest irritations on your body, you'll usually intercept ticks long before they attempt to bite.

Despite the recent interest in and the increased use of hiking trails in Los Angeles County, there is paradoxically less money (especially in Angeles National Forest) for building and maintaining them. Much of that work is left to volunteer crews nowadays. In the chaparral areas, trails can become overgrown quickly, so that travel along them can become an exercise in bushwhacking. Traveling certain trailless canyon bottoms and ridgelines also involves some bushwhacking. Blue jeans (despite their reputation as being worthless in cold, wet

Poison oak leaves

conditions) are very good at protecting your legs when you're dodging or pushing through dry chaparral.

Camping and Permits

Overnight camping in roadside campgrounds is not always a restful experience. Off-season camping (late fall through early spring) offers relief from crowds, but not from chilly nighttime weather. Campgrounds in Angeles National Forest are less well supervised than those in the Santa Monica Mountains, and therefore sometimes attract a noisy crowd. In my experience, facilities with a "campground host" promise a better clientele, and a better night's sleep.

The nice advantage of a developed campground is that you can always have a campfire there—unless the facility itself is closed. On the National Forest trails, campfires are allowed most of the year in the stoves provided at trail camps or on ground cleared to bare mineral soil to a 5' radius (campfire builders must also carry a shovel to bury the embers). Fire permits, valid for the length of a fire season, must be obtained from the Forest Service for the use of any campfire or flame device (camp stoves, gas lanterns) on the trail from May 15 to the first soaking rains of the following fall or winter. Often during that period, a "very high fire danger" is declared and Stage I restrictions go into affect which prohibit open wood fires, but allow the operation of gas stoves in the above-mentioned cleared areas. "Extreme fire danger" conditions may either close parts of National Forest areas to all entry, or result in Stage II restrictions for campers—no fire use of any kind outside of developed recreation sites.

Be aware that any jurisdiction—national forest, state, county, city, or private—may declare fire closures in which all access is prohibited during critical fire conditions. Call first if you're in doubt.

Angeles National Forest allows "remote," primitive-style camping: under it, you are not restricted to staying at a developed campground or designated trail camp. For sanitation reasons, you are required to locate your primitive camp at least 200 feet from the nearest source of water. And, of course, you must observe the fire regulations stated earlier. Contact the Forest Service to confirm these rules if you intend to do any remote camping.

Most federally managed wilderness areas around the state require special wilderness permits for entry. At present, however, permits are not required for San Gabriel Wilderness, nor for Sheep Mountain Wilderness *except* at the East Fork Station gateway, where self-registering permits are offered. Cucamonga Wilderness in San Bernardino County (included in one hike in this book) does require a wilderness permit.

Other Regulations

This book contains much trail information of interest to mountain bikers. Mountain-biking regulations, however, vary according to jurisdiction. Currently, bikes are allowed on all Angeles National Forest

Setting up at Buckhorn Campground

roads and trails except the Pacific Crest Trail and trails within wilderness areas. Elsewhere, bikes are usually permitted on fire roads, but not on "single-track" trails. Mountain bikers should yield the right-of-way to both hikers and equestrians.

Deer hunting season in Angeles National Forest occurs during mid-autumn. Although conflicts between hunters and hikers are rare, you may want to confine your explorations at that time to the state, county, and city parks, where hunting is prohibited.

Once allowed over a wide area of the mountains, target shooting is now legally restricted to private shooting ranges and to a number of designated shooting areas in Angeles National Forest. Some illegal shooting continues to take place in canyons just off some of the mountain highways. Try to report this kind of activity to the sheriff or a ranger. Shooting in the lawful pursuit of game is easy to distinguish from automatic-weapon fire in undesignated areas.

For Your Protection

There is always some risk in leaving a vehicle in an unattended area. Automobile vandalism, burglary, and theft are small but distinct possibilities. Report all theft and vandalism of personal property to the county sheriff, and report vandalism of public property to the appropriate park or forest agency.

Obviously it is unwise to leave valuable property in an automobile. To prevent theft of the car, you can disable your car's ignition system or use a locking device on the steering wheel. Many of the routes in this book are written up as one-way, point-to-point trips requiring either a car shuttle (leaving cars at both ends) or an arrangement by which someone drops you off and later picks you up. Choose the latter method if you're concerned about security.

Trail Courtesy

Whenever you travel in the natural areas of the county, you take on a burden of responsibility—keeping the backcountry as you found it. Aside from common-sense prohibitions against littering, vandalism, and illegal fires, there are some less obvious guidelines every hiker should be aware of. We'll mention a few:

Never cut trail switchbacks. This practice breaks down the trail tread and hastens erosion. Try to improve designated trails by removing branches, rocks, or other debris; but don't do this for unofficial trails or cross-country routes. Report any trail damage and misplaced or broken signs to the appropriate ranger office. When off trail, resist the temptation to build cairns or ducks (rock piles) as trail markers, except when absolutely necessary for route-finding.

When backpacking, be a "no trace" camper. Leave your campsite as you found it—or leave it in an even more natural condition.

Collecting specimens of minerals, plants, animals, and historical objects without special permit is prohibited in state and county parks. This means common things, too, such as pine cones, wildflowers, and lizards. These should be left for all visitors to enjoy. Some limited collecting of items like pine cones may be allowed on the National Forest lands—check first.

We've covered most of the general regulations associated with the use of the public lands in Los Angeles County. But you, as a visitor, are responsible for knowing any additional rules as well. The capsulized summary for each hike described in this book includes a reference to the agency responsible for the area you'll be visiting. Addresses and phone numbers for those agencies appear in Appendix 4.

Using This Book

Whether you wish to use this book as a reference tool or as a guide to be read cover to cover, you should take a few minutes to read this chapter. Herein we explain the meaning of the special symbols and other bits of capsulized information which appear before each trip description, and also describe the way in which trips are grouped together geographically.

One way to expedite the process of finding a suitable trip, especially if you're unfamiliar with hiking opportunities in Los Angeles County, is to turn to Appendix 1, "Best Hikes." This is a cross-reference of the most highly recommended hikes described in this book.

Each of the 175 hiking trips belongs to one of 32 "areas." Each area has its own introductory text and map. The areas are coded according to "regions" within Los Angeles County. Areas C-1 and C-2 are in the Coastline region of the county. Areas B-1, B-2, etc., are in the Basin and Foothills region. Letter S in the area designation refers to the Santa Monica Mountains region, letter A refers to the Angeles National Forest, and letter I refers to Santa Catalina Island. Since the easternmost Santa Monicas (Griffith Park and the Hollywood Hills) lie cheek-by-jowl next to the urban basin, I've grouped these areas with the Basin and Foothills region. The Santa Monica Mountains region of this book includes a few hikes that spill over into Ventura County, so as to preserve the integrity of coverage of the Santa Monica Mountains National Recreation Area. Also, the Angeles National Forest region picks up two hikes along the L.A.–Ventura county line (partly in Los Padres National Forest) and three hikes just beyond the L.A.–San Bernardino county line. In order to econo-mize on map space, some hikes that might be better classified as basin-and-foothill are included with mountain areas, and vice versa.

The index map of the whole county on pages xii, xiii shows the coverage of each area map, and the Table of Contents lists the page numbers for each region, area, and trip.

The introductory text for each area often includes general information about the area's history, geology, plants and wildlife not included in the trip descriptions. Information about possible restrictions or special requirements (wilderness permits, for example) may appear there too, so you should review that introductory material before embarking on a hike within a particular area.

The beginning of each area section contains an area map. On most of these maps, more than one hiking route (trip) is plotted, the numbers in the shadow boxes corresponding to trip numbers in the text. These boxed numbers refer to the start/end points of out-and-back and loop trips. For point-to-point (one-way) trips the boxed number appears twice, indicating separate start and end points. For some hikes, the corresponding area map alone is complete enough and fully adequate for navigation; for other hikes, more detailed topographical maps are recommended. A legend for the area maps appears on page 19.

The following is an explanation of the small symbols and capsulized information appearing at the beginning of each trip description. If you are simply browsing through this book, these summaries alone can be used as a tool to eliminate from consideration hikes that are either too difficult, or perhaps too trivial, for your abilities.

Easy Terrain: roads, trails, and easy cross-country hiking

 Moderate Terrain: cross-country boulder-hopping and easy scrambling

 Difficult Terrain: non-technical climbing required (WARNING: THESE TRIPS SHOULD BE ATTEMPTED ONLY BY SUIT-ABLY EQUIPPED, EXPERI-ENCED HIKERS ADEPT AT TRAVELING OVER STEEP OR ROCKY TERRAIN REQUIRING THE USE OF THE HANDS AS WELL AS THE FEET.)

Only one of these three symbols appears for a given trip, indicating the general character of the terrain encountered. A trip almost entirely on roads and trails, but including a short section of boulder-hopping or perhaps nontechnical climbing, for example, will be rated as easy terrain, and the difficulties will be duly noted in the text. As the symbols suggest, light footwear (running shoes) is appropriate for easy terrain, while sturdy hiking boots are recommended for more difficult terrain.

Nontechnical climbing includes everything up to and including Class 3 on the rock-climber's scale. While ropes and climbing hardware are not normally required, a hiker should have a good sense of balance, and enough experience to recognize dangerous moves and situations. The safety and stability of heavy hiking boots are especially recommended for this kind of trip. Hazards may include loose or slippery rocks and rattlesnakes (don't put your hands in places you can't see clearly).

Bushwhacking: cross-country travel in dense brush or riparian vegetation. This symbol is included for trips requiring a substantial amount of off-trail "bushwhacking." Wear long pants and be especially alert for rattlesnakes.

Only one of these two symbols appears:

 Marked Trails/Obvious Routes

Navigation by Map and Compass Required (WARNING: THESE TRIPS SHOULD BE ATTEMPT-ED ONLY BY HIKERS SKILLED IN NAVIGATION TECHNIQUES.)

Unambiguous cross-country routes—up a canyon, for example—are included in the first category. The hiker, of course, should never be without a map in unfamiliar territory, even if there are marked trails or the route seems obvious.

Point-to-Point Route

Out-and-Back Route

Loop Route

Only one of these three symbols appears, reflecting the trip as described. There is some flexibility, of course, in the way in which a hiker can actually follow the trip.

Suitable for Backpacking

Many of the trips in this book are not. Some parks and trails are closed at night, others allow night hiking but prohibit camping. Sometimes overnight camping is confined to areas not on the route. Angeles National Forest offers, by far, the greatest variety of backpacking experiences.

Best for Kids.

These trips are especially recommended for inquisitive children. They were chosen on the basis of their safety and ease of travel (at the time they were researched by the author), and their potential for entertaining the whole family.

Capsulized Summaries:

Distance: An estimate of total distance is given. Out-and-back trips show the sum of the distances of the out and back segments.

Total Elevation Gain/Loss: These are estimates of the sum of all the vertical gain segments and the sum of all the vertical loss segments along the total length of the route (both ways for out-and-back trips).

Hiking Time: This figure is for the average hiker, and includes only the time spent in motion. It does not include time spent for rest stops, lunch, etc. Fast walkers can complete the routes in perhaps 30% less time, and slower hikers may take 50% longer. The hiker is assumed to be traveling with a light day pack.

Optional/Recommended Map(s): The U.S. Geological Survey 7.5-minute-series topographic map or maps covering the trip are listed here. These "topo" maps are the most complete and accurate maps of the physical features of Los Angeles County. Unfortunately, many newer features, such as roads and trails do not show up on these sometimes-dated maps. Where a topo map is recommended, but it doesn't show some trails described in the text, a comparison with the area map in this book may help a lot. Other maps that may help guide your way are often available from park and forest-service offices, and from private publishers. There are about a dozen retail map shops in the greater Los Angeles area that carry USGS topos and privately published maps. For a list of maps covering L.A.'s park and backcountry areas, see Appendix 2.

Best Times: Nearly all of the short trips in this book are suitable year round. Some of the longer trips in the warmer, interior areas are simply too hot during the summer season. Hikes at high altitude can become inaccessible during the winter because of road closures, or they may be dangerous because of snow and ice. Generally, however, the range of months indicates when the hike is most rewarding.

Agency: These code letters refer to the agency, or office, that has jurisdiction over the area being hiked (for example, ANF/SD means Angeles National Forest, Saugus District). These agencies or offices can be contacted for more information. Full names,

addresses, and phone numbers are listed in Appendix 4.

Difficulty: The author's subjective overall rating takes into account the length of the trip and the nature of the terrain. The following are general definitions of the five categories:

★   **Easy.** Suitable for every member of the family.

★★   **Moderate.** Suitable for all physically fit people.

★★★   **Moderately Strenuous.** Long length, substantial elevation gain, and/or difficult terrain. Recommended for experienced hikers only.

★★★★   **Strenuous.** Long day's hike (or backpack) over a challenging route. Suitable only for experienced hikers in excellent physical condition.

★★★★★   **Very Strenuous.** Long and rugged route in extremely remote area. May require two days. Suitable only for experienced hikers/climbers in top physical condition.

Each level represents more or less a doubling of the difficulty. On average, ★★ trips are twice as hard as ★ trips, ★★★ trips are twice as hard as ★★ trips, and so on.

A final note:

In the trip descriptions, mileages along the highways (example: "mile 19.3") are keyed to the mileage markers posted at frequent intervals along most of Los Angeles County's state highways and county roads. The mileage figures are often stenciled on the roadside reflectors. In the descriptions of the hikes themselves a phrase like "at 6.3 miles" means 6.3 miles from the beginning of the hike, not from the last intersection or point of interest.

MAP LEGEND

～～～	Freeway	☁	Lake/reservoir
～～	Paved highway	♠	Ranger station/fire station
～	Paved highway	▲	Campground
～	Paved secondary road	☰	Picnic area
═ ═ ═ ═ ═	Graded dirt road	☓	Mine
▬ ▬ ▬ ▬	Foot trail/ abandoned road	P	Parking area
• • • • • • •	Cross-country route	═ ═ ═ ═ ═ ║	Locked gate: no trespassing
⠄⠄⠄⠄⠄⠄	Drainage (canyon, river, creek)	═ ═ ═ ═ ═ ╫	Gate: hikers OK
9	Start/end point with trip number	─ ─ ─ ─	County line
▲9399	Peak (elevation in feet)	∾∾∾∾∾∾∾	Wilderness boundary
■	Point of Interest		

Where and When to Go, and How to Avoid the Smog

Clearly, two of the most intractably detrimental aspects of living in most parts of Los Angeles are air pollution and traffic congestion. Air pollution affects to a greater or lesser degree all of the trips in this book, and traffic congestion affects (at least at certain times) how quickly you can escape the city and be on your merry way down the trail. In this section we'll look into some of the strategies you can use to sidestep these manmade difficulties and also take advantage of optimum conditions of weather and visibility.

Beating the traffic is not too difficult once you're out of the urban core. On weekdays, the flow of automobiles is mostly inward toward congested parts of the city during the morning, and outward during the afternoon and evening. Driving out of town early on weekend mornings is a breeze, but getting back into town later in the afternoon can be a bit problematical.

Nearly all the trails of Los Angeles County are refreshingly underutilized on weekdays. Sometimes you can walk for hours without seeing another traveler. Fair-weather weekends bring large numbers of people to a relatively small number of popular trailheads, while other trailheads have plenty of room for parking. Chantry Flat, Sunset Ridge (the approach to Millard Canyon), and Switzer Picnic Area in the San Gabriel Mountains have outside gates that can and do close to incoming traffic whenever the parking situation gets intolerable. The moral of all this is: hike on weekdays when you can, or on weekends as long as you get an early start.

There's a strong belief, even among most Southern Californians, that summer equals the hiking season. This prejudice probably comes from the fact that so many Southland residents have emigrated from other areas where this may be true. Actually, summer is the worst season to visit most of the wild lands of Los Angeles County. Summer and early fall is a time of drought, when much of the chaparral and scrub vegetation blanketing the mountain slopes turns drab and crispy, and the land bakes under a near-vertical sun. Summer hikes can be rewarding, however, if the trip is not long, and you get an early-morning start.

Summer—early summer especially—is fine for areas above 6000 feet or 7000 feet. Some of the highest elevations in the San Gabriel Mountains don't experience much of a "summer" at all, the snows of winter disappearing in July or August not long before the first subfreezing nights of September or October. Summer is also a perfectly good time to visit the beaches, and the lower slopes and canyons of the Santa Monica Mountains that benefit from coastal breezes.

Late fall brings autumn color to the oak woodlands and wet canyons of the county. The leaves of the valley oak, black oak, and walnut turn a crispy yellow in the valleys and on the hillsides. Bigleaf maples, cottonwoods, willows and sycamores contribute similar hues to canyon bottoms spotted with red-leaved poison oak vines. This is a time when the marine layer over the coastline and basin often lies low (at least in the morning) while the air above can be extraordinarily clean and dry.

Instead of suffering through days-long episodes of bad weather in winter, we Southern Californians usually experience a string of sunny days interspersed with short, rainy spells. Some storms are followed by very clear weather along with cold winds from the north. This is when you should "seize the moment": hop in the car, and head for a trail in the nearby foothills or mountains leading to some prominent high point. The views will often stretch from snow-covered peaks to the island-dotted Pacific Ocean.

Spring comes on gradually, each week a little warmer (with a heat wave or two tossed in) and a little hazier. The marine layer is thicker now, but superb views are still possible from mile-high summits in the San Gabriels such as Mt. Lowe and Strawberry Peak. Sunrises can be dramatic up there, with much of the surrounding lowland enveloped in a bank of low clouds. Annual wildflowers seem to pop up everywhere, wild lilacs paint the hillsides white and blue, and the scents of sage and nectar float on the air. When the marine layer is very deep, fogs bearing light drizzle may envelop the canyons of the Santa Monicas and San Gabriels, like the mists of Sherwood Forest. The High Country is often snowbound through May, although it may be possible to approach some of the passes and high points by way of southern routes.

In any season, the infamous Los Angeles smog can seriously affect your enjoyment of wild areas. At worst, the eye-smarting, lung-irritating air can turn an otherwise pristine watershed into one that looks like a hellish abyss. Strict, new emissions controls and other measures will almost certainly result in improvements in the air quality by the turn of the century. In the meantime (and perhaps for a very long time), a good strategy is simply to try to evade the smog by judicious choices of where and when to go.

Often, that's not very hard. Prevailing ocean breezes keep the western Santa Monica Mountains fairly clean most of the year. The High Country and northern slopes of the San Gabriels are more affected by marine air moving up the Santa Clara River valley than by dirty air blown in from the

city. For example, Charlton-Chilao Recreation Area, just 10 air-line miles from the edge of the L.A. Basin, gets an average of only about 40 smoggy days a year.

Air pollution often and seriously affects such L.A.-Basin-bordering areas as Griffith Park, the Verdugo Mountains, the Santa Susana Mountains, the Puente Hills, and the Front Range of the San Gabriels. But there are clear spells as well. Much of the smog originating in the L.A. Basin is photochemically produced (sunlight reacting on automobile exhaust gases), so morning air tends to be cleaner than afternoon air. Weekends are a little cleaner than weekdays, because traffic volumes are somewhat reduced.

When the weather is stable, and a strong temperature inversion (warmer air overlying cooler air) exists, the smog-bearing marine layer stays close to the ground until about midday. By afternoon local sea breezes are transporting it east to Riverside and San Bernardino counties, and up the Front Range canyons and slopes.

Less commonly, regional winds kick the smog north or northeast into the Antelope Valley, west along the Malibu coast to Oxnard and Ventura, or south as far as San Diego. Sometimes smog covers the whole county as a gauzy curtain, but more often it lies quite close to the ground in a localized area, leaving upwind areas with clear, blue skies.

An awareness of wind and weather patterns can help you decide where to find the cleanest air. Failing that, you can always set forth with a "plan B" as well as "plan A." While doing field work for this book, I usually kept sets of maps for at least two widely separate areas of the county in my car. Plan B was successfully invoked many times.

COASTLINE AREA

Area C-1: Malibu Coast

Fabled Malibu stretches 25 miles from the edge of the L.A. Basin at Santa Monica up-coast toward the Ventura County line. This odd, ribbon-like community—the home of many of L.A.'s rich and famous people—doggedly follows the course of the narrow, curvy Pacific Coast Highway, itself confined to a precariously unstable coastal terrace at the foot of the Santa Monica Mountains. Parts of Malibu consist of unbroken rows of townhouses perilously jammed between the highway and the surf. Just back of the coastal strip, stilted houses have gained airy footholds on precipitous, coast-facing slopes. So far, periodic fires sweeping over the mountains and the erosive battering of the ocean waves have done little to discourage urban-style growth. But a rising anti-growth sentiment among residents and recent political actions may well accomplish what nature has failed to do.

If you like strolling on crowded public beaches, or ogling fancy houses, the Malibu coastline has plenty of both. Quieter stretches of coastline, removed from the sight of houses and the roar of traffic, are a little harder to find, but well worth seeking out.

One spot worth visiting is Malibu Lagoon State Beach (Pacific Coast Highway and Cross Creek Road in the central part of Malibu, 13 miles west of Santa Monica). Here you'll find a pier, a saltwater lagoon favored by migrating birds, a famous surfing spot, and a nice stretch of sand.

If you're an avid hiker, though, you'll head a little farther afield to a stretch of coastline wrapping around the flat-topped headlands of Point Dume. This southward-pointing promontory, jutting into the Pacific Ocean 19 miles west of Santa Monica, is a widely visible landmark. Just east of the point itself, an unbroken cliff wall shelters a secluded beach from the sights and sounds of the civilized world. On this beach, you can forget about whatever else may lie just over the cliff rim; your world is simply one of crashing surf, tangy salt spray, pearly sand, and fascinating tidepools.

Area C-1, Trip 1
Point Dume to Paradise Cove

Distance	2.1 miles
Total Elevation Gain/Loss	(Flat)
Hiking Time	90 minutes
Optional Map	USGS 7.5-min *Point Dume*
Best Times	All year (passable during low tide)
Agency	DFG
Difficulty	★★

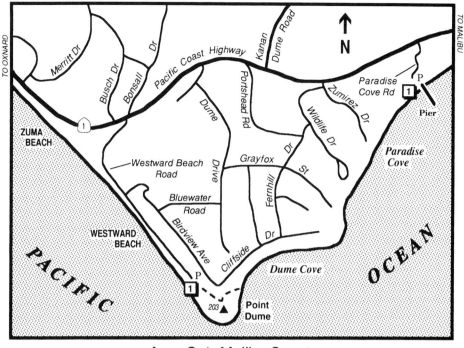

Area C-1: Malibu Coast

A pleasant walk anytime the tide is low, this trip is doubly rewarding when the tide dips as low as −2 feet. The rocky coastline below the cliffs of Point Dume harbors a mind-boggling array of marine plant and animal life, much of it underwater most of the time. Here are some of the creatures we spotted one warm October afternoon during a −1.5 foot tide: limpets, periwinkles, chitons, tube snails, sandcastle worms, sculpins, mussels, shore and hermit crabs, green and aggregate anemones, three kinds of barnacles, and two kinds of sea stars. Extreme low tides occur during the afternoon two or three times each month from October through March. Consult tide tables to find out exactly when.

Starting out at Westward Beach (open daylight hours—parking fee charged) on the west side of Point Dume, you have a choice between two routes: The shorter, much easier route (and the only practical alternative during all but extremely low tides) is the trail slanting left up the cliff. On top you'll

come to an area very popular for sighting gray whales during their southward migration in winter. You'll also discover a newly dedicated state historic monument. Point Dume, you'll learn, was christened by the British naval commander George Vancouver, who sailed by in 1793.

As you stand on Point Dume's apex, note the marked contrast between the lighter sedimentary rock exposed on the cliff faces both east and west, and the darker volcanic rock just below. Like the armored bow of an ice-breaker, this unusually tough mass of volcanic rock has thus far resisted the onslaught of the ocean swells. After you descend from the apex, some metal stairs will take you down to crescent-shaped Dume Cove.

The alternate route is open to expert climbers only. During the lowest tides, you round the point itself, making your way by hand-and-toe climbing in a couple of spots over huge, angular shards of volcanic rock along the base of the cliffs. The tidepools here and also to the east along Dume Cove's shoreline harbor some of the best displays of intertidal marine life in Southern California. This visual feast will remain for others to enjoy if you refrain from taking or disturbing in any way the organisms that live there. (WARNING: Exploring the lower intertidal zones can be hazardous. Be very cautious when traveling over slippery rocks, and always be aware of the incoming swells. Don't let a rogue wave catch you by surprise.)

The going is easy once you're on Dume Cove's ribbon of sand. Signs posted here warn against nude bathing and sunning. This was once a popular nude beach, much to the chagrin of those living in the cliffside mansions overlooking the area.

When you reach the northeast end of Dume Cove, swing left around a lesser point and continue another mile over a somewhat wider beach to Paradise Cove, site of an elegant beach-side restaurant, private pier, and parking lot (public welcome, fee charged).

Dume Cove at low tide

Area C-2: Palos Verdes Peninsula

Forged by local uplift of the seafloor roughly two million years ago, Palos Verdes lay surrounded by the ocean for hundreds of thousands of years. Today the vast sheet of alluvium filling the L.A. Basin connects Palos Verdes to the mainland—yet in a figurative sense Palos Verdes has never really lost its identity as an island.

When the South Bay cities of Torrance and Long Beach are cloaked by fog or brown haze, Palos Verdes often stands head and shoulders above the murk. Quite often you can stand on top enjoying views of faraway Santa Catalina Island and Old Baldy, but fail to make out L.A. Harbor only a few miles away.

Palos Verdes is a very distinct economic and cultural island as well. Rimmed by oil refineries, gritty industrial neighborhoods, and wall-to-wall people, the peninsula itself is dominated almost exclusively by opulent ranch-style homes and sprawling, lavishly landscaped estates. The contrast is stunning and not a little disturbing.

Fortunately, Palos Verdes offers miles of near-pristine coastline and a big patch of hillside open space for any explorer on foot to enjoy. You can start with easy Trip 1 below for an overview of the area; then graduate to one of the tougher scrambles (Trips 2–4) along the base of the coastal cliffs.

Area C-2, Trip 1
Top of the Peninsula

Distance	1.6 miles round trip
Total Elevation Gain/Loss	350'/350'
Hiking Time	1 hour
Optional Maps	USGS 7.5-min *Torrance, San Pedro*
Best Times	All year
Agency	LADPR
Difficulty	★

At Del Cerro Park on the top of the Palos Verdes peninsula, you need only climb a small, grassy hill to take in one of L.A.'s truly great ocean views. With a little bit more ambition, you can hoof it less than a mile to an even more panoramic view spot.

Ideally, you should be here when a chilly north wind (which usually follows the passage of major winter storms) cleanses the Southland of polluted air. But don't neglect the early spring. During March and April the sages, native wildflowers and

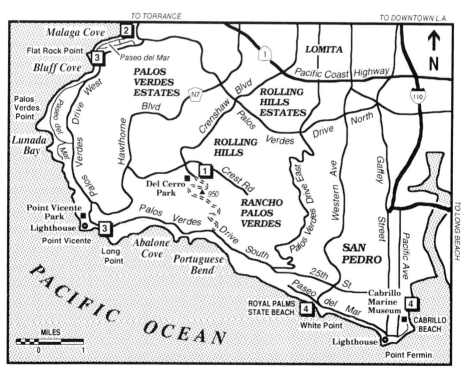

Area C-2: Palos Verdes Peninsula

weedy grasses magically transform the normally drab-colored hillsides into tapestries of velvet green.

Del Cerro Park is easy to find, as it lies very near the southern terminus (dead end) of Crenshaw Boulevard, one the L.A.'s most prominent thoroughfares. Park next to the grassy hill or find a spot elsewhere on nearby residential streets. At Crenshaw's dead end, step around the steel gate and follow the dirt fire road beyond. This road traces Crenshaw's proposed extension down to Palos Verdes Drive South at Portuguese Bend, a project that will likely never be realized.

Soon you're in a rare patch of open space surrounded by, but largely removed from, the curving avenues and palatial estates of Rancho Palos Verdes. Since the mid-50s, when more than 100 houses were destroyed or seriously damaged by landslides in the Portuguese Bend area, most of the steep area above the Bend has remained off-limits to development.

At 0.5 mile, stay right as roads branch left. Continue a curving descent until you reach a flat area about ¼ mile farther. Leave the road there and make a beeline for the top of a 950' knoll, dotted with planted pines, on the left. Atop this serene little overlook you'll enjoy a 150° view of the ocean, with Santa Catalina Island sprawling at center stage. To the right and down below, the spike-shaped Sky Tower at the defunct Marineland water park on the shoreline points upward to San Nicolas Island, about 70 miles away.

The knoll you're standing on is a remnant of one of the 13 marine terraces that have made the Palos Verdes hills a textbook example familiar to geology students. The 13 terraces, rising like rounded and broken stairs from sea level to 1300 feet, are the results of wave erosion modified by uplift and fluctuating sea levels during the past 2 million years. From this spot (despite the effects of grading and construction on some of the adjacent ridges) you will probably recognize at least seven of the terraces in the topography around you.

Area C-2, Trip 2
Malaga Cove to Bluff Cove

Distance	2.0 miles
Total Elevation Gain/Loss	200'/200'
Hiking Time	90 minutes
Optional Map	USGS 7.5-min *Redondo Beach*
Best Times	All year (only at low tide)
Agency	PVESP
Difficulty	★★

If dancing across wave-rounded boulders is your cup of tea, you'll enjoy this moderately difficult rock-hop along the northernmost edge of the Palos Verdes peninsula. With near-vertical cliffs on one side and foamy surf on the other, you'll truly feel that you're treading the edge of the continent. The only unfortunate aspect of this trip—and also the two that follow—is the appalling amount of garbage strewn about the tide line, much of it plastic debris that floats (or blows) in from the crowded beaches to the north. On this trip, as well as the next two, shoes or boots with good ankle support are recommended.

To reach the starting point, Malaga Cove, turn north on Via Corta from Palos Verdes Drive West. After 0.5 mile, make a right on Via Arroyo. One more right turn, on Paseo del Mar, takes you to a parking area in front of the Malaga Cove Intermediate School.

Find the top of the paved pathway at the far end of Paseo del Mar and walk down to the beach. Turn left along the shoreline and make your way over the obstacle course of wave-pounded rocks. After a short mile you arrive at Flat Rock Point, a popular area for tidepooling when the tide is low. Wide, curving Bluff Cove lies just ahead. From there, take the pathway on the left going back up the cliff to Paseo del Mar. You can then return to your car by strolling the four blocks of Paseo del Mar leading back to the school. Lining both sides of this street are some of Palos Verdes' most attractively landscaped mansions—very nice to admire even if you can't own one.

Area C-2, Trip 3
Bluff Cove to Point Vicente

	Distance	5.7 miles
	Total Elevation Gain/Loss	200'/200'
	Hiking Time	3½ hours
	Optional Map	USGS 7.5-min *Redondo Beach*
	Best Times	All year (low tide recommended)
	Agency	PVESP
	Difficulty	★★★

This longer trek down Palos Verdes' wild west side visits crescent-shaped Lunada Bay plus half a dozen mini-coves, and traverses the wave-torn base of the sea cliffs below Point Vicente. Time your hike so that low tide occurs when you're below the lighthouse at Point Vicente, which is one of the tighter spots along the coastline. Set up a car shuttle in advance—unless you plan to add 4½ miles to your trip by walking back on Palos Verdes Drive West. If you're out during the late morning or noon hour on a sunny day, you may want to reverse the route from that described here in order to avoid facing the sun the whole way.

Starting from the top of the Flat Rock Point trail along Paseo del Mar (to get there, follow the driving directions in Trip 2 above, but turn *left* on Paseo del Mar and go 0.5 mile), you first descend to Bluff Cove. Onward to Lunada Bay, the going is quite easy—you'll be on pebbles, and sometimes a thin ribbon of sand, as long as you stay close to the base of the cliffs. Almost any time you can walk out to tidepools that are well exposed during −1 foot tides or lower. These moderately rich pools contain green anemones, crabs, and especially purple sea urchins, but few of the more interesting creatures such as sea stars that are so abundant up the coast in the Malibu area.

At around 2 miles, short of Palos Verdes Point (a.k.a. Rocky Point) you'll come upon the dismembered remains of the freighter *Dominator,* which ran aground in 1961. Rusting pieces of the ship now litter a stretch of coastline nearly a half mile long.

Once around the point, the beautiful, semicircular Lunada Bay lies before you. The beige-tinted sedimentary cliffs encircling the bay are of Monterey shale, a thinly bedded and easily eroded formation that composes about 90 percent of the exposed rock on the Palos Verdes peninsula. The formation consists of former seafloor rich in diatoms, the skeletons of microscopic single-celled plants that float about in the ocean. A steep trail leads up the cliff at Lunada Bay to connect with Paseo del Mar. The first two of the half dozen indentations pocking the coastline beyond Lunada Bay also have steep paths going up to Paseo del Mar. Keep this in mind if you want to "bail out" and avoid the more rugged and rocky shoreline ahead.

Rock hopping becomes *de rigeur* in the last mile before Point Vicente. Some hand and foot work will get you over the piles of broken rocks just below the whale-watching overlook and lighthouse. A short way ahead you'll come to a steep path slanting up the cliff to the Point Vicente Fishing Access parking lot, the trip's end.

Before or after your hike, pay a visit to nearby Point Vicente Park. Open daily, the park features an interpretive center, which includes a nice relief map of the peninsula and offers great views of the winter-migrating gray whales from the brink of the sea cliffs.

The Point Vicente lighthouse

Area C-2, Trip 4
White Point to Cabrillo Beach

	Distance	3 miles
	Total Elevation Gain/Loss	100'/100'
	Hiking Time	2 hours
	Optional Map	USGS 7.5-min *San Pedro*
	Best Times	All year (low tide recommended)
	Agency	RPSB
	Difficulty	★★

Pressed hard and fast against the densely populated community of San Pedro, the rocky ribbon of coastline between White Point and Cabrillo Beach looks out over a 20-mile, watery gap separating Santa Catalina Island from the mainland. On clear winter days the island seems to float like a dusky shadow over the sparkling surf.

Start at Royal Palms State Beach, close to where Western Avenue meets Paseo del Mar in San Pedro. You can park inside the gate for a fee, or outside along Paseo del Mar for free. Down by the water's edge head east (down-coast) past White Point, making your way over tilted slabs of sedimentary rock and small boulders. Here, and on the bluffs above are the skimpy remains of early-century resorts and spas that capitulated to the 1933 Long Beach quake and decades of pounding surf. The checkered history of this stretch of coastline is interpreted in a display at the Cabrillo Marine Museum, which you'll find at the conclusion of this hike.

At about 1.5 miles, before the shoreline terrace you're following narrows to practically nothing at Point Fermin, you'll spot some metal steps going up the bluff. This is your safe ticket to getting past Point Fermin. (If the tide is extremely low and the surf is relatively calm—conditions that are most likely to occur on only a few afternoons during the fall—expert scramblers can try to edge around the point itself and reach the sand of Cabrillo Beach beyond. Point Fermin's cliff faces, though not the highest on the peninsula, present the wildest scene

on the peninsula. When I scooted over them during a −1 foot tide, dozens of sleek, black cormorants perched on tiny niches above observed my every move.)

At the top of the metal stairs, a path leads to the west end of Point Fermin Park, a grassy strip popular among joggers and strollers. Keep heading east along the edge of the cliffs, passing the antique Point Fermin Lighthouse, built in 1874 with materials shipped around Cape Horn. Farther east a big landslide blocks your way, so you turn inland a little to reach Shepard Street. Follow this street east, to Pacific Avenue, and continue straight ahead on Bluff Place down to Cabrillo Beach. Here you can enjoy the only true beach for miles in either direction, and pay a visit to the museum, which features some excellent marine and historical exhibits. If you want to stretch your legs further, try walking out to sea atop the San Pedro breakwater, one of several artificial barriers protecting the Los Angeles/Long Beach harbor complex from ocean swells.

BASIN AND FOOTHILLS

Area B-1: Soledad Canyon

Millions of years of geologic tumult can be read in the frozen stone exposed to casual view as you drive the Antelope Valley Freeway (California 14) between Interstate 5 and the Mojave Desert city of Palmdale. Robert P. Sharp's *Geology Field Guide to Southern California* devotes several pages to this fascinating area of fault-sliced sedimentary formations. On a geologic time scale, of course, the rocks are anything but solid and unmoving. The collapse of a freeway ramp over Interstate 5 near the Antelope Valley Freeway during the 1971 Sylmar earthquake was a pointed reminder of that.

Equally interesting perspectives can be had by getting off the freeway and following parallel roads, such as the old Sierra Highway through Mint Canyon, or the road through Soledad Canyon. Soledad Canyon drains much of the northwest flank of the San Gabriel Mountains and contains a year-round stream shaded by lush riparian vegetation. At Soledad Campground (operated by Angeles National Forest) you can look for a tiny green fish called the unarmored three-spine stickleback, an endangered species.

Soledad Canyon itself functions as a wind gap between the coastal valleys of Ventura and Los Angeles counties, and the interior desert. Often on spring and summer afternoons the canyon serves as a conduit for cool, hazy marine air flowing east toward the southwestern Mojave Desert. Less common are the hot, dry Santa Ana winds of fall and early winter that scream down the canyon in the opposite direction.

The area's main attraction for hikers is Vasquez Rocks County Park, described below. A little-used but not very scenic segment of the Pacific Crest Trail also traverses the Soledad Canyon area on its way between the high country of the San Gabriel Mountains in the south and the Sierra Pelona in the north.

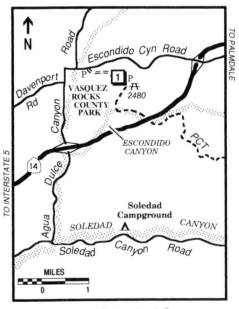

Area B-1: Soledad Canyon

Area B-1, Trip 1
Vasquez Rocks County Park

	Distance	1 to 3 miles
	Optional Map	USGS 7.5-min *Agua Dulce*
	Best Times	All year
	Agency	VRCP
	Difficulty	★ to ★★

A perennial location for filming Old West movies and sci-fi extravaganzas, the distinctive Vasquez Rocks will probably be familiar to you from episodes of "Bonanza," "Star Trek," and countless movies. Somehow these tilted slabs look impossibly high and steep when you first see them. But that illusion is dispelled when you try to climb them—none rise more than about 150 feet into the air, and there's almost always an easy way up. The best of the rocks are included in the 745-acre Vasquez Rocks County Park.

Geologically speaking, the rocks are west-dipping outcrops of sandstone and fanglomerate layers belonging to the Vasquez Formation. Here and in the surrounding area, the Vasquez Formation and the overlying Mint Canyon Formation constitute a 20,000-foot-thick sequence of sediments laid down 8–15 million years ago. The sandstone developed from fine-grained deposits laid down along gentle streams and shallow ponds. The fanglomerate (resembling conglomerate rock) developed from layers of coarse, broken rock deposited on what were probably alluvial fans at the base of steep mountains. More recently, faulting uplifted these layers, inclining them roughly 45° to the horizontal. Erosion put on the

Vasquez Rocks

final touches, producing the sheer east-facing exposures you'll see throughout the park.

Botanically speaking, the park area supports flora characteristic of habitats far to the west, south, and east. Here you find the black sage and California sagebrush common in the Santa Monica Mountains, the chamise of the San Gabriel Mountains, and the juniper of the Antelope Valley rim.

Historically speaking, the mazes of rocks hereabouts were prime hideouts of the infamous 1850s bandit Tiburcio Vasquez. Today they serve equally well as hiding places for imaginative kids. Of course it's possible for kids, as well as some adults, to become disoriented when venturing far. If so, a scramble up any of the high ridges will restore one's bearings: the Antelope Valley Freeway lies south, the picnic area and park entrance lie north.

The park, open for day use, features a single dirt access road (entrance on Escondido Canyon Road), a large picnic area, a couple of well-trampled nature trails, and a veritable spider web of informal, unsigned trails that lead into the park's far corners. South of the picnic area, you can follow a segment of the Pacific Crest Trail down into Escondido Canyon, where water trickles through after winter rains. Also try clambering about the loftier outcrops southwest of the picnic area, where you'll find a maze of ledges, pocket caves, and bizarre erosional sculptures.

Area B-2: Placerita Canyon

Barely 10 minutes drive from northern San Fernando Valley and the sprawling suburban city of Santa Clarita, Placerita Canyon County Park nestles comfortably at the foot of one of the more verdant slopes of the San Gabriel Mountains. The park's backcountry is billed as a rugged wilderness, which is certainly a fair description of the wooded ravines that slice into the mountains' flanks above the main Placerita Canyon gorge. On the civilized side, you'll find an attractive nature center—the envy of many a national park—housing exhibits on the history, pre-history, geology, plants, and wildlife of the area. A single campground on the park property is available for organized groups by reservation.

Placerita Canyon's fascinating history is highlighted by the discovery of gold there in 1842. That event, which touched off California's first gold rush (a rather trivial one at that), predated by six years John Marshall's discovery of gold at Sutter's Mill in Northern California. In the bucolic early 1900s, Placerita settlers grew vegetables and fruit, raised animals, and tapped some small reserves of a very high-grade "white" oil. Right out of the ground, the fuel was suitable for home heating and lighting purposes—and even for powering a Model T Ford. By mid-century, Placerita Canyon became one of the more popular generic Western site locations used by Hollywood's movie makers and early television producers. Like many other scenic site locations around the L.A. Basin, the canyon was eventually acquired as parkland—in this instance first by the state, then by the county.

Take the Placerita Canyon exit from Antelope Valley Freeway (California 14) at Newhall, and drive east 1.5 miles to reach the park's main gate, open 9 A.M. to 5 P.M. Adjoining the nature center and picnic area are three short, self-guiding nature trails (keyed to leaflets available at the center). The Ecology Trail, just north of the nature center, loops through the chaparral and oak-woodland habitats most representative of the area. The Hillside Trail climbs to a hillside water tank with a view of lower Placerita Canyon. The wheelchair-accessible Heritage Trail crosses under Placerita Canyon Road and leads to the "Oak of the Golden Dream," the exact site (according to legend) where gold was discovered in 1842 by a herdsman pulling up wild onions for his after-siesta meal.

For serious hikers, we describe in detail below three more-substantial trips. The longest of the three loops into the higher country of Angeles National Forest, which borders the park on the south.

Oak woodland at Walker Ranch Campground

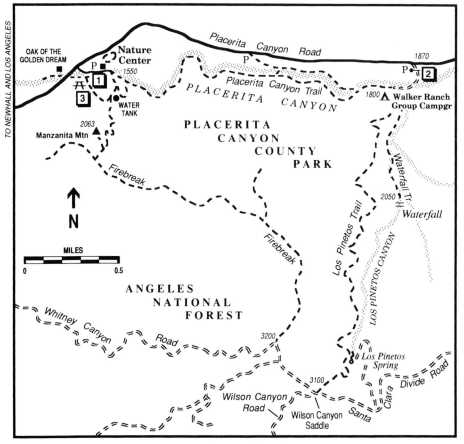

Area B-2: Placerita Canyon

Area B-2, Trip 1
Placerita Canyon

	Distance	3.6 miles round trip to Walker Ranch
	Total Elevation Gain/Loss	400'/400'
	Hiking Time	2 hours (round trip)
	Optional Map	USGS 7.5-min *Mint Canyon*
	Best Times	All year
	Agency	PCCP
	Difficulty	★★

Placerita Canyon's melodious creek flows decently about half the year (winter and spring), caressing the ears with white noise that echoes from the canyon walls. During the fall, when the creek is bone-dry, you make your own noise instead by crunching through the crispy leaf litter of the sycamores.

Starting at the nature center, cross a bridge and pick up the trail heading east up the canyon's live-oak-shaded flood plain. Down by the grassy banks you'll see wild blackberry vines, lots of willows, and occasionally sycamore, cottonwood and alder trees.

After a while, the canyon narrows and becomes a rocky gorge. Soaring walls tell the story of thousands of years of natural erosion, as well as the destructive effects of hydraulic mining, which involved aiming high-pressure water hoses at hillsides to loosen and wash away ores. Used extensively in Northern California during the latter Gold Rush, "hydraulicking" was finally banned in 1884 after catastrophic damages to waterways and farms downstream. At Placerita Canyon, several hundred thousand dollars worth of gold were ultimately recovered, but at considerable cost and effort.

At about 1 mile you reach a split. The right fork climbs a little onto the chaparral-clad slopes to the south, while the left branch connects with a trail going up to a parking area on Placerita Canyon Road and then goes upstream along the willow-choked canyon bottom. Follow either branch but take the other when you return.

Using either route you eventually reach the scant remains of some early–20th-Century cottages hand-built by settler Frank Walker, his wife, and some of his 12 children. The area is now the site of the large campground catering to organized groups (drinking water available here). Amid a parklike setting of live oaks and gentle slopes, you'll discover a sturdy chimney and a cement foundation. Back by the nature center stands another cabin built by Walker, but modified later for use in the television series Hopalong Cassidy.

Area B-2, Trip 2
Los Pinetos Waterfall

Distance	1.6 miles round trip
Total Elevation Gain/Loss	350'/350'
Hiking Time	1 hour (round trip)
Optional Maps	USGS 7.5-min *Mint Canyon, San Fernando*
Best Times	All year
Agency	PCCP
Difficulty	★★

Nourished by springs, Los Pinetos Canyon harbors at least a tiny trickle of water virtually the year round. About midway up this short tributary of Placerita Canyon is a sublime little grotto, cool and dark except when the sun passes almost straight overhead. If you come here after gully-washing rains, you'll find a true waterfall; otherwise you can just listen to water dribbling down the chute and enjoy the serenity of this private place just 3 miles—and a world away—from the edge of the L.A. metropolis.

Begin this trip at the Walker Ranch trailhead on Placerita Canyon Road (at mile 5.4 according to the roadside mileposts), 2 miles east of the county park's main entrance. Walk down to the group campground and turn south on the Waterfall Trail into Los Pinetos Canyon. Don't confuse this trail with the signed Los Pinetos Trail going up the slope west of the canyon bottom. The Waterfall Trail momentarily climbs the canyon's steep west wall, then drops onto the canyon's sunny flood plain. Presently you bear right into a narrow ravine (Los Pinetos Canyon), avoiding a wider tributary bending left (east).

Continue, now on an ill-defined path, past and sometimes over water-polished, metamorphic rock. Live oaks and bigcone Douglas-firs cling to the slopes above, and a few bigleaf maples grace the canyon bottom. The bigcone Douglas-fir (a.k.a. bigcone spruce), a Southern California variant of the Douglas-fir of the Pacific Northwest, is abundant in the San Gabriel Mountains from elevations of about 2000 feet (as here) up to about 6000 feet. The bigleaf maple, also common in the Pacific Northwest, has gained a foothold in the San Gabriels as well, especially in moist canyons and ravines.

About 0.2 mile after the first fork in the canyon, there's a second fork. Go right and continue 50 yards to the base of the waterfall—the end of the line in this branch of the canyon.

Area B-2, Trip 3
Ridgeline–Los Pinetos Loop

Distance	7.0 miles
Total Elevation Gain/Loss	1800'/1800'
Hiking Time	4 hours
Optional Maps	USGS 7.5-min *Mint Canyon, San Fernando*
Best Times	October through June
Agency	PCCP
Difficulty	★★★

The grand tour of Placerita Canyon country takes you swiftly up a steep trail and fire break to the top of a ridge spur of the San Gabriels, and then easily back downward via the Los Pinetos and Placerita Canyon trails. Start the hike early (the park gate opens at 9 A.M.) so you avoid broiling in the midday sun while ascending. If you want to make this an overnight trip, you have the option of making camp on Angeles National Forest lands, subject to the current fire regulations, of course. Contact the Tujunga Ranger District (see Appendix 4) for more information about that.

Start by picking up the Hillside Trail just behind the restroom building near the west end of the picnic area in Placerita Canyon County Park. Climb past oaks and chaparral to a point just short of the camouflage-painted water tank. There you'll find an unmarked but well-worn trail heading straight up the ridge. After 0.5 mile on this you come to a side trail on the right leading 100 yards to the top of a rounded knoll dubbed Manzanita Mountain. Not much manzanita grows hereabouts, but the area is still recovering from a 1982 wildfire. From this point on, you're on Angeles Forest lands until you reach the lower part of the Los Pinetos Trail.

Just past the side trail you come to a wide, sandy fire break. Turn left and tackle the first of several extremely steep pitches you'll encounter on the undulating fire break during the next 1.8 miles. At 2.6 miles you join Whitney Canyon Road, at the high point in elevation along the route. From there, it's downhill the rest of the way.

Turn left (east) and head for Wilson Canyon Saddle, a popular destination for equestrians and mountain bikers who come up from the San Fernando Valley via Wilson Canyon Road from Olive View Drive in Sylmar. Scramble up either of the two bumps on the ridgeline just east of here for a stupendous view (weather permitting) of the metropolis below. It's quiet here whenever the marine layer gets thick enough to smother the ridgeline in fog. At other times, when sound refracts upward through the inversion layer, the muffled roar of tens of thousands cars on the network of freeways below comes through loud and clear.

Picking up the Los Pinetos Trail on the north side of the saddle, you begin a pleasant descent through splendid live-oak woodlands. Here and there you'll find nice specimens of the California walnut (black walnut) tree, a small, deciduous tree with colorful foliage in the fall. The range of this trademark Southern California tree is limited to the margins of the L.A. Basin and the mountainous interiors of Ventura and Santa Barbara counties. Much of its habitat in Los Angeles County has been usurped by urbanization.

Down past a couple of switchbacks you come to Los Pinetos Spring, where non-potable water is stored for firefighting, and a dirt road coming down from the ridgeline. Continue your descent on the trail ahead, winding amid thick growths of chaparral— ceanothus, scrub oak, chamise, sugar bush, mountain mahogany, manzanita, and sage— along the slope west of Los Pinetos Canyon. At 5.2 miles you reach Walker Ranch campground (water available here). From there, head west down the well-trodden trail through Placerita Canyon back to the starting point.

Bigleaf maple leaves in Los Pinetos Canyon

Area B-3: Santa Susana Mountains

Barren and austere when viewed by midday light, but soft and pillowy under the sun's slanting rays, the Santa Susana Mountains rising from the northeast corner of the San Fernando Valley have long been recognized as an important reservoir of open space. Conservation organizations have spearheaded the effort to acquire from private interests bits and pieces of what will hopefully become a broad tapestry of protected land for wildlife habitat and passive recreation.

Overlooking the valley from the east end of the range is 714-acre O'Melveny Park, the second biggest (after Griffith Park) city park in Los Angeles. Noted for its picture-perfect picnic grounds with white fences and towering eucalyptus trees, the park also challenges hikers with several miles of steep, backcountry fire roads and primitive trails. The park's posted hours are 5 A.M. to 10:30 P.M.

Behind O'Melveny Park, on slopes facing north toward the Santa Clarita Valley, lie some 6000 acres of attractively wooded ridges and canyons awaiting acquisition as the future Santa Clarita Woodlands State Park.

Farther west, hikers can enjoy a network of riding and hiking paths in suburban Porter Ranch, probe the narrow confines of Devil Canyon, and trace an old stagecoach trail that preceded the 20th-Century roads through Santa Susana Pass. Worth mentioning as well is Stony Point, a spectacular but graffiti-scarred pile of sandstone boulders popular among rock-climbing enthusiasts and scramblers of all ages.

The five trips listed below give a taste of what is currently available for hikers. A decade hence, the present and future parks and open spaces of the Santa Susanas should be an integral part of the proposed "Rim-of-the-Valley Trail Corridor." The main trail in the corridor, according to current plan, will swing 100 miles around the north rim of the San Fernando Valley, stretching from Ventura County to Glendale and Pasadena.

Area B-3, Trip 1
Old Stagecoach Road

Distance	2.6 miles round trip
Total Elevation Gain/Loss	650'/650'
Hiking Time	1½ hours (round trip)
Optional Maps	USGS 7.5-min *Oat Mountain, Santa Susana*
Best Times	All year
Agency	SSMP
Difficulty	★★

Sunrises are as spectacular as they come when viewed on clear, winter mornings from the Old Stagecoach Road above Chatsworth. To the east, a hundred thousand valley lights fade while the cirrus-streaked sky cycles through a spectrum of hue and intensity. To the west, boulder-stacked hillsides materialize out of grey gloom to become perfect copies of the golden backdrops seen in so many Western movies and television productions.

Hiking the Stagecoach Road at dawn is inspiring—but not recommended unless you're familiar with the area. Pay a visit in daylight first so you can memorize the route, which (as of this writing) is not adequately marked and easy to lose.

At the entrance to Chatsworth Park South (west terminus of Devonshire Street), pick up the path signed OLD STAGECOACH ROAD on the left. After reaching the west end of the park (0.4 mile) you start climbing into the bouldered hills, where a maze of roads and old vehicle tracks complicates route-finding. Head generally southwest and uphill toward a low ridge distinguished by a row of bushy olive trees (0.6 mile). From there, turn right (northwest) up the ridge and aim toward a large, white, rectangular plaque embedded in sandstone on the hillside about 0.4 mile away. You're now on a well-preserved section of what used to be called the Devil's Slide, a key link in the 1860–90 coastal stage road linking Los Angeles and San Francisco. As you walk up the hard sandstone bed, notice the carefully hewn drainage chutes on both sides. With a little detective work you may also find a couple of old cisterns, used to capture rainwater for relay teams of horses that pulled wagons up the formidable grade.

The tiled historical plaque, placed in 1939, remains in perfect shape. Beyond the plaque, you can follow the stagecoach road bed another 0.3 mile to the Devil's Slide summit (1630'), where a fence marks the L.A.–Ventura county line. Private homes lie to the west, but to the north there's more to explore if you're willing to do some off-trail walking. The next ridge north, for example, offers a view of Santa Susana Pass, threaded by the Simi Valley Freeway and the older Santa Susana Pass Road. About 600 feet below you is the midpoint of the 1.4-mile-long Santa Susana railroad tunnel. The tunnel's east entrance can be seen back near Chatsworth Park South.

More than 800 acres of undeveloped land in the Santa Susana Pass area have been acquired by the state in the past decade for use as a state park. The next decade should see the construction of visitor facilities and marked trails through the bouldered hills.

Area B-3, Trip 2
Devil Canyon

	Distance	4.6 miles round trip
	Total Elevation Gain/Loss	450'/450'
	Hiking Time	2½ hours (round trip)
	Optional Map	USGS 7.5-min *Oat Mountain*
	Best Times	November through June
	Agency	SMMC
	Difficulty	★★

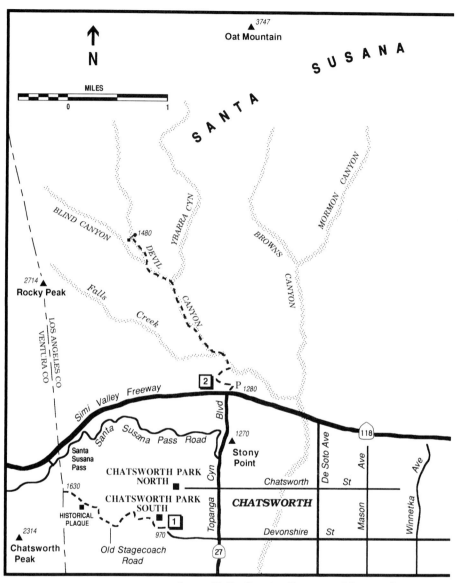

Area B-3: Santa Susana Mountains

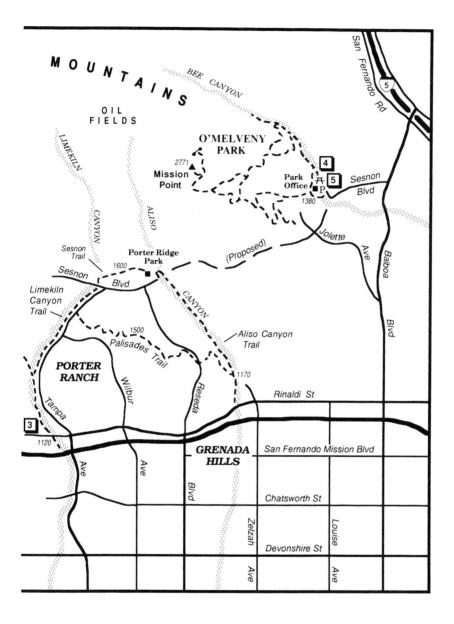

MOUNTAINS

OIL FIELDS

BEE CANYON

O'MELVENY PARK

2771
Mission Point

LIMEKILN

CANYON

ALISO

Park Office
4
5
Sesnon Blvd
1380

Jolette

San Fernando Rd

5

Sesnon Trail

Porter Ridge Park
1600

(Proposed)

Sesnon Blvd

Limekiln Canyon Trail

CANYON

1500
Palisades Trail

Aliso Canyon Trail

1170

PORTER RANCH

Wilbur

Reseda

Rinaldi St

Tampa

3
1120

Ave

Ave

GRENADA HILLS

San Fernando Mission Blvd

Blvd

Chatsworth St

Zelzah Ave

Devonshire St

Louise Ave

Jolette Ave

Balboa Blvd

A surprisingly cool and pleasant retreat just back of the hot, dry northwest corner of the San Fernando Valley, Devil Canyon sports abundant growths of live oak and willow and a small, intermittent stream. Fire and flood have long since removed almost all traces of an old auto road in the canyon; in its place hikers and mountain bikers have beaten down a narrow trail. Come here in the early spring to enjoy the blooming ceanothus on the hillsides, or in winter (wear an old pair of shoes) if you don't mind tramping through lots of good, clean mud.

The easily reached trailhead is a small, dirt parking area just north of the Simi Valley Freeway/Topanga Canyon Boulevard interchange. On foot, follow the road that curls up the hillside to the north and then descends, just east of a new housing development, into the canyon bottom (0.4 mile). Turn left and make your way up-canyon. The heretofore uninspiring scenery improves greatly as you swing around a couple of sharp bends and lose sight of the wall-to-wall condos on the bluff above.

You can go as far as a pipe gate (2.3 miles), pausing along the way to admire the wind- and water-carved sandstone bedrock along both sides of the canyon. This sandstone, a part of the same formation exposed at Stony Point and Santa Susana Pass, originated from sediments laid down in a marine environment roughly 80 million years ago. Shallow caves can be found in Devil Canyon's tributaries—especially Falls Creek—if you don't mind a little bushwhacking.

Devil Canyon wall

Area B-3, Trip 3
Porter Ranch Loop

	Distance	8.0 miles
	Total Elevation Gain/Loss	1000'/1000'
	Hiking Time	4 hours
	Optional Map	USGS 5-min *Oat Mountain*
	Best Times	November through May
	Agency	LACRPD
	Difficulty	★★★

The open spaces and trails lacing well-to-do Porter Ranch could serve as a nice model for community development anywhere in the Southland. Of course, it could be also be argued that the world would be better off without the square miles of new housing developments here and elsewhere along the rim of the San Fernando Valley. But at least local residents—and the public at large—have the opportunity to wander the remaining vestiges of two riparian canyons and a cliff-rimmed hillside blanketed with aromatic sage.

Suitable for horses and mountain bikes as well as hikers, this trip is best taken on a cool day. A look at our map (or any street map of the area) reveals ways to abbreviate the trip if you don't want to go the full 8 miles.

Park your car on Rinaldi Street, west of Tampa Avenue. Pick up the equestrian trail going north through the landscaped linear park along Limekiln Canyon's trickling creek. After crossing the creek twice on bridges you come to a split (0.7 mile) where one branch of the trail bends easily left and follows a ravine toward a new subdivision. Take the main branch (right), which goes up toward the shoulder of Tampa Avenue. You pass under a concrete bridge (a gated entrance road serving new houses west of Limekiln Canyon); pass a junction with the Palisades Trail (your return route); cross Sesnon Boulevard; and finally join the Sesnon Trail, 1.8 miles from the start.

Follow the Sesnon Trail east over a hump to Ormskirk Avenue. Turn south, walk through Porter Ridge Park, and go left on Sesnon Boulevard to where it dead ends on the edge of steep-sided Aliso Canyon. Walk around the pipe gate on the left and down into Aliso Canyon.

The 1988 Grenada Hills fire swept Aliso Canyon, as well as most of O'Melveny Park (Trips 4 and 5) to the east, so good springtime displays of fire-following wildflowers—lupine, phacelia, and California poppy—can be expected if the previous winter's rains have cooperated. After following the canyon for 1.3 miles (to 4.0 miles from the start) you turn right on the Palisades Trail, which doubles back up a ravine, climbs a slope, passes some houses, and reaches Reseda Boulevard. Cross Reseda, continue uphill on the west sidewalk for about 0.3 mile, and then veer off on the wide trail, bordered by a fancy wooden fence, descending left along a sage-covered slope.

Soon you start contouring along the base of some craggy, sedimentary bluffs—the so-called palisades. You're well above the valley floor here, so the view takes in thousands of rooftops in the foreground and the purple Santa Monica Mountains rising above the valley haze in the south.

At 6.5 miles the Palisades Trail goes over a saddle and then it drops down to Tampa Avenue. Pick up the Limekiln Canyon Trail on the far side and return to your car, retracing your earlier steps.

Area B-3, Trip 4
Bee Canyon

Distance	2.0 miles round trip
Total Elevation Gain/Loss	250'/250'
Hiking Time	1½ hours (round trip)
Optional Map	USGS 7.5-min *Oat Mountain*
Best Times	All year
Agency	OP
Difficulty	★★

O'Melveny Park's Bee Canyon is a terrific place for exploring with little ones. Presided over by sky-scraping cliffs and shaded by a veritable jungle of young willow saplings, this is natural L.A.'s answer to Disneyland's Adventureland. During most of the year water seeps, or flows, down the canyon's silty bottom, so you'd better wear old shoes if you intend to probe the canyon's upper, nearly trailless reaches.

From the park's picnic area, simply follow the path of least resistance into the hills, straight up the V-shaped gorge. On the left (southwest) side of the canyon, live oak and California walnut trees stand as battered but proud survivors of fire and flood. On the right, barren sedimentary cliffs soar 500 feet. Movements along the Santa Susana thrust fault, which cuts east-west across the Santa Susanas, have helped produce this towering feature. Water seeps out of cracks in the layered rock above and dribbles down several of the steep gullies. (Note: the cliffs are unstable and not suitable for climbing.)

At 0.5 mile beyond the picnic area, the main trail (a fire road) bends left to climb the canyon's south wall. A less-traveled trail continues ahead through willow thickets, becoming more and more obscure the farther you venture. Soon you're scrambling over eroded banks and tree roots, and squishing through mud puddles. By the time the going gets really rough, you'll be at or near the north boundary of the park—a good turnaround point.

Area B-3, Trip 5
Mission Point

Distance	4.7 miles
Total Elevation Gain/Loss	1450'/1450'
Hiking Time	3 hours
Optional Map	USGS 7.5-min *Oat Mountain*
Best Times	November through May
Agency	OP
Difficulty	★★★

Two centuries ago the barren bump called Mission Point overlooked an arid valley dotted with Indian villages. One century ago, the same vantage point would have revealed an early housing boom amid the citrus groves on the valley floor. Today (whenever the smog chances to clear away) the 150°-wide view of the San Fernando

Valley takes in a seemingly endless grid of rectilinear streets and avenues, plus all the visible infrastructure of a city-within-a-city of 1.5 million people.

To reach Mission Point from O'Melveny Park, walk up the fire road west (beyond a wooden fence) of the old ranch house that serves as the park office. The road goes steeply up a narrow, barren ridge dividing two parallel ravines. Most of the California walnut trees in the ravine bottoms survived the 1988 Granada Hills wildfire; elsewhere the grass and sage-scrub hillsides are recovering quickly. Chances are good you'll spot a deer or a coyote, or perhaps a roadrunner flitting across your path.

Keep straight where a nature trail joins on the left, and keep straight again where a side road splits left. After another 300 feet of elevation gain, your road veers left and then descends a little to join a wider fire road (0.8 mile). Turn right and continue climbing, on looping curves, toward Mission Point. (You can shave off some distance, if not effort, by following a footpath going straight up the mountain along the easement of an underground gas pipeline.) Near the summit you pass through a break in a chain-link fence (O'Melveny Park's boundary) and swing around a knoll topped by a cluster of four live-oak trees. This tiny oak copse makes a fine picnic spot with a good view to boot.

A small, stone monument atop Mission Point's shadeless summit (2.2 miles) memorializes physician Mario De Campos, a lover of the local mountains. Down in the valley 3 miles southeast, you'll spot the new Los Angeles Reservoir as well as the dry bed of its predecessor, the Van Norman Reservoir, whose dam very nearly failed during the 1971 Sylmar quake. To the west, carved into the dry, south slopes of the Santa Susanas, are oil wells and a tangle of cliff-hanging roads built to serve them.

For a look at the much-more-agreeable north slopes of the Santa Susanas, walk farther north on the fire road to a locked gate, posted no trespassing. From there, you can get a glimpse of canyon country dotted with live oak, valley oak, walnut, and bigcone Douglas-fir trees. Most of this will be incorporated into the future Santa Clarita Woodlands State Park.

On your return to O'Melveny Park, retrace your steps as far as the park boundary fence. Once past the fence, take the first road to the left, trending northeast toward Bee Canyon. After about a mile on this road, you pass an unmarked junction with a path that descends into the upper canyon. From that junction on, the road tilts very steeply downward, offering a dizzying perspective of the sheer sandstone wall on Bee Canyon's far side. When you reach the canyon floor, turn downstream and hike the remaining short distance out to the picnic area and your starting point.

Area B-4: Simi Hills

Only a decade ago the pastoral grazing lands of the Simi Hills seemed remote from the city. Today, spill-over growth along the Ventura Freeway from the San Fernando Valley to Thousand Oaks is making substantial inroads. An orgy of grading and construction threatens to further usurp the habitat of the valley oak (the stately, spreading tree for which the nearly city of Thousand Oaks is named), and snuff out an important wildlife corridor between the coastal Santa Monica Mountains and the remaining wild lands of the interior.

On the brighter side, 2150 acres of Simi Hills ranchland—nearly the entire upper watershed of Cheeseboro Canyon—have been purchased by the National Park Service for inclusion in the Santa Monica Mountains National Recreation Area. This has assured protection for most of the canyon's valley-oak savannah habitat and created a new recreational resource much needed by residents of the region.

Cheeseboro Canyon and a small patch of open space a few miles east along the rim of the San Fernando Valley—Bell Canyon Park—are the focus of the two hikes in this section. A number of other parcels of Simi Hills land, bordering Thousand Oaks, have recently been acquired for use as parks and open space as well.

Area B-4, Trip 1
Castle Peak

Distance	1.4 miles round trip
Total Elevation Gain/Loss	650'/650'
Hiking Time	1 hour (round trip)
Optional Map	USGS 7.5-min *Calabasas*
Best Times	All year
Agency	LACRPD
Difficulty	★★

Topped by craggy blocks of white conglomerate rock, Castle Peak affords what is probably the most expansive view of San Fernando Valley's west side. From the top, a sea of ground-hugging subdivisions is seen lapping at the foot of the mountain and stretching toward a vaporous horizon. In the middle distance, a bevy of new skyscrapers at Warner Center rises up starkly, symbolizing the valley's evolution toward what will likely be a more vertical type of metropolitan environment in the next century.

To the Chumash Indians living in the Simi Hills centuries ago, Castle Peak was known as Huan, a gigantic monument used to keep track of repetitive celestial and earthly cycles. Every year during the winter solstice, Huan's pointed afternoon shadow swept across a Chumash village located near the mouth of Bell Canyon. Even today,

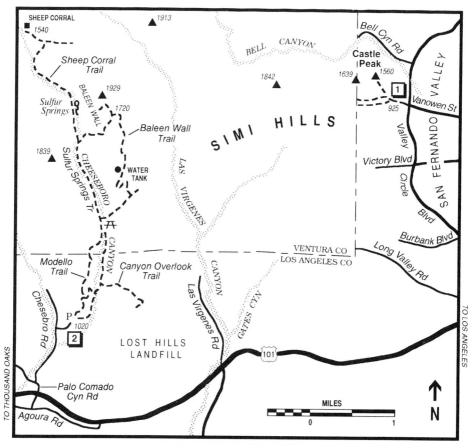

SHEEP CORRAL
■ 1540

▲ 1913

BELL   CANYON

Bell Cyn Rd

Sheep Corral
Trail

Castle
Peak

1842
▲

1639
▲

▲ 1560

1

Vanowen St

VALLEY

1929
▲

Sulfur
Springs

1720

Baleen Wall
Trail

S I M I   H I L L S

925

Valley

SAN FERNANDO

BALEEN WALL

1839
▲

CHEESEBORO

Sulfur Springs Tr

● WATER
TANK

LAS

VIRGENES

Victory Blvd

Circle

Blvd

VENTURA CO
LOS ANGELES CO

Long Valley Rd

Burbank Blvd

Modello
Trail

CANYON

Canyon Overlook
Trail

CANYON

Las Virgenes Rd

GATES CYN

Chesebro Rd

P
1020

2

LOST HILLS
LANDFILL

101

TO LOS ANGELES

TO THOUSAND OAKS

Palo Comado
Cyn Rd

MILES

Agoura Rd

0   1

N

Area B-4: Simi Hills

there's a sense of timeless drama on Huan's summit as you watch (on a crystal-clear December or January afternoon especially) the shadows of the Simi Hills stretch across the urban plain.

Although Castle Peak's summit can be reached from all sides, the shortest and most direct route is by way of the southeast slope. You start walking from the west terminus of Vanowen Street, where Vanowen meets Sunset Ridge Drive, ¼ mile west of Valley Circle Boulevard. Follow an old dirt road going west into a broad, valley-oak-dotted canyon—a part of the undeveloped Bell Canyon Park. Go right where the road divides into two parallel branches, and right again on a steeply inclined path heading

straight up toward Castle Peak's craggy summit. Some scrambling gets you atop the highest outcrop.

Hawks and ravens patrol the air spaces above—and often below—you as you survey the landscape. If you wish, you can follow the trailless ridgeline east to peak 1639 for a better view of the rolling, and as yet undeveloped Simi Hills to the west.

The parallel dirt roads leading west a way from Vanowen Street are blocked by a tall chain-link fence running along the west park boundary and the L.A-Ventura county line A huge, cavernous formation in sandstone lies just beyond, inaccessible on privately owned land.

Area B-4, Trip 2
Cheeseboro Canyon

	Distance	6.5 miles
	Total Elevation Gain/Loss	850'/850'
	Hiking Time	3 hours
	Optional Map	USGS 7.5-min *Calabasas*
	Best Times	November through May
	Agency	NPS
	Difficulty	★ ★

Instantly a hit when it first opened to the public in the late 1980s, Cheeseboro Canyon now draws a mix of hikers, mountain bikers, equestrians, and even wheelchair explorers—an estimated 30,000 visitors yearly—to its network of old roads and newer trails. Friendly rangers patrol the roads and trails on horseback, eager to tell anyone willing to lend an ear about the park's natural features and wildlife (deer and coyotes, especially).

For a good overview of the entire area, follow the 6.5-mile route described here, which goes up the canyon floor and back along the east ridge. Two optional, worthwhile side trips could add another 5 miles—if you're up to it.

Take the Chesebro (sic) Road exit from the Ventura Freeway, go north about 200 yards, and then turn right on the country road signed Chesebro Road. Drive 0.7 mile north to the park's entrance and trailhead on the right. From there, the popular Sulfur Springs Trail goes east and then bends north up the wide, nearly flat canyon floor, while the Modello Trail slants left and curves up along the canyon's rounded west wall. Stay on the Sulfur Springs Trail, passing statuesque valley oaks, which are deciduous, and gnarled coast live oaks, which retain their leaves year round. The extension of a major east-west road (Thousand Oaks Boulevard) across this part of Cheeseboro Canyon may one day spoil the serenity, but for now you see and hear almost nothing of the world beyond the canyon rim.

After 2.5 miles, turn right on the steep, narrow Baleen Wall Trail—no mountain bikes allowed—and begin climbing the grass- and sage-covered east canyon wall. (From this junction you could make an out-and-back side trip: By keeping straight on the main trail, you would pass some sulfurous-smelling seeps and later emerge in an open valley dotted with sandstone boulders. An old sheep corral made of wire lies at trail's end in the upper reaches of Cheeseboro Canyon, 2 miles from the Baleen Wall turnoff.)

After some huffing and puffing up the Baleen Wall Trail, you come to a powerline access road roughly following the east ridgeline. (Here begins a second side trip: You could go north along the road 0.5 mile to the lip of the Baleen Wall, a whitish sedimentary outcrop, for an impressive view of the upper canyon.)

To continue on the main route, walk south on the access road past a large water tank and down to a T-intersection. Turn right and continue descending toward the main trail on Cheeseboro Canyon's floor. From there retrace your steps an easy 1.5 miles back to the trailhead.

Area B-5: Verdugo Mountains

Like a ship caught fast on a sandbar, the Verdugo Mountains protrude above what would otherwise be an unbroken sheet of alluvial deposits slanting down from the foot of the San Gabriel Mountains toward the San Fernando Valley. The narrow, sloping La Crescenta valley divides the Verdugos from the San Gabriels to the east, while the pancake-flat San Fernando Valley stretches nearly 20 miles to the west.

The Verdugos are, in fact, geologic cousins of the San Gabriels; they're only about half as high, but similar in origin and form. Both are youthful, fault-block ranges of unconsolidated crystalline (granitic and metamorphic) rocks, pushed skyward by vertical movements along faults at their bases.

The Verdugo Mountains stand as a remarkable island of undeveloped land—a haven for wildlife such as deer and coyotes—completely encircled by an urbanized domain. Public access is by foot, horse,

or mountain bike, great news if you're looking for a quick escape from the ubiquitous automobile and the pressures of city life. About half of the main part of the Verdugos (a 20-square-mile area south of La Tuna Canyon Road) has so far been set aside as protected open space and parkland. Housing developments have made inroads along some of the lower slopes, but because of steep and unstable slopes further development is all but precluded elsewhere in the range.

Like any dry, interior range, the Verdugos are subject to instant conflagration about half the year. Because of this, a network of wide, smooth fire roads was constructed decades ago to slow the spread of wildfire, and to facilitate access by fire trucks. These roads, along with a new riding and hiking trail on the north end, are your ticket to hours of healthy exercise and enjoyable views whenever the air turns clean and transparent.

Area B-5, Trip 1
South End Loop

	Distance	5.5 miles
	Total Elevation Gain/Loss	1500'/1500'
	Hiking Time	3 hours
	Optional Maps	USGS 7.5-min *Pasadena, Burbank*
	Best Times	November through May
	Difficulty	★★★

From the south end of the Verdugos' summit ridge, your gaze takes in the San Gabriel Mountains, much of the L.A. megalopolis, and even the ocean on occasion. Do this trip late in the day if you want

to enjoy both a spectacular sunset and a blaze of lights after twilight fades. At best, try this on any cloud-free, smog-free day that falls within two weeks on either side of the winter solstice (December 21). During

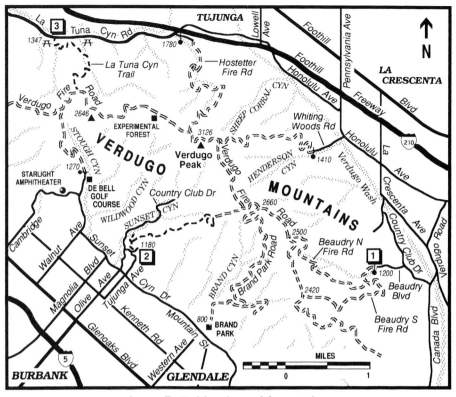

Area B-5: Verdugo Mountains

that period, the sun sets on the flat ocean horizon behind Santa Monica Bay. At other times of year, the sun's sinking path is likely to intersect the coastal mountains. The seemingly strange fact of the sun setting over land most of the year is a consequence of the east-west orientation of California's coastline in the first miles "up-coast" from Los Angeles.

You'll find the starting point on Beaudry Boulevard, 0.4 mile west of Country Club Drive in the city of Glendale (not to be confused with Country Club Drive in Burbank). Park on the street, walk up a paved segment of fire road, bypass a vehicle gate, and continue on dirt past a debris basin to where the fire road splits (0.3 mile). Choose for your way the shadier but less viewful right branch, Beaudry North Fire Road. You'll

return to this junction by way of the left branch, the Beaudry South Fire Road. About halfway up the north road you'll come to a trickling spring and a water tank nestled in a shady ravine, a good place for a breather.

When you reach the summit ridge (2.3 miles), turn sharply left on Verdugo Fire Road and continue climbing another 0.4 mile toward a cluster of brightly painted radio towers atop a 2656' bump—the highest point along this hike. From the towers, continue south along the ridge 0.6 mile to a road junction. The right branch descends to Sunshine Drive in Glendale; you take the left branch and return along an east ridge to the split just above the debris basin.

Area B-5, Trip 2
West Side Loop

	Distance	7.8 miles
	Total Elevation Gain/Loss	2000'/2000'
	Hiking Time	4 hours
	Recommended Map	USGS 7.5-min *Burbank*
	Best Times	November through May
	Agency	BP
	Difficulty	★★★

This is one of the more adventurous trips in this book, even though when you're on it you're almost never out of sight or earshot of the suburbs below. You climb the Verdugo crest by way of an old road—abandoned and washed out in several places, but not ignored by hikers and a few intrepid mountain bikers. The old road is plotted on the currently available (1966, photorevised 1972) *Burbank* topo map. Wear long pants, or else you'll be benignly scourged by the scratchy buckwheat and sage vegetation taking root in the road bed.

Start from the T-intersection of Via Montana and Camino de Villas in the foothills above Burbank. (This can be reached most quickly by driving north on Country Club Drive from the end of Olive Avenue, and turning right at Via Montana.) Across the street from a row of new condos, cross a patch of grass and pick up an old dirt road bed going north. The road contours across a hillside toward some houses in the bottom of Sunset Canyon. At 0.2 mile, turn right where another old road goes sharply up the ridge. Stay on the same for the next 1.7 miles, picking your way past bushes and occasional rock slides, Near the top of this difficult stretch, at a spot with a nice view southwest, look for a rock cairn concealing an informal register (notebook). You can leave a record of your passage there.

At 1.9 miles from the start you come upon a maintained dirt road which goes left a short distance to a water tank, and right to Verdugo Fire Road on the crest. Walk 0.5 mile up to the crest, where you arrive at an unmarked, four-way junction. Take the middle branch (the road on the right quickly dead-ends). Continue another 0.3 mile to a junction with Brand Park Road, where a wooden bench on the shadeless ridgeline invites you to sit a spell (if it's not too hot) and enjoy the view.

Brand Park Road, a fairly new addition to the fire-road network, is somewhat less scenic than what you've traveled so far. Follow its turns and twists 3.3 miles to the green lawns of Brand Park in the valley below. You'll loop around a small landfill near the bottom and perhaps dodge a couple of garbage trucks.

In a corner of Brand Park stands Glendale's architecturally noted Brand Library, originally a Spanish-Moorish-style mansion built by early 1900s civic booster Leslie Brand. Near the library and for some distance up the canyon behind it are the remnants of the tropical gardens that once graced Brand's estate.

To complete this loop hike, walk along pleasantly shaded Mountain Street (which becomes Sunset Canyon Drive as you pass into the city of Burbank) for 1.2 miles to Tujunga Avenue. Turn right on Tujunga (which later becomes Camino de Villas) and walk 0.4 mile uphill to Villa Montana and your waiting car.

Area B-5, Trip 3
North End Traverse

	Distance	9.5 miles
	Total Elevation Gain/Loss	2050'/2050'
	Hiking Time	4 hours
	Optional Map	USGS 7.5-min *Burbank*
	Best Times	October through May
	Agency	SMMC
	Difficulty	★★★

Less sunshine and more moisture make the north slopes of the Verdugo Mountains more appealing that the sun-blasted southern slopes. On this trek you'll pass by luxuriant growths of aromatic chaparral and visit a couple of surprisingly attractive oak- and sycamore-shaded mini-canyons. On clear days, the best part is the walk along the Verdugo ridgecrest. There you can "bag" 3126' Verdugo Peak, the tallest bump in the range.

You start on the delightful new La Tuna Canyon Trail, a meandering, hand-built pathway through acreage newly acquired as parkland by the Santa Monica Mountains Conservancy. It begins at a small picnic site on the south side of La Tuna Canyon Road, 1.4 miles west of the La Tuna Canyon Road exit from Foothill Freeway, and 3.3 miles east of Sunland Boulevard in Sun Valley. Don't confuse this picnic spot with a similar one 0.3 mile east.

Follow the La Tuna Canyon Trail up along a small canyon about 100 yards to a fenced viewpoint overlooking a natural declivity, where water cascades after a good rain. From there you double back and undertake an easy switchback ascent of the canyon's east wall. Rooted to the steep slopes are a tangled assortment of mature chaparral shrubs—scrub oak, hollyleaf cherry, ceanothus, and toyon.

After about 0.6 mile the trail starts to contour across a slope immediately above La Tuna Canyon Road, and afterward drops quickly to the bottom of another small canyon, parallel to the first. (Down this canyon is the top of a 20' waterfall, the bottom of which lies just above the picnic site east of your starting point.) For a while you're engulfed in a cool tunnel of over-arching live oak and bay laurel limbs. Wild blackberry vines and poison oak thrive in this intimate little glen.

At 1.3 miles the newly cut trail tread joins an old jeep road that quickly gains the ridge between the two canyons and then connects with Verdugo Fire Road. A heart-pounding climb (600 vertical feet in 0.6 mile) puts you on the wide fire road. Turn left and head east toward Verdugo Peak.

Next stop (worth the short side trip if the air is clear) is a 2646' knoll on the right, 0.6 mile from the top of the La Tuna Canyon Trail. Scramble up the fire break on the knoll's east side and enjoy what is likely the most complete view of the San Fernando Valley available from any land-based vantage point. The pseudo-aerial perspective reveals flat grids of linear streets slashed by curving freeways, huge complexes of industrial buildings that look like giant computer circuit boards, endless rows of stuccoed single-family homes half-hidden in a green haze of street trees, and spiky clusters of high rises. The valley's geographic connection to the main Los Angeles Basin is plainly revealed. In the gap where the connection is made (between the Verdugo and Santa Monica mountains), sunlight gleams on the concrete banks of the Los Angeles River flood channel.

Farther east you pass several antenna sites and enter a cool grove of pine, cedar, and cypress trees planted for experimental purposes after a major fire in 1927. Out of their element on these naturally scrubby ridgetops, the trees are nonetheless a welcome addition.

A right turn at the next fire-road junction (4.3 miles from the start) and a short climb south take you to the high point unofficially known as Verdugo Peak. Walk around the antenna facility at the top for a 360° view. The San Gabriel Mountains and La Crescenta valley to the east are especially striking. On the far side of the valley, subdivisions completely cover most of the classically formed alluvial fans that spill from the foot of the San Gabriels. Debris dams at the apex of nearly every fan do their best (but sometimes fail) to catch the muddy slurry that sweeps down the canyons whenever storms unleash torrents of water on the slopes above.

After visiting the peak, backtrack to the aforementioned junction, but bear right (north) on Hostetter Fire Road. Three miles of easy descent take you down to a large, steel gate just short of La Tuna Canyon Road. Follow the left (south-side) shoulder of that road to return to your car—an easy half-hour walk or 15-minute jog.

Experimental forest atop the Verdugo Mountains

Area B-6: Griffith Park

Why shouldn't one of the world's most expansive cities boast one of the world's biggest city parks? It does, in fact. Griffith Park's 4100 acres—about five times the size of New York's Central Park—rate as the nation's largest municipal park completely surrounded by urban areas.

Griffith Park is L.A.'s "park for the people," where Angelenos (and not very many tourists) come to spread a picnic blanket, visit the homegrown zoo or the observatory and planetarium, and explore the chaparral-covered hills and scenic vistas. Over half of the park's area consists of terrain too steep to be developed as parkland in the conventional manner, so it remains as a kind of in-city wilderness, albeit of a mostly dry and scrubby kind.

More than 50 miles of fire roads and foot trails lure those on foot and horseback; while bicyclists can explore more than 20 miles of twisting pavement, or take to the dirt wherever such use is permitted. The trails are busy on sunny weekends, yet it can be amazingly quiet here as long as you get an early start (the park's several gates swing open at 6 A.M. for access by automobile). By starting early you can also take advantage of the day's coolest temperatures and generally the cleanest air.

Our area map of Griffith Park (p. 55), though adequate for the purposes of navigating the routes described in detail below, omits a multitude of lesser paths, many of them worn in by people making their own way through the brush. Hileman's *Recreation and Geological Map of Griffith Park*, available at the observatory gift shop, is your best source for information about the lesser trails. The map's geologic overlay, showing faults and various features, is quite instructive as well. You can also pick up a free sketch map of the trails at the ranger station and information center on the park's east side. Trail names and numbers keyed to the sketch maps are of little use, though, since nearly all the trail signs have been stolen or rendered illegible by graffiti. This is not to say that Griffith Park is an urban jungle; on the contrary it is kept surprisingly tidy considering its role as a playground in the midst of a pressure-cooker city.

Griffith Park occupies the eastern tip of the Santa Monica Mountains, a fact difficult to discern until you climb one of the park's high points and look west along the crest of the range. The higher and wilder parts of the Santa Monicas, west of Sepulveda Pass, are covered later in the Santa Monica Mountains section of this book.

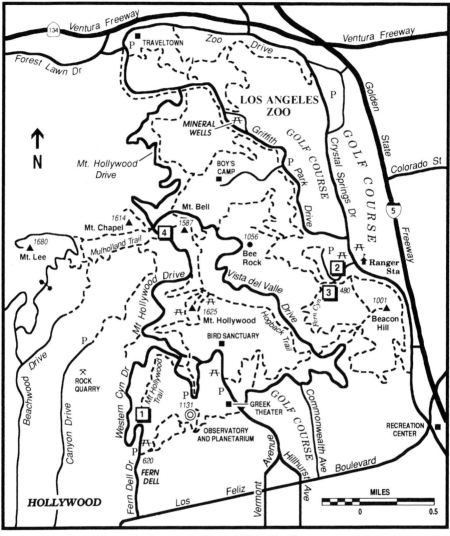

Area B-6: Griffith Park

Area B-6, Trip 1
Fern Dell–Mt. Hollywood Loop

	Distance	4.7 miles
	Total Elevation Gain/Loss	1050'/1050'
	Hiking Time	2 hours
	Optional Maps	USGS 7.5-min *Hollywood, Burbank*
	Best Times	All year
	Agency	GP
	Difficulty	★★

The bald, flattish summit of Mt. Hollywood would scarcely be something to write home about except for its strategic location overlooking just about everything. Hikers approach from all directions, but the most popular starting point is the observatory parking lot. On the somewhat longer trek described here, you'll start out a bit below the observatory so you can enjoy the exotically landscaped Fern Dell area too. The dell features picnic tables, a year-round brook (a part of the observatory's cooling system, but appealing nonetheless), plenty of succulent plants and shade trees, and a nature museum.

From Fern Dell's main parking lot, walk across the lowermost horseshoe curve on Western Canyon Road and continue on the wide, dirt fire road heading uphill (north) into sunny chaparral country. A bit trampled and trashy at first, the landscape improves immensely as you climb. Along the trail are larger shrubs such as toyon, elderberry, laurel sumac, sugarbush, and ceanothus; and smaller ones such as black sage, buckwheat, and fuchsia-flowered gooseberry— all very typical of the drier, south- and west-facing slopes in the park. Here, too, are common weedy plants such as fennel, tree tobacco, and castor bean. Planted eucalyptus and pines stand high on the nearby slopes, while a handful of native live oaks tucked into the bigger creases on the sun-seared slopes draw just enough moisture from the soil to survive.

After passing under a couple of shade-giving oaks, the trail curves left and crosses the west observatory road. Soon you're on the ridgeline south of Mt. Hollywood, passing high over a road tunnel. Listen for horns blaring as cars barrel through below.

A couple of long, lazy switchback legs take you to a trail junction not far below Mt. Hollywood's summit. Make a sharp left, pass the shady Captain's Roost picnic area (drinking water here), and continue to a wide trail junction just north of the summit. Make a hard right there and walk over to the picnic tables on the top. Your gaze takes in (among many other things) the downtown L.A. skyline and the antenna-topped Mt. Lee with its famous HOLLYWOOD sign facing south over "Tinseltown." Just beyond Mt. Lee is the top of Cahuenga Peak (1820'), the highest summit in this corner of the Santa Monica Mountains.

On your return, backtrack to the wide junction and go right, circling Mt. Hollywood's east side. Retrace your steps on the two switchback segments, but keep south along the ridgeline after you reach the top of the tunnel. Walk across the observatory parking lot toward the monumental, copper-domed building that houses a 500-seat planetarium and two massive but antique refractor telescopes. Swing around the back side of the building to discover some intimate little observing decks with commanding views of the L.A. Basin.

For the final leg of the trip, follow the trail that descends the slope just east of the observatory. It starts from the left side of the building as you face its grand entrance. After 0.2 mile, swing right at a trail junction. Immediately afterward bear left at a second junction, avoiding a right fork that dead-ends. Go either way at the third junction—both trails meet later at Fern Dell. The left (lower) trail, however, is a bit more scenic. After winding past golden-blossomed silk oak trees, you arrive at Fern Dell's bubbling brook. Your starting point is just up the road.

Toyon—the "holly" of Hollywood

Area B-6, Trip 2
Beacon Hill

Distance	1.9 miles
Total Elevation Gain/Loss	550'/550'
Hiking Time	1 hour
Optional Map	USGS 7.5-min *Burbank*
Best Times	All year
Agency	GP
Difficulty	★★

Sharply terminated by the Los Angeles River flood channel and Interstate 5, Beacon Hill stands as the last eastward gasp of a 50-mile-long mountain range—the Santa Monicas. Back in the Teens and Twenties it served a utilitarian purpose as the site of an illuminated beacon for Grand Central Airport in Glendale. Today it presides over flatlands overrun by industrial buildings. Commercial air operations have long since shifted to LAX and four other big airports around the L.A. Basin. On this looping trip up to Beacon Hill's seldom-visited summit, you'll have a unique view of Glendale's industrial tracts, its emerging medium-rise downtown skyline, and the looming Verdugo Mountains beyond.

From the entrance to the large parking lot west of the ranger station and south of the merry-go-round, head south across a paved road onto a parallel fire road. Contour 0.1 mile east, and then turn sharply right up the narrow but obvious footpath that goes straight up the hill. A very steep but short climb takes you up past twisted live oaks and tree-sized toyons. When you reach a ridgetop path lined with pine trees, turn left and walk up to Beacon Hill's summit dome. The top is grown over with laurel sumac, but you need only descend a little to the east for an unobstructed view of Glendale.

You can return by a much more gradual but longer route, entirely on fire road. From Beacon Hill, walk west on the ridge to a five-way junction on a shady saddle. Take the right branch, and wind easily down the sides of a steep, north-flowing ravine called Fern Canyon. You pass through some of the park's densest growths of vegetation—an agreeable mixture of native chaparral, oaks, and various non-native trees. Near the bottom, stay right at both of two closely spaced intersections. Your starting point lies directly ahead.

Area B-6, Trip 3
East Side Loop

	Distance	5.9 miles
	Total Elevation Gain/Loss	1350'/1350'
	Hiking Time	3½ hours
	Optional Map	USGS 7.5-min *Hollywood, Burbank*
	Best Times	October through June
	Agency	GP
	Difficulty	★★★

Botanically and geologically, this is perhaps Griffith Park's most interesting hike. It's no slouch when it comes to good views either. The route tops out on the very crest of the park at Mt. Hollywood.

When we last took this hike on a warm March afternoon, my companions and I appreciated the shade-giving live oak, pine, eucalyptus, and California walnut trees. The walnut trees were just leafing out at that time. We also noted both blue and white varieties of blooming ceanothus, and four relatives in the family of sumacs that frequent the Southern California chaparral—laurel sumac, lemonade berry, sugarbush, and poison oak.

As in Trip 2 above, start at the parking lot just south of the merry-go-round. Cross the paved road but head southwest up the Fern Canyon fire road. Keep straight at the first of two closely spaced junctions, but go right at the second, 0.1 mile after crossing the pavement. In the next 0.7 mile you pass the site of the old L.A. Zoo, and a side trail leading left (west) toward Bee Rock, an impressive outcrop of cavernous sandstone poking out of the ridge above. Bee Rock is a good example of the types of marine sedimentary rock that are widely exposed throughout the middle and eastern Santa Monica Mountains. Up around Mt. Hollywood, the bedrock consists of volcanic rocks more characteristic of the west end of the Santa Monicas.

Just past the Bee Rock trail, turn left on the fire road going up along the side of a ravine. You zigzag around a chaparral-covered ridge overlooking the Griffith Park Boy's Camp and arrive, after 1.2 miles, at Vista del Valle Drive. Swing right, walk about 0.1 mile down the shoulder, then veer left on the wide trail that ascends sharply up the slope to the south. Turn sharply left at the next junction and continue south along the ridge between Mts. Bell and Hollywood.

From the wide intersection just below Mt. Hollywood's summit, you will eventually go east along the sunny ridgeline. But first pay a visit to the summit itself, and later cool off and refill your water bottle at the irrigated spot east of the summit known as Dante's View. Eucalyptus trees and succulent plants frame a view to the south at this little hideaway.

The view-rich but sometimes steep trail along the ridgeline to the east, sometimes called the Hogback Trail, meanders down to meet Vista del Valle Drive. Cross the pavement there, walk down along the shoulder for about 100 feet, and pick up the trail going left past a water tank and down into the upper reaches of Fern Canyon. A delightfully shaded descent leads to a five-way junction. Make a hard left there and descend along Fern Canyon's shady slopes to your starting point below.

Area B-6, Trip 4
Mulholland Ridge

	Distance	1.6 miles
	Total Elevation Gain/Loss	300'/300'
	Hiking Time	1 hour
	Optional Map	USGS 7.5-min *Burbank*
	Best Times	All year
	Agency	GP
	Difficulty	★★

If the scenic highway following the crest of the Santa Monica Mountains (Mulholland Drive/Highway) were ever extended eastward, it would probably snake along the sharply defined ridge between Mt. Lee and Mt. Chapel. But for now, and probably forever, the phenomenal views both north and south from this ridge remain the privilege of self-propelled travelers alone.

The starting point, the intersection of Mt. Hollywood Drive and Vista del Valle Drive, has no formal parking lot, but there's plenty of roadside space nearby. From the intersection, walk 0.1 mile southeast on Mt. Hollywood Drive and then make a 180° turn to the right on the dirt fire road known as the Mulholland Trail (Mulholland Highway on some maps). Contour for about 0.8 mile, passing two intersections where fire roads join from the south. At a point 50 yards past the second intersection, look for a narrow but deeply eroded path going north up a steep ridge. Take this for 0.2 mile to a rugged trail running east-west along the ridge between Mt. Chapel and the paved (private) service road to Mt. Lee. Go right (east) on this trail.

On the ridge, you almost feel like you're flying as you gaze a thousand feet down on the Hollywood foothills to the south and the tidy green spaces of Forest Lawn Memorial Park to the north. Near Mt. Chapel a steep path slants sharply up to the summit, one of several ways to scramble up this rocky peaklet if you feel like it. Our route, however, bends right, contours the south slope,

connects with a service road to a water tank high on Mt. Chapel's north shoulder, and arrives back at the starting point.

Area B-7: Hollywood Hills

The scraggly ridges and precipitous canyons separating San Fernando Valley from Hollywood and Beverly Hills harbor more than just a tangled net of serpentine streets and the homes of the rich and famous. Here and there a few pockets of open space remain where one can roam over sage-scented trails and partake, however briefly, of some of the perks—like great vistas on a clear day—afforded to Hollywood's most privileged residents.

The as-yet mostly unconnected parks and open spaces covered here are included within the sinuous boundaries of the Santa Monica Mountains National Recreation Area, a mosaic of federal, state and local parkland and private lands stretching from Cahuenga Pass above Hollywood to Point Mugu in Ventura County. The remainder of the national recreation lands will be treated separately in the Santa Monica Mountains section of this book. Here on the east side of the Santa Monicas, even diminutive parcels of land mean a lot for an area whose last unprotected ridges and canyons are being cut and filled by massive development.

Literally minutes away from L.A.'s most congested districts, the hikes described below offer remarkable opportunities to escape noise, traffic, and on some occasions, low-lying smog.

Area B-7, Trip 1
Runyan Canyon

Distance	1–2 miles
Hiking Time	½ to 1 hour
Optional Map	USGS 7.5-min *Hollywood*
Best Times	All year
Agency	LACRPD
Difficulty	★

The former estate of actor Errol Flynn, now called Runyan Canyon Park, is slowly reverting back to nature. Fire and erosion have erased all but some old foundations, and damaged but not destroyed palms, pines, eucalyptus, and other exotic vegetation that once graced the site. The native vegetation is of the typical chaparral variety—dry and unappealing during summer's drought, but verdant and aromatic in the springtime.

Entrance gates for the park at the north ends of both Fuller Avenue and Vista Street are open during daylight hours only. There are basically two hikes you can take here, each ending at an overlook.

The first (a total of 1 mile out and back), goes straight up the old driveway from Fuller Avenue. It curves up the ridge east of the canyon bottom, passes above an abandoned tennis court, and ends on a flat spot overlooking most of Hollywood and the Wilshire corridor from a point roughly 600 feet higher.

The second (2 miles out and back, with a gain of 500 feet) follows an old asphalt road up the canyon's west side and circles to the east ridge near the head of the canyon. There you meet a dirt road going south along the ridge to another viewpoint, this one on the same ridge as the overlook mentioned earlier, but about 200 feet higher.

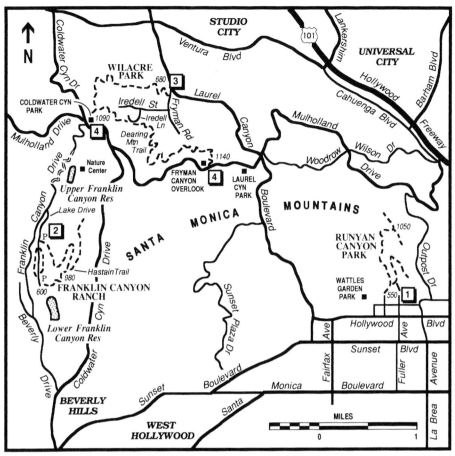

Area B-7: Hollywood Hills

Area B-7, Trip 2
Franklin Canyon

	Distance	1.8 miles
	Total Elevation Gain/Loss	400'/400'
	Hiking Time	1 hour
	Optional Map	USGS 7.5-min *Beverly Hills*
	Best Times	All year
	Agency	NPS
	Difficulty	★

Franklin Canyon Ranch is the southern-most part of Cross Mountain Park, an emerging recreational complex straddling the Santa Monica Mountains crest. The other units include Upper Franklin Canyon Reservoir, Coldwater Canyon Park, Wilacre

Park, and the Fryman Canyon Natural Area. The ranch, which is under the jurisdiction of the National Park Service, draws plenty of families and kids for nature walks led by rangers and volunteer docents. It's a good place to drop by for a picnic, or a hike or a run before or after work.

Tucked into a fold in the mountains above the newly refurbished (but closed to the public) Lower Franklin Canyon Reservoir, the ranch is a bit off the beaten path. From Beverly Hills, go north on Beverly Drive—but be careful to fork left on the lesser-traveled north end of Beverly Drive where the main Coldwater Canyon Drive goes straight. After 0.8 mile, bear right on narrow Franklin Canyon Drive. Go 1.2 miles farther along the canyon-side to Lake Drive. Turn right and backtrack 0.3 mile south to a small parking area at the ranch's entrance sign. The Hastain Trail begins there, on the left.

You can also reach Lake Drive and the entrance to the ranch by driving south from Mulholland Drive on Franklin Canyon Drive. Part of that stretch is unpaved and becomes a muddy morass after heavy rains.

From the parking area, walk the twisting Hastain Trail (a fire road) 0.9 mile along chaparral-covered slopes to a hairpin turn (980') with a panoramic view of the city. Looking over green-mantled Beverly Hills estates and the office towers of the Wilshire corridor, you can sometimes see a blue horizon beyond.

From the hairpin turn, the fire road continues climbing toward Coldwater Canyon Drive. You veer right on the narrow switchback trail descending to the green lawn and ranch house below. Somehow this old gentleman's ranch managed to retain its rustic, rural charm before being acquired for parkland a decade ago.

From the ranch house you can walk back to your car on either of two trails that parallel Lake Drive. The trail on the right passes under a shady canopy of live oak, while the trail on the left meanders among scattered oaks and sycamores down along Franklin Canyon's usually dry stream bed.

Amphitheater at Franklin Canyon Ranch

Area B-7, Trip 3
Wilacre-Coldwater Loop

Distance	2.7 miles
Total Elevation Gain/Loss	500'/500'
Hiking Time	1½ hours
Optional Map	USGS 7.5-min *Van Nuys*
Best Times	All year
Agency	SMMC
Difficulty	★★

A 129-acre island of open space in the midst of Studio City's more lavish residential areas, Wilacre Park (the former estate of silent movie star Will Acres) offers a wide-ranging view of San Fernando Valley and a peaceful, quiet atmosphere. This loop route goes up through Wilacre Park and visits Coldwater Canyon Park, which is the headquarters of TreePeople, a grassroots organization that is spearheading efforts to plant millions of trees in the urban Los Angeles area.

Find a curbside parking spot near where Fryman Road diverges from Laurel Canyon Boulevard, and walk west up the gated trail—at first a curving, hardtopped driveway flanked by pine and cypress trees. After passing the slab foundation of Acres' old house, the road turns to dirt. You ascend, more easily now, along north-facing slopes dotted with live oak and walnut. After a

while you turn south, descend slightly, and arrive at a wide junction (1.4 miles) on the edge of Coldwater Canyon Park. Take the Magic Forest Trail on the right, or use some steps a little way to the left to reach the old fire station above that serves as headquarters for TreePeople. Pick up a brochure at the parking lot and make your own self-guided tour of TreePeople's exhibits and nursery.

Return to the wide junction and continue east (downhill) on Dearing Mountain Trail (a.k.a. Betty B. Dearing Trail), named in honor of the late advocate of Santa Monica Mountains trails. After 0.5 mile you hit pavement at Iredell Lane, a cozy, residential cul-de-sac. The last 0.6 mile is along lightly traveled streets—down Iredell Lane to Iredell Street, down Iredell Street to Fryman Road, and down Fryman Road to the starting point.

Area B-7, Trip 4
Coldwater to Fryman Canyon

Distance	2.5 miles
Total Elevation Gain/Loss	500'/450'
Hiking Time	1½ hours
Optional Maps	USGS 7.5-min *Van Nuys, Beverly Hills*
Best Times	All year
Agency	SMMC
Difficulty	★★

The Dearing Mountain Trail commemorates Betty B. Dearing (1917–77), a conservationist who foresaw a trail stretching from Los Angeles along the mountain crests to the sea. When the Backbone Trail is completed across the Santa Monica Mountains National Recreation Area sometime in this decade, her wish will be fulfilled.

The Dearing Mountain Trail, which is not a part of the Backbone Trail or even near it, runs roughly parallel to the motorist's equivalent of the Backbone Trail—Mulholland Drive. Mulholland Drive, along with Mulholland Highway to the west, is the main scenic roadway stretching 50 miles through the National Recreation Area.

Do this as a car-shuttle trip by leaving cars at both Coldwater Canyon Park (open for parking 9 A.M. to dusk) and Fryman Canyon Overlook; or leave one car and go out and back on the same route for a somewhat rugged 5 miles of ups and downs. Another alternative would be to make a loop by walking or jogging over or back along Mulholland Drive—a good option if you can do the road-walking part very early on a Sunday morning to avoid traffic.

Pay careful attention to our directions. In places this poorly marked trail is like rabbit run through the brush, with plenty of intersecting roads and false paths to lead you astray.

From the east side of the TreePeople complex in Coldwater Canyon Park (see the previous trip), descend a stone staircase and hook up with the dirt road—Dearing Mountain Trail—below. Go downhill 0.5 mile to where you meet Iredell Lane. Walk 100 yards down the sidewalk there and then veer off on the fire road that slants up to the right. After only 0.1 mile, turn left and follow a foot trail. You soon bend right and begin climbing straight up a slope over wooden water bars. The trail levels along a brushy slope and soon intersects a disused dirt road bed overlooked by some towering, opulent, new residences. Turn left on the road bed, curve past a private, fenced exercise yard and descend into the eucalyptus-shaded upper reaches of Fryman Canyon. This shady little ravine is a part of the small Fryman Canyon Natural Area between Mulholland Drive and the edge of the residential area below. Part of the year a tiny stream enhances this cool and appealing spot.

After curving sharply left to cross the ravine, you ascend gradually on an old road bed another 0.3 mile, then take the steep foot trail (Dearing Mountain Trail) going up the slope to the right. This meanders generally eastward, staying about 150–200 feet below Mulholland Drive. Near the end you pass a morgue of old, wrecked cars jettisoned from the road above, and settle into switchbacks leading up to a fire road just east of the mini-park called Fryman Canyon Overlook.

Area B-8: Puente Hills

The rambling Puente Hills, overlooking the San Gabriel Valley to the north and Orange County to the south, interrupt what would otherwise be a continuous spread of flat, nondescript suburbs. Rising no higher than 1500 feet in elevation, they host a growing collection of hillside homes; the sprawling, mostly undeveloped Rose Hills Memorial Park; and several large patches of open space. L.A. County's Skyline equestrian trail skips over the west end of the Puente Hills from one rounded summit to the next, joining a number of spur trails that connect to suburbs below.

Unfortunately, the Puente Hills lie near the geographic center of the worst-polluted air basin in the U.S.A. Nonetheless, even here, sparkling weather does come on rare occasions. All you have to do is wait and be ready to take advantage of it. Whenever the L.A. Basin is swept clear of smog and moisture by offshore winds, parts of the Skyline Trail offer truly mind-blowing views of almost everything from the mountains to the sea. Don't miss the spectacular sunrises over the San Bernardino and San Jacinto mountains, and sunsets over the Pacific Ocean.

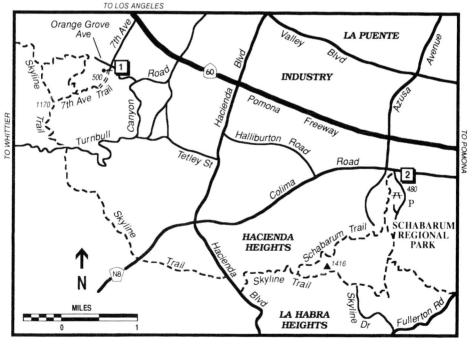

Area B-8: Puente Hills

Area B-8, Trip 1
West Skyline Loop

	Distance	4.3 miles
	Total Elevation Gain/Loss	1100'/1100'
	Hiking Time	2 hours
	Optional Maps	USGS 7.5-min *Baldwin Park, El Monte*
	Best Times	October through May
	Agency	LADPR
	Difficulty	★★

The west end of the Puente Hills was hit hard during the 1989 Hacienda Heights fire. A few months later the same slopes were sprouting new growths of wild grass and mustard. Fire-following wildflowers came in modest numbers by the following spring (they should put on an even better show in future years if winter rains bring plenty of moisture). For the most part the flames skipped over, or merely singed, the mature live oaks and California walnut trees hidden in the north-side ravines. Amazingly, some of the oaks completely denuded of their evergreen leaves were sprouting new ones within weeks, even as the smell of charcoal lingered in the air.

On this trip you'll explore these hardy little pockets of oak woodland, and also get a close look at the marine sedimentary bedrock of the Puente Hills, which dates back about 15–30 million years. Mostly this consists of silty, layered deposits, but you'll also find some conglomerate rock in the ravines.

This is an especially fun trip to take on an evening lit by the full moon. You'll make your way along spooky ravines where moonbeams filter through the twisted oaks and glance off the cobbled rock formations.

The easy-to-find trailhead for this hike is the south terminus of 7th Avenue, 0.7 mile south of the Pomona Freeway. Park along any nearby street and walk south on the gated, unpaved roadway (7th Street will one day carry traffic over this stretch toward

Whittier). After 0.3 mile you veer right up an asphalt strip that leads to an abandoned hillside reservoir. From there, pick up the switchback trail going up the ridge.

At 0.8 mile from the start you reach a small flat with a hitching post. Keep going straight up the ridge (you'll later return to this spot by way of the trail coming up from the right). At 1.3 miles you arrive at the Skyline Trail, which at this point follows the wide Puente Hills crest. Turn right and follow the trail's right-of-way, fenced on both sides, roughly paralleling some high-voltage powerlines. Long views (hopefully) west toward downtown L.A.'s Oz-like skyline and the blue Pacific atone for the atrociously ugly, 'dozer-scraped foreground.

At 1.8 miles, turn right on a trail that goes briefly up a little hill and then steadily down along oak-dotted slopes overlooking a deep ravine. After several switchbacks you arrive at the mouth of that ravine (2.7 miles) and traverse to the right around a hillside just above the edge of a subdivision. The trail steers you into another shade-dappled ravine, similar to the first. You ascend moderately along the bottom, veer left (south) up a tributary, and climb switchbacks to the hitching post on the ridge above (3.5 miles). From there retrace your earlier steps past the hillside reservoir to 7th Avenue.

Area B-8, Trip 2
Schabarum Trail

	Distance	5.2 miles
	Total Elevation Gain/Loss	900'/900'
	Hiking Time	2½ hours
	Optional Map	USGS 7.5-min *La Habra*
	Best Times	October through May
	Agency	LADPR
	Difficulty	★★

Schabarum Regional Park (formerly known as Otterbein Park before its dedication to county supervisor Peter Schabarum in 1989) features a green-grass strip extending nearly a mile into the Puente Hills, and lots of steep, brushy hillsides affording some great panoramas of the San Gabriel Valley and the San Gabriel Mountains. You'll share these views with hawks and ravens who ride the hillside thermals.

After parking in any of the park's spacious lots (open 8 A.M. to sunset), start your hike on the signed Schabarum Trail. It starts near the park entrance and twists and turns along dry, prickly-pear-covered slopes west of the park's long strip of green turf. At 0.8 mile you come to a split; the left branch goes over to an equestrian ring at the south end of the turf strip, while the right branch, your route, takes you up through dense chaparral toward the Puente Hills crest. The panorama below includes nearby subdivisions in Hacienda Heights, the linear City of Industry (which, it is manifestly clear, specializes in industry), and assorted other suburban sprawl stretching to the foot of the San Gabriel Mountains. The winter-white-capped summit of Mt. San Antonio (Old Baldy) floats serenely above it all.

As you approach the ridgeline, you contour below an antenna-topped, 1416' peak. A short-cut to the Skyline Trail is possible up and around this.

After 2.5 miles from the park entrance, bear left as you're approaching a water tower and antenna site served by a paved service road coming up from below. Follow the dirt road going east, which is the Skyline Trail. You climb some more, passing the 1416' peak, and then descend. To the south you look over the wooded community of La Habra Heights, and across the coastal plains of Orange County.

After winding down a steep hillside, you reach a north-south dirt road in a saddle (3.8 miles). Go left and continue 0.7 mile down a draw to the equestrian ring. From there you can follow an asphalt walkway down the middle of the turf area to reach the park entrance.

Old Baldy from the Schabarum Trail

Area B-9: San Gabriel Valley

The million or so residents of the greater San Gabriel Valley area are fortunate to have easy access to dozens of higher-country trails in the San Gabriel Mountains. In this section, however, we're going to concentrate on three worthy hikes on the rim of the valley itself—two in the San Jose Hills at San Dimas, and a third along the base of the San Gabriel Mountains just above La Verne. Two more lowland hikes, in the Puente Hills, have already been described in Area B-8. All five make fine winter and spring additions to your repertoire of favorite hiking spots—especially if you're a resident of these parts.

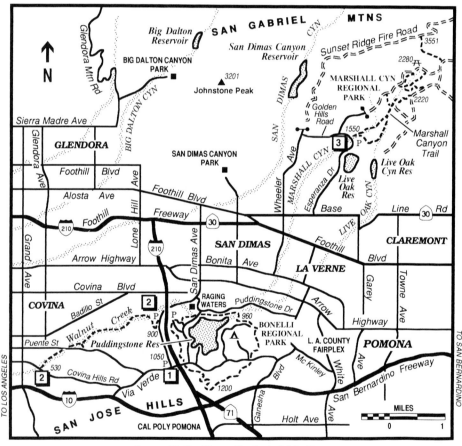

Area B-9: San Gabriel Valley

Area B-9, Trip 1
Around Puddingstone Reservoir

	Distance	7.0 miles
	Total Elevation Gain/Loss	1050'/1050'
	Hiking Time	3½ hours
	Optional Map	USGS 7.5-min *San Dimas*
	Best Times	November through May
	Agency	LADPR
	Difficulty	★★★

Girded by freeways and busy streets, and perched above the world's first five-level freeway interchange (the intersection of routes 10, 210, and 71), the trails of Bonelli Regional Park are hardly the place to get away from it all—unless, of course, you arrive here early on a Saturday or Sunday morning. During those quiet times you can get a sense of how peaceful a spot this was before World War II. In those distant days, Puddingstone Reservoir nestled among serene hills overlooking a patchwork quilt of citrus groves.

Today the reservoir and the surrounding county-operated regional park are a big tourist draw, with attractions such as the Raging Waters aquatic amusement park, a golf course, acres of RV camping and picnic grounds, horse stables, hot tubs, and even motorboat drag races on occasion. For hikers, what remains of the dry, grassy hills above the reservoir can be very attractive in March and April, especially if California poppies brighten the velvety green slopes.

Although most of the trails at Bonelli Park are designed to serve equestrians, hikers (and especially mountain bikers of late) have discovered them as well. About 14 miles of dirt roads and bridle trails lace the outer perimeter of the park, not including some pedestrian and bike paths that follow parts of the reservoir's shoreline.

Our "grand tour" of the park circles the lake in a roundabout but scenic way. It's convenient to start outside the park in a Park and Ride lot on Via Verde, just west of

Interstate 210. On weekends this lot has plenty of space, and you don't have to pay.

From the Park and Ride lot, walk east on Via Verde over the freeway toward Bonelli Park's west entrance booth and nearby administration center, where you can get a detailed trail map for the asking. Just after crossing the overpass you'll see a trail, passing through a tunnel under Via Verde, going southeast up onto a grassy hillside dotted with planted pines. Take it, and let the EQUESTRIAN TRAIL signs be your guide for the next couple of miles. The trail dips momentarily, almost touching Via Verde, and then swings right and later left as it climbs to the top of the ridge. Keep climbing and ignore side trails to the left. Topping out at about 1200 feet elevation (1.4 miles from where you parked), there's a fine view over the Puente Hills to the south and across the flat lands stretching interminably east toward San Bernardino and Riverside.

Continue following the ridge, generally east, for the next mile. You'll arrive at a road intersection close to the park's east entrance booth. Cross the pavement and climb north and east around some horse stables to a gap in the ridge to the north (restrooms here). Continue north down a draw, and bear left to join McKinley Avenue (3.5 miles), which is gated to the left. Near the gate pick up a signed bridle trail that briefly follows a shoreline access road. The trail soon swings north, follows a fence delimiting Brackett Field (a small airport), and then crosses a muddy creek (Live Oak

Wash) to join a paved walkway through grassy picnic and play areas along the reservoir's north shore.

Continue west on the walkway—or across the lawns—to the boat-launching area. Just beyond that, climb up over the spillway, cross a paved road, and descend sharply into a shady ravine (Walnut Creek) below the spillway's snout. Like Sisyphus you immediately start a steep, zigzagging

ascent back up the far wall—but at least that passage takes you through an enchanting little grove of live oaks.

After topping out, follow a paved road west to a large parking lot (equestrian staging area) below. From there, head generally south (parallel to the I-210 freeway), up and over an oak and walnut-dotted ridge, and down to the tunnel beneath Via Verde at Bonelli Park's west entrance.

North shore, Puddingstone Reservoir

Area B-9, Trip 2
Walnut Creek Trail

Distance	3.7 miles
Total Elevation Gain/Loss	100'/500'
Hiking Time	1½ hours
Optional Map	USGS 7.5-min *San Dimas*
Best Times	All year
Agency	LADPR
Difficulty	★★

Tucked away in a surprisingly unspoiled canyon just below Puddingstone Reservoir is Walnut Creek Park, a ribbon of open space stretching through the cities of San Dimas and Covina. A wide and well-traveled bridle trail goes the length of the park, crossing the stream several times (expect to get your feet soaked in winter and spring!). Plenty of oaks, sycamores, willows, and assorted non-native ornamental trees—but relatively few walnut trees—line the banks.

Steep south walls along most of this stretch of Walnut Creek make it a cool haven on all but the hottest days. Often on winter mornings the canyon bottom is a frosty wonderland, since it acts as a sink for cold, dense night air slinking down along the slopes of the nearby San Gabriel Mountains.

Start at the roadside parking area on the west side of San Dimas Avenue, 1 mile north of Via Verde. (Across the street, a trail goes under I-210 to the big equestrian staging area on the west side of Bonelli Regional Park.) Our trail zigzags down the road embankment to the west, and into the shady canyon. Down along the bottom there are several splits in the trail: the first three are merely alternate routes that go along the opposite bank or up onto the steep south slope before returning to the main trail; the fourth is a spur trail that connects with Puente Street.

Past Puente Street there's not much of a trail at all, and you may well find yourself sloshing through the shallow water. In a while the water enters a cement flood-control channel to be whisked efficiently away. You climb up on the left bank of the flood-control channel. Covina Hills Road lies just ahead—a good place to end this trip provided you've planted a second car there in advance.

Area B-9, Trip 3
Marshall Canyon Trail

	Distance	5.0 miles
	Total Elevation Gain/Loss	1100'/1100'
	Hiking Time	2½ hours
	Optional Map	USGS 7.5-min *Mt. Baldy*
	Best Times	October through June
	Agency	LADPR
	Difficulty	★★★

Although it's been in county ownership for more than a quarter century, Marshall Canyon Regional Park remains obscure—omitted, even, from some of the popular street maps. This is all the better for hikers and horsemen, who can enjoy these undeveloped 600 acres in peace and quiet.

The park encompasses the upper watersheds of two small canyons—Marshall and Live Oak—which are smothered by a leafy canopy of live oak, sycamore and alder. In some areas luminescent curtains of poison oak and wild grape cling to the trees, while carpets of blackberry vines and vinca (an ornamental ground-cover gone wild) coat the stream banks. Steep, chaparral-covered slopes, dotted here and there with planted pines, eucalyptus and incense cedar, round out the scene.

On the intricate, figure-eight route described here you'll explore parts of both canyons and pay a visit to a shady picnic spot perched high in the foothills of the San Gabriel Mountains.

You begin at the equestrian parking area on Golden Hills Road, 1 mile east of

Wheeler Avenue in La Verne. (You can also get there by driving north on Esperanza Drive from Base Line Road.) After only a few steps, you're enveloped in a shade-dappled milieu—Marshall Canyon. Bear left at the first split at 0.1 mile. You'll return to this point later on the fork to the right.

In a little while, you leave Marshall Canyon's shady creek bed and rise to the perimeter of a fenced nursery (0.7 mile), atop the low ridge that divides Marshall and Live Oak canyons. You contour into the latter, where you hook up with a trail coming up along its bottom. Continue upstream to another trail junction (1.2 miles). Stay right and go another 0.1 mile to yet another junction. Take the equestrian trail on the left, ignoring the dirt road that curves right up the hillside. After gaining 400 vertical feet on switchbacks you reach a dirt road atop a ridge-running fire break (1.7 miles, 2220') offering rare, clear-day vistas extending all the way to downtown L.A.'s skyscrapers.

Turn left, continue on the fire break 0.2 mile, and then veer sharply left on a trail that takes you back down into the shady depths of Live Oak Canyon (2.2 miles). Swing right at the bottom (remaining on trail) and continue uphill 0.4 mile to a dirt road. Turn left and follow the road 200 yards down to the picnic area (2.8 miles), which sits in a shady draw at the head of Live Oak Canyon. A restroom and horse trough are here, but there's no potable water.

(The Mt. Baldy topo map shows an old pack trail ascending the ridge east of the picnic area to Sunset Ridge Fire Road above. This path is now overgrown, but a wide, very steep fire break farther east accomplishes the same thing. See Area A-12, Trip 3 for more details.)

From the picnic area, keep descending along the dirt road, which at this point follows Live Oak Canyon's mostly sun-exposed north wall. About ¼ mile below, don't miss the pleasant trail that conveniently short-cuts a couple of curves in

the road. On the road again you pass above the point where you turned uphill a mile earlier. Farther ahead, at 3.7 miles, you leave the road and veer left on a path going down a shallow draw. This soon hooks up with the trail through Live Oak Canyon. Retrace your earlier steps for 0.2 mile, then fork left, remaining in Live Oak Canyon. A murmuring stream swishes through here most of the year. At 4.5 miles, the trail abruptly switches back and climbs to an open flat with two large water tanks. Pass to the left of the first, to the right of the second, and pick up the path that descends into Marshall Canyon. You arrive back at the first split you encountered, 0.1 mile east of the parking area.

Walnut Creek Trail

SANTA MONICA MOUNTAINS

Area S-1: Topanga

Topanga—"The place where the mountains meet the sea." That simple and descriptive Gabrielino Indian name aptly applies to both the famous canyon and to the big state park sprawling along its east rim. The ocean is your almost perpetual companion here, if not in sight, at least in the feel of the cool, marine air flowing up along the sunny slopes and through the dark, wooded canyons.

Assembled from purchases of public and private lands in the late '60s and early '70s, Topanga State Park's 9000 acres (which are almost entirely within the Los Angeles city limits) rate as one of the world's largest wildlands adjacent to an urban area. The park also serves as a key anchor in the patchwork quilt of public and private lands known as the Santa Monica Mountains National Recreational Area. (The next four areas in this book cover the somewhat more remote middle and western sections of the SMMNRA.)

Perhaps nowhere else in Southern California is the attack on the integrity of large open spaces so graphically illustrated as right here. The park's ragged boundary necessarily excluded lands earmarked for development in two of the coastal canyons—Santa Ynez and Pulga. Today, massive grading and construction in and along the walls of these canyons have marred the otherwise open vistas. (On the flip side, of course, you need only look east to the Hollywood Hills to imagine how these mountains would probably look decades hence if they lacked any protection at all.)

Topanga State Park's only area developed specifically for visitors centers around the Trippet Ranch, off Topanga Canyon Boulevard on Entrada Road. The ranch (open during daylight hours) was originally one of the many second-home and resort properties developed in the Topanga Canyon area early in the century. There you'll find a tiny administrative office, a pond, oak-shaded picnic tables, a 1-mile self-guiding nature trail (ill-maintained as of this writing), and trailheads for several of the wide-ranging routes we describe in detail below. The trail system is also accessible from several other points on or near the periphery of the park.

Rounding out our coverage of this area are hikes originating at Will Rogers State Historic Park in Pacific Palisades, and trips through Rustic and Sullivan canyons on lands owned by the Los Angeles County Sanitation District. The county-owned lands are presently open to the public for non-motorized recreation.

The adjoining sketch map includes fire roads and established trails, but does not show dozens of miles of firebreaks and informal paths threading some of the canyons and going up or along most of the ridges. Since the last major fire (1978) in this area, many of these seldom-trod pathways have become overgrown; others pass through private lands for which there is no public access.

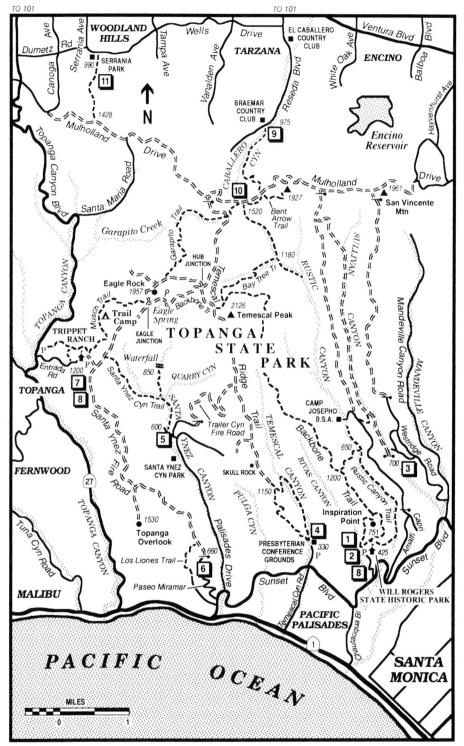

Area S-1: Topanga

Area S-1, Trip 1
Will Rogers Park

	Distance	2.0 miles
	Total Elevation Gain/Loss	350'/350'
	Hiking Time	1 hour
	Optional Map	USGS 7.5-min *Topanga*
	Best Times	All year
	Agency	WRSHP
	Difficulty	★

Drive up a short mile from the speedway known as Sunset Boulevard toward Will Rogers State Historic Park, and you'll instantly leave the rat race behind. Especially on weekdays or early on weekend mornings, this quiet spot is perfect for getting some exercise and taking advantage of multimillion-dollar views of Santa Monica, West L.A. and downtown. The park is open daily, except certain holidays, from 8 A.M. to 5 P.M. A parking fee is charged.

Newspaperman, radio commentator, movie star and pop-philosopher Will Rogers purchased this 182-acre property in 1922 and lived with his family here from 1928 until his death in 1935. Historic only by Southern California standards, his 31-room mansion is nevertheless interesting to tour.

Our main goal, however, is to reach Inspiration Point, a flat-topped bump on a ridge overlooking the entire spread. Follow the main, wide, riding and hiking trail that makes a 2-mile loop, starting at the north end of the big lawn adjoining the Rogers home. Or use any of several shorter, more direct paths. You may want to obtain a copy of the detailed hikers' map, available at the gift shop in a wing of the home. Printed on the map is one of Will's memorable aphorisms, ". . . if your time is worth anything, travel by air. If not, you might just as well walk."

Relaxing on the benches at the top on a clear day, you can admire true-as-advertised, inspiring vistas stretching east to the front range of the San Gabriel Mountains and southeast to the Santa Ana Mountains. South past the swelling Palos Verdes peninsula you can sometimes spot Santa Catalina Island, rising in ethereal majesty from the shining surface of the sea.

L.A.'s amazing skyline seen from Inspiration Point

Area S-1, Trip 2
Lower Rustic Canyon

Distance	4.6 miles
Total Elevation Gain/Loss	900'/900'
Hiking Time	3 hours
Optional Map	USGS 7.5-min *Topanga*
Best Times	October through June
Agency	TSP
Difficulty	★★★

Get set for an adventurous trek along a hardscrabble ridge and down through a once-busy but now wild canyon—all of this no more than a mile by crow's flight from the outermost suburbs of west-side Los Angeles. Rustic Canyon, the retreat of Will Rogers and his cohorts, later a hideout of Nazi sympathizers, and still later an artist's colony, is fast reverting to wildness under Nature's one-two punch—fire and flood.

As in the previous trip, you begin and end at Will Rogers State Historic Park. Take the eucalyptus-lined east branch of the Inspiration Point loop trail 0.8 mile to a signed junction with the Backbone Trail, just north of Inspiration Point. This far-eastern segment of the Backbone Trail is also called the Rogers Trail in honor of Will Rogers. When completed, the Backbone Trail will run approximately 60 miles along the crest of the Santa Monicas to Point Mugu State Park.

As soon as you start climbing the well-defined ridge, you'll realize how appropriate the name "Backbone" is—not only in the grand sense, but also on a smaller scale. The trail skips up, over, or around cobbled sandstone "vertebrae" along a stretch known variously as Chicken Ridge and Gobbler's Knob. At 1.5 miles you cross a bridge overlooking a knife-edge saddle between Rivas Canyon on the west and Rustic Canyon on the east. Just ahead at another saddle (1.8 miles) you turn right on a trail that wastes no time descending into Rustic Canyon.

On the way down you make your way through a mini-forest of chaparral, including green-bark ceanothus, mountain mahogany, chamise, manzanita, toyon, sumac, and buckwheat—all of it regrown from the October 1978 Mandeville Canyon fire which destroyed 270 houses. Down in a little glade at the bottom (2.5 miles) is an old barn spared by the fire, now undergoing restoration. If no one's around, you may spook a deer—they're abundant in this neck of the canyon.

Upstream lies the Boy Scouts' Camp Josepho, named after Will Rogers' friend Anatol Josepho, inventor of the pay telephone. Our route—an informal and partly overgrown path—turns south (down-canyon) past the site of one of Rogers' cabins and an assortment of other structures, burned or abandoned. Plenty of ornamental trees and shrubs mix with the native live oak and sycamores along the trickling stream.

On the left a way down stands the cement shell of a power-generator building (remarkably intact aside from the unsightly graffiti). This, along with a diesel-fuel bunker and sheet-metal buildings, was part of the pre-World-II "Murphy Ranch," which was protected by a high fence and patrolled by armed guards. Short-wave broadcasts beamed to Germany from the site finally convinced authorities of its true nature and led to the arrest of a German spy. The spy, it seems, had duped a wealthy couple and convinced them to finance construction of this stronghold, which was to serve as a haven for true believers in the Third Reich. After the war, this section of the canyon became an artists' colony, until ravaged by fire and flood. Today it is owned by the City of Los Angeles.

Past an old flood-control dam (3.6 miles) the canyon narrows and the trail becomes merely a muddy track through a tight constriction in the canyon—impassable during floods. Conglomerate walls soar

eerily on both sides. Watch out for poison oak and slippery rocks. At 4.1 miles, the canyon abruptly widens. On the right a wide trail curves uphill toward the polo field across from Will Rogers' home, your starting point.

Area S-1, Trip 3
Sullivan Canyon

	Distance	10.0 miles
	Total Elevation Gain/Loss	1600'/1600'
	Hiking Time	4½ hours
	Optional Maps	USGS 7.5-min *Topanga, Canoga Park*
	Best Times	October through May
	Agency	TSP
	Difficulty	★★★

In serene Sullivan Canyon you can hike for at least an hour without catching sight of any manmade improvements, save for a gravelly service road and some markers indicating a buried pipeline. All this could change if Sullivan and neighboring upper Rustic Canyon become, as envisioned by county planners, a huge dump for solid waste. Both canyons are, however, considered priority items for purchase as permanent open space. Hopefully they will be added to the growing list of protected properties within the Santa Monica Mountains National Recreation Area.

This comprehensive tour goes up along Sullivan Canyon's sycamore-lined bottom and touches upon Mulholland Drive, where on clear days a hiker can view the ocean and the San Fernando Valley from a single stance. It concludes with an easy descent on the long, sinuous ridge just east of the canyon. The route, and variations of it, is ideally suited for long-distance runners, mountain bikers, and horse riders, as well as walkers.

The route lies almost entirely on a geologic formation called Santa Monica

Slate, a grey, bluish-grey or black rock. These 150 million-year-old rocks of marine origin, the oldest found in the Santa Monica Mountains, are exposed in a broad area stretching almost continuously from Coldwater Canyon and Franklin Canyon behind Beverly Hills into the east half of Topanga State Park.

Since the road in Sullivan Canyon is at best only semi-shaded, you may want to choose a time that takes advantage of early-morning or late-afternoon shadows. You could, for example, walk up the canyon late in the day, catch the setting sun from Mulholland, and watch the city lights twinkle on as you walk down the east ridge.

To reach the starting point, turn north from Sunset Boulevard onto Mandeville Canyon Road. Make a left on the first intersecting street, Westridge Road, and go 1.2 miles to Bayliss Road. Turn left on Bayliss and continue 0.3 mile to Queensferry Road, a dead-end street on the left.

Step around a gate and walk down to the service road going up along the bottom of Sullivan Canyon. Oaks, willows, and sycamores cluster along the usually dry creek bed. At 0.7 mile a narrow path comes down from the left, giving access to Sullivan Canyon's west-ridge fire road, an alternate route used by some people.

The almost imperceptible climb on the road takes you past thinning sycamores to a fork in the canyon (3.4 miles), where the main canyon branch heads northeast. You follow the road up a smaller, steeper ravine going northwest. Climbing in earnest, you swing around some sharp turns and then hook up with the west-ridge fire road (4.3 miles). Continue north to unpaved Mulholland Drive, then follow Mulholland east along the Santa Monica Mountains divide toward the wreckage of the abandoned Nike missile base atop San Vicente Mountain (5.5 miles). This vandalized, sorry site awaits restoration as an L.A. City park. The view from here, when uncompromised by smog or haze, is undeniably spectacular. Look north to glimpse the Tehachapi Mountains, 70 miles distant, through the gap between the Santa Susana and San Gabriel mountains.

From the missile site, head south along the fire road. It curves around several rounded bumps on the ridge between Mandeville and Sullivan canyons, climbing on occasion, but mostly descending. You'll have outstanding views of the L.A. Basin to the east and south, marred only by some foreground powerlines.

At 9.0 miles you hook up with Westridge Road in a suburban housing development. Walk 0.5 mile down Westridge, turn right on Bayliss, and continue another 0.5 mile down to Queensferry.

Area S-1, Trip 4
Temescal Canyon

	Distance	2.8 miles
	Total Elevation Gain/Loss	850'/850'
	Hiking Time	1½ hours
	Optional Map	USGS 7.5-min *Topanga*
	Best Times	All year
	Agency	SMMC
	Difficulty	★★

A favorite of west-side L.A. hikers, this short ramble includes both wonderful views from high places and a shady passage through riparian and oak woodland.

Park at the entrance to the Presbyterian Conference Grounds just north of Sunset Boulevard on Temescal Canyon Road. Since part of the route ahead passes through church property, you must sign a register at the hiker's booth provided. Don't forget to *sign out* in the same register upon your return.

I enjoy making the loop clockwise, climbing the scrubby canyon wall west of Temescal Canyon on the way up, and then making a nice, easy descent down through the canyon. To do that, simply take the steep path going left just beyond the booth. After eight short switchbacks, the trail sticks to an open ridge with a 180° view of distant horizons. Pause often so you can admire the coastline curving from Santa Monica Bay to Malibu. One winter afternoon on this ridge, I watched a leaden cumulus cloud drop its load over Temescal Canyon and then move on, leaving a vivid rainbow in its wake.

At 1.3 miles, the trail meets the Temescal Ridge Trail, a fire road that follows a viewful but shadeless ridge north all the way to Mulholland Drive. At this point you have the option of making a side trip north 0.5 mile to a wind-carved, sandstone outcrop known as Skull Rock.

Staying on the loop route, turn right and start down the eroded bed of the former Temescal Fire Road. When you hit the shady canyon bottom (1.7 miles), scramble around the stonework buttresses of a fallen bridge and pick up a better section of the old fire road on the far side of the creek. Above and below this crossing are small, trickling waterfalls and shallow, limpid pools. Poke around the creek a bit for a look at its typical denizens—water striders and newts.

The final stretch follows the canyon bottom, then contours along a slope to the right of the church buildings. Lots of live oak, sycamore, willow, and bay trees, their woodsy scents commingling on the ocean breeze, highlight your return.

Area S-1, Trip 5
Santa Ynez Waterfall

	Distance	2.4 miles round trip
	Total Elevation Gain/Loss	250'/250'
	Hiking Time	1½ hours (round trip)
	Optional Map	USGS 7.5-min *Topanga*
	Best Times	All year
	Agency	TSP
	Difficulty	★★

Twisted oaks and sycamores and pungent bay laurel trees highlight this brief trek up the L.A. coast's most easily accessible wild canyon. The modest goal is an 18' cascade tucked into one of the several upper branches of Santa Ynez Canyon.

From Sunset Boulevard, drive 2.4 miles north on Palisades Drive to Vereda de la Montura. Turn left and park along the curb near the bridge over Santa Ynez Canyon's creek. Pick up the trail going up-canyon from the east side of the bridge. After a couple of minutes you're dodging stray willow branches, stepping across the soggy creek, and forgetting about the civilized world behind you.

At 0.5 miles there's a fork—wide Quarry Canyon, site of an old limestone quarry goes right. You stay left and go another 100 yards to a second fork, where the main trail goes west up a tributary toward Trippet Ranch. Take the lesser-traveled trail right (north) up the main upper Santa Ynez Canyon.

After some mild bushwhacking, foot-wetting fords, and a slippery scramble over some conglomerate boulders, you arrive at the grotto below the falls. The cascade itself is impressive only after heavy rains, but the cool and damp air is always refreshing. Unfortunately this otherwise magical spot is simply too close to (and until now, unprotected from) urban decay. "Party animals" have trashed the place, and it will take a mighty big flood to erase the spray paint and clear out the myriad shards of glass. Park authorities have established a nighttime curfew for minors in this area, which should curb any further abuse.

On your way back, near the two junctions mentioned earlier, you can look for the stone chimney of a burnt-out cabin and a sandstone boulder pocked by Indian mortars.

Area S-1, Trip 6
Topanga Overlook

Distance	5.0 miles round trip
Total Elevation Gain/Loss	1200'/1200'
Hiking Time	2½ hours (round trip)
Optional Map	USGS 7.5-min *Topanga*
Best Times	All year
Agency	TSP
Difficulty	★★

From the perch known as Topanga Overlook, Parker Mesa Overlook, or simply the "Overlook," you get a bird's-eye view of surfers off Topanga Beach, the crescent shoreline of Santa Monica Bay, L.A.'s westside cityscape—and much, much more if the air is really transparent. You can reach the overlook by walking south along Topanga Canyon's east ridge from Trippet Ranch, but we'll describe a shorter and more interesting route from a street called Paseo Miramar, west of Pacific Palisades.

This trip is especially rewarding when done early on certain fall or winter mornings, when tendrils of fog fill the canyons, leaving the mountains to rise above a cottony sea. It's also excellent as a sunset or night hike. For a special treat, do it on any clear, full-moon evening between May and August. In the fading twilight you'll watch the moon's pumpkin-like disk silently materialize in the east or southeast, hovering over a million glittering lights.

To reach the trailhead, turn north on Paseo Miramar from Sunset Boulevard 0.3 mile north of Pacific Coast Highway. This intersection is one block north of a turnoff for Los Liones Drive. Drive up narrow Paseo Miramar to its end, where limited parking is available just short of a vehicle gate. Walk up the dirt fire road that continues up along a ridge, passing after 0.2 mile a foot trail coming up from Los Liones Drive. Farther ahead you briefly traverse a cool, north-facing slope overlooking Santa Ynez Canyon and neighboring ridges. You arrive at a road junction (2.0 miles) overlooking Topanga Canyon to the west. Turn south and walk out along the bald ridge to Topanga Overlook. Down below are Parker and Castellammare mesas, parts of a striking marine-terrace structure that continues east into Pacific Palisades. When it's time to go back, return the way you came.

Area S-1, Trip 7
Eagle Rock Loop

Distance	6.7 miles
Total Elevation Gain/Loss	1200'/1200'
Hiking Time	3½ hours
Optional Map	USGS 7.5-min *Topanga*
Best Times	October through May
Agency	TSP
Difficulty	★★★

Eagle Rock, the most impressive landmark in all of Topanga State Park, affords hikers an airy perch overlooking the upper watershed of Santa Ynez Canyon and the ocean beyond. Make it your destination for lunch during a lazy day's hike, but do it on a cooler day—there's little shade on the route. This is a figure–8 route, so if you have smaller kids along, you can cut the distance to about 4 miles by avoiding the far loop.

You begin at Trippet Ranch, which is reached by taking Topanga Canyon Boulevard to Entrada Road (just north of the community of Topanga), and driving 1 mile east. From the large parking lot at Trippet Ranch, walk north on a paved drive about 100 yards to where the signed Musch Trail slants to the right across a grassy hillside. You soon plunge into the shade of oak and bay trees. Enjoy the shade—there's not much more ahead. After contouring around a couple of north-flowing ravines, the trail rises to meet a trail campground at the former Musch Ranch (1.0 mile). This camp, along with others to be established along the unfinished Backbone Trail, serves equestrians and through-hikers. For now this is the only public camping area in the Santa Monica Mountains east of Malibu Creek State Park.

Beyond the campground, the trail soon starts climbing through sun-blasted chaparral. After a crooked ascent you reach a ridgetop fire road at Eagle Junction (2.5 miles), from which Eagle Rock can be seen looming over the headwaters of Santa Ynez Canyon. This layered sandstone outcrop, pitted with small caves, is an outstanding example of the 15-million-year-old Topanga Canyon Formation. Turn left and follow the fire road up to the gentler north side of Eagle Rock. Walk to the top for the best view. Some of the areas below look a little ragged—they were scorched by a 1989 fire.

Back on the fire road, continue east up along a ridgeline and then down to a four-way junction of fire roads at 3.9 miles, called "Hub Junction" because of its central location in the park. On a side trip south from here you could visit Cathedral Rock and Temescal Peak (see Trip 8), but our way goes sharply right on the Backbone Trail (a fire road) leading west under Eagle Rock and back to Eagle Junction. Before you reach the junction, there's a side path on the right to Eagle Spring, where water trickles out of the sandstone bedrock beneath oaks and sycamores.

When you reach Eagle Junction again (5.3 miles), turn left and return to Trippet Ranch the fast and direct way: Go 1.2 miles down the ridge-running fire road to the south, and then 0.2 mile northwest on a road leading down to the picnic area and parking lot.

Eagle Rock, landmark of Topanga State Park

Area S-1, Trip 8
East Backbone Trail

	Distance	9.2 miles
	Total Elevation Gain/Loss	1700'/2500'
	Hiking Time	4½ hours
	Optional Map	USGS 7.5-min *Topanga*
	Best Times	October through May
	Agency	TSP
	Difficulty	★★★

On a cool, clear day, the easternmost section of the Backbone Trail—Trippet Ranch to Will Rogers State Historic Park—yields dazzling and ever-changing perspectives of the meeting of mountains and sea. A lesser benefit of this one-way trip is that you get to walk downhill most of the time. Arrange a car shuttle, or better yet, have someone drop you off at Trippet Ranch (opens at 8 A.M.) and later pick you up in front of the Rogers home or at some other agreed-upon spot in Will Rogers Park (closes at 5 P.M.)

From the picnic area at Trippet Ranch, head southeast on the fire road going up the hill to the Santa Ynez Fire Road. Turn left at the top and climb to Eagle Junction (1.4 miles). Go right there, pass under Eagle Rock, climb some more, and arrive at Hub Junction (2.7 miles). Turn right on the Temescal Ridge Trail and walk 0.5 mile south, passing a cavernous sandstone outcrop on the left called Cathedral Rock, to another junction. The Backbone Trail goes left here on an old fire road. Nearby Temescal Peak, whose summit can be reached by way of a short, steep fire break on its west side, is worth climbing if the visibility is good. This somewhat undistinguished looking bump on the Temescal Ridge holds the distinction of being the highest peak in the Santa Monicas east of Topanga Canyon.

The Backbone Trail (originally the Rogers Trail from here on down to Will Rogers Park) goes east for about 1 mile, then veers south to loosely follow an undulating ridgeline that always lies west and well above Rustic Canyon and its tributaries. For a couple of miles the upper reaches of Temescal Canyon lie to the west, but then you bear left (southeast) to join the ridge between Rivas and Rustic canyons. On a flat overlooking the head of Rivas Canyon at 6.5 miles, there's a live oak tree that provides welcome shade.

Past the oak, 2 more miles of foot trail lead down to a junction just above Inspiration Point in Will Rogers Park. Turn right on the wide trail. After about 0.3 mile, make a left on the shortcut path signed BACKBONE TRAIL. That will take you straight down to the big lawn above Will Rogers' home.

Area S-1, Trip 9
Caballero Canyon

	Distance	4.2 miles round trip (to peak 1927)
	Total Elevation Gain/Loss	1000'/1000'
	Hiking Time	2 hours (round trip)
	Optional Map	USGS 7.5-min *Canoga Park*
	Best Times	October through June
	Agency	TSP
	Difficulty	★★

Caballero Canyon's convenient trailhead allows San Fernando Valley hikers to gain easy access to the trails of Topanga State Park without having to drive either the curvy Topanga Canyon Boulevard or the notoriously rutty dirt section of Mulholland Drive. It is also the starting point for the Sierra Club's popular "Twilight Hikes in Caballero Canyon." New construction around the area, including the extension of Reseda Boulevard toward Mulholland Drive on the Santa Monica Mountain crest, has destroyed some of the favorite paths of local hikers, and has made access to the canyon a little awkward. A bulletin board, down in the canyon opposite the Braemar Country Club clubhouse, marks the start.

The once-quiet hike up the sycamore-dotted canyon is now a bit noisier, with bulldozers scraping and hammers pounding on the surrounding ridges. But some of the wildlife is still around—I spotted a bobcat bounding through the brush down near the bulletin board. After about a mile you pass a sign indicating the state park boundary. All land north of here could be developed sometime in the future.

At 1.5 miles you come up to a saddle traversed by unpaved Mulholland Drive. There's a much better view of everything if you climb a little farther. To the east you'll notice a very steep fire break going up a ridge. Go up this a short distance, then contour to the right to pick up the unsigned Bent Arrow Trail. This narrow path takes you on a winding route up a south-facing slope, crosses a wide fire break, and finally tops out on a rounded, nearly flat ridge. There's a 1927' knoll immediately to the east, and a slightly higher point overlooking Mulholland Drive 0.4 mile east. Late in the day you can watch evening shadows elongate across the San Fernando Valley, and clouds form along the coast as the chill of evening descends upon the land.

Area S-1, Trip 10
Upper Rustic-Garapito Loop

	Distance	6.8 miles
	Total Elevation Gain/Loss	1500'/1500'
	Hiking Time	3½ hours
	Optional Maps	USGS 7.5-min *Canoga Park, Topanga*
	Best Times	October through June
	Agency	TSP
	Difficulty	★★★

The secret recesses of upper Rustic Canyon, its shady "bay tree" tributary, and Garapito Creek invite your attention. With rudimentary navigational skills you can find and follow this circle tour through some of the most remote and rugged terrain in the Santa Monica Mountains. Expect to encounter some indistinct or partially overgrown sections of trail, and watch for poison oak down in the canyons.

You start hiking from unpaved Mulholland Drive at a point 4.9 miles east of Topanga Canyon Boulevard and 2.6 miles west of the old missile site on San Vicente Mountain. More specifically, this point is 0.3 mile west of the trail (old fire road) coming up through Caballero Canyon. Parts of Mulholland are like a third-world highway, fairly wide but full of mudholes after heavy rains, rough and rutty otherwise. A high-clearance or 4-wheel-drive vehicle may be required. At the expense of an extra 3.5 miles round trip, you can avoid the dirt-road driving by starting from Reseda Boulevard and using the Caballero Canyon route (see Trip 9) to reach Mulholland.

On the brushy slope south of Mulholland, find and follow the narrow trail going due south. Steep and eroded at first, it drops into an upper tributary of Rustic Canyon, then descends more moderately as it joins the tributary's dry bed. The canyon deepens and the chaparral is joined by scattered live oaks, and then by a nice mixture of sycamores, willows, bay laurels, ferns, and assorted riparian plants—the hallmarks of a year-round water supply, at least underground. Some fine examples of dark-grey Santa Monica Slate are exposed along the canyon sides.

After 1.1 miles there's an easily missed, unmarked trail junction. You'll turn right here on the unsigned Bay Tree Trail, which goes up a narrow west fork. Down-canyon 0.4 mile from this junction is another fork, where the main Rustic Canyon heads north. When the streams are really flowing, you may want to make a side trip up this canyon to see "Blue Gorge," a moss-covered constriction in the canyon bottom where water tumbles over a series of cascades.

Follow the Bay Tree Trail along the bottom of the west fork for 0.4 mile, then start an ascent on an obvious trail up the steep south wall. A dense grove of bay laurel trees has stump-sprouted here after the 1978 Mandeville Canyon fire, creating what is today surely one of the most densely shaded spots in the Santa Monica Mountains. Water from a tiny spring seeps over the trail at one point, just below a multi-trunked bay tree. After a steady but delightfully shaded climb, you break out of the trees and soon thereafter hook up with the Backbone Trail (2.4 miles). Go right and walk 0.2 mile to Temescal Ridge Trail. Temescal Peak—highest point in Topanga State Park—lies within easy reach, if you desire, on the left.

Go north on the Temescal Ridge Trail to Hub Junction and take the middle of the three roads ahead, signed north loop trail. Follow this ridge-running fire road 0.8 mile east to the obscure junction of the Garapito Trail (just short of Cheney Fire Road, which descends west onto private lands outside the park). Turn right here.

The Garapito Trail, the newest in the park, cuts a sinuous course through mature chaparral—mostly mountain mahogany and ceanothus up to 20 feet tall. The blossoms of the ceanothus exude a wild-honey scent in spring, attractive to bees as well as humans. You contour along a west-facing slope, then descend along a sharply falling ridgeline, crisscrossing on many tight switchbacks. At the bottom, the trail swings around to cross a south fork of Garapito Creek, and then contours a short distance over to an east fork. A steady climb up along this east fork takes you to a wide dirt road, the Temescal Ridge Trail. Cross over to the far side of this road and you'll see a footpath that takes you down and then back up to Mulholland Drive. You join Mulholland at a point 0.1 mile west of where you started your descent into the Rustic Canyon tributary.

Area S-1, Trip 11
Woodland Ridge

	Distance	2.2 miles round trip
	Total Elevation Gain/Loss	500'/500'
	Hiking Time	1 hour (round trip)
	Optional Map	USGS 7.5-min *Canoga Park*
	Best Times	All year
	Agency	SMMC
	Difficulty	★★

At sunset the weird chorus of sharp-pitched shrieks and howls started up, with echoes that reverberated off the walls of the houses below. The coyotes were defiantly laying claim (so it seemed when I was there) to one of the dwindling number of open spaces remaining on San Fernando Valley's south rim.

That little patch of public land, known variously as Woodland Ridge and Serrania Ridge, features a ridge-running trail connecting Serrania Park with Mulholland Highway. The park can be reached by turning south at the De Soto Avenue exit from the Ventura Freeway and continuing 1 mile south on Serrania Avenue to where Serrania Avenue becomes Wells Drive.

The trail climbs along the park's east boundary, tops a couple of rises offering nice views across the valley, and finally arrives at Mulholland Drive a little below the Santa Monica Mountains crest. To the right as you climb are views of the Woodland Hills Country Club golf course and hillside housing developments characteristic of the '50s and '60s. On the left is a late '80s version of suburbia—a small canyon jam-packed with hulking pseudo-mansions, ridiculously out of proportion to the postage-stamp-sized lots on which they sit. Behind that development, the clay hills have been elaborately graded and stabilized to protect against mudslides. The contrast between the older and the new illustrates how valuable even marginally buildable land has become in this well-to-do corner of the valley.

Polo Grounds at Will Rogers State Historical Park

Area S-2: Malibu Creek

Nosing its way around an obstacle course of upraised and tilted sandstone, conglomerate and volcanic rock formations, Malibu Creek clearly has been successful in adapting to the tectonic creaks and groans of Mother Earth. It's the only stream that has managed to cut entirely through the Santa Monica Mountains. Its tentacle-like tributaries reach far west and north, draining parts of the north edge of the Santa Monicas, as well as about one third of the Simi Hills. Lower Malibu Creek has cut an impressively deep gorge, followed most of the way by the fast, two-lane highway called Malibu Canyon Road.

Hikers and other self-propelled travelers can enjoy 6000-acre Malibu Creek State Park, which features a quiet stretch of Malibu Creek and picturesque outcrops of sandstone and volcanic rock. Several newly acquired parcels of park and open-space land lie adjacent to the state park, and these are included as well in the 12 trips in the following pages.

In contrast to the previous area covered in this book (Topanga), full-blown urbanization is not as much of a factor here. Still, urban-style housing developments have crept into the mountain valleys along Las Virgenes Road and along Mulholland Highway near San Fernando Valley. Timely efforts by park advocates in the 60s and 70s resulted in the present substantial inventory of park and open-space areas, and these efforts continue, even as land prices spiral upward. A quick historical review will be helpful in understanding the area's value as parkland and open space:

Bedrock mortars (grinding holes) and other archaeological evidence indicate thousands of years of prehistoric use of the Malibu Creek area, most recently by the coast-dwelling Chumash. These Indians maintained a presence here up to at least the mid-1800s. Some say that Chumash descendants cast the adobe bricks for construction of the Sepulveda Adobe (still standing near Mulholland Highway and Las Virgenes Road) in 1863.

At the turn of the century, a group of wealthy individuals bought property along Malibu Creek and formed the exclusive Crag's Country Club. A clubhouse and several private homes were built, but a more lasting effort involved the erection of a dam across a rocky defile on Malibu Creek. The 7-acre lake created by the dam was later named Century Lake by the succeeding owner of the property, Twentieth Century Fox.

By the mid-1900s, much of Malibu Creek country was a kind of annex for Hollywood studios, with sets strategically placed to take advantage of a great variety of exotic backdrops. A vestige of this activity continues today, though most of the sets in the present state park and elsewhere have been removed.

The land owned by Twentieth Century Fox was purchased by the state in 1974, and adjoining parcels acquired soon after. In 1976 Malibu Creek State Park was opened to the public. Then, in 1978, Congress established the Santa Monica Mountains National Recreation Area to "preserve and enhance its scenic, natural, and historical setting and its public health value as an airshed for the Southern California metropolitan area while providing for the recreational and educational needs of the visiting public." To date these goals have been partially realized through the cooperation of several government agencies as well as private landowners. Malibu Creek State Park grew to encompass 6000 acres. Meanwhile, the state-funded Santa Monica Mountains Conservancy, the National Park Service, and private organizations have been busily buying key parcels of land in the Malibu Creek area and elsewhere for use as open space and parkland. About 40 percent of the land shown on our map of the Malibu Creek area is in public ownership so far.

The state park (and nearby Paramount Ranch) harbors some of the southernmost valley-oak habitat in California. You can see beautiful specimens of this sprawling, deciduous tree in Liberty Canyon north of Mulholland Highway, and along the Nature Trail, located near the state park's main entrance off Las Virgenes Road.

Malibu Creek State Park also features a large, new campground with cold showers, quiet in the off-season but often full on spring and summer weekends. Even if you live rather close by in the L.A. area, you might choose to use the campground as a base for early morning or evening hikes. The park's hours for day users are 8 A.M. until dusk.

Several of the hikes described below include parts of the Backbone Trail. This range-spanning trail has been completed from Topanga State Park through Malibu Creek State Park, with the exception (as of this writing) of a segment between Old Topanga Canyon and Saddle Peak.

Rock Pool on Malibu Creek

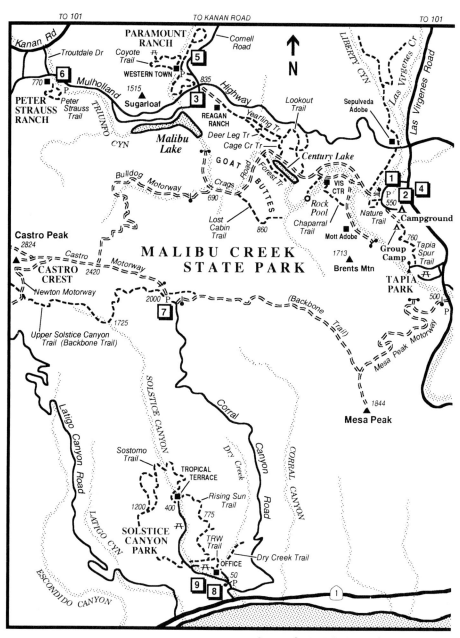

Area S-2: Malibu Creek

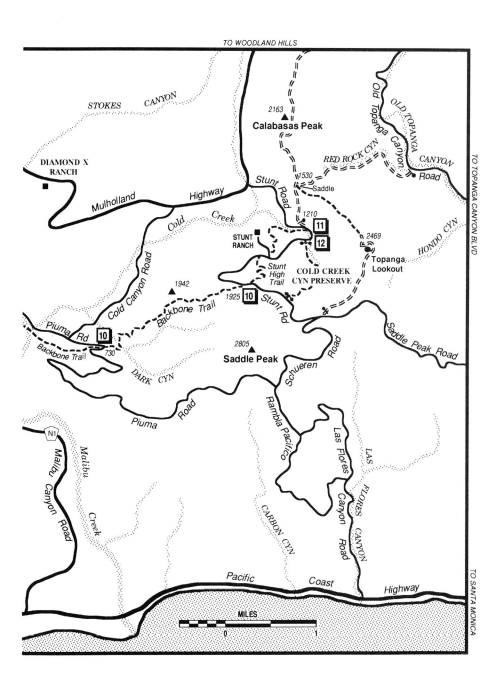

Area S-2, Trip 1
Century Lake/Rock Pool

Distance	3.0 miles round trip
Total Elevation Gain/Loss	250'/250'
Hiking Time	1½ hours (round trip)
Optional Map	USGS 7.5-min *Malibu Beach*
Best Times	All year
Agency	MCSP
Difficulty	★

If you only have time for a single hike at Malibu Creek State Park, this is the one to take. In 3 miles of easy walking you can explore the park's main attractions, and also drop by the visitor center (open Saturdays and Sundays 1–4), which is not accessible by car. Picnic tables and water are available along the route.

Start at the main parking lot (open 8 A.M. until dusk; day-use fee charged) just beyond the park entrance booth on Las Virgenes Road, 0.4 mile south of Mulholland Highway. Walk west on unpaved Crags Road. After 0.5 mile you come to a concrete-ford crossing of Malibu Creek. Youngsters come here to toss in a line for bass, bluegill, and catfish. A right at the fork in the road just beyond leads you most directly to the visitor center. (A more interesting, roundabout and arduous alternative is to turn south at the fork, visit the burned-out ruin of the Mott adobe home, backtrack to the Chaparral Trail, and follow it up and over a saddle to the visitor center. At the saddle you're rewarded with a great view of the Goat Buttes.)

The visitor center is housed in a grand old home once occupied by a member of the Crag's Country Club, and later by the groundskeeper for Twentieth Century Fox. Even if the center isn't open, you can peruse the interpretive panels set up outside beneath the oaks.

From the visitor center, cross over Malibu Creek on a sturdy bridge and continue up the hill on Crags Road, gaining about 200 feet in elevation. The effects of a 1982 fire are still obvious, especially on the rolling hills to the north where battered-looking oaks are staging a slow comeback. This 42,000-acre fire burned all the way from the Simi Hills in Ventura County to the Malibu coast, and consumed about two thirds of Malibu Creek State Park's vegetation.

When you reach the crest, look for the path descending left. In a minute or two, you'll reach the shady east shoreline of Century Lake, created in 1901 by damming Malibu Creek with a tall concrete structure. Subsequent silting-in has allowed a freshwater marsh to overtake much of what was previously open water. Ducks, coots and herons frequent the lake, their squallings and callings reverberating off the weathered, honeycombed volcanic cliffs rising from the reservoir's far shore. Redwing blackbirds flit among the cattails and rushes.

When you've had your fill of these engaging sights and sounds, backtrack to the bridge over Malibu Creek. Just before you reach it, though, turn south onto a footpath signed gorge trail. In a few minutes you'll come upon the Rock Pool, a placid stretch of water framed by volcanic cliffs. This generically wild-looking site has served as a backdrop for outdoor sequences filmed for *South Pacific, Tarzan, Swiss Family Robinson,* and many other productions. A serious effort involving swimming and boulder-hopping could take you past the rock portals to as far as the base of Century

Lake dam, but don't try it if the water's flowing fast.

To return to the starting point, simply backtrack to Crags Road, and walk east on it for a scant mile until you reach the day-use parking lot.

Area S-2, Trip 2
Lost Cabin Trail

	Distance	6.2 miles round trip
	Total Elevation Gain/Loss	700'/700'
	Hiking Time	3 hours (round trip)
	Optional Map	USGS 7.5-min *Malibu Beach*
	Best Times	October through June
	Agency	MCSP
	Difficulty	★★

It's been said that the number of people on a wilderness trail diminishes in proportion to the square of the distance and the cube of the elevation gain from the nearest road. Perhaps that explains why only about one in every hundred visitors to Malibu Creek State Park bothers to check out the dead-end Lost Cabin Trail.

In truth, when you reach the end, there's no "there" there—just a trickling brook, a line of willows and oaks, lots of fragrant chaparral on the hillsides, plus the overarching dome of the blue sky. (The cabin, if there ever was one, seems to be truly lost.) This placid scene, however, lies in the heart of the 1900-acre Kaslow Natural Preserve, the largest of three areas in the park managed for research and low-level public use. The Kaslow (meaning golden eagle in the language used by the Chumash Indians) preserve harbors mountain lions, golden eagles, and a rare native plant—the Santa Susana tarweed. (The other natural preserves, incidentally, cover the valley oak habitat in Liberty Canyon, and a small amount of oak-and-chaparral country along Udell Creek, north of Crags Road and south of the Reagan Ranch.)

Begin, as in Trip 1, by walking west on Crags Road. At the summit just above Century Lake (1.2 miles) keep going west on the road. On the right is the marine sedimentary Calabasas Formation, consisting of light-colored, easily eroded rocks roughly 15 million years old. On the left is the north wall of the Goat Buttes, which consist of the erosion-resistant Conejo Volcanics, also about 15 million years old. Ahead on the Lost Cabin Trail you'll get a look at the south side of the buttes, which features a weird assortment of pock-marked outcrops and boulders.

At 1.7 miles you come to a bridge over Malibu Creek. There's a water fountain on the near side—the last water available until you return to this point on your way back. (Just ahead, the Forest Trail goes left, providing access to Century Lake's south shore. The extra, flat mile out to there and back is well worth it. Huge live oaks, redwood trees planted in the early 1900s, volcanic boulders and ledges half-hidden by shadows and shrubbery on the slopes, velvety grass, and wildflowers give this little neck of the woods a park-like ambience unique in the Santa Monicas. By dodging some poison oak at the trail's far end, it's possible to traverse a rock wall and reach a point close to the concrete dam.)

From the Forest Trail intersection, follow Crags Road another 0.6 mile, to where an old bulldozed road goes left up along a

draw. This is the Lost Cabin Trail, formerly
an access road for sites used in the filming
of the MASH television series. The main
MASH site, dismantled upon the conclusion of filming in 1982, is marked by a sign
along Crags Road. Little remains of the site
of the fictional 4077th tent hospital other
than an old burned-out jeep amid the
encroaching brush.

Follow the Lost Cabin Trail up to a
divide and then down to the bank of Lost
Cabin Creek, a small tributary of Malibu
Creek. At the trail's end a sign advises you
to go no farther. Downstream, the trickling
creek tumbles over a precipice to join
Malibu Creek in the gorge between Century
Lake and the Rock Pool.

Coast live oak, Lost Cabin Trail

Area S-2, Trip 3
Lookout Loop

	Distance	3.8 miles
	Total Elevation Gain/Loss	500'/500'
	Hiking Time	2 hours
	Optional Map	USGS 7.5-min *Malibu Beach*
	Best Times	November through June
	Agency	MCSP
	Difficulty	★★

If it's springtime, you'll want to have
your camera, plus macro lens or close-up
attachment, with you on this trip. With an
average of about 20 inches of rain falling
between the months of November and April,
these gentle meadows and oak-dotted hillsides can muster quite a showing of wildflowers from March into May or June. Keep
an eye out for lupine, larkspur, California
poppy, wild pansy, Chinese houses, gold-
fields, creamcups, wallflower, wild rose,
and the ever-present, but weedy mustard.
You're seldom out of sight or sound of
nearby Mulholland Highway, but there's
plenty of botanical variety to make the trip
an enjoyable one.

A good place to start is the intersection
of Mulholland Highway and Cornell Road,
where limited roadside parking is available
(there's virtually unlimited parking space at
Paramount Ranch, 0.3 mile north). Walk
southeast on the eucalyptus-lined, unpaved
driveway to the park headquarters buildings, which are on the site of the ranch
owned by former president Ronald Reagan
prior to his election as California governor
in 1966. Bypassing the ranch buildings, pick
up the signed Yearling Trail, which runs for
more than a half mile through a grassy
meadow. After just 0.1 mile, bear right on
the Deer Leg Trail (later you'll return to this
intersection on the Yearling Trail, the path to

the left). The Deer Leg Trail rambles through a strip of oak woodland and then descends to cross tiny Udell Creek. A side path slants left to reconnect with the Yearling Trail, but you stay right on the narrow path that climbs up a brushy slope. In a few minutes, you arrive on top of a ridge overlooking Century Lake and Malibu Creek. In the background, the Goat Buttes soar into a milky blue sky. Strong backlight during most of the day makes this a difficult landscape to capture properly on film. Late afternoon side-light, however, does justice to the majesty of the scene.

From the ridgetop, the trail veers north to join the Yearling Trail in the meadow below. Turn right at the bottom, go 0.1 mile

east, and go right again on the Cage Creek Trail. After an abrupt 250' loss of elevation, you arrive at Crags Road. Turn left, and continue 0.3 mile east past Century Lake to the Lookout Trail, on the left. The Lookout Trail swings up a dry ridge to the north, offering more views of the lake and the buttes to the south. You cross an intersecting trail (the left branch dead-ends; the right branch goes to a turnout along Mulholland Highway—an alternate starting point for this hike), and then contour through patches of cool oak woodland and toasty chaparral. Leaving the chaparral, you traverse a grassy saddle and rejoin the Yearling Trail. Follow it back toward the Reagan Ranch and your starting point.

Area S-2, Trip 4
Bulldog-Backbone Loop

Distance	13.7 miles
Total Elevation Gain/Loss	2700'/2700'
Hiking Time	7 hours
Optional Maps	USGS 7.5-min *Malibu Beach, Point Dume*
Best Times	November through May
Agency	MCSP
Difficulty	★★★★

This is the classic grand tour of Malibu Creek State Park's rugged backcountry. Along the way you'll tramp along the crestline of the Santa Monicas, circling high above the park's most conspicuous landmarks. Mountain bikers, who use a slight variation of the route, typically make this a 3- or 4-hour task, but you'd better allow about double that amount of time on foot. There's little shade, so be prepared with plenty of water (two quarts or more on a warm day) and sun protection.

You'll be traveling two alternatives of the Backbone Trail over most of the route. The Backbone Trail's main branch uses Mesa Peak Motorway and the Upper Sol-

stice Canyon Trail, while the other branch consists of Tapia Spur Trail, Crags Road, Bulldog Motorway, and part of Castro Motorway.

You may prefer other trailheads (Tapia Park or Corral Canyon Road, for example) but we'll assume you're going to start from Malibu Creek's State Park's main, east-side parking lot off Las Virgenes Road. Begin, as in Trips 1 and 2 above, by following Crags Road west past Century Lake and the Lost Cabin Trail. After 2.7 miles, bear left on Bulldog Motorway, a fire road that also serves as a powerline access road. The road ascends along a small, oak-shaded creek, then rises crookedly along slopes thickly clothed in chaparral. As you climb, you'll pass three side roads leading to electrical transmission towers. Stay left at the first two intersections, and go right at the third. The physical effort of negotiating the last, steep, uphill mile is rewarded by ever-expanding views over and beyond the now-shrunken-looking Goat Buttes. You'll also pass close to some interesting outcrops of sandstone, looking much like gigantic incisor teeth. Turn left when you reach Castro Motorway at 5.8 miles.

While you descend east, the Malibu shoreline soon comes into view. Visible in clear weather are several of the Channel Islands, Palos Verdes, and the west and south parts of the L.A. Basin.

As you approach the Corral Canyon parking lot (6.7 miles), stay left on the pathway that goes up a hogback ridge bristling with sandstone pinnacles. Walk east along this ridge for 0.5 mile, passing an old home-site and several gargantuan sandstone outcrops—worth climbing if you want to take the time. On the east end of the ridge, you drop down to Mesa Peak Motorway.

At 9.4 miles there's a split. The road to Mesa Peak goes right; you bear left, staying on Mesa Peak Motorway. You now begin a 1350' descent along the precipitous west wall of Malibu canyon. Malibu Creek and the curving highway come into view occasionally, seemingly straight down. At 11.2 miles, the fire road abruptly ends at a locked gate just above a water-treatment plant. You sidestep this closure by going right (east) on a more primitive road, part of the Backbone Trail. After contouring a while, the trail descends very quickly to a turnout along Malibu Canyon Road (11.8). Follow Malibu Canyon Road north to Tapia Park, crossing a bridge over Malibu Creek. Be careful of fast traffic on this short stretch. The bridge has a sidewalk on the east side only; in order to use it you must cross the road twice.

When you reach the edge of Tapia Park, head northwest through the picnic grounds and pick up a narrow, paved road leading to the private entrance of a Salvation Army camp. Just before reaching the Salvation Army gate you'll see a pathway on the right—the Tapia Spur Trail (closed to bikes). On this you wend your way past a fenced honor camp, and eventually reach a low saddle. From there a short descent takes you to a group campground in Malibu Creek State Park. Walk out the access road and over to your car in the valley ahead.

Sandstone cave above Corral Canyon Road

Lower Rustic Canyon

Area S-2, Trip 5
Paramount Ranch

	Distance	1 to 3 miles
	Optional Map	USGS 7.5-min *Point Dume*
	Best Times	All year
	Agency	NPS
	Difficulty	★

For most of this century, Paramount Ranch has served the needs of an entertainment industry always hungry for rustic outdoor scenery. Since 1980, however, the core of this property has been in the hands of the National Park Service. The park service set about restoring Western Town, a set where exteriors for hundreds of TV western episodes were shot in the 50s and 60s. Today the false fronts and dusty streets serve both as an interpretive facility and as a working set for television productions.

Paramount Ranch is a popular spot for guided walks, but you can explore on your own just as easily. About 4 miles of trails lace the 326-acre property. A good bet during the springtime is the 0.5-mile Coyote Trail. It starts behind Western Town, goes up a ravine, and circles back along a chaparral-dotted slope. Wildflowers abound in a good year—woolly blue curls, owl's clover, verbena, mallow, and more. About halfway along the trail, there's a short spur leading up to a single picnic table perched on a spot with a commanding view of Western Town, the brooding Goat Buttes, and the dark summit ridge of the Santa Monica Mountains.

Several shorter trails, plus portions of a former auto racetrack, have been linked together in the 5-km Run Trail, identified in several places by logo-like markers. From a scenic standpoint, the southern part of the Run Trail is more worthwhile. There's a passage along the bank of Medea Creek, and an easy climb of a hillock near the intersection of Cornell Road and Mulholland Highway. At the top of that hillock you can look upon the soaring profile of Sugarloaf Peak, which is made of the same stuff as the Goat Buttes—Conejo Volcanics. Hearsay has it that Sugarloaf Peak was the inspiration for the familiar mountain in the Paramount Pictures logo.

Area S-2, Trip 6
Peter Strauss Trail

	Distance	1.0 mile
	Total Elevation Gain/Loss	200'/200'
	Hiking Time	½ hour
	Optional Map	USGS 7.5-min *Point Dume*
	Best Times	All year
	Agency	NPS
	Difficulty	★

The 65-acre Peter Strauss Ranch (owned by actor-producer Peter Strauss prior to its purchase for inclusion in the national recreation area in 1983) has an interesting past. In the 30s and 40s this was Lake Enchanto, a popular resort and amusement park, boasting the largest swimming pool west of the Rockies, a terrazzo dance floor, and amusement rides. The upper reaches of Malibu Creek (known here as Triunfo Canyon) were dammed to create the lake itself, a popular draw for boaters and fishermen. During the 60s—long after Lake Enchanto's commercial demise—plans were afoot to develop the property as an elaborate Disneyland-style park, but they were never realized.

Today's Lake Enchanto bears scant resemblance to the resort it used to be. The dam washed out in 1960 and has not been rebuilt. The great swimming pool lies unfilled. A picturesque stone-and-wood bath house is undergoing restoration. Other than guided walks, and occasional special events such as dances, plays, art shows, and musical performances held on the grounds, this quiet refuge caters to a relatively small number of hikers, picnickers, and curious folk.

Kids will find plenty to keep them busy here. From spring into early summer the shallow, sluggish stream is alive with thousands of tadpoles. Careful investigation may reveal crayfish, newts, and pond turtles. Just south of the ranch house, there's a playground in a eucalyptus grove overlooking the remains of Lake Enchanto's dam. The Peter Strauss Trail, probably the most attractive short trail in the Santa Monica Mountains, begins here. Shaded by live oaks and flanked by a ground-hugging carpet of ferns and poison oak, the easy-to-follow path zigzags up a hillside and loops back toward the ranch house.

Peter Strauss Ranch, open 8 A.M. to 5 P.M. daily, is located 3 miles south of Highway 101 at Agoura Hills by way of Kanan Road and Troutdale Drive. When you reach Mulholland Highway at the end of Troutdale, turn east, cross the bridge spanning the creek, and then turn into the large dirt lot on the south side. Go back over the bridge on foot to reach the ranch entrance. If the water level in the creek is low enough, you can make a beeline to the ranch house or the playground by wading or boulder-hopping across the creek.

Area S-2, Trip 7
Upper Solstice Canyon

	Distance	5.0 miles
	Total Elevation Gain/Loss	1000'/1000'
	Hiking Time	2½ hours
	Optional Map	USGS 7.5-min *Point Dume*
	Best Times	October through June
	Agency	NPS
	Difficulty	★★★

A splendid sense of isolation pervades the upper reaches of Solstice Canyon—thanks to the purchase of lands along the Castro(Peak crest some years ago by the National Park Service. This brushy and dry country may look a bit unfriendly under harsh midday sunshine, but it's really quite intriguing when soft morning or evening shadows drape the hillsides and hollows.

Ideally you would start this loop hike in the late afternoon, and go clockwise to take advantage of evening shadows while climbing through the canyon below. If you can leave about 2 hours before sunset, you'll hit the Castro crest by sundown. The distant lights of L.A. will be in view by the time you arrive back at your car.

To reach the trailhead parking area,

drive 5½ miles north from Pacific Coast Highway on Corral Canyon Road. From the west edge of the parking lot, follow the path (which may or may not be signed BACK-BONE TRAIL) that switchbacks downward along the rim of a bowl drained by several upper tributaries of Solstice Canyon. Mostly the trail makes use of old roads, but some of it is newer trail tread—watch out for false trails. After about 1 mile of indecisive descent, you join a ravine bottom and then descend decisively to the main tributary of Solstice Canyon (1.3 miles). Turn sharply right and walk up-canyon 200 yards to a small meadow sporting a colorful assortment of wildflowers during the spring. A break may be in order here, since the next 2.1 miles will include 900 feet of elevation gain.

Above the meadow, the trail passes under the charred limbs of live oaks still recovering from a 1982 fire. Farther ahead, as the oaks thin, you start climbing out of the canyon bottom. After rounding some switchbacks you come up to Newton Motorway (2.8 miles) on a saddle south of, and well below, Castro Peak. The Backbone Trail contours west toward Latigo Canyon Road at this point, but you go uphill on Newton Motorway, traversing Castro Peak's south slope.

When you reach the top of the grade (atop Castro Peak's east ridge) walk east about 50 yards on a side path to the top of a barren knoll. On clear days, the view encompasses almost the entire coastline from Ventura County to Palos Verdes. At least four of the Channel Islands can be seen poking out of the sea offshore. Near winter solstice, the sun sinks to an ocean horizon as seen from here.

Just past the knoll you'll hook up with Castro Motorway (3.6 miles). Turn right and let gravity repay you for your previous efforts. Within a half-hour your car in the parking lot should be in view.

Area S-2, Trip 8
Lower Solstice Canyon

	Distance	3.0 miles round trip (to Tropical Terraces)
	Total Elevation Gain/Loss	400'/400'
	Hiking Time	1½ hours (round trip)
	Optional Maps	USGS 7.5-min *Malibu Beach, Point Dume*
	Best Times	All year
	Agency	SMMC
	Difficulty	★

Solstice Canyon, one of the newest and most attractive additions to the Santa Monica Mountains National Recreation Area, invites your attention. Since its unveiling in June 1988, workers have been busy transforming these 556 acres into a hiker's showplace. Old buildings have been restored, junk has been hauled away, weedy plants have been replaced by native ones,

new trails have been cut, and old roads have been either revegetated or incorporated into the trail system. Except for the ruins of the architecturally noted "Tropical Terrace" home built by the previous owners of the property (the Roberts family), not much remains of the devastation wrought by the 1982 Malibu fire.

It would be hard to find a better-

The remains of Tropical Terrace

maintained public park or preserve anywhere in Los Angeles County—perhaps because the Santa Monica Mountains Conservancy (a state-funded operation charged with acquiring land for public use) maintains its headquarters here.

For all of its virtues, Solstice Canyon Park is not well advertised. Its simple gateway is found along Corral Canyon Road, 0.2 mile north of Pacific Coast Highway. There's parking space here for about 6 cars. On busy weekends, it's often possible to drive past the gate to a larger lot near the park office. The mileages quoted for this hike and the next refer to the outer lot as the starting point. Posted park hours are 8 A.M. to 5 P.M.

A few minutes' walk up the paved road to the right take you to the park's office, housed in a beautifully restored 1940s cottage. There you can obtain a map and lots of printed (or oral) information about the area.

Across from the office, the Dry Creek Trail goes northeast up an oak-shaded ravine for about 0.6 mile before entering unposted private property. An outrageously cantilevered "Darth Vader" house overlooks the ravine as well as a 100'-high precipice that on rare occasions becomes a spectacular waterfall.

The TRW Trail, heading north from the office, loops up to the hillside headquarters of the Santa Monica Mountains Conservancy, housed in a silo-shaped building formerly used by TRW, Inc. as a test facility for satellite instrumentation.

On our way to Tropical Terrace, however, we ignore these side trips and further follow the paved road (or a parallel trail through a creekside picnic area) up-canyon through a fantastic woodland of sycamore, bay, and live oaks—the latter with trunks up to 18 feet in circumference.

At 1.0 mile you pass a circa 1865 stone cottage on the right, soon to become a museum upon full restoration. Just beyond is another picnic area nestled alongside the melodious creek. At 1.5 miles, you arrive at Tropical Terrace, 90 percent burned in the 1982 fire. In a setting of palms and giant bird-of-paradise, curved flagstone steps sweep toward the roofless remains of what was for 26 years one of Malibu's grand homes. Beyond the house, crumbling stone steps and pathways lead to what used to be elaborately decorated rock grottoes, and a waterfall on Solstice Canyon's creek. Large chunks of sandstone have cleaved from the canyon walls, adding to the rubble. For all its perfectly natural setting, Tropical Terrace's destiny was that of a temporary paradise, defenseless against both fire and flood.

Area S-2, Trip 9
Rising Sun-Sostomo Loop

	Distance	5.8 miles
	Total Elevation Gain/Loss	1800'/1800'
	Hiking Time	3 hours
	Optional Maps	USGS 7.5-min *Malibu Beach, Point Dume*
	Best Times	October through May
	Agency	SMMC
	Difficulty	★★★

This roller-coaster-like ramble over the hillsides overlooking lower Solstice Canyon can be an exhilarating but sweaty affair if the day is sunny and warm. But with an early enough start (park hours are 8 A.M. to 5 P.M.), you can finish in time for lunch under the oaks in the cool, shady canyon bottom.

Start by walking to the park office (0.3 mile), as in Trip 8 above. From there take the TRW Trail, which winds uphill toward the silo-shaped building. Walk past the building and continue climbing on an old road curving up the hillside—the Rising Sun Trail. With every step, a wider slice of the ocean comes into view. After 400 feet of ascent, the signed Rising Sun Trail (a footpath) veers left, while the road continues about 200 yards to a chain gate—private property beyond. There's a fine view of the coastline up near the gate; if you're there by 8:30 A.M. on or near winter solstice, the risen sun should be gleaming above the Palos Verdes peninsula, its light scattered into a thousand watery pinpoints on the ocean's surface below.

Resuming your travel on the Rising Sun Trail, you contour above a snaggle-toothed outcrop called Lisa's Rock, and then descend sharply to the Tropical Terrace site (2.1 miles). Cross Solstice Canyon's creek, walk down past the ruins of the house, and pick up the Sostomo Trail on the right.

On the Sostomo Trail, which is an old road to start with, you ascend the west wall of Solstice Canyon, cross the creek (2.4 miles), and then start up the east wall. About 0.1 mile beyond the creek crossing, take the side trail to the left. This little shortcut across a bend in the road visits a tiny, burnt-out cabin, its forlorn brick chimney bravely poking above the encroaching chaparral. Starting at 2.8 miles, you drop down and cross the creek again. Going up the west bank you pass another cabin fatality—a roofless stone-and-mortar shell. Looming over the canyon ahead is a spectacular outcrop of sedimentary rock, but our trail circles south away from it and climbs to a trail junction (3.2 miles). Take the left fork—the easier way; both trails converge ahead—and contour through a small pocket of oak woodland known as Deer Valley. After more climbing you reach the shoulder of a ridge (3.9 miles, 1200'), where the other trail rejoins. Point Dume and the coastline sprawl ahead, but the view is marred somewhat by high-voltage powerlines in the foreground.

You've now reached the highest point on the hike, and it's downhill all the way back to your starting point. Follow the Sostomo Trail as it swings south to follow a ridge, and then east down a steep slope to meet the paved road in Solstice Canyon.

Area S-2, Trip 10
Saddle Peak Traverse

	Distance	3.5 miles
	Total Elevation Gain/Loss	350'/1550'
	Hiking Time	1½ hours
	Optional Map	USGS 7.5-min *Malibu Beach*
	Best Times	All year
	Agency	NPS
	Difficulty	★★

One of the newest sections (built in 1987) of the Backbone Trail cuts across the northwest flank of Saddle Peak, accomplishing in 3.5 indirect miles what a bird in flight could traverse in about 1.5 miles. Along its winding, scenic course, the trail passes massive sandstone boulders, slices through tangled thickets of chaparral, penetrates secret copses of live oak and bay laurel, and dips to cross a clear-flowing brook in what is appropriately called Dark Canyon. In my opinion, this is the most scenic section of the Backbone Trail in place so far.

Easy road access on both ends makes this a good car-shuttle trip. Plant one car along Piuma Road near mile-marker 1.2 (1.2 miles east of Malibu Canyon Road). Take the other car to a turnout at mile 3.0 on Stunt Road (3 miles up from Mulholland Highway), where the hike begins.

From the turnout on Stunt Road, walk west along the road shoulder about 100 yards and pick up the signed Backbone Trail on the left. Wide-open views to the north are interspersed with shady passages across seasonal rivulets descending from Saddle Peak's boulder-studded heights. At 1.2 miles you traverse a grassy meadow astride a small saddle. Northwest of this meadow a 1942' peaklet promises a great view at the expense of a short, leg-scratching climb.

From the saddle you begin a crooked, more-or-less steady descent (1100 feet in 2 miles) down through mostly chaparral—hot going on a sunny afternoon. A cool and

pleasant but brief passage across a north-facing slope precedes a final switchbacking plunge down the steep wall of Dark Canyon. There are lots of opportunities to admire Malibu Creek country spread before you—the upthrust Goat Buttes, Brents Mountain, and the green or gold (depending on the season) valleys below. At the bottom, fern-draped Dark Canyon is like a paradise, but the shady passage is a brief one. A final zigzag climb takes you back up into the sunny chaparral, where you come upon Piuma Road.

Equestrians on Sostomo Trail

Area S-2, Trip 11
Calabasas Peak

	Distance	3.6 miles round trip
	Total Elevation Gain/Loss	1000'/1000'
	Hiking Time	2 hours (round trip)
	Optional Map	USGS 7.5-min *Malibu Beach*
	Best Times	October through June
	Agency	SMMC
	Difficulty	★★

The climb to Calabasas Peak should appeal to both exercise buffs and landscape photographers. The non-trivial gain and loss of elevation make a great workout, and the geologic formations passed along the way are some of the most photogenic in the Santa Monica Mountains. In any case, an early or a late start is almost always preferred over a midday excursion. The exercise-minded will find the cool morning air most refreshing. Photographers will appreciate the three-dimensional effect of low-angle sunlight on the rock formations and the long shadows slanting across the shaggy mountainsides.

Park in the large turnout at mile-marker 1.0 on Stunt Road (1 mile from Mulholland Highway). Cross the pavement and pick up the fire road that cuts across a hillside to the north. Bear left when you reach a road junction at a saddle (0.7 mile), where you'll get a first look at aptly named Red Rock Canyon to the east. From there you continue north, wending your way past a fascinating collection of tilted sandstone slabs and fins.

At 1.6 miles, just beyond a couple of horseshoe curves in the road, you reach the summit ridge, south of the Calabasas Peak summit. Most of Old Topanga Canyon, to the east, is visible below. The road goes on to traverse the peak's east shoulder, so you leave it and hop onto a fire break going up toward the peak itself on your left. A low thicket of chaparral guards the rounded summit.

The foreground view, marred at many points around the compass by massive grading and home construction, may be disappointing. But on clear days, the long views west toward Castro Crest and east to the San Gabriel Mountains are inspiring all the same.

Area S-2, Trip 12
Topanga Lookout-Stunt High Loop

🥾	**Distance**	6.5 miles
	Total Elevation Gain/Loss	1800'/1800'
	Hiking Time	3½ hours
	Optional Map	USGS 7.5-min *Malibu Beach*
🏳️ 🏔️ ↺	**Best Times**	October through May
	Agency	NPS
	Difficulty	★★★

This wide-ranging loop has a bit of what feels like genuine mountaineering—a mere class 2½ or 3 in climber's parlance, but exciting all the same. Save the trip for an exceptionally clear day, as I did, and you'll be rewarded with vistas that must be seen to be believed.

Begin, as in Trip 11, by hiking to the saddle at the head of Red Rock Canyon, 0.7 mile from Stunt Road. Take neither the road north to Calabasas Peak nor the road east into Red Rock Canyon below. Instead, turn sharply right and climb up a steep bulldozed road. The road soon peters out, but you can continue climbing to a 1766' knoll. There you can see what lies ahead: an undulating, brushy, knife-edge ridge, buttressed by tilted sandstone slabs and fins. A narrow, but well-beaten trail up the ridge testifies to its popularity as a mountaineer's route.

Make your way for a painstaking mile up and over or around the sandstone obstacles and through the brush until you reach the terminus of a fire road. Continue on this for an easy-going 0.4 mile, past a couple of striking columnar rock formations, to the foundation of the long-abandoned Topanga Fire Lookout (2.2 miles). Try to ignore the tons of discarded bottles and trash (it looks like a thousand drunken fools descended on the place) and concentrate instead on the stupefying view. A big section of the San Fernando Valley is visible, along with parts of the L.A. Basin and Santa Monica Bay. Downtown L.A.'s office towers point the way toward a low spot on the east horizon— San Gorgonio Pass—flanked by Southern California's highest peaks (San Gorgonio and San Jacinto), over 100 miles away.

From the lookout site, walk south on the fire road to Saddle Peak Road (3.1 miles), where there's a better view of Santa Monica Bay and Santa Catalina Island. Over at the intersection of paved roads immediately west, bear right on Stunt Road. Walk easily downhill along Stunt Road for a bit over a mile, a not-unpleasant task since the road carries only light traffic and offers nice views throughout. (The future Backbone Trail, which will parallel this stretch, will someday provide an alternative to walking the road.) On the way down you'll pass by the upper gate for a trail through Cold Creek Canyon Preserve. The property is open for guided hikes, and may also be used by individuals if reserved three days or more in advance (see Appendix 4).

At a turnout on the right at mile-marker 3.0, you'll discover the top end of the Stunt High Trail. Follow the trail's winding course downhill for 0.8 mile through tall chaparral until you hit Stunt Road again. Turn right and walk 0.1 mile east along Stunt Road's left shoulder to the Stunt Ranch entrance road. Follow this for 0.1 mile north, then veer right to continue on the signed Stunt High Trail. Only a mile of walking remains: You wind through more chaparral, go down across a meadow to Cold Creek, and meet an old road paralleling the stream. The final, delightfully shaded stretch goes up along the creek and ends at your starting point, the large turnout at mile 1.0 on Stunt Road.

Area S-3: Zuma Canyon

Although it slices only 6 miles inland from the Pacific shoreline near Point Dume, Zuma Canyon harbors one of the deepest gorges in the Santa Monica Mountains. Easily on a par with Malibu and Topanga canyons in scenic wealth, Zuma Canyon holds a further distinction of never having suffered the invasion of a major road.

Recent and future acquisitions of open space in Zuma Canyon (and in neighboring Trancas Canyon to the west and Ramirez Canyon to the east) by the National Park Service will serve two goals relevant to the needs of hikers. First, there is now public access to lower Zuma Canyon—gateway to the most wild and isolated stretch of canyon bottom in the Santa Monicas. Second, a public right-of-way is being established so that an important missing link of the Backbone Trail can be constructed in the near future. Starting at Kanan Dume Road, this segment will dip past upper Zuma Canyon's waterfalls, climb to cross the Zuma Ridge Trail, and then wind west across the upper tributaries of Trancas Canyon to intersect Encinal Canyon Road.

Future editions of this book will surely have more to offer in this area. For now, we're including a couple of hikes in lower Zuma Canyon, plus a visit to nearby Rocky Oaks Park, a good spot for a short hike, a picnic, wildflower hunting, or birdwatching.

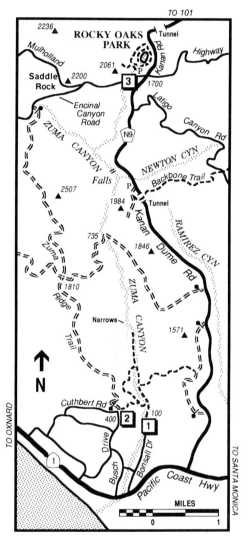

Area S-3: Zuma Canyon

Area S-3, Trip 1
Lower Zuma Canyon

	Distance	2.5 miles round trip
	Total Elevation Gain/Loss	100'/100'
	Hiking Time	1 hour (round trip)
	Optional Map	USGS 7.5-min *Point Dume*
	Best Times	All year
	Agency	NPS
	Difficulty	★

Officially opened to public use in 1989, the mouth of Zuma Canyon offers a small network of riding and hiking trails, and plenty of space to wander along the gravelly bed of the canyon's small creek. For starters, we suggest you try this easy walk.

Park at the end of Bonsall Drive (1 mile north of Pacific Coast Highway). Walk past a gate and into the sycamore-dotted flood plain ahead. When you reach a split in the trail after 0.2 mile, stay right. Continue along the winter-wet, summer-dry creek, crossing it several times in the next mile. You'll pass statuesque sycamores, tall laurel sumac bushes, and scattered wildflowers in season. This is a promising area for spotting wildlife anytime—squirrels, rabbits,

and coyotes are commonly seen, deer and bobcats less so.

After about a mile, the canyon walls close in tighter, oaks appear in greater numbers, and you'll notice a small grove of eucalyptus trees across the creek on a little terrace. A short while later, the trail abruptly ends at a pile of sandstone boulders. During the dry months, surface water may get only this far down the canyon. Usually, however, the water trickles or tumbles past here, disappearing at some point downstream into the porous substrate of the canyon floor. Further travel through the V-shaped canyon ahead is possible only by rock-hopping (Trip 2), so this is a good spot to turn around.

Area S-3, Trip 2
Zuma Canyon Loop

	Distance	8.0 miles
	Total Elevation Gain/Loss	1700'/1700'
	Hiking Time	6 hours
	Optional Map	USGS 7.5-min *Point Dume*
	Best Times	October through June
	Agency	NPS
	Difficulty	★★★★

Caught between walls soaring 1500 feet or more, the green, riparian strip along the bottom of Zuma Canyon's mid-section lies undisturbed (save for the crossing of a single

dirt road built to give access to electrical towers). Under cover of jungle-like growths of willow, sycamore, oak and bay, the canyon's small stream cascades over sculpted sandstone boulders and gathers in limpid pools adorned with ferns. These natural treasures yield their secrets begrudgingly, as they should, only to those willing to scramble over boulders, plow through sucking mud and cattails, and thrash through scratchy undergrowth.

Zuma Canyon is passable all the way to the bottom of a 25′ waterfall just above Newton Canyon. For variety, however, we'll route you part of the way up the canyon, and then back on the powerline road and the Zuma Ridge Trail (a fire road). The roads are shadeless, but offer great vistas of the canyon and the ocean.

Hiking the canyon bottom is least problematical in the fall season before the heavy rains set in. The stream may have shrunk to isolated pools by then, and you'll step mostly on dry rocks with good traction. Winter flooding can render the canyon impassable, but such episodes are rare and short-lived. During spring, the stream flows heartily and there's plenty of greenery and wildflowers; at the same time there's an increased threat of exposure to poison oak (which is found in fair abundance along the banks) and you're more likely to surprise a rattlesnake. Summer days are usually too oppressively warm and humid for such a difficult hike. Whatever the season, take along plenty of water; the water in the canyon is not potable.

A good starting place is the dirt parking area at the north end of Busch Drive, one mile from Pacific Coast Highway. There's a fire road on your left, which is your return route. Take the path across the hillside to your right (east). You lose about 300 feet of elevation as you zigzag down to the flat flood plain at the mouth of Zuma Canyon.

When you reach the bottom, go a little farther east to a trail junction. Turn left there and walk up along Zuma's creek bed for about a mile. Now you begin a nearly 2-mile stretch of boulder-hopping, 2 or 3 hours worth depending on the conditions. Other than a few rusting pieces of pipeline from an old dam and irrigation system at the lower

end, you may find that the canyon is completely litter-free; please keep it that way.

The great variety of rocks that have been washed down the stream or fallen from the canyon walls says a lot about the geologic complexity of the Santa Monicas. You'll scramble over fine-grained siltstones and sandstones, conglomerates that look like poorly mixed aggregate concrete, and volcanic rocks of the sort that make up Saddle Rock (a local landmark near the head of Zuma Canyon) and the Goat Buttes of Malibu Creek State Park. Some of the larger boulders attain the dimensions of mid-sized trucks, presenting an obstacle course that must be negotiated by moderate hand-and-foot climbing.

About 0.5 mile shy of the dirt road crossing, you'll pass directly under a set of high-voltage transmission lines—so high they're hard to spot. These lines, plus the service road built to give access to the towers, represent the major incursion of civilization into Zuma Canyon. If you can ignore them, however, it's easy to imagine what all the large canyons in the Santa Monicas were like only a century ago.

From the service-road crossing, more scrambling and bushwhacking could potentially take you all the way to Kanan Road via Newton Canyon. Going our way, however, you turn left and climb up the twisting service road to the top of the west ridge. From there, the Zuma Ridge Trail, a fire road, takes you back down to the starting point.

Area S-3, Trip 3
Rocky Oaks Park

	Distance	1.0 mile
	Total Elevation Gain/Loss	150'/150'
	Hiking Time	½ hour
	Optional Map	USGS 7.5-min *Point Dume*
	Best Times	All year
	Agency	NPS
	Difficulty	★

Diminutive Rocky Oaks Park is typical of the many small properties that have been purchased or earmarked for future acquisition by the National Park Service in the continuing effort to flesh out the Santa Monica Mountains National Recreation Area. This property, a former cattle ranch, was burned over in 1978, was purchased by the NPS in 1980, and has now largely reverted to nature. There are restrooms, a parking lot, and a picnic area (off Mulholland Highway, just west of Kanan Road), and about 200 acres of chaparral, sage scrub, grassland, and oak woodland to explore.

An easy, 1-mile loop hike begins across the stream from the parking lot. Go left and walk 0.2 mile to a 4-way intersection, then continue straight ahead up a steep slope to reach an overlook at the top of some wood

steps. The cattle pond in the valley below may or may not contain water, depending on recent rains. In the opposite direction is peak 2061 (a.k.a. Mitten Mountain), which itself blocks from view Saddle Rock. These two crags, as well as the summit you're standing on, consist of the roughly 15-million-year old Conejo Volcanics rock formation.

The trail continues north, contouring through mature chaparral. Here dead twigs are accumulating beneath the new growth. In the natural scheme of things, this vegetation is about ready for the next burn, its ashes providing nutrients for the next, almost identical generation of plants.

Bear right at the next fork, descend to the meadow below, and make your way past the pond back to the parking lot.

The wilds of Zuma Canyon

Area S-4: Arroyo Sequit-
Sandstone Peak

Toward the western end of the Santa Monica Mountains, the pulse of life slows. Human population is scattered and sparse. People live on little ranches tucked in the canyons, or in modest cottages perched on the hillsides. A growing number are busy building ostentatious versions of the perfect, hilltop dream house. Lots of day-trippers and campers come this way to enjoy the ocean, the fresh coastal breezes, and the picturesque, mostly unspoiled backcountry.

The area depicted on our map, straddling the Los Angeles-Ventura county line, is dominated by a small stream called Arroyo Sequit. An escarpment stands tall at the northern headwaters of Arroyo Sequit, culminating in a craggy outcrop called Sandstone Peak. At 3111 feet, it's the highest point in the Santa Monicas. The peak, really an outcrop of volcanic rock that looks like sandstone, is just one of several similar-looking summits that make up Boney Mountain, which stretches west into Point Mugu State Park (Area S-5).

Much of this area is protected open space, in big chunks of land like Circle X Ranch and Leo Carrillo State Beach, and also more modest-sized parcels, like Malibu Springs, Arroyo Sequit, and Charmlee parks. Leo Carrillo State Beach, named after the actor, encompasses a mere 6000 feet of ocean frontage, but 2000 acres of interior hillsides and canyons.

Readily accessible from either the Ventura Freeway (U.S. 101) in the north or Pacific Coast Highway in the south, the area is convenient to day hikers, campers, and backpackers. Opportunities for camping here (and also in nearby Point Mugu State Park) help make up for the sore lack of campsites in the eastern Santa Monicas. You may pull into either of Leo Carrillo's two developed campgrounds (Leo Carrillo and North Beach—the former has hot showers), or brave a stretch of winding, dirt road to reach the rustic and underutilized Happy Hollow Campground at Circle X Ranch. Leo Carrillo has a hiker-biker campground annex. You can also backpack into the higher country of Circle X Ranch for a stay at a secluded trail camp there (see Trip 9).

Generally speaking, hiking is good the year round immediately next to the coast where the sea breezes take the heat off the south-facing slopes. Inland, at places like Circle X Ranch, the temperature can climb to 100° on summer days and drop to well below freezing on calm winter nights.

In addition to hiking, the coastline in and next to Leo Carrillo State Beach offers some of the finest beachcombing, surfing, swimming, and sailboarding on the L.A. County coast. At Sequit Point you'll find a jagged stretch of sea bluffs, and rocky pools to explore when the tides are low. Sequit Point is an especially good vantage for spotting gray whales during their winter migrations. Sometimes they can be seen swimming just beyond the surf line.

The nine trips below encompass many diverse environments and span 3000 feet of elevation change. This is my favorite area of the Santa Monicas; you may agree after exploring it a bit.

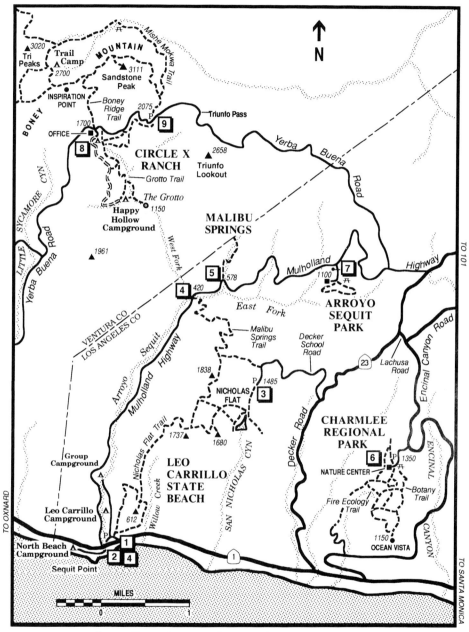

Area S-4: Arroyo Sequit/Sandstone Peak

Area S-4, Trip 1
Leo Carrillo Ocean Vista

	**Distance**	2.0 miles
	Total Elevation Gain/Loss	600'/600'
	Hiking Time	1 hour
	Optional Map	USGS 7.5-min *Triunfo Pass*
	Best Times	All year
	Agency	LCSB
	Difficulty	★★

For the modest effort of climbing a 612' hill, you can enjoy one of the best ocean views available anywhere in the Santa Monica Mountains. If the morning is fog-free and you're ambitious enough, I'd recommend trying to make the top in time for sunrise. (The sun rises around 7 A.M. in October, November and December, so you don't have to lose much sleep, especially if you're camped nearby). That's what I did one clear, autumn morning when warm Santa Ana winds were sweeping out to sea. To the sound of booming surf, I watched as the sun's golden beams spilled over Palos Verdes and glanced off the whitecaps below—a very memorable experience.

Day-use parking (for a fee) is available just past the entrance booth at Leo Carrillo Campground, but you may also park, for free, along the shoulder of Pacific Coast Highway. The trail begins just beyond the booth. Almost immediately there's a split—go either way to reach the top of the hill.

The slightly more direct right branch slants across a hillside overlooking the highway, then ducks inland along a slope overlooking the V-shaped ravine of Willow Creek. Near the top, you reverse direction three times and arrive at a 4-way junction of trails on a saddle. Turn left and walk the remaining distance to the 612' hilltop. In addition to the nearby coastline stretching out to Point Dume, you might see the Palos Verdes peninsula, Santa Catalina Island, and several of the Channel Islands. In the north, the toothy crest of Boney Mountain barely peeks over a rounded ridge opposite the Arroyo Sequit. Below, in the west, you'll look down on the sycamore-dotted Leo Carrillo Campground, stretching for almost half a mile along a flat terrace just above Arroyo Sequit's parched bed.

When it's time to go, return to the 4-way junction. Take the left branch this time, returning by way of the lower Nicholas Flat Trail.

Coastline, Leo Carrillo State Beach

Area S-4, Trip 2
Lower Arroyo Sequit

	Distance	3.0 miles round trip
	Total Elevation Gain/Loss	200'/200'
	Hiking Time	1½ hours (round trip)
	Optional Map	USGS 7.5-min *Triunfo Pass*
	Best Times	All year
	Agency	LCSB
	Difficulty	★★

For thousands of years, lower Arroyo Sequit and most of the other canyons of consequence in the Santa Monica Mountains were inhabited by resourceful Native Americans—most recently by the people called the Chumash. Before the coming of the Spanish, the Chumash settled into a comfortable existence here and apparently lived peaceably with neighboring tribes. They gathered seeds and acorns from the land, captured fish by hook and net, and traded with other Native Americans all over California. They also fashioned canoes, water-proofed with tar, which took them on seafood-collecting trips along the local coastline and out as far as the Channel Islands. For them, Arroyo Sequit was both a source of fresh water and a travel corridor to inland hunting grounds and oak woodlands. Today, when you hike up the narrows of lower Arroyo Sequit, you get an inkling of what the prehistoric world of the Chumash was like.

Start from the day-use parking area at the entrance to Leo Carrillo Campground, or from Pacific Coast Highway. Walk north, either through the campground or up along the gravelly bed of the stream itself, which is dry in this lowermost stretch most of the year. Once past the campfire circle and the group campground, the canyon walls begin to assume a sheer posture, and oaks, sycamores, bays, and willows offer cool shade. Poison oak grows in a few places on the banks. There's at least some surface water flowing here, even in the dry season.

Make your way over multicolored, stream-worn boulders, mostly of volcanic origin. Most have washed down from Arroyo Sequit's East Fork and West Fork tributaries, which themselves drain the largest formation of volcanic rock in the Santa Monicas. The rock walls of the canyon itself are not volcanic at all, but sedimentary in origin.

A little ahead, you pass a spot where the water tumbles or trickles over an obstacle course of rounded boulders. Beyond, the canyon floor widens, the trees all but disappear, and the walls soar even higher.

After about 1.5 miles from Pacific Coast Highway, there's a large, cave-like hollow on the left—the last really interesting sight in this part of the canyon. This is a good place to make a U-turn and head back to the group campground. If you followed the creek upstream another 0.3 mile, you would come to a bridge on Mulholland Highway, 1.6 road miles up from Pacific Coast Highway.

Area S-4, Trip 3
Nicholas Flat

Distance	1.5 miles round trip
Total Elevation Gain/Loss	100'/100'
Hiking Time	1 hour (round trip)
Optional Map	USGS 7.5-min *Triunfo Pass*
Best Times	All year
Agency	LCSB
Difficulty	★

Nicholas Flat harbors a small oasis of live oaks and an old cattle pond backed by picturesque sandstone outcrops. During the spring, the grassy meadows above the pond may put on an eye-popping wildflower show. Because so many plant communities converge in this one area—coastal sage scrub, grassland, chaparral, and oak woodland—Nicholas Flat is a good bet for bird- and wildlife-watching too.

You begin on Decker School Road, which intersects Decker Road (Highway 23) at a point 2.5 miles north of Pacific Coast Highway and 1.4 miles south of Lachusa Road. Drive to the west end of Decker School Road, opposite an abandoned ranch, and park in the space provided without blocking gates. From there, a pleasant, oak-lined path (old road) leads south to an intersection just above the pond. Bear

right to visit the oak-dotted west shore or the grassy area north of the pond. Amid the oaks you can look for a bedrock metate, where the Chumash milled acorns. In wetter times, the pond (which is artificial) brims with water, while in drought years (as in the late 80s) it may be bone-dry by late summer. When I visited in October 1989, there were gaping cracks up to 2 feet deep in the abobe mud at the bottom.

To explore a little further, you can work your way around the lake to the top of the sandstone outcrops on the south side (watch out for poison oak as you do so). From there you get a fine view through the gorge of San Nicholas Canyon to the blue ocean below. A somewhat better view can be had by hiking up to a 1680' knob on the ridge to the west (an extra gain and loss of 300 feet, entirely on trail).

Area S-4, Trip 4
Leo Carrillo Traverse

Distance	5.2 miles
Total Elevation Gain/Loss	1500'/1900'
Hiking Time	2½ hours
Optional Map	USGS 7.5-min *Triunfo Pass*
Best Times	October through June
Agency	LCSB
Difficulty	★★★

This one-way hike goes from the confluence of Arroyo Sequit's East and West forks to Leo Carrillo Beach—the hard way.

Mulholland Highway is the easy way. You can quickly set up a car shuttle by leaving one car at Leo Carrillo Beach, and taking the other to mile 3.2 on Mulholland Highway. There you'll find roadside parking for two cars, and an old road bed—now a marked hiking trail—slanting up the slope to the south. (Even if you don't have two cars, you could walk or bicycle, as I did, the 3.2 miles of narrow pavement. Early morning is a good time to try this. Before 7 A.M. there's virtually no traffic on this remote and scenic stretch of Mulholland.)

In essence you'll be going up and over Arroyo Sequit's east ridge, starting out in oak woodland and chaparral, and ending in coastal sage-scrub vegetation as you approach the ocean. The value of an early-morning start will be apparent as you begin with a bang: 1400 feet of ascent in 2 miles. On the way up, you swing around several hairpin turns, discovering ever-more-impressive vistas of Boney Mountain and the deep crease in the mountains below it—Arroyo Sequit's West Fork. In the north you'll spot the Triunfo Lookout site, now occupied by a huge, boxy structure serving as a passive reflector for microwave transmissions. Down in the valley to the east are the big, white "ears" of a GTE satellite tracking station.

Before reaching the top of the ridge, with about 200 vertical feet to go, you pass a trail that forks left and contours eastward. Take it only if you want to extend your hike by circling around to visit Nicholas Flat. This junction also marks the spot where you leave National Park Service land (Malibu Springs open-space area) and enter Leo Carrillo State Beach property.

The 1838' summit is the highest point on the whole ridge, but you'll have even better ocean views ahead. Drop down to a junction at a saddle (2.4 miles), keep right, and continue south along a brushy ridge overlooking Nicholas Flat. At the next trail junction, where the Nicholas Flat Trail comes in from the left, stay right again. On the saddle just southwest, the Nicholas Flat Trail descends to the right, and a fire break continues south to a 1737' knoll. Detour to the top for the best ocean and coastline view of all.

The final, bone-jarring descent to Leo Carrillo Beach features almost 1700 feet of elevation loss in 2.4 miles. A mile from the end, you have a choice: go left down along Willow Creek, or right down the slope overlooking the campground. Both paths are scenic and about equally direct.

Area S-4, Trip 5
Malibu Springs

	Distance	1.0 mile round trip
	Total Elevation Gain/Loss	200'/200'
	Hiking Time	½ hour (round trip)
	Optional Map	USGS 7.5-min *Triunfo Pass*
	Best Times	October through June
	Agency	NPS
	Difficulty	★

A secret little hideaway lies just north of Mulholland Highway on a tributary of the Arroyo Sequit. There you'll find a trickling, sycamore- and oak-bowered stream, crickets chirping in a meadow, and parapets of ruddy volcanic rock soaring into the blue vault of the sky: an hour spent quietly contemplating such purity and simplicity can bring on a feeling of profound peace, and leave you in a relaxed state of mind.

To find this intriguing spot, drive to a hairpin turn at mile 3.7 on Mulholland Highway, where there's space for about three parked cars. Squeeze around the fence and go north up a gorge on a battered, abandoned dirt road. You bend right to cross a creek, then left to resume travel upstream on the other side. Look for the remains of cabins on the shady banks (but watch out for poison oak, too).

After about a half mile, the canyon divides and the road fades. From there, determined hikers can go on to explore either branch, first on rabbit trails through the sage shrubbery, then through heavy chaparral. All around you, reddish brown walls—made of the same stuff as Boney Mountain and Sandstone Peak—rise impressively. Almost all of what you can see here lies within the NPS-administered Malibu Springs open-space area. Hence it will probably remain undisturbed for the foreseeable future.

Area S-4, Trip 6
Charmlee Regional Park

Distance	2.8 miles
Total Elevation Gain/Loss	500'/500'
Hiking Time	1½ hours
Optional Map	USGS 7.5-min *Triunfo Pass*
Best Times	All year
Agency	CRP
Difficulty	★

Charmlee Regional Park's 460 acres of meadow, oak woodland, sage scrub, and chaparral were opened to the public in 1981. Never designed to accommodate a large number of visitors, its parking lot is nonetheless often full on the weekends. Charmlee is a great place to take family and friends wildflower hunting in the spring, or ocean watching on a cool, clear winter day.

The park's well-marked entrance is on Encinal Canyon Road, 4 miles north of Pacific Coast Highway and a little over 1 mile south of Lachusa Road. Gates are open 8 A.M. to sunset daily. From the park's maze of footpaths and old ranch roads, I've chosen a route that more or less follows the perimeter:

From the parking lot, walk on pavement to the nature center (inside, pick up a guide for the Fire Ecology Trail and other interpretive materials). Bear right on a paved road, soon dirt, that bends north up a slope. Make an acute left turn at the top, follow a ridge road past a hilltop water tank (detour and walk around the tank for a good overview of the park and the ocean), and then curve down to a T-intersection. Jog right, then go left on the Fire Ecology Trail. After a few minutes you be passing under some fire-singed coast live oaks, which are well known for their ability to survive fast-moving wildfires.

At post 10 on the Fire Ecology Trail, go right on a road that winds along the west edge of Charmlee's large, central meadow. Continue all the way to a dry ridge topped by some old eucalyptus trees and a concrete-lined cistern, both relics of cattle ranching days. From there descend south (stay right at the next junction) to the "Ocean Vista," which really delivers in a big way what its name suggests, especially on clear days. In addition to miles of surf seemingly at your feet, there may easily be a thousand square miles of open ocean in view—most of it extremely foreshortened, of course.

Circle north from Ocean Vista around the hill with the cistern and then along the east side of the meadow. When you come to the northeast part of the meadow and the dirt road curves west, pick up the hard-to-spot Botany Trail on the right. It winds through mostly chaparral vegetation and takes you to the picnic area just above your starting point.

If it's a spring day and you've kept a tally of wildflowers spotted on the hike, you may be surprised to find your list includes as many as two dozen or more.

Area S-4, Trip 7
Arroyo Sequit Park

	Distance	1.2 miles
	Total Elevation Gain/Loss	150'/150'
	Hiking Time	½ hour
	Optional Map	USGS 7.5-min *Triunfo Pass*
	Best Times	November through June
	Agency	SMMC
	Difficulty	★

With a little detective work you can successfully locate this obscure little park, 155 acres of meadow and canyonside. You'll find it on Mulholland Highway at mile 5.6 according to the roadside markers, or by the address on the mailbox out front: 34138. The property, a former ranch, is open only on weekends for day use.

Like much of the Santa Monica Mountains, this patch appears drab and dry at least half the year—but fall or winter rains can transform it instantly into an emerald paradise. Bring the kids here for a little hiking, picnicking, wildflower hunting, or bird watching.

Park along Mulholland's shoulder or in the driveway (taking care not to block the closed gate), and walk up toward an old ranch house on the macadam driveway. Veer left toward a restored barn (used for meetings) and pass a small picnic area shaded by oaks. On the right, you'll see a marked hiking trail slanting up and across a meadow. You'll circle to the rim of a little canyon (an upper tributary of Arroyo Sequit), then curve back down through more grassland toward the house.

Other unmarked trails lace the area, including one that descends to the bottom of the little canyon below. These can be rewarding if the day is cool and runoff is coursing down the canyon.

Winter surf, Leo Carrillo State Beach

Area S-4, Trip 8
The Grotto

Distance	2.6 miles round trip
Total Elevation Gain/Loss	650'/650'
Hiking Time	1½ hours (round trip)
Optional Map	USGS 7.5-min *Triunfo Pass*
Best Times	All year
Agency	CXR
Difficulty	★★

The 1655-acre Circle X Ranch, formerly run by the Boy Scouts of America but now administered by the National Park Service, is positively riddled with Tom Sawyer-esque hiking paths. Some have succumbed to encroaching brush, but two that are in good shape—the Grotto and Mishe Mokwa (see Trip 9) trails—are among the most interesting in the whole Santa Monica Mountain range.

For the hike on the Grotto Trail, start at Circle X park headquarters, on Yerba Buena Road 5.4 miles north of Pacific Coast Highway, or 5.5 miles west of Mulholland Highway. (Either way you face a white-knuckle drive, with sharp curves and a lack of guard rails where they're really needed.) Leave your car either in the upper parking area just off Yerba Buena Road, or 0.1 mile below in the lot next to the ranger office.

From the office, start off on the dirt road leading down toward Happy Hollow Campground. At a point about 100 yards down, veer left at the entrance to a group campground. Walk through or skirt the campsites, and pick up a trail heading south down along a shady, seasonal creek. Keep heading downhill as you pass, in quick succession, two trails coming in from the left. Very shortly afterward, you cross the creek at a point immediately above a 30' ledge which becomes a trickling waterfall in winter and spring. You then go uphill, gaining about 50 feet of elevation, and cross an open meadow offering fine views of both Boney Mountain

above and Arroyo Sequit's West Fork gorge below. Pass a short trail going over to Happy Hollow road on the right, and descend a steep stretch leading to the bottom of the gorge.

When you reach an old road at the bottom, bear left, cross the creek, and continue downstream on trail along the shaded east bank. Pass some campsites (part of Happy Hollow Campground) and then curve left when you reach a grove of fantastically twisted live oaks at the confluence of two stream forks. On the edge of this grove, an overflow pipe coming out of a tank discharges tepid spring water. Continue another 200 yards down the now-lively brook to The Grotto, a narrow, spooky constriction flanked by sheer volcanic-rock walls. If your sense of balance is good, you can clamber over grey-colored rock ledges and massive boulders fallen from the canyon walls—just as thousands of Scouts have done before you. At one point you can peer cautiously into a gloomy cavern, where the subterranean stream is more easily heard than seen. Water marks on the boulders above are evidence that this part of the gorge probably supports a two-tier stream in times of flood.

When you've had your fill of adventuring, return by the same route, uphill almost the whole way. As an option you could hike west through the campground and then follow the dirt road up. This alternative is longer, more gradual, and less scenic than the trail.

Live-oak woodland above The Grotto

Area S-4, Trip 9
Sandstone Peak

Distance	5.8 miles
Total Elevation Gain/Loss	1400'/1400'
Hiking Time	3½ hours
Optional Maps	USGS 7.5-min *Triunfo Pass,* *Newbury Park*
Best Times	October through June
Agency	CXR
Difficulty	★★★

Sandstone Peak, *the* destination for peak baggers in the Santa Monicas, can be reached in as little as 1½ miles (by way of the short, very steep Boney Ridge Trail from Circle X park headquarters). Much more rewarding and relaxing is the looping route outlined below. Take a picnic lunch and plan to make a half day of it. At best you should come on a crystalline day in late fall or winter to take best advantage of the skyline views. Spring is dependably good because

of the wildflowers. In addition to blue-flowering stands of ceanothus, the early to mid-spring bloom includes monkey flower, nightshade, Chinese houses, wild peony, wild hyacinth, morning glory, and phacelia. Delicate, orangish Humboldt lilies should be unfolding by June.

Backpacking is good in just about any season. In summer, you can travel during the cooler late afternoon and early morning hours, with a layover at the backcountry trail camp about halfway along the route. Reservations are required—call (818) 597–9192 for details.

Start hiking at the large parking lot on the north side of Yerba Buena Road, 1 mile east of Circle X park headquarters. Proceed past a gate and up a fire road 0.3 mile to where the marked Mishe Mokwa Trail branches right. Right away you plunge into brush so thick and tall it's often hard to see the outside world. The hand-tooled route is delightfully primitive, but requires prompt maintenance every year or so to keep the chaparral from knitting itself together across the path. Both your hands and feet will come into play over the next 40 or 50 minutes as you're forced to scramble a bit over rough-textured outcrops of volcanic rock. You'll make intimate acquaintance with mosses and ferns and several of the more attractive chaparral shrubs: toyon, holly-leaf cherry, manzanita, and red shanks (a.k.a ribbonwood), which is identified by its wispy foliage and perpetually peeling, rust-colored bark. You'll also pass several bay trees, under which the temperature seems to fall about 10°. After about a half hour on the Mishe Mokwa Trail, keep an eye out for an amazing balanced rock that rests precariously on the opposite wall of the canyon that lies just below you.

By 1.7 miles from the start you will have worked you way around to the north flank of Sandstone Peak, where you suddenly come upon a couple of picnic tables and "Split Rock," a fractured volcanic boulder with a gap wide enough to walk through (please do so to maintain the Scouts' tradition). At this point you pick up a dirt road that crosses the aforementioned canyon and turns west (upstream). You pass beneath some hefty volcanic outcrops and at 2.5 miles come to a junction with a trail on the right which goes over a summit and down to the Old Cabin Site in Pt. Mugu State Park. (See Area S-5, Trip 3.) Continue on the road and circle south to the trail campground (2.8 miles) on the left, nestled in a little draw. This draw embraces the westernmost headwaters of Malibu Creek. Rainwater falling here makes

its way about 12 miles east through Lake Sherwood and Triunfo Canyon before turning south to descend the deep gorge cut by Malibu Creek.

A side trail leads west from the campground and then north to the bouldery summit of Tri Peaks, one of several peaks that make up the skeletal ridge aptly named Boney Mountain. The half-hour climb is worth it if you have the time and energy. Most of Point Mugu State Park, to the north and west, is visible from the top.

Our route continues south, then east on the main trail, still a dirt road. About 200 yards beyond the junction of a spur road leading past some water tanks, look for an obscure side path going right. This takes you about 50 yards to the top of an outcrop—Inspiration Point. The direction-finder there indicates local features as well as distant points such as Mt. Baldy and Santa Catalina and San Clemente islands.

Press on and pass the junction of the Boney Ridge Trail, but don't miss the junction of the Sandstone Peak summit trail, just past two closely spaced hairpin turns in the road. Make your way up the slippery path to the windswept top. The plaque on the summit block honors W. Herbert Allen, a long-time benefactor of the Scouts and Circle X Ranch. To the Scouts this mountain is "Mt. Allen," although that name has not, so far, been accepted by cartographers. In any event, the peak's real name is misleading. It, along with Boney Mountain and most of the western crest of the Santa Monicas, consists of beige- and rust-colored volcanic rock, not unlike sandstone when seen from a distance.

On a clear day the view is truly panoramic from here, with distant mountain ranges, the hazy L.A. Basin, and the island-dimpled surface of the ocean occupying all 360° of the horizon. Before you leave the summit, don't forget to sign in at the register, housed in a little cubbyhole. To return, go back down to the road and resume your travel eastward. One and a half miles of twisting descent will take you back to the trailhead.

Area S-5: Point Mugu

Mugu, a corruption of the Chumash word *muwu,* meaning beach, lends its name to a rocky promontory jutting into the ocean, a bald peak towering behind it, and one of the larger state parks in California—16,000-acre Point Mugu State Park.

Geographically speaking, the Point Mugu area is the last gasp of the Santa Monica Mountains up the coast from Los Angeles. Geologists, however, say that the underpinnings of these mountains really extend as far west as the Channel Islands off Santa Barbara. The intervening low area, occupied by the flat, silty Oxnard Plain and part of the continental shelf offshore, is a structurally huge syncline, or downfold of crustal rocks. Paleontological evidence has shown that for a long period ending one or two million years ago the islands were linked to the mainland by an isthmus. This ancient feature is named the Cabrillo Peninsula, after the 16th century explorer Juan Rodriguez Cabrillo, who was buried on the westernmost island, San Miguel.

Point Mugu State Park lies entirely outside Los Angeles County's boundary, but I've included it in this book because it's an integral and important part of the Santa Monica Mountains National Recreation Area. Almost half the park's area comprises the Boney Mountain State Wilderness, so far the only area managed as wilderness in the Santa Monica Mountains.

The two principal park entrances—both off Pacific Coast Highway—are Big Sycamore Canyon and the Ray Miller Trailhead at La Jolla Canyon. Big Sycamore Canyon, in particular, is one of the favored areas on the California coast for overwintering Monarch butterflies.

Abutting the north end of the park, next to suburban Newbury Park, is the Rancho Sierra Vista/Satwiwa open space and cultural park, managed by the National Park Service. In addition to serving as a northern trailhead for the state park (easily accessible from the Ventura Freeway), Rancho Sierra Vista features the Satwiwa Native American Indian Culture Center (open Sundays, 10 A.M. to 4 P.M.). Currently quartered in a former ranch house, the center awaits the construction of a new, specially designed building that will provide a place for Native Americans to teach visitors about their cultures.

With about 100 miles of trails lacing the Point Mugu area, it's possible to devise more than a dozen loop trips significantly different from one another. Trails range from paved service roads and graded fire roads (on which mountain bikes are welcome) to primitive pathways suitable for hikers only. Out of this plethora of possibilities, I've chosen to describe four, non-overlapping loop routes that cover nearly all of Point Mugu's most scenic areas.

Although they are not discussed in detail below, it may be helpful to note certain connections between Point Mugu State Park and Circle X Ranch (Area S-4) that can be used by hikers. A fairly well-used route is a steep trail that leads south of the Old Cabin Site into Circle X Ranch near Tri Peaks. A second, mostly trail-less route goes along Boney Mountain's crest between Old Boney Road and the trail camp at Circle X.

Camping opportunities in the Point Mugu area are plentiful. There are developed campgrounds at La Jolla Beach and Sycamore Canyon (hot showers at the latter). Backpackers can pitch a tent at La Jolla Valley Walk-in Camp, a 2.5-mile hike by the shortest route.

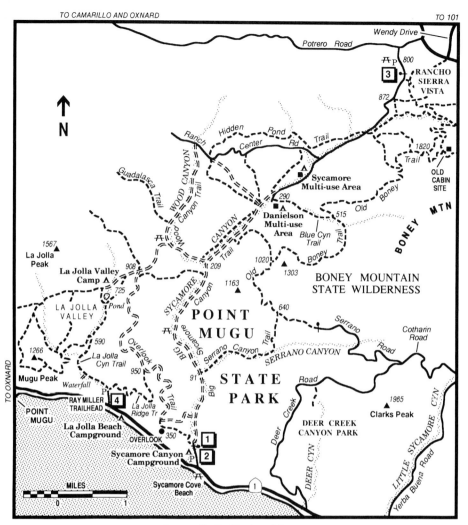

Area S-5: Point Mugu

Area S-5, Trip 1
Overlook Loop

Distance	2.6 miles	
Total Elevation Gain/Loss	350'/350'	
Hiking Time	1½ hours	
Optional Map	USGS 7.5-min *Point Mugu*	
Best Times	All year	
Agency	PMSP	
Difficulty	★	

The Overlook above Sycamore Canyon Campground offers an almost straight-down view of white, foamy surf and turquoise-tinted shallows. When the tide and surf conditions are just right, and the water's glassy, you can watch the swells reflect off the shore and head back out to sea, producing an ever-changing interference pattern on the surface of the water.

This is an easy loop trip; not the much longer one that hikers and mountain bikers often take by linking the whole, ridge-running Overlook Trail with trails in Wood and Big Sycamore canyons. This more leisurely approach will give you time to pay closer attention to the wildflowers and wildlife. Deer frequent these slopes in the early morning and evening. Fire swept these coastal slopes in the fall of 1989, and drought parched them through 1990. Seeds are in the ground, waiting to germinate, so spring wildflower displays could be spectacular if the rains return in the early 1990s.

Day-use parking (for a fee) is available at the starting point, Sycamore Canyon Campground, but you may also park, for free, in a dirt lot outside the entrance, next to Pacific Coast Highway.

North of the campground, just past a vehicle gate, start up the Scenic Trail on the left. You curve up a hillside and arrive after about 15 minutes at a saddle overlooking the ocean. Walk down to a little flat below for a better view. If you're game for it, you can make your way along the narrow ridge that rises to the southeast, for an even better perspective. Nestled against the cliff below is a sloping blanket of sand called The Great Sand Dune. Prevailing sea breezes from the west and south keep it in place.

When it's time to go, pick up the fire road that curves down the high ridge to the north—the Overlook Trail. Follow its winding course downhill to Big Sycamore Canyon, turn right, and walk back to the campground.

Area S-5, Trip 2
Serrano-Big Sycamore Loop

Distance	9.8 miles
Total Elevation Gain/Loss	1250'/1250'
Hiking Time	4½ hours
Optional Maps	USGS 7.5-min *Point Mugu, Triunfo Pass*
Best Times	October through July
Agency	PMSP
Difficulty	★★★

There's always something nice about this hike in just about any season. October through December brings warm, dry winds and fall color—muted yellows and oranges—to the sycamores. During the rainy season, mostly December through March, runoff cascades through the canyon bottoms, and the grasslands come to life. March, April and May are great for wildflowers—even as the grass bleaches to white and gold. June and July are warm, but

tolerable under the shade of the spreading oaks in Serrano Canyon, where delicate, orange Humboldt lilies sway in the breeze.

Two caveats: Bring all the water you'll need, and watch out for poison oak, especially in Serrano Canyon. Begin, as in Trip 1 above, at Sycamore Campground. Head past the vehicle gate and up along the wide dirt road (Big Sycamore Canyon Trail) through park-like Big Sycamore Canyon. Once past the area singed by the 1989 fire, the landscape looks a bit more lush. Proceed to a major fork in the canyon, 1.5 miles from Pacific Coast Highway, and bear right on the Serrano Canyon Trail. After a rather dry, open stretch you enter the steep-walled canyon.

Serrano Canyon is a real treasure, narrow, private, filled with thickets of dark live oaks, pale sycamores, pungent bay laurels, and a green carpet of wild blackberry, ferns, and poison oak. The stream carves its way in a couple of spots through bedrock and gathers in shallow pools. A little off-the-trail scrambling to explore the pools is well worth it, especially if the stream is running vigorously.

At 2.9 miles, the Serrano Canyon Trail leaves the canyon, bearing left up a ravine and onto a grassy slope. Heading almost due north, you pass an old metal shed and come to a T-intersection (3.5 miles) with the Old Boney Trail. Turn left, wind around a ravine, and continue uphill through chaparral to a gap in the ridge above you. At this gap (4.5 miles) you can look down upon a slice of Big

Sycamore Canyon. You're now on the far west shoulder of Boney Mountain; the way east leads directly to the craggy peaks above and ultimately to Sandstone Peak. Follow the Old Boney Trail uphill along this ridge for about 300 yards. From that point a mountaineer's path to Circle X Ranch continues east over peak 1303 and beyond, but you swing left on Old Boney Road and go downhill to a junction 200 yards farther on (4.8 miles, 1020'). Bear left at that junction and descend sharply to Big Sycamore Canyon—750 feet down in 1 mile.

Four pleasant, easy miles remain in Big Sycamore Canyon. The park's brochure boasts of the canyon as being "the finest example of a sycamore savanna in the State Park System." It's true enough. Some of the gangly sycamores soar to heights of about 80 feet. Look for deer, bobcats and coyotes in the grass, and owls and hawks nesting in the trees. If it's fall or early winter, you may see masses of Monarch butterflies in some of the trees.

Serrano Canyon sycamores in late afternoon

Area S-5, Trip 3
Old Boney Loop

	Distance	10.0 miles
	Total Elevation Gain/Loss	2000'/2000'
	Hiking Time	5 hours
	Optional Maps	USGS 7.5-min *Newbury Park, Triunfo Pass*
	Best Times	November through June
	Agency	PMSP
	Difficulty	★★★

This trip takes you through the heart of the Boney Mountain State Wilderness, which encompasses nearly all the Point Mugu State Park lands east of the Big Sycamore Canyon Trail. As in wilderness areas under federal management (those in the Angeles National Forest and elsewhere), policy here prohibits travel by any mechanical conveyance—even bicycles. Old roads exist from the ranching days, but they are not maintained or improved anymore, except to allow for the passage of hikers and horses.

Boney Mountain, which is the top part of a mass of volcanic rock that solidified roughly 15 million years ago and was later uplifted to its present dominant position, overshadows the area. You'll pass beneath its craggy heights while hiking the Old Boney Trail during the latter part of this trip.

You enter the state park the back way, from Rancho Sierra Vista/Satwiwa park. To get there, exit Highway 101 at Wendy Drive in Newbury Park, just west of Thousand Oaks. Drive south to where Wendy ends at Potrero Road. Turn right and proceed 0.5 mile to Reino Road, then go left (staying on Potrero Road) another 0.4 mile to Rancho Sierra Vista's entrance on the south side of Potrero Road.

Park inside and head south on foot up the main road, passing a locked vehicle gate. You'll soon enter state park property and reach an 872' summit with a water tank on the right (0.6 mile). You can now look down on Big Sycamore Canyon and the ribbon of pavement you'll be following for the next 2.5 miles. Walking this paved service road is not unpleasant at all, but if you tire of it there are dirt paths that parallel it from time to time.

Just before the road's end at a ranger residence (3.1 miles), turn left into the Danielson Multi-use Area, one of two such facilities in the park that cater to organized groups of campers, backpackers, and equestrians. The Danielson facility lies on the grounds of the former Danielson Ranch, which was incorporated into Point Mugu State Park in 1973. There are restrooms, a pay telephone, and a beautiful, oak-shaded barbecue pit and patio, which is great for a picnic if it's not occupied. Top off your water bottles here with enough to last the rest of the trip.

Now the harder part begins. Head east on the Blue Canyon Trail, under an oak- and sycamore-canopy, until you reach an intersection with the Old Boney Trail, (4.1 miles). Make a sharp left there and trudge uphill through hot, dry chaparral to an open ridge. You'll follow the undulating ridge for a while, under the gaze of Boney Mountain's crags, then climb in earnest to another, higher ridge (5.8 miles).

You're going against the grain of the land now, and it feels like it. There's a steep descent of about 200 feet and then another climb of about 550 feet to an 1820' summit (6.8 miles). En route you pass two trails leading down to Big Sycamore Canyon; stay right at both junctions. On a clear day all this labor is offset by the tremendous view of the Oxnard Plain, the Channel Islands, the far-off ridges of the Los Padres National Forest, and the discontinuous urban sprawl of Ventura County before you.

Two trails split at the 1820′ summit. Take the right branch and descend beneath huge outcrops on Boney Mountain's north flank. You may spot a side path worn in by rock climbers on the right. Presently you'll pass a trickling spring down in a ravine and arrive at a little oak-shaded flat (7.3 miles) where the foundation and rock chimney of an old cabin stand. Nearby is a beautiful monument to Richard E. Danielson made of rock and wrought-iron. Danielson and his family donated a part interest in the lands, which were acquired to expand the state park and create the Rancho Sierra Vista/ Satwiwa park. In one corner of the flat you'll spot a steep trail going east up the slope of Boney Mountain. This goes up underneath Tri Peaks and into Circle X Ranch (see Area S-4, Trip 9).

From the cabin site, contour over to a junction with the trail coming down from the 1820′ summit, and then descend a twisting 0.8 mile to a hairpin turn (8.3 miles) that wraps around upper Big Sycamore Canyon's stream. At the turn a side path goes east a short distance to some beautiful cascades in a tributary ravine. You won't want to miss this short detour if the water's flowing decently.

Back on the Old Boney Trail, continue west 0.2 mile to a Y-junction and go right. You'll climb to a ridge with Big Sycamore Canyon on the left and the meadows of Rancho Sierra Vista ahead and right. Several paths lace the grassland below; choose the shortest way back to your starting point, less than a mile away.

Area S-5, Trip 4
La Jolla Valley-Mugu Peak

Distance	10.8 miles
Total Elevation Gain/Loss	1950′/1950′
Hiking Time	5½ hours
Optional Map	USGS 7.5-min *Point Mugu*
Best Times	October through June
Agency	PMSP
Difficulty	★★★

Lazily curving up the rumpled, rounded slopes east of La Jolla Canyon, the La Jolla Ridge Trail takes in sweeping views of the Point Mugu coastline and the distant Channel Islands. Completed in December 1989, this westernmost link in the unfinished Backbone Trail system offers a well-graded and scenic approach to the ridge dividing La Jolla and Big Sycamore canyons. Most of the area traversed by the trail was burned in the October 1989 fire, but within a few months the trail sides were dotted with flowers—paintbrush, lupine, phacelia, shoot- ing stars, wild hyacinth, mariposa lily, prickly phlox, and star lily.

The La Jolla Ridge Trail is just the start of the big loop we're suggesting here: a comprehensive trek through the western quadrant of Point Mugu State Park. If this is too big a chunk to bite off for a single day, there are plenty of short cuts, as our map suggests. You could also break up the trip by staying overnight at La Jolla Valley Walk-in Camp. No reservations are needed, but you must register with a park ranger first.

Two trails start from the Ray Miller

Trailhead at the mouth of La Jolla Canyon. The wide one going up along the dry canyon floor ahead is the La Jolla Canyon Trail— your return route. You will take the narrow, inconspicuous La Jolla Ridge Trail to your right. It starts by curling up along the toe of a ridge, where it meets a short spur trail going down to an equestrian staging area. It then doggedly climbs 2.4 miles to a junction with the Overlook Trail, a wide fire road. Keep going north on the Overlook Trail, wend your way around several bumps on the undulating ridge, and arrive at a saddle (4.5 miles from the start), from where roads descend east into Wood Canyon and west into La Jolla Valley. Go left (west) and descend moderately into the green-or flaxen-colored (depending on the season) floor of the valley.

The valley is managed by the state park as a natural preserve to protect the native bunch grasses that flourish there. Because so much of California's coast ranges have been biologically perturbed by grazing for more than a century, opportunistic, non-native grasses have taken over just about everywhere. The authentic California "tall-grass prairie" here in parts of La Jolla Valley is a notable exception.

La Jolla Valley Walk-in Camp (5.0 miles) has piped water, restrooms, and oak-shaded picnic tables. Just south of there, along a trail leading directly back to the Ray Miller Trailhead, you'll find a tule-fringed cattle pond, seasonally dry in some years. Look for chocolate lilies on the slopes around it.

From the walk-in camp, continue west in the direction of a military radar installation on Laguna Peak (off-limits to hikers). Ignore trails going left, right, and left; you'll want to gradually circle to the southwest and south, heading for a saddle on the right (northwest) shoulder of rounded Mugu Peak. Attaining that saddle at 6.8 miles, you'll have a great view of the Pacific Ocean. The popping noises below are from a military shooting range, on the coastward side of Pacific Coast Highway. Up the coast lies the Point Mugu Naval Air Station.

From the saddle, the trail contours south and then east around the south flank of Mugu Peak. You arrive (7.7 miles) at another saddle just east of Mugu's 1266' summit. Five minutes of climbing on a steep path put you on the barren top, where hikers have fashioned a large rock cairn and planted pine saplings. You can look down upon The Great Sand Dune and Pacific Coast Highway where it barely squeezes past some coastal bluffs. On warm days there's a desert-like feel to this rocky and sparsely vegetated mountain, oddly juxtaposed with the sights and sounds of the surf below.

Return to the saddle east of the peak and continue descending to a junction (9.0 miles) in a wooded recess of La Jolla Canyon. Turn right, proceed east along a hillside, and then hook up with the La Jolla Canyon Trail, where you turn right.

There's an exciting stretch down through a rock-walled section of La Jolla Canyon, where you'll see magnificent springtime displays of giant coreopsis. This plant is quite common in the Channel Islands, but found only in scattered coastal locales from far western Los Angeles County to San Luis Obispo County. Some coreopsis plants have forked stems towering 10 feet, head and shoulders above the surrounding scrub. The massed, yellow, daisylike flowers are an unforgettable sight in March and April.

Nearing the canyon's mouth, you'll pass a little grove of walnut trees and a small, seasonal waterfall. You descend to join a dirt road built to haul stone out of the area for the construction of the coast highway, and arrive about 15 minutes later at the Ray Miller Trailhead.

ANGELES NATIONAL FOREST

Area A-1: Piru Creek

Although relatively unknown among hikers, Piru Creek and its tributaries offer a rugged, wilderness experience barely one hour's drive away from the San Fernando Valley and Santa Clarita Valley suburbs. Los Padres National Forest and Angeles National Forest share administrative responsibilities for the area, which lies west of Interstate 5 along the Los Angeles-Ventura county line. Today most of the area, which has few roads and trails, is being managed primarily for its value as watershed and wildlife habitat. The area borders the Sespe Condor Sanctuary, which currently harbors no condors.

Much of the area from Whitaker Peak west is included within the boundary of the proposed Sespe Wilderness—200,000-plus acres of wildlands centered on Sespe Creek in Ventura County. Parts of Sespe Creek and Piru Creek (specifically the section detailed in Trip 2 below) are also being considered for federal designation as wild and scenic rivers.

Some years ago you might have been able to see some of the last remaining California condors in this, the edge of their last stronghold. Today, all remaining native condors have been removed from their native habitat and are participating in captive breeding programs at the Los Angeles Zoo and San Diego Wild Animal Park. With a population rebounding from a low of 26 in 1986 to 40 by 1990, it is expected that reintroduction efforts will occur sometime in the next few years. Meanwhile, an experiment is taking place involving Andean condors, a related species prevalent in parts of South America. Since 1988, at least 13 female-only Andean condors have been released at the Hopper Mountain National Wildlife Refuge (5 miles west of Lake Piru). These condors, of course, cannot breed, but their behavior, which mimics that of the native condors, is being monitored by biologists in an effort to recognize the possible pitfalls of the reintroduction process. If not for condors themselves, you can keep an eye on the skies above Piru Creek for the more prevalent golden eagles, turkey vultures, and red-tailed hawks.

Car campers can make use of the developed Oak Flat Campground (water available) and Blue Point Campground (no water). Undeveloped Frenchmans Flat Campground is a popular jumping off spot for fishermen who seek trout in the waters of Piru Creek.

Backpackers can make camp, as they prefer, along Piru Creek or its tributaries. Fire regulations apply; during the drier months you'll need a fire permit (from Los Padres National Forest) in order to have a campfire or operate a camp stove. When and if the Sespe Wilderness is created you will probably need a wilderness permit for either day or overnight use as well.

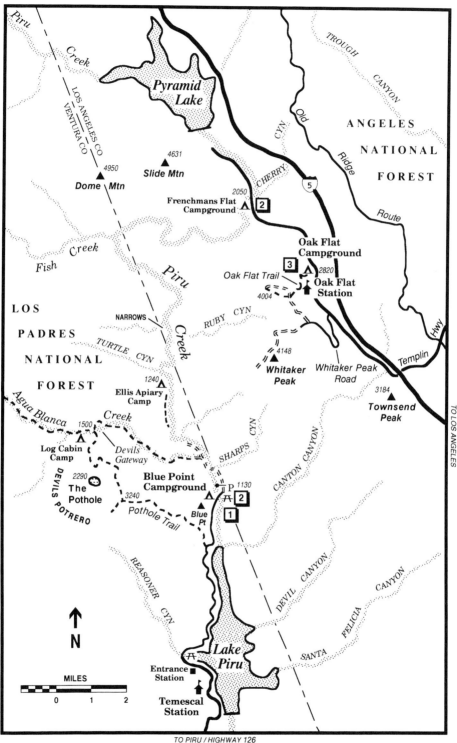

Area A-1: Piru Creek

Area A-1, Trip 1
The Pothole

	Distance	11.4 miles
	Total Elevation Gain/Loss	2900'/2900'
	Hiking Time	6 hours
	Recommended Map	USGS 7.5-min *Cobblestone Mtn.*
	Best Times	November through May
	Agency	LPNF/OD
	Difficulty	★★★

Space in this book does not permit many forays beyond the L.A. County line. But I've included this trip as an instructive and gratifying sampler of the charms of the vast Sespe country stretching west through Ventura County. You'll enjoy the erosion-whittled ridges, gentle *potreros* (pastures), and sandstone gorges where pond turtles sun themselves on rocks overlooking emerald pools.

To reach the starting point, exit Interstate 5 at westbound Highway 126 (just north of Santa Clarita). Drive 11 miles west to the town of Piru and follow the signs to Lake Piru. Pass the entrance station for the recreation area at the lake (you do not have to pay if you are camping at Blue Point Campground or using national-forest lands ahead) and continue 6 miles farther on narrow pavement to Blue Point Campground. If Piru Creek isn't flowing heavily, you'll be able to drive over a wide ford just beyond the campground and reach a parking and picnic area. Otherwise you can park at the campground.

Start by walking back along the paved road to a point 1.3 miles south of the campground. There you'll find the signed, newly reconstructed Pothole Trail. Follow it straight up a ridge where cattle have grazed amid the chaparral, and a few small walnut trees stand like lonely sentinels. Soon there are expansive views of the sandstone outcrops, including Blue Point, on neighboring ridges. Pass a wildlife guzzler on a hilltop (3.4 miles from the campground, 3000') and continue down and then up the ridgeline to a

junction (4.0 miles, 3240'), where remnants of an old fire break continue up the ridge. There you veer right, following the circuitous Pothole Trail down along a ridge overlooking a spread of chaparral and grassland to the west—Devils Potrero.

Where the trail hits bottom on the edge of the potrero itself, there's a sharp turn north (5.7 miles). Find the obscure path going 0.2 mile south, through tall chaparral, to The Pothole. This large, flat, perfectly isolated basin—a true topographical depression, is filled with grasses and rimmed by cottonwoods and willows. It's easy to imagine a painter with paintbrush and palette at work here under the big sky. Bring your camera with wide-angle lens, or a sketchpad. Geologically, this strange formation is a "sag pond," owing its existence to the Agua Blanca thrust fault paralleling Agua Blanca Creek to the north.

Return to the Pothole Trail and descend another mile to Agua Blanca Creek. On the way you'll pass an old abandoned cabin, a fern-draped brook, lots of oak trees, masses of poison oak, and a few bigcone Douglas-firs. When you arrive at the creek, Log Cabin trail camp (with stoves) lies a short distance upstream, while the sheer-walled Devils Gateway lies just below. The trail itself detours around the Gateway by rising some 250 feet up and around the north wall, but as an option you can wade through the 20'-wide Gateway itself—in water that's likely to be waist-deep or more during the spring.

Past Devils Gateway, the trail follows a

well-graded route, mostly along the steep, shaded south wall of the canyon cut by the creek, or down in the flood plain itself. At several creek crossings, you can admire (during times of good flow in winter and spring, at least) the extraordinary transparency of the water.

At the mouth of the canyon (10.1 miles) you pass a couple of buildings at Kesters, a small, private inholding in the national forest, and then hook up with a dirt road leading down along Piru Creek to Blue Point Campground.

Area A-1, Trip 2
Piru Creek

Distance	14.8 miles
Total Elevation Gain/Loss	300'/1200'
Hiking Time	11 hours
Recommended Maps	USGS 7.5-min *Whitaker Peak, Cobblestone Mtn.*
Best Times	October through June
Agency	LPNF/OD
Difficulty	★★★★

Piru Creek's middle section is hardly a river on the scale of those that tumble from grander mountains such as the Sierra Nevada. But it does live up to the honor of being selected for consideration as a federally designated Wild and Scenic River—the only one in Los Angeles County. During the winter and spring, upstream releases of water from Pyramid Lake plus normal runoff from lower tributaries keep it bubbling and wide. Even without much water, the canyon itself is still impressive, lined with cottonwoods, willows, sycamores and oaks, and flanked by rock walls that sometimes rise a sheer 500 feet.

The creek isn't normally navigable by watercraft, but it's tailor-made for a hiking adventure. There's no trail for the most part, so you'll spend a lot time battling willow thickets, sidestepping scratchy brush, and wading through knee-deep crossings.

You should resign yourself right away to walking in squishy boots. It won't be worth the constant effort of seeking out boulders to hop across, or taking off your boots and socks in order to keep them dry. Once you

get used to it, the crossings will feel refreshing.

Too much of a good thing, of course, is dangerous. During wet periods you should seek the advice of Los Padres National Forest rangers before going. You can also check conditions for yourself: When you arrive at Blue Point Campground to leave your first car (the trip works well as a shuttle trip), try crossing the stream on the concrete ford just north of the campground. Knee-high or deeper waters there could spell potential trouble. Remember, there are dozens of crossings like this or worse upstream. If you don't feel confident enough to undertake the journey through the canyon, try something else in the area, like the Pothole Trail.

Make this a very long day hike, or plan an overnight stay somewhere along the way. Ellis Apiary trail camp, with oak-shaded sites and stoves, is a pleasant place to spend the night, but it's rather near the end. North of Ellis Apiary—and especially north of the narrows indicated on our map—the canyon floor is rocky, but some small campsites can be found on terraces above the stream. Travel is considerably easier south of Ellis Apiary trail camp, where there are some segments of old trail in place, and a dirt road along the final 1.5 miles. During spring's warmer and longer days you can get away with a midmorning start if you don't mind some night hiking at the end. We started at midmorning and finished by flashlight in pitch darkness, though an evening moon to light the way would have been nice.

The water in Piru Creek is both colder and murkier than you might expect. Either bring all the drinking water you'll need or use a water filter.

After leaving your first car at Blue Point Campground (see Trip 1 for details), drive the second car back to Interstate 5 and north to Templin Highway. Drive up the west frontage road (old Highway 99) to a point 2 miles past Oak Flat Campground's entrance. There you'll find Frenchmans Flat— a large, dirt lot on the left. Fishermen by the score park here (or camp) and then hike down the canyon in search of trout fishing holes. The stream is artificially stocked.

Make your way down the cottonwood- and willow-fringed banks, crossing whenever necessary. The stream slips over water-worn boulders, some the size of cars, and collects in silt-bottomed pools. The seamed and shattered walls down the length of the gorge disclose at least five distinct changes in the bedrock as you progress. These rocks reflect a variety of ages, from older than 600 million years (Precambrian gneiss) to tens of millions of years old (Eocene sedimentary rocks). Several faults cross the route, including the northernmost end of the San Gabriel Fault. If you care to keep apprised of your progress down the canyon, be sure to keep updating your position on your topographic maps. The Fish Creek confluence at 5.2 miles is a major milestone; there you change your general direction of travel from west to south.

The most interesting part of the canyon is an otherworldly passage just north of the confluence of Ruby Canyon (9.5–10 miles).

There you make your way between grotesquely sculpted conglomerate-rock walls, wading most of the time.

South of the narrows the canyon widens considerably and you sometimes have the luxury of walking on flat, sandy benches on either side of the creek. After passing Ellis Apiary Camp (on an oak-shaded bench to the right—11.5 miles), you can follow a remnant of an old trail on the canyon's west side for some distance before being forced back into the rocky bed of the creek. At 13.2 miles, you pick up an old road that will take you to the parking and picnic area opposite Blue Point Campground.

Narrows of Piru Creek

Area A-1, Trip 3
Oak Flat Trail

Distance	2.8 miles round trip
Total Elevation Gain/Loss	950'/950'
Hiking Time	90 minutes (round trip)
Optional Map	USGS 7.5-min *Whitaker Peak*
Best Times	All year
Agency	ANF/SD
Difficulty	★★

The Oak Flat Trail, the only developed trail along the Interstate 5 corridor through the Angeles Forest, offers ever-widening vistas of fault-tortured canyon country, and a close look on the way up at some interesting outcrops of breccia—a rock resembling conglomerate in appearance, except that the imbedded stones are not so rounded.

The trail originates near Oak Flat Campground, tucked away in a large oak grove. To reach it, exit I-5 at Templin Highway, about 45 miles northwest of central Los Angeles. Pick up the frontage road on the west side of I-5 (old Highway 99, formerly the main highway) and drive an additional 3 miles northwest to the campground entrance. Turn left and continue 0.3 mile to a parking area next to the Oak Flat Ranger Station, just short of the Verdugo Oaks Boy Scout camp.

The signed Oak Flat Trail begins on the left side of the big, grassy area just inside Camp Verdugo Oaks. Newly constructed switchbacks take you under a shady canopy of valley oaks and live oaks. Soon, however, you'll rise up to scrub-covered slopes exposed to the morning and midday sun. Mileposts every ¼ mile and trailside benches (including a picnic table halfway up) are nice touches along the way.

After surmounting a final set of steeply inclined switchback segments, you reach the Whitaker Spur Road (1.4 miles). From there you can look west into the gorge of Piru Creek, and, if it's clear, farther west into the remote Los Padres country where Cobblestone Mountain, White Mountain, and a half dozen other summits over 5000 feet raise their shaggy heads. In the foreground is a breccia outcrop with a window in it. Turning north and east, you'll be able to trace the long hogbacks of Liebre and Sawmill mountains and the gashed face of Redrock Mountain (these areas are covered in Area A-2).

At this point you're standing just east of the San Gabriel Fault, whose trace is not obvious here. The fault continues southeast and east about 70 miles into the San Gabriel Mountains, where it parallels the West and East forks of the San Gabriel River, roughly dividing the so called "Front Range" of the San Gabriels from the "High Country."

You'll return down the same trail. In the meantime, you may want to try following the Whitaker Spur Road 0.7 mile west to a 4004' summit offering a nice view of Pyramid Lake to the north. You can also go 0.4 mile south on the same road to see a large outcrop of pock-marked breccia.

Area A-2: Liebre Mountain/ Fish Canyon

I made my first acquaintance with Angeles National Forest as a child, while riding in the family car north of L.A. on Highway 99 (yesterday's version of Interstate 5). The signs said "National Forest," but my obvious question (probably voiced by millions before and since) was simply "Where are the trees?"

There are trees aplenty, if you know where to look for them—high on the ridges, down in the canyons, tucked away on north-facing slopes. If you take the poetic name of the chaparral—*elfin forest*—literally, there's plenty of that along Interstate 5 as well. In fact, 78 percent of the entire Angeles National Forest is covered by either chaparral or sage-scrub vegetation.

It's a truism that in Southern California, the best scenery lies far from the major routes of travel. Cienaga and Fish canyons and their many tributaries are cases in point. Billowing ridgelines suggest a gentle aspect to the landscape, but down inside these canyons, you'll find cliff-like walls and hidden recesses where riparian vegetation flourishes. These drainages compose one of the more isolated and pristine roadless areas within the Angeles Forest—good places to get away from it all with a minimum of travel. The headwaters of Cienaga and Fish canyons drain the south slopes of Liebre and Sawmill mountains, whose higher elevations support patches of vegetation reminiscent of that found farther north in the foothill country of central California.

The area mapped for this section, as well as the Sierra Pelona country (Area A-3), occupies a triangular-shaped area bounded by the south edge of Antelope Valley on the north, Interstate 5 on the southwest, and Antelope Valley Freeway on the southeast. In a geological sense this triangle is simply an extension of the San Gabriel Mountains, though you don't usually find that name attached to it on maps. Administratively it belongs to the Saugus Ranger District of Angeles National Forest, whose boundary is detached from the four other, contiguous districts covering the San Gabriels.

Saugus District lands are generally well laced with both paved and dirt roads (except for the large roadless areas in the Fish and Cienaga canyon drainages). There are 18 national-forest campgrounds in the district, as well as target-shooting and off-road vehicle areas—mostly clustered near the south end. The ORV and plinking activities, mostly incompatible with hiking, do not seriously affect any of the trips described below. Plans call for a large increase in the number of ORV trail miles in this district, but funding cutbacks have slowed (and probably will slow) their construction. Cutbacks have also affected the maintenance of hiking trails, especially those that are not used very often. Here, as elsewhere in the Angeles National Forest, "use it or lose it" is a good adage.

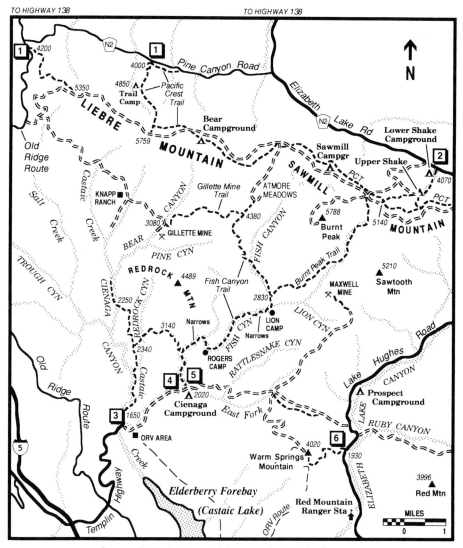

1   4200

N2

1

4000

Pine Canyon Road

4850 ▲   Pacific
Trail   Crest
Camp   Trail

5350

Elizabeth Lake Rd

N2

Lower Shake
Campground

LIEBRE

Bear
Campground
▲

Old
Ridge
Route

Castaic Creek

5759

MOUNTAIN

Sawmill
Campgr ▲

Upper Shake

2

4070

Salt Creek

KNAPP
RANCH ■

BEAR CANYON

Gillette Mine
Trail

ATMORE
MEADOWS

SAWMILL

PCT

PCT

3080 ⚒ GILLETTE MINE

4380

FISH CANYON

5788
▲
Burnt
Peak

5140

MOUNTAIN

PINE CYN

REDROCK MTN   4489
▲

Fish Canyon
Trail

Burnt Peak Trail

TROUGH CYN

CIENAGA

2250

Narrows

2830

MAXWELL
MINE ⚒

5210
▲
Sawtooth
Mtn

3140

REDROCK CYN

CANYON

2340

Narrows

FISH CYN

LION
CAMP

Narrows

LION CYN

RATTLESNAKE CYN

Hughes

Road

ROGERS
CAMP

CANYON

Old
Ridge

4

5

▲ 2020
Cienaga
Campground

East Fork

LAKE

▲ Prospect
Campground

Castaic

Route

3

1650

ORV AREA ■

RUBY CANYON

5

4020

6

Creek

Templin Highway

Elderberry Forebay
(Castaic Lake)

Warm Springs
Mountain

1930

ELIZABETH

3996
▲
Red Mtn

ORV Route

Red Mountain
Ranger Sta

MILES

0   1

↑
N

Area A-2: Liebre Mountain/Fish Canyon

Area A-2, Trip 1
Liebre Mountain

	Distance	9.0 miles
	Total Elevation Gain/Loss	2100'/1900'
	Hiking Time	5 hours
	Recommended Map	USGS 7.5-min *Liebre Mtn.*
	Best Times	October through June
	Agency	ANF/SD
	Difficulty	★★★

The cool, forested north slopes of Liebre Mountain rear up in stark contrast to the wide, brown Antelope Valley at their feet. The San Andreas Fault, which lies along Liebre Mountain's north base, is responsible for this juxtaposition. Vertical movements have occurred along the fault, as well as the more familiar horizontal movements.

Atop Liebre Mountain's sparsely wooded, mile-high crest you can gaze north to the rolling Tehachapis and the southern Sierra, west toward the Sespe country and the highest (8000+ feet) summits of Los Padres National Forest, and south and southeast over much of Angeles National Forest. Seemingly at your feet is the flat, arid floor of the Mojave Desert, stretching to a hazy vanishing point on the eastern horizon.

This unique view of so much of California is yours to enjoy if you do this hike on a clear late-fall or winter day. Winter storms spinning out of the Pacific can hit Liebre Mountain hard, leaving lasting snow cover, so check the weather forecast or with rangers first. On the warmer days of the year, be sure to bring along plenty of water.

This is a shuttle trip requiring two cars. (If you have a single car, you can elect to walk—or send the fastest runner of your group—down the 5 miles of pavement between the two points to close the loop.) From central Los Angeles, drive northwest on Interstate 5 about 65 miles to the Highway 138 exit. After 4 miles on 138, turn right on Old Ridge Route (County Route N2). Go 2.2 miles south, to where Pine Canyon Road (West Oakdale Road on older maps) goes east. Leave one car 0.5 mile south of this intersection on the shoulder of Old Ridge Route, and take the other 4.2 miles east of the intersection to a small summit on Pine Canyon Road (mile 13.5, according to the mile markers). Park off the pavement in the dirt area to the south.

The San Andreas Fault closely follows Pine Canyon Road, so when you start this hike you'll literally be standing atop the boundary between two of the earth's largest tectonic plates—the Pacific and North American plates. Liebre Mountain, on the east edge of the Pacific Plate, is creeping northwest an average of about 2 inches a year relative to the Antelope Valley.

Just south (uphill) of where you parked, you'll find the Pacific Crest Trail. Go right (west), and begin a leisurely switchback ascent through red-barked manzanitas, wispy digger pines, and deciduous black oaks. Patches of Great Basin sagebrush remind you that the high desert is not far away.

The mix of mountain-desert vegetation is soon enhanced by many large California buckeye shrubs. Leafless and grey until about April, buckeye becomes one of California's most handsome blooming plants by June, showing off myriad sprays of white blossoms. Botanically, this slope resembles much of central California's Coast Ranges and the lower Sierra foothills. Here on

Liebre Mountain, both buckeye and digger pine are very close to their southern geographical limits.

Nearly 2 miles up, the trail becomes steeper amidst closely spaced digger pines. On a little flat to the right, you'll discover a wilderness campsite, with a picnic table, for hikers on the PCT. There's no water, but the breeze soughing through the long, thin pine needles overhead sets a peaceful mood, and the desert air, whether warm or cool, feels nice on the skin.

Past the campsite, you continue over the broad top of a 4923' peaklet and descend to a wooded saddle. From there the trail switchbacks up through bigcone Douglas-fir and joins an old road bed. You enter a grassy clearing dotted with black oaks (5400')—a good place to admire the view of the Antelope Valley while catching your breath.

Ahead another half hour (3.5 miles from the start) you arrive at a junction where the PCT veers east toward Sawmill Mountain. Keep straight and walk up to Liebre Mountain Truck Trail (5759'), which is open to motor traffic when road conditions allow. Turn right and follow this road west along the oak-dotted crestline. An overgrown, abandoned segment of the PCT lies right and then left of the road. Originally PCT travelers were to have used this alignment, passing near Quail Lake, to reach the Tehachapis. Later the PCT was rerouted on the path you followed up the hill.

At mile 6.6, exactly where the topo map indicates a campground (non-existent now), take the narrow, unmarked trail that forks right. This point is 0.3 mile short of a 5345' peaklet labelled "Sandberg" on the topo map, where the road bends left and starts descending quickly toward Old Ridge Route. Use by hikers and equestrians keeps this abandoned section of the PCT in fairly good shape.

As you descend through the chaparral you'll spot the weathered concrete ribbon of Old Ridge Route winding like a snake down below. This venerable roadway was a key

(and dreaded) link in the original "Valley Route" linking Los Angeles with the Central Valley and points north. Paved with a narrow ribbon of concrete in 1919, the Ridge Route between Castaic and Gorman featured 642 turns in 38 miles, the equivalent of 97 complete circles! Widening and additional asphalt paving in the 1920s eliminated about one third of the turns. The road was virtually abandoned in 1933 when a new bypass (U.S. 99) opened to the west. Today a third-generation Ridge Route—8-lane Interstate 5—carries virtually 100 percent of the through traffic.

The trail ends on Old Ridge Route's shoulder, 0.2 mile south of the defunct townsite of Sandberg, which was a popular stopover on the old highway.

Area A-2, Trip 2
Sawmill Mountain

	Distance	4.8 miles
	Total Elevation Gain/Loss	1000'/1000'
	Hiking Time	2½ hours
	Optional Map	USGS 7.5-min *Burnt Peak*
	Best Times	All year
	Agency	ANF/SD
	Difficulty	★★

Sawmill Mountain shares many characteristics with its neighbor to the west—Liebre Mountain. Both have elongated summit ridges, parallel to the San Andreas Fault. Both have steep north slopes supporting a delightful mix of black oaks, canyon live oaks, and drought-resistant conifers. Sawmill Mountain's tired-looking, dark Precambrian (more than 600 million years old) metamorphic rock, however, contrasts with the lighter and younger (roughly 100 million years old) bedrock that constitutes most of Liebre Mountain.

The starting point for this hike to Sawmill's summit ridge is Lower Shake Campground, a tiny drive-up-and-walk-in facility at the mouth of Shake Canyon on Sawmill Mountain's north slope. To get there exit Interstate 5 at Lake Hughes Road, 40 miles northwest of central Los Angeles. Follow Lake Hughes Road 23 miles north from I-5 to Elizabeth Lake Road (County N2). Turn left (west) and go 4.2 miles to the short dirt road (at mile-marker 4.56) leading south to the campground.

From the back of the campground, follow the trail up the cool, alder-lined, V-shaped canyon, crossing the bottom several times. In the springtime a little brook flows here, and the trailside is dotted with greenery and flowers—miner's lettuce, poison oak, stinging nettles, lupine, and baby blue eyes. The trail is susceptible to erosion, so you may have to scramble in a couple of places.

After 0.6 mile, the canyon widens and the trail comes up to a spacious, gently sloping bowl. This perfect site for a campground is indeed occupied by one—Upper Shake Campground—accessible to cars via a dirt road from Elizabeth Lake Road. During most of the non-summer season, the campground and the road leading to it are closed. (If you have small kids, and don't wish to go farther, simply retrace your steps from here.)

Walk through the campground and continue west on the access road. In a few minutes you'll come to a concrete ford in the road. Just short of the ford, veer left on a spur road to the left. The road soon ends, but a footpath continues up through stands of black oak along Shake Canyon's upper reaches. Half a dozen switchbacks take you up the head of the canyon to an intersection with the Pacific Crest Trail (2.0 miles), just below a saddle traversed by the Maxwell Truck Trail. The view south from the truck trail includes parts of the lonely Fish Canyon drainage (see Trip 5).

Turn east on the PCT. Ahead is one of the most pleasant PCT segments in the Angeles Forest—rather level throughout and shaded by canyon oaks and towering bigcone Douglas-firs. Breaks in the shady cover allow vistas over flat Antelope Valley and the distant Tehachapi Mountains. Watch for an obscure trail, intersecting the PCT at 3.6 miles (the trail comes up obliquely from the left and is easy to miss). It takes you down to the uppermost campsites in Upper Shake Campground. From there, retrace your earlier steps to Lower Shake Campground.

Area A-2, Trip 3
Cienaga Canyon

	Distance	8.5 miles
	Total Elevation Gain/Loss	1200'/1200'
	Hiking Time	5 hours
	Recommended Maps	USGS 7.5-min *Whitaker Peak, Liebre Mtn.*
	Best Times	November through May
	Agency	ANF/SD
	Difficulty	★★★

Cienaga Canyon (*cienaga* in Spanish means marsh) delivers what it promises. Here, amid the arid-looking mountains north of Castaic Lake, Castaic Creek flows the better part of the year through a sinuous gorge flanked by picturesque sandstone outcrops. The creek is perfect for wading—shallow, slow-moving, and warmed by the sun. Wear an old pair of boots. You'll find it easier and more fun to wade the creek than to thrash through the shrubbery along its banks.

To reach the starting point, take the Templin Highway exit from I-5, and drive 5 miles east to the end of the pavement. Cross the bridge over Castaic Creek and immediately make a hard left on a dirt road going north along a wide terrace overlooking Castaic Creek. The road becomes washed out a short distance ahead. Park and continue on foot, mostly on the remnants of the old dirt road, but occasionally up the wide, flood-scoured bed of the creek itself.

The canyon walls assume gorge-like proportions by 1.0 mile, and at 1.4 miles you pass a 15-foot waterfall. Just beyond the fall you'll catch sight of Redrock Mountain, its tan- and rose-colored walls glowing in the bright sunshine ahead.

At 1.8 miles the canyon forks, Castaic Creek (Cienaga Canyon) on the left and Redrock Canyon on the right. Follow the old road—now a trail—that slants up along the chaparral-clad ridge dividing the two. Soon you'll be treated to a more impressive panorama of Redrock Mountain. A streak of brick-red rock on the south face gave the mountain its name.

At 2.5 miles, the Red Rock Trail intersects on the right. You go left, staying high, and soon pass a cream-colored outcrop of sandstone pocked with wind caves. The rock here consists of sediments laid down in a shallow sea some 10 million years ago.

At 3.6 miles, just as the road bed begins a sharp descent toward Cienaga Canyon, take note of more sandstone outcrops on the right. A short scramble up to the ridgecrest reveals the best view yet of Redrock Mountain. Adventurous hikers have bushwhacked 0.4 mile northeast from this point into Redrock Canyon to reach a shady grotto, lined with ferns and poison oak and adorned (in winter at least) with a 20' waterfall.

When the road bed reaches the bottom of Cienaga Canyon (4.2 miles), leave it and turn sharply left, heading down-canyon. Road-builders eschewed this most rugged section of the canyon in favor of the route you've already taken. The next 2.5 meandering miles can be really fun if there's lots of water. You can either splash through pools 1–2' deep (winter and spring), or pick your way along animal trails through the willows and mule-fat. This is prime habitat for rattlesnakes to be out and about in the spring, so proceed cautiously.

After about a mile down the canyon, the

wide, sandy bed of Salt Creek intersects on the right. From this point on, Cienaga Canyon's floor resembles that of a desert wash—flood-scoured and smothered with rocks and sand—save for the narrow ribbon of water down the middle. A few live oaks, sycamores, and alders stand on terraces high enough to have escaped the reach of floodwaters.

Just above the confluence with Redrock Canyon and the road bed you came in on, you'll walk beneath a towering, near-vertical wall of conglomerate rock—the most dramatic feature seen on the whole trip. This alone is a worthy destination for those who might want to try an abbreviated version of the trip.

Area A-2, Trip 4
Fish Canyon Narrows

Distance	4.4 miles round trip
Total Elevation Gain/Loss	400'/400'
Hiking Time	3 hours (round trip)
Optional Maps	USGS 7.5-min *Whitaker Peak, Liebre Mtn.*
Best Times	October through June
Agency	ANF/SD
Difficulty	★★

In the trench-like confines of middle Fish Canyon, aridity and moisture stand side by side, separated by a matter of a few yards. Mountain mahogany, manzanita and other drought-resistant chaparral shrubs cling to the walls, while a shallow stream gurgles merrily past a line of oaks, sycamores, willows, and cottonwoods. It's almost as if a little slice of the Pacific Northwest were transplanted to Southern California. Around the time of winter solstice, sunbeams fail to reach the innermost confines of the canyon and frost can linger on the creeping blackberry vines till mid-morning.

From the end of Templin Highway (see driving directions in Trip 3 above), drive across the narrow Castaic Creek bridge and continue generally east through a desolate ORV camping area. Drive through a gate (which may be closed if the road ahead is badly flooded) into lower Fish Canyon. Continue another two miles on dirt to Cienaga Campground, crossing the stream

several times on concrete fords. Just below the campground, walls of conglomerate rock pinch in tightly, forming the lowermost of the three scenic "narrows" in the canyon.

Park at the campground and begin hiking north up the main Fish Canyon on an old road bed, closed to motor traffic. (Take care not to head east up Fish Canyon's east fork.) The oak-shaded road takes you 1.0 mile to a sharp bend to the right, where the second (middle) narrows of Fish Canyon begins. Opposite an old mining prospect, "The Pianobox," on the right, you'll note on the left a trail (see Trip 5 below) coming down from the south shoulder of Redrock Mountain.

The narrow section ahead is flanked by towering walls made of a strange, battered-looking, grey- and tan-colored rock. They're part of a 15-mile-wide formation of Precambrian gneiss (metamorphosed granite) covering most of Redrock Mountain, Sawmill Mountain, Fish Canyon, and upper Elizabeth Lake Canyon.

Only the merest pretense of a trail threads through the narrows, but the going is usually fairly easy along flat benches to either side of the creek. You'll cross the shallow creek perhaps two dozen times in the next mile.

After four sharp bends in the canyon, you arrive at unmaintained Rogers Camp (2.2 miles), perched atop a grassy, oak-shaded bench on the right—opposite an old mining tunnel bored in the north wall. The site, used often by Scouts, has picnic tables and stoves. More opportunities for camping (without amenities) can be found a few hundred yards ahead, where the canyon widens.

Rogers Camp is a good turnaround point for a first hike or backpack into Fish Canyon. Read on (Trip 5 below) for more about the area.

Area A-2, Trip 5
Around Redrock Mountain

Distance	20.5 miles
Total Elevation Gain/Loss	4300'/4300'
Hiking Time	12 hours
Recommended Maps	USGS 7.5-min *Whitaker Peak, Liebre Mtn., Burnt Peak*
Best Times	November through April
Agency	ANF/SD
Difficulty	★★★★

This grand circle-tour of the Fish-Cienaga canyons area takes you completely around Redrock Mountain, a sprawling complex of ridges and canyon slopes in the most remote part of the Saugus Ranger District. If you're very strong, fast and motivated, and start before sunrise on a spring day, you could complete the 20.5-mile loop—a feat roughly equivalent in effort to walking about 35 miles of flat city streets—before nightfall. Overnight backpacking allows a more leisurely pace, but is still a challenge by virtue of the poor (even nonexistent) condition of some of the trails along the route.

The topographic maps listed above are essential aids for navigation. The trails you'll be traveling are accurately depicted on these maps, except that a newer switchback trail just northwest of The Pianobox prospect has replaced the steeper former route. Water (potable with treatment) is abundant in Fish, Bear, and Cienaga canyons during winter and spring, and may be present year round in parts of Fish Canyon.

Begin, as in Trip 4 above, with the walk up through the second narrows of Fish Canyon to Rogers Camp (2.2 miles). Beyond Rogers Camp, the canyon becomes wide and straight, and the stream alternately flows above ground and disappears under a sheet of gravel. The trail, too, disappears from time to time on the sandy banks, and darts (sometimes unobviously) up the brush-covered sidewalls to avoid tight spots in the canyon floor. There's a confusing spot at 3.5 miles, where the trail shortcuts a tight series of meanders. If you miss it, don't worry; just keep going up the main, wide wash and you'll recover it soon enough.

At 4.4 miles the trail passes, on the right, a third narrows, where water collects in knee-deep pools between low walls of polished rock. It's fun but also time-consuming to wade through this section, later picking up the trail some 300 yards upstream.

Lion Camp (5.0 miles) appears on an

oak-shaded bench above the confluence of
Lion and Fish canyons. A couple of old
wood stoves can be found at this isolated
and unmaintained camping spot. From
there, remnants of the Fish Canyon Trail
continue north up the willow-choked creek
bed, passing the Burnt Peak Trail at the
mouth of the next small canyon on the right.
Thereafter, the canyon opens as a broad,
sand-and gravel-drowned flood plain, fully
exposed to the warm (or hot, as the case
may be) rays of the midday sun. Fill up
canteens—you're not likely to see much
water beyond the last of the willow thickets.

At 6.5 miles you turn northwest into a
tributary canyon, but soon switchback out
of it to begin a mile-long, steep climb up the
sun-baked ridge to the right. The landscape
all around looks harsh and desert-like,
except for a few ragged patches of bigcone
Douglas-fir clinging tenaciously to some
far-off, north-facing slopes. After about
1000 feet of ascent, you contour over to a
wooded ravine, whereupon the cool breath
of the high country hits you like a wet
sponge. Scattered groves of digger pines and
bigcone Douglas-firs offer welcome shade.

You continue over a saddle and arrive at
a Y-junction (8.3 miles), from where the
trail straight ahead goes to the site of the

former Atmore Meadows Campground, and
the trail doubling back to the left leads to the
Gillette Mine. A boxed-in spring nearby,
indicated on the topo map, offers un-
appealing-looking water.

You turn west on the Gillette Mine Trail,
contour through a multi-textured sea of
chaparral, and arrive at a 4350' saddle (9.5
miles). There, a new vista can be seen
stretching north and east toward the high
peaks of the Los Padres National Forest in
Ventura County.

Next comes a steady drop of 1300 feet
that takes you down to the bottom of Bear
Canyon. About half-way down, take note of
the California buckeyes on the north-facing
slopes—crabapple-sized buckeye fruits litter the trail. These particular buckeye
colonies are among the southernmost found
naturally in California.

In Bear Canyon you meet a graded
access road to Gillette Mine coming down
from Old Ridge Route. Turn left and follow
this road down-canyon past some old dig-
gings on the right and an active prospect on
the left (respect this private claim). Keep
going past the last remnant of road, then
drop into the narrow, willow-choked stream
bed. You now face almost two miles—
perhaps two hours—of fairly rigorous bush-

Sandstone formation below Redrock Mountain

whacking and stream-hopping down the remainder of Bear Canyon. Strategically placed ribbons or other markers occasionally guide you along sections of long-neglected trail. This is prime rattlesnake habitat, so watch you step, especially in early spring, when the snakes are hungry and irritable. Camp could be made on any of several small benches tucked against the steep walls of this wild and isolated canyon.

Your pace will accelerate when you reach wide Cienaga Canyon at 13.5 miles. Follow remnants of an old road south for 0.9 mile, then bear left to follow a well-defined jeep road up a ridge to the east. After another 1.7 miles, make a sharp left

on the Redrock Trail.

The Redrock Trail crosses the marshy bottom of Redrock Canyon and meanders a short while amid an enchanting mini-maze of sandstone slabs. The south face of Redrock Mountain, its characteristic red streak visible, presides over this starkly beautiful landscape reminiscent of Arizona canyon country.

The final hurdle must now be negotiated: a 1000' climb and descent over the south shoulder of Redrock Mountain. Switchbacks take you up and over to The Pianobox and the road back to Cienaga Campground—your starting point.

Area A-2, Trip 6
Warm Springs Mountain

Distance	6.0 miles round trip
Total Elevation Gain/Loss	2100'/2100'
Hiking Time	3½ hours (round trip)
Optional Map	USGS 7.5-min *Warm Springs Mountain*
Best Times	November through April
Agency	ANF/SD
Difficulty	★★★

The hike up Warm Springs Mountain is a good antidote to the urban doldrums, particularly if you choose a crisp, fresh-air day during late autumn or winter. The trailhead is quite close to the L.A. Basin (40 minutes from San Fernando Valley) and the view from the top takes in a good part of the Saugus District lands and the rest of Angeles National Forest. To the south, framed by a gap between the San Gabriel and Santa Susana mountains, you can sometimes spot Santa Catalina Island, floating like a mirage 70 miles away.

The Ruby Fire of 1987 reduced the entire surface of the mountain to ashes, leading to considerable erosion on some of the steeper slopes during subsequent rains. The Warm Springs Trail, the hiker's route up

the mountain, was severed in several places. But even if the trail hasn't been repaired by the time you use it, you'll probably find it easy to follow except in a few spots near the lower end. There it carves through crumbling Precambrian rock similar to that seen in the Fish Canyon drainage to the north. A group of mountain bicyclists is rehabilitating the trail, and it will soon become a designated, although very difficult bike route.

The unmarked bottom of the trail is located at mile-marker 11.23 on Lake Hughes Road, 12 miles north of Interstate 5. Parking space along the road shoulder can be found just north of this point. The trail goes a short distance up a small ravine, and then veers right, climbing obliquely across a cliff-like slope. After 2.5 miles of steady climbing (and ever-widening vistas), you arrive at a saddle just south of Warm Springs Mountain's summit. Ignore the off-road-vehicle trail that goes along the west slope and touches this saddle. Instead, turn sharply right and scramble up the broad, open ridge leading to the summit. The burned-out fire-lookout structure at the summit is a sorry sight, but not far away you'll find a small grove of fire-singed pines offering a measure of shade.

Redrock Mountain

Shake Canyon Trail

Area A-3: Sierra Pelona/Green Valley

This small area within the Saugus Ranger District (Angeles National Forest) contains several roadside campgrounds (some just off the edge of our map), hiking trails, and an off-road-vehicle trail that connects with the popular Rowher Flat ORV area south of Sierra Pelona. A section of the Pacific Crest Trail winds through here as well, mostly across dry and uninspiring south-facing slopes.

Parts of the area burned in 1964, and again in 1989. A few pockets of canyon live oak are found in protected hollows, some riparian vegetation clusters along Bouquet Canyon, but mostly there's wave after wave of chaparral—the ultimate survivor of periodic conflagrations. Our two trips below stick mainly to the cooler and more interesting north-facing slopes.

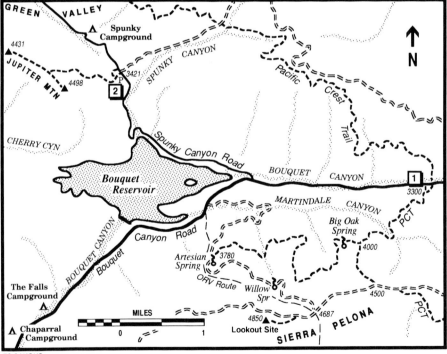

Area A-3: Sierra Pelona/Green Valley

Area A-3, Trip 1
Sierra Pelona Loop

	Distance	11.2 miles
	Total Elevation Gain/Loss	2300'/2300'
	Hiking Time	5 hours
	Recommended Map	USGS 7.5-min *Sleepy Valley*
	Best Times	October through May
	Agency	ANF/SD
	Difficulty	★★★

More popular with off-road-vehicle drivers than with hikers, the Sierra Pelona crest nevertheless offers some hidden haunts and unexpected adventures, especially for those willing to step off the tire-beaten path. Wildlife seems to abound here. At dusk one evening, I tailed a fox-like creature for half a mile down the Pacific Crest Trail, never learning exactly what it was. Earlier I'd seen half a dozen deer foraging around Willow Spring.

An obscure hiking trail on the slope above Bouquet Reservoir makes possible the loop trip described here. Since both legal and illegal off-road trails cross the area, you'll find hiking here a lot more pleasant if you come on a weekday, when the area is virtually deserted. Although Big Oak Spring, near the beginning of the hike, trickles most of the year, it's safer to carry all the water you'll need.

To reach the trailhead, first drive to the Santa Clarita community of Saugus (exit either I-5 or State 14). From Saugus, follow Bouquet Canyon Road northeast up scenic Bouquet Canyon for 16 miles, to where Spunky Canyon Road intersects on the left. Go 2.2 miles farther east to a turnout on the right (south) side of Bouquet Canyon Road. The Pacific Crest Trail crosses the roadway just east of this turnout.

From the turnout, pick up a short spur trail that goes 50 yards south to the PCT. Turn right and follow the PCT southwest through the dense chaparral characteristic of Sierra Pelona's lower north-facing slopes. Cross a fire break at 1.0 mile,

descend a little, and cross Martindale Canyon, a ravine dotted with a few oaks. Climb again to a trail junction at 1.8 miles. There you leave the PCT simply by keeping straight on a less-used trail. Contour 0.2 mile over to Big Oak Spring, which is up a short path to the left. Amid a thicket of elderberry and poison oak around the spring, you'll discover the hulking skeleton of what used to be the world's largest known canyon live-oak tree (37 feet in trunk circumference), killed by fire more than two decades ago.

From the spring, a narrow trail continues crookedly west, winding along Sierra Pelona's north flank for 3.5 miles. Mountain bikers occasionally use it, and help keep it open. The trail climbs, contours, descends, and contours again, finally reaching a dirt road at Artesian Spring. Along the way, there are sunny vistas north and west over a sea of chaparral, and passages across spooky ravines deeply shaded by live oaks.

Capped-off Artesian Spring stands amid a pleasant little flat (formerly a campground) dotted with live oaks and planted pines and cedars. From there follow the dirt road upward 1.4 miles to Willow Spring, marked by a water tank and a lone black oak tree. Another 1.0 mile of uphill takes you to an intersection with a road that winds along the nearly bald Sierra Pelona crest. Along much of the crest you can look down into Mint Canyon and across to the highest summits of the San Gabriel Mountains. But if time allows, the weather's very clear, and you want a somewhat broader view, you can turn right and make a side trip to the old Sierra Pelona lookout site, 0.7 mile away. There and elsewhere along the crest you'll find some strangely contorted outcrops of Pelona Schist, a roughly 200-million-year-old metamorphic basement rock that makes up the entire Sierra Pelona ridge and underlies much of the San Gabriel Mountains.

From the intersection, proceed east for 0.8 mile, then make a sharp left on the PCT. Follow the PCT for another 0.8 mile, down along a grassy slope dotted with wild-flowers in the early spring, to reach the spot where you left the PCT earlier. The remaining 1.8 miles, mostly downhill through the chaparral, go quickly.

Area A-3, Trip 2
Jupiter Mountain

	Distance	3.0 miles round trip
	Total Elevation Gain/Loss	1050'/1050'
	Hiking Time	2 hours (round trip)
	Optional Map	USGS 7.5-min *Green Valley*
	Best Times	All year
	Agency	ANF/SD
	Difficulty	★★

Clad in chaparral, Jupiter Mountain's swayback summit ridge presides regally over a landscape of fault-churned ridges and linear canyons. A little-known trail cuts along the mountain's cool north slope, giving access to its viewful crest, high above Bouquet Reservoir and the valley and little hamlet that share the name Green Valley.

The trail starts on the shoulder of Jupiter Mountain, where Spunky Canyon Road rolls over a pass halfway between Green Valley and Bouquet Canyon Road. Park on the west side of the road, next to a plantation of pine, cedar, and cypress trees established in 1964. Take the upper (left) road through the grove, and look for the foot trail striking left along the edge of the trees.

Steep at first and then more moderately inclined, the trail slants upward along brush-smothered north-facing slopes. With barely enough room to get by, you'll get to know intimately several of the most common chaparral plants seen around Southern California: chamise, manzanita, mountain mahogany, scrub oak, and ceanothus. Loose,

decomposed-granite soil underfoot will also slow you down a bit.

On the crest, you'll meet a pathway threading an overgrown fire break between Jupiter Mountain's two main summits. Turn left and go sharply uphill to reach the higher and closer east summit, 1.5 miles from the start. There, a makeshift bench invites you to sit a while and enjoy the view. In the southwest foreground are ridges and canyons underlain by offshoots of the San Andreas Fault. One of these, the San Francisquito Fault (running southwest down Bee Canyon and San Francisquito Canyon) was implicated in one of California's worst disasters—the collapse of the St. Francis Dam at San Francisquito Canyon in 1928. The culprit in this case was not an actual movement along the fault (earthquake), but rather weaknesses in the rocks of the fault zone which were supporting the huge concrete dam.

Area A-4: Tujunga District

Rising starkly behind the San Fernando and La Crescenta valley communities of Sylmar, San Fernando, Sunland and Tujunga, the westernmost ridges of the main San Gabriels have a lean and hungry look— at least from a distance. As seen at closer range—as along Big Tujunga Canyon Road—that impression is certainly reinforced. Canyon walls, some soaring half a mile in height, bear scraggly growths of brush and widely scattered trees. Sharply cut ravines, filled with accumulated rock rubble, appear to sweep down from the rounded ridgelines above. There's an almost palpable sense of violent events past and future. Fires, floods, and landslides keep material on these slopes moving downward even as fault movements heave the whole mountain mass upward.

This dramatic if unforgiving landscape (which we'll call the "Tujunga District" since all of it lies within the Tujunga Ranger District of the Angeles National Forest) has a gentler, mostly hidden side too. That's what you'll discover off the main roads and

especially on the trails. The Tujunga District boasts mile-high peaks (including Mt. Lukens, highest point within L.A.'s city limits), one of the more picturesque waterfalls in the county (in Trail Canyon), riparian glens, and pocket forests of oaks and conifers.

Three large drainage systems penetrate the Tujunga District. Pacoima Canyon, on the north, stretches east to Mt. Gleason and drains the south slopes of the mile-high Santa Clara Divide (the north slopes shed water to the Santa Clara River in Soledad Canyon). Little Tujunga Canyon, along with its biggest tributary, Gold Creek, drains the rolling foothill country between two prominent ridges—Mendenhall and Yerba Buena. Big Tujunga Canyon, the largest of the three, penetrates deep into the High Country of the San Gabriels (Area A-7). Big Tujunga Canyon Road threads the lower reaches of this canyon, permitting almost instant access to the canyon's lower trails by San Fernando Valley residents.

Area A-4, Trip 1
Yerba Buena Ridge

Distance	7.8 miles	
Total Elevation Gain/Loss	2300'/2300'	
Hiking Time	4½ hours	
Recommended Map	USGS 7.5-min *Sunland*	
Best Times	October through May	
Agency	ANF/TD	
Difficulty	★★★	

There's a double symmetry of place names associated with this trip: you start at Gold Creek near its confluence with Little

Tujunga Canyon, climb and follow the watershed divide of Yerba Buena Ridge, and descend to the confluence of Gold Canyon

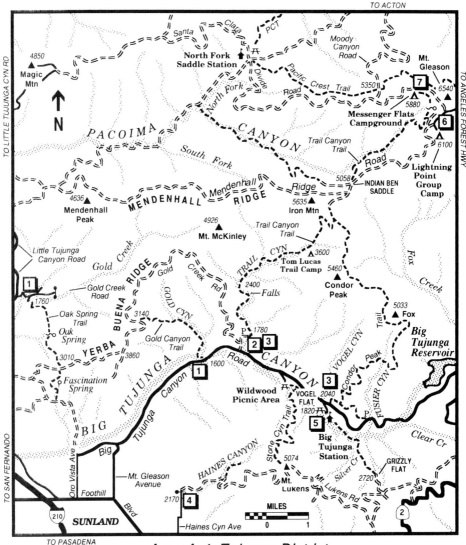

Area A-4: Tujunga District

and Big Tujunga Canyon. As implied by
their names, both "gold" drainages were
combed by prospectors in days past.

Although city-close, this one-way route
could throw you a curve ball or two. The
Gold Canyon Trail may be overgrown and
difficult to follow. At the very end you may
have difficulty crossing Big Tujunga Canyon
if the water level's too high. Call the Forest
Service, or do some advance planning yourself, especially if you'll be leading a group.

If you're going to do the trip from east to
west (opposite to the way we describe),
allow plenty of time to find and follow an
overgrown section of trail starting 1.3 miles
up Gold Canyon from Big Tujunga Canyon.
Try for a cool and clear, an overcast, or even
a foggy day—there's little shade en route.

Leave one car at a turnout on the west
(down-canyon) end of the Big Tujunga
Canyon bridge, at mile-marker 1.3 on Big
Tujunga Canyon Road. This is a popular

parking area for people who fish or picnic along the stream below. Check out the water level below; if the creek looks unfordable, try descending from the up-canyon side of the bridge to see if the north bank is passable. During times of high water you may want to finish the hike that way.

Drive the second car up Little Tujunga Canyon Road (the extension of Osborne Street east of Interstate 210). At about 4 miles from I-210, turn right on Gold Creek Road. Continue exactly 0.7 mile to the signed trailhead for the Oak Spring Trail on the right. Park off the pavement here.

The newly refurbished Oak Spring Trail goes steadily uphill, switching back seven times, crosses a hillside, goes over a saddle, and then drops into a grassy bowl containing Oak Spring (1.4 miles). The spring itself lies hidden beneath a cluster of live oaks. From there, the trail contours south for a while, and resumes climbing up ceanothus-smothered slopes that can become waves of white blossoms during the late winter or early spring.

When you reach Yerba Buena Road (2.3 miles), turn left and continue uphill. This wide, graded fire road is hardly scenic in itself, but it does offers a rim-of-the-world view of La Crescenta and San Fernando valleys below. At 3.8 miles, there's a major split, with a dead-end road branching right

(it drops about 1 mile and 400 feet down to a crest overlooking Tujunga Canyon and the community of Sunland). Two other roads go straight and quickly dead end on a hilltop. You continue on the far-left road, which descends generally north.

At 4.9 miles, you round a bend to the left and catch sight of some raw, white cliffs at the head of Gold Canyon (a feature produced by movements along the Sierra Madre Fault). About 300 yards farther ahead (at the spot shown precisely on the topo map) the Gold Canyon Trail, indicated by a steel post half-hidden in chaparral, intersects on the right. This old pack trail was overgrown in spots by encroaching chaparral in 1990, but readily passable. It zigzags down some rather steep slopes, dotted with a dozen varieties of wildflowers in early spring. Near the bottom (6.3 miles) you reach a pleasant grove of oaks and bigcone Douglas-firs.

There's no trail beyond, just an easy walk down the wide-open, flood-scoured bed of Gold Canyon, which is covered by a porous sheet of white rocks and sand—dry except after rains. Farther down-canyon, water is squeezed upward and flows across the surface. When you reach Big Tujunga Canyon, turn left, cross Big Tujunga's Creek wherever convenient, and walk up to the west abutment of the bridge.

Area A-4, Trip 2
Trail Canyon Falls

Distance	3.0 miles round trip
Total Elevation Gain/Loss	700'/700'
Hiking Time	1½ hours (round trip)
Optional Map	USGS 7.5-min *Sunland*
Best Times	December through May
Agency	ANF/TD
Difficulty	★★

When soaking rains come, Trail Canyon's normally indolent flow becomes a lively torrent. After tumbling through miles of rock-bound constrictions and sliding across many gently inclined declivities, the water comes to the lip of a real precipice.

There the bubbly mixture momentarily attains weightlessness during a free-fall of about 30 feet. If you can manage to ignore the vastly smaller scale of this spectacle, you might easily imagine yourself in Yosemite Valley during spring runoff.

The falls in Trail Canyon are easy to approach, except during the most intense flooding, when the several fords you must cross on the way may be dangerously deep. Sturdy footwear (which is not needed during the drier summer months) may be helpful at some of the deeper crossings in high water.

To reach the trailhead, drive 5 miles up Big Tujunga Canyon from Sunland to a dirt road on the left (mile 2.0), indicated by a sign reading TRAIL CANYON TRAIL. Drive 0.2 mile uphill on this road to a fork, go right, and descend 0.2 mile to an oak-shaded parking area on the right, just above Trail Canyon's melodious creek. Continue up the same road on foot, passing a few cabins and fording the creek for the first time. The now-very-deteriorated road goes on to follow an east tributary for a while, doubles back, contours around a ridge, and drops into Trail Canyon again (0.6 mile). The road ends there, and you continue up-canyon on a footpath. The path clings to the banks for 0.5 mile, crossing the stream several times, and then climbs the west wall to avoid a narrow, alder-choked section of the canyon. The falls come into view as you round a sharp bend about 1.5 miles from the parking area.

Trail Canyon Falls

Although many people have obviously done so, it's difficult and dangerous to slide down from the trail to the base of the falls. The falls can also be reached by bush-whacking up the canyon from the point where the trail begins its ascent of the west wall; this is fun scrambling during low water, hazardous during high water.

Area A-4, Trip 3
Condor Peak-Trail Canyon

Distance	14.0 miles	
Total Elevation Gain/Loss	4260'/4520'	
Hiking Time	9 hours	
Recommended Maps	USGS 7.5-min *Condor Peak, Sunland*	
Best Times	October through May	
Agency	ANF/TD	
Difficulty	★★★★	

This all-day trip has a little of everything: long, winding passages across fragrant chaparral-clothed slopes, outstanding views from the open summit of Condor Peak, and a soothing, foot-wetting descent along Trail Canyon's delightful stream. The elevation gains and losses, however, are punishing to all but well-conditioned hikers and backpackers. The first half of the route (Condor Peak Trail) is infrequently maintained, sometimes eroded, and often overgrown, so lug soles and long pants or lightweight leg coverings are recommended. An early start, ideally before sunrise, is advised too. That way you can be off the lower, south-facing slopes before midday's heat.

A five-minute car shuttle will connect together the start and end points. (Alternatively you can take only one car and have someone in your party sprint 3 miles along Big Tujunga Canyon Road to close the loop.) Leave one car at the trailhead parking area in Trail Canyon (see Trip 2 above) and take the other car to the roadside turnout opposite the entrance to Big Tujunga Station and Vogel Flat Picnic Area, mile 4.3 on Big Tujunga Canyon Road. Walk east on the north shoulder to the mile 4.5 marker, where you will find the Condor Peak Trail going up a gully.

About 0.5 mile up the trail, a lateral of the Condor Peak Trail comes in from the right. This 1-mile-long trail was constructed in 1980 after rock slides had closed a section of Big Tujunga Canyon Road. Stay left at the trail junction and continue winding steadily uphill along the ridge between Vogel and Fusier canyons. In March, thousands of white-flowering ceanothus shrubs burst into bloom on these slopes, suffusing the air with a sublime perfume. A few conifers, the survivors of past fires, rise above the ubiquitous blanket of chaparral.

After 2.0 miles the trail bends around several gullies draining into Fusier Canyon. The biggest gully you cross (3.2 miles) is a cool, ferny oasis with surface water present until at least April or May. At 5.5 miles (4600'), the Condor Peak Trail joins an old fire break coming down from Fox Peak—one of several bumps on the ridge running northwest toward Condor Peak. Follow the fire break up and over the undulating ridge 1.2 miles more to a point just below the east brow of Condor Peak. Leave the trail and scramble 300 feet up the slope on sandy soil and over fractured granite (watch for loose rocks). On the windswept summit plateau, there are two small peaklets, each containing a climbers' register hidden in a cairn.

A pleasant, but dry camp could be made here on the summit plateau or on any neighboring ridge, if the weather is calm. Wind-sheltered campsites lie about 3 miles ahead at Tom Lucas trail camp in upper Trail Canyon.

From Condor Peak, the Pacific Ocean sprawls more than a quarter of the way around the compass. To the south, barely clearing the broad profile of Mt. Lukens, Santa Catalina Island floats in serene splendor on the hazy blue horizon. To the west, over the San Fernando Valley and through the low gap of Santa Susana Pass, rises Santa Cruz Island, the biggest and tallest of the Channel Islands, about 90 miles away.

If time allows, consider scrambling 0.8 mile down the ridge west of Condor Peak to a 5250' knob. From there you can peer almost straight down on upper Trail Canyon, threaded by a dark-green line of riparian vegetation.

After soaking in the view, retrace your way back to the Condor Peak Trail and continue going north on the old fire break. At 8.3 miles, you come to a 4840' saddle at the head of Trail Canyon and the intersection of the Trail Canyon Trail. Make a sharp left

and zigzag steeply down the scrubby slopes to a dry, sloping bench. At 9.7 miles you reach the line of willow and bay trees making up Big Cienaga, the source of Trail Canyon's almost-perennial stream. Down-canyon another 0.3 mile, on a small, grassy flat surrounded by oaks and jungle-like riparian vegetation, is cozy Tom Lucas trail camp (tables and stoves), often occupied by Scouts or other groups.

The last 4 miles along the trench-like confines of the canyon are thoroughly delightful if you don't mind occasional rocky stretches and foot-wetting fords. On clear afternoons, warm sunlight filters through the alders, casting flitting shadows amid the crystalline pools and stream-side boulders. The soothing music of water flowing over stone assuages the weariness almost every hiker feels at this point.

Area A-4, Trip 4
Haines Canyon

	Distance	3.4 miles round trip
	Total Elevation Gain/Loss	1100'/1100'
	Hiking Time	2 hours (round trip)
	Optional Map	USGS 7.5-min *Sunland*
	Best Times	October through June
	Agency	ANF/TD
	Difficulty	★★

Coyotes howl, water splashes down a willow-lined creek, hummingbirds flit about in search of nectar. All of this takes place barely a mile from the grid of suburban streets on L.A.'s fringe. I'm talking about Haines Canyon here, but it sounds a lot like the dozens of other small canyon streams that give up their water to the concrete storm channels of the city below. At the mouth of almost every one yawns a debris basin, often 50–100' wide, designed to catch the slurry of silt, sand, rocks, and boulders that roar down the mountain slopes during infrequent cloudbursts.

Haines Canyon, at least, has a roadway accessible to the non-motorized traveler. On it you can climb all the way to the summit of Mt. Lukens (see Trip 5 below for a more interesting route to the top). Our goal here is merely to reach a secluded middle section of Haines Canyon, removed from both the improvements of the L.A. County Flood Control District and the sight and sound of the city.

Park at the north end of Haines Canyon Avenue, 1 mile north of Foothill Boulevard, in suburban Tujunga. Walk past two vehicle gates; past a typical, ugly debris basin and dam; and up along the creek on a dirt road. Civilization quickly fades, except for the 12 check dams ("crib dams") down along the creek, all constructed of the same kind of pre-cast concrete "logs." (If you follow the rest of the trips in this book you'll run into many more of them.) After more than a quarter century of growth, willows, live oaks, and sycamores do a good job of softening their impact.

After 1.2 miles, the road curves abruptly right and climbs out of the canyon toward Mt. Lukens. You take the old road to the left, up the main branch of the canyon. It soon becomes a trail, and then nothing but an informal, brushy path, with patches of asphalt underfoot here and there. Remnants of the old road end beneath a large live oak, 1.7 miles from the start. A seasonal stream trickles by. You can picnic at this secluded spot, or press on to explore one source of the water, a spring a couple hundred yards upstream (watch out for poison oak). From here, the old Sister Elsie Trail, which may be rebuilt by volunteer efforts someday, climbs east to join the Stone Canyon Trail near Mt. Lukens. As of 1990, it was overgrown and virtually invisible.

Area A-4, Trip 5
Mount Lukens-Grizzly Flats Loop

Distance	12.2 miles
Total Elevation Gain/Loss	3400'/3400'
Hiking Time	8 hours
Recommended Map	USGS 7.5-min *Condor Peak*
Best Times	October through May
Agency	ANF/TD
Difficulty	★★★★

Unlike the relatively tame and tedious approach of Mt. Lukens' summit from Tujunga, this all-day adventure lets you walk on the wild side. After a grueling climb up the north slope from Big Tujunga Canyon, you circle back by way of a long, gradually descending route that passes through secluded Grizzly Flats. The hike feels best on a cool day, but beware of periods following heavy rain: the trip begins and ends with crossings of Big Tujunga creek, which can be hazardous in high water. If you're in doubt, call the Forest Service to check on flood conditions.

From Sunland, drive up Big Tujunga Canyon Road 7 miles to the Vogel Flat Picnic Area/Big Tujunga Station turnoff on the right (south side of road). Drive to the bottom of the hill, turn right, and park at the Vogel Flat parking lot, open from 8 A.M. to 10 P.M.

On foot, head west down a narrow, paved road (private, but with public easement) through the cabin community of Stonyvale. When the pavement ends after 0.7 mile, continue on dirt for another ¼ mile or so. Choose a safe place to ford Big Tujunga creek, wade across, and find the Stone Canyon Trail on the far bank. From afar you can spot this trail going straight up the sloping terrace just left (east) of Stone Canyon's wide, boulder-filled mouth. Once on the terrace, settle into a pace that will allow you to persevere over the next 3 miles and 3200 feet of vertical ascent.

From the vantage point of the first switchback, you can look down on the thousands of storm-tossed granitic boulders filling Stone Canyon from wall to wall. Although the boulders are frozen in place, you can almost sense their movement over geologic time. Indeed, floods continue to reshape this canyon and many others in the San Gabriels during every major deluge.

Ahead, you twist and turn along precipitous slopes covered by a thick blanket of chaparral—the result of growth since the last fire in 1975. At or near ground level, a profusion of ferns, mosses, and herbaceous plants forms its own pygmy understory.

The dizzying view encompasses a long, obviously linear stretch of Big Tujunga Canyon. This segment of the canyon is underlain by the San Gabriel Fault and its offshoot, the Sierra Madre Fault. The latter fault splits from the former near Vogel Flat and continues southeast past Grizzly Flat, following a course roughly coincident with the final leg of our loop hike. According to current understanding, the San Gabriel Fault is presently inactive and not likely to be the cause of major movement or earthquakes in the foreseeable future. The depth of Big Tujunga Canyon and the steepness of its walls are due primarily to stream cutting following uplift of the whole mountain range.

Between 1.8 and 2.6 miles (from the start), the trail hovers above an unnamed canyon to the east, nearly equal in drainage to Stone Canyon, but very steep and narrow. Down below you can often hear, and barely glimpse, an inaccessible waterfall. Long and short switchback segments take you rapidly higher to a steep, bulldozed track leading to the bald summit ridge of Mt. Lukens. Go 0.5 mile farther (connecting with Mt. Lukens Road along the way) to reach the highest point on the ridge (4.2 miles), which is occupied by several antenna structures. Technically the summit lies within the city limit of Los Angeles, and is the highest point in any incorporated city in the county. Glendale almost claims this honor, as its corporate limit reaches within 300 yards of the summit. Both cities encompass parts of the Angeles National Forest, of course. The view, needless to say, can be fabulous—but only on a clear day.

The remaining two-thirds of the hike is almost entirely downhill—a little monoto-nous at times, but mostly easy on the knees. Follow Mt. Lukens Road southeast down the main ridge, keeping left at the next two road junctions. At 7.2 miles you begin dropping toward a saddle. At the four-way junction there (9.0 miles), choose the road to the far left and continue on a zigzag course past beautiful oaks and bay laurels to Grizzly Flat (10.0 miles), where planted pines fill most of a terrace sloping down to a ravine called Vasquez Creek. The leftmost of several diverging roads on the flat leads to a water tank. Behind that you'll find a maintained remnant of the old Dark Canyon Trail from Angeles Crest Highway to Big Tujunga Canyon—roughly the escape route used by the outlaw Tibercio Vasquez and his unsuccessful pursuers during a hot chase over a century ago.

From the water tank, follow the maintained trail down to a creek bedecked with woodwardia fern and wild strawberry. You then descend moderately through oak forest, descend sharply down a ridge overlooking the pit-like gorge of Silver Creek, and finally reach a wildflower-dotted bench along Big Tujunga creek. Wild fruit trees and eucalyptus there silently speak of former homesteads. Head downstream, crossing the creek five times in the next mile, to reach Stonyvale Picnic Area, ¼ mile upstream from your car at Vogel Flat.

Trail below Grizzly Flats

Area A-4, Trip 6
Upper Pacoima Canyon

	Distance	7.3 miles
	Total Elevation Gain/Loss	1700'/1700'
	Hiking Time	3½ hours
	Optional Map	USGS 7.5-min *Condor Peak*
	Best Times	March through November
	Agency	ANF/TD
	Difficulty	★★★

Despite the scars of recent wildfires, Pacoima Canyon's uppermost reaches are as inviting as ever. Down in the depths of the canyon, sword and bracken ferns sway in the breeze, touched by sunbeams filtering through a fluttering leaf canopy. A little brook trickles by, adding its tiny voice to that of a dozen varieties of birds flitting through the brush, perching on treetops, and gliding overhead.

To get to the starting point, Lightning Point Group Campground, you can either drive east from Little Tujunga Canyon Road at Bear Divide on Sand Canyon Road (which becomes Santa Clara Divide Road east of Magic Mountain), or west on paved Mt. Gleason Road from Angeles Forest Highway at Mill Creek Summit. The route from Bear Divide is slower, with 16 miles of dirt-road travel, perhaps requiring the use of a truck or 4-wheel-drive vehicle. Parking space is available where a paved extension of Mt. Gleason Road ends, opposite the campground entrance.

From the campground, walk southwest on dirt-surfaced Mendenhall Ridge Road, which follows the divide between Pacoima Canyon on the right and several tributaries of Fox Creek (draining toward Big Tujunga Canyon) on the left. Do this part early in the morning, if possible, to take advantage of the clearer air and wide-ranging views.

After 3.5 miles, and a loss of a little over 1000 feet of elevation, you'll come to Indian Ben Saddle, where three dirt roads meet at a wide intersection. At the north edge of the intersection, make a sharp right turn on narrow path signed TRAIL CANYON TRAIL. This infrequently used route, an extension of the popular trail through Trail Canyon to the south, descends the steep south wall of Pacoima Canyon to join and then follow upstream the fern-fringed brook at the bottom. Huge, thick-barked live oaks, big-cone Douglas-firs, and incense cedars tower over the canyon bottom, while the stark, grey skeletons of fire-killed trees cling to upper slopes blanketed by youthful, aggressive growths of chaparral. One fallen giant by the trail side, probably done in more by age than fire, shows more than 300 annual growth rings.

After a couple of cool, enchanting miles alongside the brook, the trail leaves the canyon bottom and begins switchbacking up the slope to the right, gaining 700 feet in less than a mile. Fragrant Jeffrey pines and gracefully drooping sugar pines provide welcome shade on the heart-pounding ascent. Presently the trail levels, contours around a steep ravine, and meanders up to a trail junction. One mile down the left branch lies Messenger Flats Campground. Our way, to the right, signed DEER SPRING, goes 0.1 mile to join a dirt access road going down to Deer Spring. Turn right (uphill) on the road, walk 0.2 mile to Mendenhall Ridge Road, and turn sharply left to return to the starting point.

Area A-4, Trip 7
Messenger Flats

	Distance	3.3 miles
	Total Elevation Gain/Loss	800'/800'
	Hiking Time	1½ hours
	Optional Map	USGS 7.5-min *Acton*
	Best Times	March through November
	Agency	ANF/TD
	Difficulty	★★

Tucked amid a lovely grove of pines on the remote north ridge of the San Gabriels is tiny Messenger Flats Campground, the starting point for this ramble over a short section of the Pacific Crest Trail. You'll go out on the PCT and circle back on Santa Clara Divide Road, taking advantage of long-range vistas you can't get from the campground or the road alone.

Messenger Flats Campground is a nice, quiet retreat from the city, at least during the cooler months, when it's uncrowded. Snow renders the campground inaccessible by car for at least part of every winter. To reach the campground from Mill Creek Summit on Angeles Forest Highway, go west on Mt. Gleason Road 9 miles to unpaved Santa Clara Divide Road on the right (the pavement itself veers left and continues on to Lightning Point Campground 0.2 mile away). Follow this dirt road 1 mile to Messenger Flats Campground. By using a truck or a 4-wheel drive, you can also get to the campground from the west by way of Bear Divide and Magic Mountain.

The PCT parallels Santa Clara Divide Road at a point 20 yards north of the campground entrance. Go left (west) and follow the trail as it veers away from the road and starts to descend along steep, north-facing slopes. This is a narrow, rough-cut, seldom traveled section of the PCT. Conifers and oaks provide welcome shade at frequent intervals. Far below is Soledad Canyon, the broad, east-west gash separating the main block of the San Gabriel Mountains from

outlying ranges to the northwest. In the hills beyond Soledad Canyon, the tilted sedimentary slabs known as the Vasquez Rocks glow a bright beige amid the otherwise muted grey-green and brown land.

After 1.5 miles, the PCT dips into a shady ravine and crosses Moody Canyon Road. Leave the trail and follow the road 0.2 mile uphill to Santa Clara Divide Road. Turn left there and return to Messenger Flats, uphill all the way.

Ponderosa Forest at Messenger Flats

Area A-5: Arroyo Seco/Front Range

Despite regular invasions by noxious air (mostly at lower elevations), Angeles National Forest's Arroyo Seco District can be a hiker's and backpacker's paradise. Here, and in the next two sections (Areas A-6 and A-7), we'll cover a host of trail trips featuring fantastic views from high ridges, passages through lush forests, and visits to sparkling waterfalls and mirror-like pools.

Although hardly qualifying as wilderness by bureaucratic standards (because it's so heavily roaded), much of the area has the look and feel of wilderness. Most of the fire roads that have been built over the past few decades are now blocked to unauthorized vehicle traffic. Once off the pavement, travelers must get around on their own power, much as people did during the so-called Great Hiking Era of the early 1900s. Then, the mountains behind Pasadena and the higher country beyond it were regarded as a local frontier for weekend exploration and recreation. Scenic trails were constructed, and dozens of trailside camps and

hostelries sprang up to serve the needs of overnight guests. The road-building era that followed in the late '30s and the '40s ended that idyllic chapter of the mountains' history.

There's a renewed interest in rambling the mountains of the Front Range today, with the focus on day hiking. Volunteers have teamed up with the Forest Service to refurbish the old trails and construct new ones. Several of the old resorts have been replaced by trail camps that are popular on weekends among youth groups and backpackers.

A clear advantage of the Front Range trails is that many of them can be reached so quickly and easily from the metropolitan basin below. Down in the canyon recesses, a hiker can quickly forget the sights and sounds of the city, hardly aware that his or her peaceful, uncrowded world lies only a few miles from the edge of one of the world's largest cities.

Area A-5, Trip 1
Switzer Falls

Distance	3.6 miles round trip
Total Elevation Gain/Loss	700'/700'
Hiking Time	2 hours (round trip)
Optional Map	USGS 7.5-min *Condor Peak*
Best Times	All year
Agency	ANF/ASD
Difficulty	★★

Amid a precarious setting of crumbling diorite walls, the waters of the upper Arroyo Seco slide some 50 feet down a steep incline

known as Switzer Falls. Normally a modest dribble, but occasionally an exuberant cascade, the falls are tantalizingly secretive—

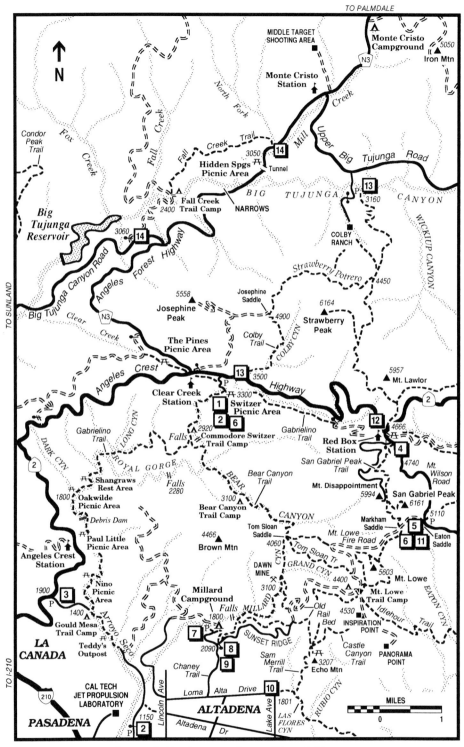

Area A-5: Arroyo Seco/Front Range

they can be approached at close range only by some foolhardy scrambling over unstable or slippery rock (definitely not recommended—many people have been seriously hurt this way). Our route takes you by trail around the main falls and down to a lesser cascade in the canyon below.

The starting point, Switzer Picnic Area, is one of the most popular destinations in the San Gabriels. Plan to arrive early—gates normally swing open at 8 A.M. By 10 A.M. on weekends the picnic area's adjacent parking lot is usually filled to capacity. Overflow and off-hours parking is available at the well-marked entrance at mile-marker 34.2 on Angeles Crest Highway (10 miles from I-210 at La Canada). If you park there you must hike down the entrance road (0.4 mile, 250' loss) to reach the picnic area.

On weekends the picnic area resembles a multicultural extravaganza, with many ethnic groups present. The sounds of rap music, revivalist preaching, and whooping children waft up through the trees with the smoky plumes of barbecues.

From the west end of the picnic area, pick up the signed Gabrielino Trail. Make your way past outlying picnic tables, and then down along the alder-shaded stream. Soon nothing but the clear-flowing stream and rustling leaves disturb the silence. Remnants of an old paved road are occasionally underfoot. In a couple of spots you ford the stream by boulder-hopping—no problem except after heavy rain.

One mile down the canyon you come upon the foundation remnants of Switzer's Camp—now the popular Commodore

Lower falls below Switzer's

Switzer Trail Camp. Established in 1884, the camp became the San Gabriels' premier wilderness resort in the early 1900s, patronized by Hollywood celebrities as well as anyone who had the gumption to hike or ride a burro up the tortuous Arroyo Seco trail from Pasadena. After the completion of Angeles Crest Highway as far as Red Box in 1934, and then a severe flood in the 1938, the resort lost its appeal. It was finally razed in the late '50s.

Below Switzer's Camp the stream slides 50 feet over Switzer Falls—but don't go that way. Instead, cross the stream and continue on the Gabrielino Trail as it edges along the canyon's right (west) wall. To the left are glimpses of the falls, a dark pit below them, and the crumbled foundation of a miniature stone chapel (a part of the resort) that perched on a ledge above the falls. Continue 0.2 mile to a trail junction. Take the left fork (the trail to Bear Canyon) and descend to the canyon bottom (1.5 miles). There's a severe, unfenced dropoff on the left on the way down, so watch your step and that of your kids.

Leave the trail there and walk along the banks, or rock hop through the stream itself, 0.2 mile up-canyon. You'll come upon a dark, shallow pool, fed by a 15'-high cascade just below the main Switzer Falls. This is a peaceful and secluded spot for a picnic. Signs here warn against climbing farther up the canyon, and that is advice well-taken.

Area A-5, Trip 2
Down the Arroyo Seco

Distance	9.6 miles
Total Elevation Gain/Loss	450'/2600'
Hiking Time	5 hours
Optional Maps	USGS 7.5-min *Condor Peak,* *Pasadena*
Best Times	October through June
Agency	ANF/ASD
Difficulty	★★★

The Spanish colonists who christened Arroyo Seco ("dry creek") evidently observed only its lower end—a sweltering, boulder-strewn wash emptying into the Los Angeles River. Upstream, inside the confines of the San Gabriels, Arroyo Seco is a scenic treasure—all the more astounding when you consider that its exquisite sylvan glens and sparkling brook lie just 12–15 miles from L.A.'s city center. If you haven't yet been freed from the notion that Los Angeles is nothing but a seething megalopolis, walk down the canyon of the Arroyo Seco. You'll be convinced otherwise.

A botanist's and wildflower seeker's dream, the canyon features generous growths of canyon live oak, western sycamore, California bay, white alder, bigleaf maple, bigcone Douglas-fir, and arroyo willow. A quick census one spring day (in a dry year, no less) yielded for me the following blooming plants: golden yarrow, prickly phlox, western wallflower, Indian pink, liveforever, wild pea, deerweed, bush lupine, Spanish broom, baby-blue-eyes, yerba santa, phacelia, chia, black sage, bush poppy, California buckwheat, shooting star, western clematis, Indian paintbrush, sticky monkey flower, scarlet bugler, and purple nightshade.

You'll be traveling the westernmost leg of the Gabrielino Trail, one of four routes in the Angeles Forest specially designated as "National Recreation Trails." The others are the High Desert, Silver Moccasin, and West Fork trails, all catering to a variety of uses (hiking, biking, horseback riding). A fifth "national" trail that crosses the Forest, the Pacific Crest National Scenic Trail, is not open to any kind of mechanical means of travel. The Arroyo Seco stretch of the Gabrielino Trail described here receives considerable use—and also a lot of much-needed maintenance—by mountain-bike club members. The upper and middle portions, which are in places narrow with steep drops to one side, are challenging even for expert riders, although not at all hard for hikers. The lower end consists of remnants of an old road built as far up the canyon as the Oak Wilde resort (now Oakwilde Picnic Area) in the '20s.

Several rest stops and picnic sites line the trail's lower half, making this a great route for a leisurely saunter. Most of these stops are located on the sites of early tourist camps or cabins erected in the early 1900s. Virtually all the structures were either destroyed by flooding in 1938 or removed through condemnation proceedings (based on water and flood-control needs) in the '20s, '30s, and '40s. Carry along whatever drinking water you'll need for the duration of the trip; there may be piped water at Paul Little Picnic Area, but don't count on it.

Begin, as in Trip 1 above, at Switzer Picnic Area. You'll finish, nearly 10 miles later, at the corner of Windsor Avenue and Ventura Street, a mile north of Interstate 210, opposite the sprawling California Institute of Technology/Jet Propulsion Laboratory.

As in Trip 1, walk down to the trail fork 0.2 mile beyond Commodore Switzer Trail Camp (1.2 miles from Switzer Picnic Area). Now bear right and begin a mile-long

The Gabrielino Trail above Oakwilde

traverse through chaparral, well above Royal Gorge, a twisting, trench-like stretch of the Arroyo Seco. Trail builders wisely avoided going through that part of the canyon (see Trip 3 for a Royal Gorge adventure).

At 2.3 miles (from the start) the trail joins a shady tributary of Long Canyon, and later Long Canyon itself, replete with a trickling stream. Alongside the trail you'll discover at least five kinds of ferns, mosses, poison oak, and Humboldt lilies (in bloom during early summer).

At 3.4 miles, the waters of Long Canyon swish down through a sculpted grotto to join Arroyo Seco. The trail descends to Arroyo Seco canyon's narrow floor and stays there, crossing and recrossing many times over the next few miles. The stretch from Long Canyon to Oakwilde Picnic Area (4.5 miles) is perhaps the most gorgeous of all, flanked by soaring walls and dappled with shade cast by the ever-present alders. Bigleaf maples put on a great show here in November, their bright yellow leaves boldly contrasting with the earthy greens, grays, and browns of the canyon's dimly lit bottom.

Beyond Oakwilde Picnic Area (4.5 miles) the canyon widens a bit and the trail assumes a more gentle gradient. There's a sharp climb at 5.3 miles—to bypass the large Brown Canyon Debris Dam—then a long trek out to the mouth of the canyon with no further significant climbing. Toward the end, the trail becomes a dirt road, and finally a paved service road, complete with bridged crossings of the Arroyo Seco (purists can follow a narrow, equestrian trail alongside). During the last couple of miles you're likely to run into lots of cyclists, joggers, parents pushing strollers, and even skateboarders.

Area A-5, Trip 3
Royal Gorge

	Distance	12.4 miles round trip
	Total Elevation Gain/Loss	1600'/1600'
	Hiking Time	7 hours (round trip)
	Optional Maps	USGS 7.5-min *Pasadena, Condor Peak*
	Best Times	All year
	Agency	ANF/ASD
	Difficulty	★★★★

Easy trail hiking, then moderate boulder-hopping, and finally some knee-deep wading will take you deep into the sublime hide-away of the Royal Gorge, the narrow, rock-walled section of Arroyo Seco that has repelled trail builders for over a century. There you'll come upon a small waterfall and a deep, dark, swimmable pool whose setting suggests to me the name "Royal Pool" or perhaps "King's Bathtub."

As of this writing, the easiest way in is by way of Gould Mesa Campground. (If and when a new trail through Dark Canyon is built from Angeles Crest Highway to Oak-wilde Picnic Area, the round trip will become about 4 miles shorter.)

Start from the parking area and trail-head at mile 26.4 on Angeles Crest High-way (2 miles north of I-210). Step around the locked gate and descend 1 mile on a paved service road to reach the Gabrielino Trail, just upstream from Gould Mesa Campground. Follow the Gabrielino Trail upstream (north) past Oakwilde Picnic Area

(3.6 miles) to the point where the Gabrielino Trail leaves Arroyo Seco and starts going up Long Canyon (4.7 miles). Abandon the trail at this point and start boulder-hopping up the main stream to the right—this is Royal Gorge. (Note: abandon the idea of reaching the Royal Pool if the first couple of creek crossings are difficult; that would indicate that the water level was extraordinarily high.)

After following the stream around several horseshoe bends, you enter (at about 6.0 miles) a section of the gorge where the sheer walls pinch in tight. Clamber over some boulders and wade through a couple of pools to reach the Royal Pool ahead. Fed by water that slides about 8 feet down a 45° incline, then 10 feet more almost vertically,

the rock-bound pool measures about 50 feet long, 30 feet wide, and 10 feet deep at the middle.

Don't try climbing around the falls to reach the upper gorge. The south wall may look "do-able," but it consists of horrendously loose, battered Precambrian metamorphic rock (it looks its age).

It is possible to approach the upper lip of the falls from the upstream side (an hour's walk and an easy boulder-hop from the Bear Canyon Trail), but there's no safe way to descend from there—even by sliding over the precipice into the pool. A small rock ledge juts from the base of the falls near the pool's surface. Anyone using the falls as a water slide would probably experience a very hard (possibly lethal) landing.

Royal Pool in Royal Gorge

Area A-5, Trip 4
San Gabriel Peak

Distance	4.2 miles round trip
Total Elevation Gain/Loss	1450'/1450'
Hiking Time	2½ hours (round trip)
Optional Maps	USGS 7.5-min *Chilao Flat, Mt. Wilson*
Best Times	All year
Agency	ANF/ASD
Difficulty	★★

The new San Gabriel Peak Trail, built by JPL (Jet Propulsion Laboratory) Hiking Club volunteers in 1987–88, bypasses a less-interesting, paved service road to Mt. Disappointment used by hikers in the past.

Disappointment was the name given to the peak in 1875 by surveyors who were trying to establish a triangulation point on the area's highest promontory. After a laborious struggle through brush they discovered they'd reached a false summit. San Gabriel Peak, 100 feet higher, lay beyond.

Today's Mt. Disappointment is a disappointing shadow of its former self. The U.S. Army blasted off its top in the '50s, installed a Nike missile base, and built a service road to the top. Currently the flattened summit serves as an antenna site. San Gabriel Peak's summit is not so abused, and makes a fine destination for a high-country hike anytime.

Drive to Red Box Station, 14 miles from I-210 at La Canada, and turn right on Mt. Wilson Road. Proceed just 0.4 mile to a turnout for the gated Mt. Disappointment service road on the right. This is also the trailhead for the San Gabriel Peak Trail, which wastes no time in zigzagging straight up the steep, oak- and conifer-shaded slopes to the west. Starting at about 0.5 mile, the trail come abreast of and parallels for a while a stretch of the service road. It then resumes switchbacking, offering occasional conifer-framed views of the Mt. Wilson and West Fork (San Gabriel River) country to

the east. You come up alongside the service road again at about 1.5 miles. Soon afterward, the trail switchbacks up and joins the service road.

You can turn north on the service road for a side trip to Mt. Disappointment, if you like. Our route to San Gabriel Peak, however, continues southeast over the broad saddle between Mt. Disappointment and San Gabriel Peak. You come to a trail junction: the right branch goes south, dropping to Markham Saddle. Take the left branch, going east up San Gabriel Peak's flank, gaining 400 feet in about 0.4 mile. The view from the top is panoramic, but not quite so impressive as that from Mt. Lowe, which is about a mile closer to the great L.A. Basin below.

San Gabriel Peak can also be climbed by way of Eaton Saddle and Markham Saddle—a shorter and slightly easier but less scenic approach through the chaparral.

Area A-5, Trip 5
Mount Lowe

	Distance	3.2 miles round trip
	Total Elevation Gain/Loss	500'/500'
	Hiking Time	1½ hours (round trip)
	Optional Maps	USGS 7.5-min *Mt. Wilson*
	Best Times	All year
	Agency	ANF/ASD
	Difficulty	★★

Late in the year, when the smog lightens, but temperatures still hover within a moderate register, come up to Mt. Lowe to toast the setting sun. You can sit on an old bench, pour the champagne, and watch Old Sol sink into Santa Monica Bay.

Start from the roadside parking area at unmarked Eaton Saddle, mile 2.4 (counted from Red Box Station) on Mt. Wilson Road. This popular trailhead may be jammed with cars on the weekends. Walk past the gate on the west side and proceed up the dirt road (Mt. Lowe fire road) that carves its way under the precipitous south face of San Gabriel Peak. Rainwater shed from these slopes falls to Eaton Canyon below, where it quickly tumbles down-canyon toward the L.A. Basin near Altadena.

As you approach a short tunnel (0.3 mile) dating from 1942, look for the remnants of a former cliff-hanging trail to the left of the tunnel's east entrance. At Markham Saddle (0.5 mile) the fire road starts to descend slightly—don't continue on the road. Instead, find the unmarked Mt. Lowe Trail on the left (south). You contour southwest above the fire road for about 0.6 mile, and then start climbing across the east flank of Mt. Lowe without much change of direction.

At 1.3 miles, make a sharp right turn. Proceed 0.2 mile uphill, then go left on a short spur trail to Mt. Lowe's barren summit. Mt. Lowe was the proposed upper terminus for Professor Thaddeus Lowe's famed scenic railway (see Trip 10). Funding ran out, however, and tracks were never laid higher than Ye Alpine Tavern (later named Mt. Lowe Tavern), 1200 feet below. During the railway's heyday in the early 1900s, thousands disembarked at the tavern and tramped Mt. Lowe's east- and west-side trails for world-class views of the basin and the surrounding mountains. Some reminders of that era remain on the summit of Mt. Lowe and along some of the trails: volunteers have repainted, relettered, and returned to their proper places some the many sighting tubes that helped the early tourists familiarize themselves with the surrounding geography.

Area A-5, Trip 6
Bear Canyon

Distance	7.4 miles
Total Elevation Gain/Loss	1000'/2800'
Hiking Time	4 hours
Optional Maps	USGS 7.5-min *Mt. Wilson, Pasadena, Condor Peak*
Best Times	All year
Agency	ANF/ASD
Difficulty	★★★

Bear Canyon, as secluded and beautiful as any small canyon in the Front Range country, enjoys the added benefit of good trail access from two sides. Graced by a sparkling rivulet of water, and shaded by beautiful sycamore, alder, bigcone Douglas-fir, bigleaf maple, and bay trees, the canyon's innermost confines are scarcely disturbed at all by the little-improved remains of the historic Tom Sloan Trail—built in 1923 to serve the needs of hikers traveling between Mt. Lowe Tavern and Switzer's Camp. The stretch through the canyon is a special delight in November, when the leaves of the maples turn crispy yellow, and you scuff through leaf litter so thick it's hard to recognize the path.

This one-way hike goes between Eaton Saddle and Switzer Picnic Area (see Trips 1 and 5 for driving directions). If you'll be leaving a car overnight on the Switzer end, ask the Forest Service where to park it (the Switzer gate is locked overnight).

From Eaton Saddle, take the Mt. Lowe fire road west to Markham Saddle (0.5 mile). Continue southwest and west without leaving the fire road until you reach a 180° bend to the left (1.8 miles) atop the long west ridge coming down from Mt. Lowe's summit. Leave the road there and continue, on trail now, westward along the same ridge. Here and there along the way you can look south over Millard Canyon and across the usually hazy lowlands to Palos Verdes and Santa Catalina Island. Upper Bear Canyon

lies to the north, its rugged, chaparral-clad slopes hardly suggesting the beauty that exists down along the hidden stream. After a few downhill switchbacks, you arrive at Tom Sloan Saddle (2.8 miles), where several newly reconstructed trails meet: a trail coming up from Dawn Mine, the east leg of the Tom Sloan Trail from the Mt. Lowe Tavern site, and the west leg of the Tom Sloan Trail (a.k.a. the Bear Canyon Trail) coming up from Bear Canyon. In addition, there's a ridgetop fire break, sometimes followed by hikers, leading west to the summit of Brown Mountain.

From Tom Sloan Saddle, you go north, descending reworked switchbacks through chaparral until you reach Bear Canyon's stream (3.5 miles). There you'll discover the remains of a small, stone shed and cabin foundations hidden amid the poison oak and wild blackberry vines.

The trail deteriorates as you turn down-canyon, and progress slows. From time to time, boulder-hopping becomes the way to travel until you reach Bear Canyon Trail Camp (tables and stoves on an oak-shaded terrace to the left—4.2 miles), after which the pathway becomes easier to follow. A section of trail carved precariously into a sheer wall on the right (mile 5.4) heralds your arrival at Bear Creek's confluence with Arroyo Seco. From there on the path is wide and obvious, and you'll be climbing for almost all of the remaining 2 miles. You follow Arroyo Seco upstream past some sparkling mini-falls and rock-bound pools (unfortunately the priceless beauty of these cascades was spoiled by spray-painted graffiti in 1988). Half a mile later you start an ascent up the slope to the left, and soon

thereafter join the Gabrielino Trail. You pass Switzer Falls, skirt Commodore Switzer Trail Camp, and go on to finish at Switzer Picnic Area.

Area A-5, Trip 7
Millard Canyon Falls

Distance	1.4 miles round trip
Total Elevation Gain/Loss	300'/300'
Hiking Time	1 hour (round trip)
Optional Maps	USGS 7.5-min *Pasadena*
Best Times	All year
Agency	ANF/ASD
Difficulty	★★

During heavy rains, Millard Canyon's modest watershed gathers enough runoff to stage a real spectacle near its lower end—Millard Canyon Falls. Even in the dry season, when the water dribbles over the rock by way of several serpentine paths, the steep-walled grotto containing the falls is pleasantly cool, and worth a visit.

From Loma Alta Drive in Altadena, drive up the Chaney Trail (a paved road) toward Sunset Ridge. (A sturdy gate along the way is closed and locked every night from 10 P.M. to 6 A.M., allowing neither entrance nor exit to or from the area above. This has apparently solved the problem of rowdy individuals using Millard Canyon at

night. Millard Campground, I found, was a pleasant place to sleep overnight.)

The Chaney Trail goes over the top of Sunset Ridge and then down to a large, new parking lot alongside the stream. Walk upstream, past a vehicle gate, and through Millard Campground (a walk-in facility with tables, stoves, and piped water). Continue up the canyon, boulder-hopping from time to time, beneath oaks and alders, until you reach the falls. Part of the falling water is blocked from view by several large boulders wedged like chockstones high above. It's difficult to take a photograph that does justice to this cool, dark or sun-dappled, pleasant place.

Area A-5, Trip 8
Dawn Mine Loop

Distance	6.0 miles
Total Elevation Gain/Loss	1600'/1600'
Hiking Time	3½ hours
Optional Maps	USGS 7.5-min *Pasadena*
Best Times	October through June
Agency	ANF/ASD
Difficulty	★★★

Millard Canyon's happily splashing stream, presided over by oaks, alders, maples, and bigcone Douglas-firs, is the main attraction on this hike. But you can also do a little snooping around the site of the Dawn Mine, one of the more promising gold prospects in the San Gabriels, worked intermittently from 1895 until the early '50s.

An early start is emphatically recommended. That way you'll take advantage of shade during the climbing phase of the hike, and you'll be assured of finding a place to park your car at the trailhead (which is as popular with mountain bikers as with hikers).

From Loma Alta Drive in Altadena, drive up the Chaney Trail (past the gate that opens at 6 A.M.) to the top of Sunset Ridge, where there's parking by the roadside. Walk east on the gated, paved Sunset Ridge fire road. After about 100 yards, pass a foot trail on the left leading down to Millard Campground. Continue another 300 yards to a second foot trail on the left (Sunset Ridge Trail). Take it. On it you contour north and east along Millard Canyon's south wall, passing above the 50'-high falls. You begin climbing in earnest at about 0.9 mile and soon reach a trail fork. The left branch (your return route) goes down 100 yards past a private cabin to the canyon bottom. You go right, uphill. Switchbacks long and short take you farther up along the pleasantly shaded canyon wall to an intersection with Sunset Ridge fire road (2.4 miles), just below a rocky knob called Cape of Good Hope.

Turn left on the fire road, and walk past Cape of Good Hope. The trail to Echo Mountain, intersecting on the right, and the fire road ahead are both part of the original Mt. Lowe Railway bed (see Trip 10)—now a self-guiding historical trail. Continue your ascent on the fire road/railway bed to post #5 on the left (2.9 miles). There you'll find a trail descending to Dawn Mine in Millard Canyon. This is a recently reworked but primitive version of the mule path once used

to haul ore from the mine to the railway above. On the way down you may encounter a dicey passage or two across perpetually sliding talus.

After reaching the gloomy canyon bottom (3.6 miles), the trail goes upstream along the east bank for about 100 yards to the long-abandoned Dawn Mine, perched on the west-side slope. The gaping entrance to the lower shaft may seem inviting to explore, but it's subject, of course, to collapse without warning.

From the mine, head down-canyon past crystalline mini-pools, the flotsam and jetsam of the mining days, and storm-tossed boulders. Much of the original trail in the canyon has been washed away, but a new generation of hikers has beaten down a pretty good semblance of a path. About ½ mile below the mine a wider area of the canyon, with a high and dry terrace on the right, could be used as a wilderness campsite.

After swinging around an abrupt bend to the right, the canyon becomes dark and gloomy once again. After another 0.5 mile you'll come to the aforementioned trail climbing up to the left. Pass the private cabin and hook up with the Sunset Ridge Trail, which will take you back to the Sunset Ridge fire road and your car.

Area A-5, Trip 9
Upper Millard Canyon

	Distance	10.6 miles
	Total Elevation Gain/Loss	2700'/2700'
	Hiking Time	6 hours
	Optional Maps	USGS 7.5-min *Pasadena,*
		Mt. Wilson
	Best Times	October through May
	Agency	ANF/ASD
	Difficulty	★★★★

On this longer version of the Dawn Mine loop described in Trip 8 above, you'll climb all the way to Tom Sloan Saddle at the head of Millard Canyon, and then take the newly reconstructed east leg of the Tom Sloan Trail down toward Mt. Lowe Trail Camp (formerly Mt. Lowe Tavern). If this is your first visit to the area, it's better to travel around the loop in a clockwise direction as we describe here, returning via the Mt. Lowe Railway bed. Route finding is easier that way.

Begin as in Trip 8 by walking up the Sunset Ridge fire road and veering left onto the Sunset Ridge Trail after 400 yards. Bear left at 1.0 mile (where the Sunset Ridge Trail climbs right), descend to Millard Canyon's stream, and work your way up along the banks to Dawn Mine (2.4 miles).

Continue upstream another 0.2 mile to a confluence where a large tributary, Grand Canyon, branches east. On the left you should find a narrow switchback trail going up the shady ravine heading north. You cross the ravine five times and negotiate several switchbacks before arriving at Tom Sloan Saddle (3.6 miles) atop the high ridge shared by Brown Mountain and Mt. Lowe. Of the many paths that converge there, take the one farthest right—you will see its trace slanting across the chaparral-covered north wall of Grand Canyon. Reworked in 1988–89, this 1923 trail retains much of the charm of the original. Just wide enough for hikers, it climbs on a constant, moderate grade,

chiseling across rock faces, ducking beneath oaks, tunneling through tall chaparral. South across Grand Canyon, you'll spot the old railway bed cutting across the opposing canyon wall—you'll be walking on it before long.

When you reach the Mt. Lowe fire road (5.2 miles), turn right and walk about ¼ mile. You'll probably hear voices from Mt. Lowe Trail Camp, 150 feet below, on the right. Find a good place to cut down the slope—you'll save almost half a mile of road-walking this way. Year-round water is available at the trail camp, but it must be filtered or purified.

From the trail camp it's downhill virtually all the way back. Follow the fire road/old railway bed 2.6 miles west and south, down past a couple of hairpin turns, to Cape of Good Hope, where the pavement begins. Just past the Cape, use the Sunset Ridge Trail to return to the starting point. Alternatively you can can walk down the paved Sunset Ridge fire road, which is slightly shorter, but sun-exposed and a lot less scenic.

Area A-5, Trip 10
Mount Lowe Railway

	Distance	11.2 miles
	Total Elevation Gain/Loss	2800'/2800'
	Hiking Time	5½ hours
	Optional Maps	USGS 7.5-min *Mt. Wilson,* *Pasadena*
	Best Times	October through May
	Agency	ANF/ASD
	Difficulty	★★★

An engineering marvel when built in the 1890s, the Mt. Lowe Railway has lived a checkered past full of glory and destruction. Before its final abandonment in the mid-'30s, the line carried over 3 million passengers—virtually all of them tourists. Unheard of by millions of Southland newcomers today, the railway was for many years the most popular attraction in Southern California.

Today hikers are taking a new interest in the old road bed; the Rails-to-Trails Conservancy (which promotes the conversion of abandoned rail corridors into recreation trails) ranked the Mt. Lowe Railway as one of the nation's 12 most scenic and historically significant recycled rail lines.

The line consisted of three stages, of which almost nothing remains today. Passengers rode a trolley from Altadena into lower Rubio Canyon, then boarded a steeply inclined cable railway which took them 1300 feet higher to Echo Mountain, where two hotels, a number of small tourist attractions, and an observatory stood. At Echo Mountain, non-acrophobic passengers hopped onto the third phase, a mountain trolley that climbed another 1200 vertical feet along airy slopes to the end of the line—Ye Alpine Tavern (later Mt. Lowe Tavern, on whose ruins stands today's Mt. Lowe Trail Camp).

The Forest Service and volunteers have put together a self-guiding trail, featuring ten sturdy markers fashioned from railroad rails, along the route of the mountain trolley. As we've already seen (Trip 8), the old railway bed can be reached by hiking either the Sunset Ridge fire road or the Sunset Ridge Trail. The more direct, easier, and more exciting way to reach Station 1 at Echo Mountain, however, is to go by way of the Sam Merrill Trail from Altadena.

The trailhead lies on the grounds of the long-demolished Cobb Estate, easily found at the north end of Lake Avenue in Altadena. Walk east past the stone pillars at the entrance and continue 150 yards on a narrow, blacktop driveway. The driveway bends left, but you keep walking straight (east). Soon you come to a water fountain on the rim of Las Flores Canyon and a sign indicating the start of the Sam Merrill Trail. This trail goes left over the top of a small debris dam and begins a switchback ascent of Las Flores Canyon's precipitous east wall, while another trail (the Altadena Crest equestrian trail) veers to the right, down the canyon.

Inspired by the fabulous views (assuming you're doing this early on one of L.A.'s clear winter days), the 2.5 miles of steady ascent on the Sam Merrill Trail may seem to go rather quickly. Turn right at the top of the trail and walk south over to Echo Mountain, which is more like the shoulder of a ridge. There you'll find a historical plaque and some picnic tables near a grove of incense cedars and bigleaf maples. There's also a water faucet, which cannot be

Los Angeles from the Sam Merrill Trail on a clear day

depended upon. (It's unwise to count on the availability of pure water anywhere along the trails of the Front Range.) Poke around and you'll find many foundation ruins and piles of concrete rubble. An old "bull-wheel" and cables for the incline railway were thoughtfully left behind after the Forest Service cleared away what remained of the buildings here in the '50s and '60s. After visiting Echo Mountain, you'll go north on the signed Echo Mountain Trail, where you'll walk over railroad ties still imbedded in the ground.

Since the self-guiding brochure for the rail bed ahead is not always available from the Forest Service, I'll briefly summarize the stops. Numbers in parentheses refer to hiking mileage starting from Echo Mountain.

Station 1 (0.0) Echo Mountain. This was known as the White City during its brief heyday in the late 1890s, but most of its tourist facilities were destroyed by fire or windstorms in the first decade of the 1900s. The mountain remained a transfer point for passengers until the mid-'30s.

Station 2 (0.5) View of Circular Bridge. You can't see it from here, but passengers at this point first noticed the 400'-diameter circular bridge (Station 6) jutting from the slope above. As you walk on ahead, you'll notice the many concrete footings that supported trestles bridging the side ravines of Las Flores Canyon.

Station 3 (0.8) Cape of Good Hope. You're now at the junction of the Echo Mountain Trail and Sunset Ridge fire road. The tracks swung in a 200° arc around the rocky promontory just west—Cape of Good Hope. (Walk around the Cape, if you like, to get a feel for the experience.) North of this dizzying passage, riders were treated to the longest stretch of straight track—only 225 feet long. The entire original line from Echo Mountain to Ye Alpine Tavern had 127 curves and 114 straight sections.

Station 4 (1.0) Dawn Station/Devil's Slide. Dawn Mine (Trip 8) lies below in Millard Canyon. Gold-bearing ore, packed up by mules from the canyon bottom, was loaded onto the train here. Ahead lay a treacherous stretch of crumbling granite, the Devil's Slide, which was eventually bridged by a trestle. (The current fire road has been shored up with much new concrete, and cement-lined spillways seem to do a good job of carrying away flood debris.)

Station 5 (1.2) Horseshoe Curve. Just beyond this station, Horseshoe Curve enabled the railway to gain elevation above Millard Canyon. The grade just beyond Horseshoe Curve was 7 percent—steepest on the mountain segment of the line.

Station 6 (1.6) Circular Bridge. An engineering accomplishment of worldwide fame, the Circular Bridge carried startled passengers into midair over the upper walls of Las Flores Canyon. Look for the concrete supports of this bridge down along the chaparral-covered slopes to the right.

Station 7 (2.0) Horseshoe Curve Overview. Passengers here looked down on Horseshoe Curve, and could also see all three levels of steep, twisting track climbing the east wall of Millard Canyon.

Station 8 (2.4) Granite Gate. A narrow slot carefully blasted out of solid granite on a sheer north-facing slope, Granite Gate took 8 months to cut. Look for the electric wire support dangling from the rock above.

Station 9 (3.4) Ye Alpine Tavern. The tavern, which later became a fancy hotel, was located at Crystal Springs, the source that still provides water (which now requires purification) for backpackers staying overnight at today's Mt. Lowe Trail Camp. The rails never got farther than here, although it was hoped they would one day reach the summit of Mt. Lowe, 1200 feet higher.

Station 10 (3.9) Inspiration Point. From Ye Alpine Tavern, tourists could saunter over to Inspiration Point along part of the never-finished rail extension to Mt. Lowe. Sighting tubes (still in place there) helped visitors locate places of interest below.

Inspiration Point is the last station on the self-guiding trail. The fastest and easiest way to return is by way of the Castle Canyon Trail, which descends directly below Inspiration Point. After 2 miles you'll arrive back on the old railway grade just north of Echo Mountain. Retrace your steps on the Sam Merrill Trail.

Area A-5, Trip 11
Inspiration Point

	Distance	6.0 miles
	Total Elevation Gain/Loss	1500'/1500'
	Hiking Time	3½ hours
	Optional Maps	USGS 7.5-min *Mt. Wilson*
	Best Times	October through June
	Agency	ANF/ASD
	Difficulty	★★★

This trip rambles down to Inspiration Point the back way—via Mt. Lowe. It's a down-and-up route, so save most of your energy for the trip back. On the way down and later back, you'll have a chance to use both the east and west trails on the slopes of Mt. Lowe. These were among the best-used trails during the era of the railway, and both have been brought back into service in recent years.

As in Trip 5 above, proceed 1.3 miles to the trail junction on Mt. Lowe's east flank. Go either way (straight for the east trail, sharply right for the west trail), but plan to use the other trail on your return.

Either way you'll end up descending to meet the Mt. Lowe fire road at a point above Mt. Lowe Trail Camp. Go south on the fire road to Inspiration Point, where the view, I'm happy to report, is still inspiring whenever the marine inversion layer lies low across the L.A. Basin—a fairly common occurrence early in the day. On clear, dry days the ocean horizon can be seen *behind* the gap at Two Harbors on Santa Catalina Island, and San Clemente Island sprawls indistinctly just left of the leftmost tip of Santa Catalina.

If you're interested in side trips, you can climb the 4714' peaklet just west of Inspiration Point. Or you can travel 1 mile southeast on the flat fire road going out to Panorama Point—the ridge overlooking Eaton Canyon. Starting around 1915, tourists could traverse this stretch on board a mule-pushed (not drawn, so passengers could avoid dust) observation car that rolled along narrow-gauge rails. This O. M. & M.

(One Man and a Mule) Railroad became a popular side attraction for Mt. Lowe Tavern guests and day-trippers.

Today's fire road out toward Panorama Point curls south and ends at a cement water tank, where views of the L.A. Basin are more fantastic (in my experience) than from any other land-based vantage point. On a clear night, the view of millions of lights almost a mile of elevation lower is surreal. From this close-in point, less than two beeline miles from the edge of the city, the soft droning of a hundred thousand engines, accented now and again by an accelerating motorcycle or unmuffled car, floats upward on the updrafts.

Return the way you came, except in circling Mt. Lowe.

At Inspiration Point

Area A-5 Trip 12
Strawberry Peak

	Distance	6.6 miles round trip
	Total Elevation Gain/Loss	1900'/1900'
	Hiking Time	4 hours (round trip)
	Optional Map	USGS 7.5-min *Chilao Flat*
	Best Times	October through June
	Agency	ANF/ASD
	Difficulty	★★★

Strawberry Peak's 6164' summit beats by a smidgen 6161' San Gabriel Peak, thus claiming the honor of being the highest peak in the Front Range. Although its profile appears rounded as seen from most places, in reality its flanks fall away sharply on three sides, leaving only one relatively easy route to the top.

In March 1909, Strawberry Peak garnered national attention when a gas balloon and gondola carrying six passengers over Tournament Park in Pasadena was swept by violent gusts into storm clouds over the San Gabriel Mountains. After being tossed to as high as 14,000 feet, the balloon descended in white-out conditions and crash-landed just below Strawberry's snow-covered summit—its gondola coming to rest just 10 feet from a vertical precipice. Nearly three days later, a telephone call from Switzer's Camp brought news to the world below that the riders had survived.

On this hike you'll climb Strawberry by way of the fastest and easiest way—first by trail, then on a well-beaten but sometimes steep path along an old fire break. You'll be traveling mostly along hot, south-facing slopes and open ridges exposed to the sun, so an early-morning start is best.

Park at Red Box Gap, 14 miles from I-210 in La Canada. The gap, named for a red box of fire-fighting tools placed there around 1908, lies on the divide between Arroyo Seco and the West Fork of the San Gabriel River. Six trails converged there in the early 1900s; today it's an important crossroads for auto traffic. Park in either the ranger station or picnic-ground lots.

From Red Box, walk east along the left shoulder of Angeles Crest Highway 0.1 mile to an abandoned fire road slanting left up the hillside. Continue up the eroded bed of that road for 0.6 mile to reach a trail on the left. From there, newly cut switchbacks through chaparral take you northwest to a saddle due south of Mt. Lawlor's summit. Afterward, the trail gains elevation very gradually.

When you reach a saddle on the northwest shoulder of Mt. Lawlor (2.2 miles from Red Box) and the trail starts to descend north, leave the maintained trail and start climbing along the overgrown fire break slanting left along an undulating, chaparral-covered ridge. Work your way north and finally west to Strawberry's shaggy-looking summit—rocky and slippery going in places.

Scattered Coulter pines and bigcone Douglas-firs struggle for existence near the summit, their wind-blown limbs swept back in gestures that seem defiant. The view from the top is panoramic, but not so exciting as from peaks such as Mt. Lowe or Mt. Lukens, which rise dramatically from the L.A. Basin. On the other hand, Strawberry often basks in clean air while the basin-bordering ramparts are wreathed in smog.

Another popular way to reach Strawberry Peak is by way of the northwest ridge from the Colby Trail (see Trip 13 below), which involves some Class 3 scrambling over huge granitic boulders.

Area A-5, Trip 13
Colby Canyon to Big Tujunga

Distance	8.4 miles
Total Elevation Gain/Loss	1700'/2040'
Hiking Time	5 hours
Optional Maps	USGS 7.5-min *Condor Peak, Chilao Flat*
Best Times	October through May
Agency	ANF/TD
Difficulty	★★★

A new bypass of the old Colby Trail through Colby Ranch now allows hikers to swing by Strawberry Peak and descend all the way to the bank of Big Tujunga Canyon's creek. (Formerly, the trail ended inside the ranch property—now a private Methodist camp.) For the most part you'll be following a route hewn over the mountains in the 1890s by pioneer Delos Colby. The trail connected Switzer's Camp in the Arroyo Seco with Colby's ranch in Coldwater Canyon, a tributary of Big Tujunga. Around the turn of the century, the ranch catered to hikers, hunters, and fishermen independent and determined enough to travel beyond the fancy resorts of the Arroyo Seco and Mt. Lowe areas.

The highlight of the trip is Strawberry Potrero, a series of gentle depressions tucked under the granite cliffs and talus of Strawberry Peak's sheer north flank. Those who are motivated can try either of two optional side trips—a scramble up Strawberry Peak from Josephine Saddle, or a much easier walk-up of Josephine Peak. See John Robinson's *Trails of the Angeles* for more details about either of those routes.

With two cars, leave one at the site of the old Wickiup Campground in upper Big Tujunga Canyon. To get there drive 1.2 miles east from Angeles Forest Highway on the newly paved Upper Big Tujunga Road, turn right on the road signed COLBY CAMP, and descend on narrow and sharply twisting pavement to a large unpaved lot along Big

Tujunga creek. The area upstream is a favorite haunt of anglers seeking native trout.

Take the other car to an unpaved turnout on the north side of Angeles Crest Highway, 0.7 mile east of Clear Creek Station (mile-marker 34.5). This serves as the trailhead for the popular pathway up Colby Canyon.

During the first half mile you'll be charmed by the woodsy atmosphere and (in season at least) the brook trickling down the narrow canyon bottom. All too soon you're struggling up slopes thickly grown with chaparral and punctuated by the giant white plumes of blooming yuccas. The well-graded but at times rock-strewn trail zigzags expeditiously to Josephine Saddle, 2.0 miles. There you meet a fire road going west toward Josephine Peak, and a footpath going northeast, gently uphill, left of the ridge leading to Strawberry Peak. Take the latter. Almost immediately you'll notice the well-worn climbers' route to Strawberry's summit veering right; our route follows the trail contouring ahead.

For 2 more miles the trail stays close to the 5000' contour, bending around several precipitous gullies that often serve as chutes for rockfall. Unlike Strawberry Peak's wind-beaten, nearly barren top (unseen more than 1000 feet above), oaks, pines, and bigcone Douglas-firs cling tenaciously to this level of the mountain—wherever the soil is stable enough to retain moisture. Clusters of prickly phlox and Indian paintbrush brighten the muted tones of earth and forest.

Following a moderate descent, you arrive (4.6 miles) at the westernmost clearing of Strawberry Potrero (the Spanish word *potrero* means pasture), a sandy basin ringed by live oaks and Coulter pines. The sheer, granite cliffs and talus of Strawberry Peak's north face preside over this superb camping/picnic spot. Amenities include an old picnic table and plenty of flat, sandy space for pitching tents. Depending on the season, water might be obtained from runoff or snowmelt on the slopes above.

A trail (Colby's original route) continues north down to Colby Ranch. Our way, however, *contours east* along the base of the talus slope, passes through a second clearing, and descends through a shady ravine to a third, open basin—this one a true meadow filled with sedges and grasses.

At the next trail junction, 5.6 miles from the start, go left (north). When you come to the next fork, 0.2 mile farther, keep right (northeast) to follow the new trail down to Big Tujunga.

At 6.6 miles the trail comes to the nose of a ridge offering a view of cars in the unpaved lot at the trail's end, 1000 feet below but almost 2 miles away via the trail. Two steep firebreaks diverge here, one to the northwest, the other to the northeast. Our route follows the latter. Slip and slide down, losing about 150 feet, and find the continuation of the trail going left (northwest) along an oak-bowered slope. Gentle switchbacks take you from there to Big Tujunga Canyon.

Area A-5, Trip 14
Fall Creek Trail

	Distance	5.5 miles
	Total Elevation Gain/Loss	1600'/1600'
	Hiking Time	2½ hours
	Optional Map	USGS 7.5-min *Condor Peak*
	Best Times	October through June
	Agency	ANF/TD
	Difficulty	★★

Threading the steep, north wall of Big Tujunga Canyon above Big Tujunga Reservoir, the Fall Creek Trail offers unique vistas of Big Tujunga's Narrows and the looming "skyline" beyond—Josephine and Strawberry peaks. This makes a good one-way trip—down into Big Tujunga Canyon, and back up the other side. Remember, though, that flood conditions could render Big Tujunga's creek unsafe to ford.

Both end-points of the hike lie on virtually the same elevation contour, so it makes little difference which way you go. Mornings, you may prefer going west to keep the sun out of your eyes; afternoons,

going east is probably better. Assuming you go from east to west, you'll start the hike at Hidden Springs Picnic Area, on Angeles Forest Highway just north of the tunnel. The trail doesn't start here, but rather from the road shoulder about 300 yards north. It goes up along a small canyon (North Fork Mill Creek) a short distance and then veers left along a brushy hillside. After gaining roughly 800 feet in 1 mile, the trail levels, contours for another mile, and then begins dropping steadily into Big Tujunga Canyon.

You're almost never out of sight or sound of the curling ribbons of asphalt and traffic below, but at least the trail smells of wilderness and wild chaparral. The sun-warmed slopes reek of pungent yerba santa and sage. While you're descending, enjoy the view up the V-shaped gash of Big Tujunga's Narrows to the east.

At 3.5 miles, the footpath you're on ends at a junction of dirt roads. The left branch leads 200 yards east to Fall Creek Trail Camp (a former work camp—tables, stoves, and ornamental plantings gone wild), while the middle branch (our route) descends to the gravelly floor of Big Tujunga Canyon.

After fording the normally shallow creek, continue west on the fire road that crookedly ascends Big Tujunga Canyon's steep south wall. On the way up, look across the canyon to see water shooting (or dribbling) down a moss-covered ledge in Fall Creek. The fire road ends at a turnout on Big Tujunga Canyon Road, 0.7 mile west of Angeles Forest Highway.

Colby Trail north of Josephine Saddle

Area A-6: Mount Wilson/Front Range

In the lush and shady recesses of Big Santa Anita Canyon, Eaton Canyon, and other drainages at the foot of Mt. Wilson, you can easily lose all sight and sense of the hundreds of square miles of dense metropolis lying just over a single ridge. With very easy access, by city street or mountain road and then by trail, these are perfect spots to discover the San Gabriel Mountains' beguiling charms.

The flattish, rambling summit of Mt. Wilson, a sort of centerpiece for the area covered in this section, is hardly notable for its elevation of about 5700 feet. But its long history of use, dating back to 1864, has made it a major node in the trail network of the San Gabriels. Today the drive to Mt. Wilson is an easy one—half an hour at best from I-210 at La Canada. You can play tourist (10 a.m to 5 P.M. daily) by visiting Skyline Park and Mt. Wilson Observatory, or you can get serious and set off on one of the steep trails down its flank.

Chantry Flat, above Arcadia, is the hikers' hub on the lowland side. Chantry Flat is also the jumping-off spot for cabin owners who must walk down to their homes away from home in Big Santa Anita Canyon. At Chantry Flat, you'll find spacious (although often inadequate) parking space, a ranger station, a picnic ground, and a mom-and-pop refreshment stand. There's also a freight business—the last pack station operating year round in California. Almost daily, horses, mules and burros carry building materials and other supplies to canyon residents.

A sturdy gate on Santa Anita Avenue just above Arcadia clangs shut every night at 10 P.M. and doesn't open till 6 A.M. the next morning. This has curbed most of the nocturnal rowdiness that used to take place in the Chantry Flat parking lots, along with what in these parts is sometimes called "he-in' and she-in'." On the weekends, it's wise to arrive early at Chantry Flat; otherwise parking is hard to come by.

Gabrielino Trail above Winter Creek

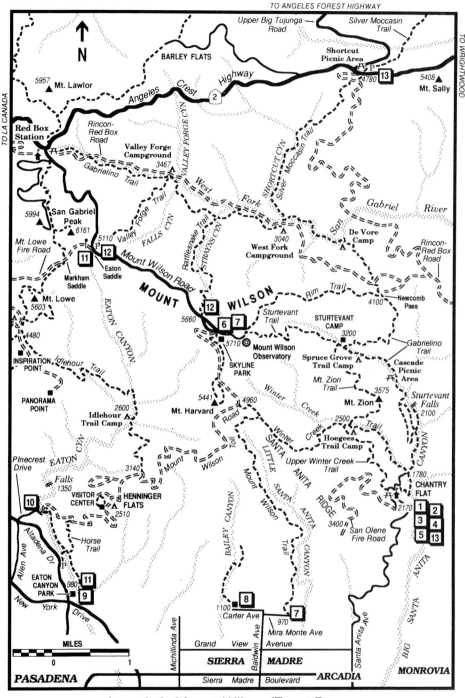

Area A-6: Mount Wilson/Front Range

Area A-6, Trip 1
Santa Anita Ridge

👟	**Distance**	7.5 miles round trip
	Total Elevation Gain/Loss	1350'/1350'
🏳	**Hiking Time**	3½ hours (round trip)
	Optional Map	USGS 7.5-min *Mount Wilson*
	Best Times	November through May
➹	**Agency**	ANF/ASD
	Difficulty	★★★

Winding its way lazily upward from the crowded parking lots at Chantry Flat, San Olene Fire Road leads to a shoulder of Santa Anita Ridge—the viewful divide between Big and Little Santa Anita canyons. From the top of the road, the sweeping view takes in the Santa Anita Park race track (only 3 miles to the south), a good chunk of the San Gabriel Valley, and parts of the San Gabriel Mountains' High Country to the north and northeast.

The road climbs 3.5 miles at an almost steady 6 percent grade—a bit tedious at walking pace; probably better for running or mountain biking. On clear days, the scenery is uniformly pleasant, especially after winter storms have dusted the surrounding summits. Edging along north-facing slopes much of the way, the road twists and turns through stands of mature chaparral and mini-groves of bay and maple. Best of all, you're likely to meet no one at all beyond the first half-mile. The route is ideally suited

for a late afternoon or early evening stroll. From the top you could catch the sunset, watch the city lights turn on, then return by the light of a three-quarter or full moon (but remember, the gate below Chantry Flat closes at 10 P.M. daily).

Route finding could scarcely be more simple. Follow the paved service road upward from the picnic area. At 0.7 mile you pass the Chantry Flat Air-Attack Station (heliport), where the pavement ends and a dirt road continues. (Those who would prefer a much shorter, but gut-busting, approach can follow an old fire break straight up the ridge west of the heliport. It leads to the uppermost hairpin turn on San Olene Fire Road.) At 3.5 miles the road levels. There's a microwave reflector structure on the left and a water tank signed SANTA ANITA RIDGE on the right. Proceed another ¼ mile down the ridge to the south for the best view of the valley below.

Area A-6, Trip 2
Hoegees Loop

👟	**Distance**	5.4 miles
	Total Elevation Gain/Loss	1300'/1300'
🏳	**Hiking Time**	2½ hours
	Optional Map	USGS 7.5-min *Mount Wilson*
	Best Times	All year
↻ 🚶	**Agency**	ANF/ASD
	Difficulty	★★

California magazine called it "a rustic Xanadu, where groceries come by burro." Unlike Coleridge's dream city, however, the anachronistic community of cabins tucked into Big Santa Anita Canyon and its main tributary, Winter Creek, needs no imagination to behold. On foot is the only way in for the owners of the 82 cabins, dating from the early 1900s and as yet unclaimed by catastrophic flood or wildfire. Most of the residents are weekenders; Forest Service regulations prohibit continuous habitation of structures on leased land. Most are delighted to have to settle for amenties typical of a century ago: kerosene lamps, drinking water carried in by the jugful, and one-hole privies. A crank-operated, emergency telephone system strung throughout the canyons provides a tenuous link with the outside world.

On this rambling loop hike to and from Hoegees Trail Camp on Winter Creek, you'll get a good feel for the riparian splendor that attracted early residents and day-trippers, and that still attracts legions of hikers today. (Since there are about a dozen stream crossings on the route without benefit of bridges, you'll want to avoid this trip after heavy rain.) Native alders, oaks, bays, and willows cluster along the bubbling, cascading streams. Ivy and vinca, planted by the early settlers, have run rampant in some areas, climbing high into the trees in a fashion reminiscent of the kudzu-vine invasion of the American Southeast. Both canyons have been plugged in many places with crib dams—check dams constructed of precast concrete logs—but more than 30 years of steady regrowth have softened their visual impact.

Start at the south edge of the lower parking lot at Chantry Flat, where a gated, paved road (the Gabrielino Trail) starts descending into Big Santa Anita Canyon. After rounding the first sharp bend (0.2 mile), veer right onto an unmarked trail (First Water Trail), which was once a lateral branch of the original Sturtevant Trail between the San Gabriel Valley and Sturtevant Camp (see Trip 4). Descend on pre-cipitous switchbacks (watch your step!) to the stream below, where an appropriately named First Water Camp welcomed hot and footsore hikers in the '20s and '30s. Turn left (upstream) and follow the rudiments of a trail amid streamside cabins and boulders to the confluence of Big Santa Anita Canyon and Winter Creek, where a paved drive comes down from Chantry Flat. Today, only a small restroom building occupies a flat area nearby (1780') where the largest resort of the area, Roberts' Camp, sprawled early during the century. During the peak of its popularity, a branch of the L.A. County Library and a post office were established here to serve guests and passing hikers.

From the confluence, head west into the steep-walled confines of Winter Creek. The well-traveled trail snakes upward, sometimes along the stream, otherwise up on the canyon walls in order to bypass crib dams or to swing by cabins. After 1.5 miles (from the confluence) you come to Hoegees Trail Camp (tables, stoves), tucked into a shady nook on Winter Creek's south bank. Nearby are the scattered foundation ruins of Hoegee's Camp (later called Camp Ivy), a hiker's resort established in 1908, and destroyed by wildfire in 1953. Today, Hoegees is one of the more popular trail camps in the San Gabriels—charming, rustic, and easy to reach by way of the Upper Winter Creek Trail from Chantry Flat.

Your looping return is by way of the Upper Winter Creek Trail. From Hoegees, continue upstream on the north bank, passing the Mt. Zion Trail on the right. Presently, the trail swings left to cross the stream and climb obliquely up Winter Creek's south canyon wall. In a short while you reach a signed junction—right toward Mt. Wilson, left back to your starting point a crooked 2.6 miles away. About 0.3 mile from the end, the trail joins a paved section of San Olene Fire Road; it will take you down past the picnic area to the upper parking lot at Chantry Flat.

Area A-6, Trip 3
Sturtevant Falls

	Distance	3.4 miles round trip
	Total Elevation Gain/Loss	700'/700'
	Hiking Time	1½ hours (round trip)
	Optional Map	USGS 7.5-min *Mount Wilson*
	Best Times	All year
	Agency	ANF/ASD
	Difficulty	★★

At Sturtevant Falls, the waters of Big Santa Anita Canyon leap (or dribble, depending on the season) over a 50' precipice into a shallow pool. Sturtevant Falls ranks, along with falls of a similar stature in Millard and San Antonio canyons, as one of the more impressive and yet easily reached waterfalls in Southern California. A local attraction since the days of the early resorts, it still draws hundreds of visitors on some fair-weather weekends. To avoid the crowds and gain some feeling of majesty in this special spot, it's best to pay a visit on a weekday. Better yet, come on an overcast day, when flat lighting enhances the subdued colors of the rocks, the trees, and the frothing water.

From the south edge of the lower parking lot at Chantry Flat, hike the first, paved segment of the Gabrielino Trail down to the confluence of Winter Creek and Big Santa Anita Canyon (0.6 mile). Pavement ends at a metal bridge spanning Winter Creek. Pass the restrooms and continue up alder-lined Big Santa Anita Canyon on a wide road bed following the left bank. Edging alongside a number of small cabins, the deteriorating road soon assumes the proportions of a foot trail.

At 1.4 miles, amidst a beautiful oak woodland, you come to a 4-way junction of trails. Take the right fork and continue upstream, boulder-hopping over the clear-flowing stream part of the way (and perhaps getting your feet wet for the first time), to the foot of the falls. Don't be tempted to

climb the sidewalls; the two trails going left back at the 4-way junction can take you safely past the falls if you want to press on farther up the canyon.

Sturtevant Falls

Area A-6, Trip 4
Mount Zion Loop

	Distance	9.4 miles
	Total Elevation Gain/Loss	2100'/2100'
	Hiking Time	5½ hours
	Optional Map	USGS 7.5-min *Mount Wilson*
	Best Times	October through June
	Agency	ANF/ASD
	Difficulty	★★★

Sturtevant Camp is both the oldest (1893) and the only remaining resort of the Big Santa Anita drainage. Run by the Methodist Church as a retreat (but available to other groups by reservation), the camp remains accessible only by foot trail. Supplies are packed in from Chantry Flat on the backs of pack animals, not unlike a century ago. Today's pack trains ply the Gabrielino Trail up Big Santa Anita Canyon past Sturtevant Falls. Around the turn of the century, however, travelers and supplies came by way of a trail hacked out by Wilbur M. ("Sturde") Sturtevant and some associates. Beginning in Sierra Madre, this original Sturtevant Trail worked its way along the high, west wall of lower Big Santa Anita Canyon; crossed a shady spot later known as Chantry Flat; traversed Winter Creek at a point near today's Hoegees Trail Camp; ascended a hot, dry slope to a notch just below Mt. Zion; and finally slanted downward to Sturtevant's camp in Big Santa Anita's headwaters.

In this scenic loop trip from Chantry Flat, you'll climb by way of the newer Gabrielino Trail to Sturtevant Camp, and return by way of the Mt. Zion and Upper Winter Creek trails—the original Sturtevant route. Do it in a day, or take your time on an overnight backpacking trip, with a stay at Spruce Grove Trail Camp. The trail camp is a popular one, so plan to get there early to secure a spot on the weekend—or go on a weekday.

As in Trip 3 above, proceed on the Gabrielino Trail to the 4-way junction of trails below Sturtevant Falls (1.4 miles). The right branch, as we've seen, goes up-canyon to the foot of the falls; the middle and left branches join again about a mile upstream. The left, upper trail is recommended for horses. Take the middle, or lower, trail—the more scenic and exciting alternative—unless you fear heights. The lower trail slices across a sheer wall above the falls and continues through a veritable fairyland of miniature cascades and crystalline pools bedecked with giant chain ferns.

A half mile past the reconvergence of the upper and lower trails, you come upon Cascade Picnic Area (2.8 miles—tables and restrooms here), named for a smooth chute in the stream bottom just below. Press on past a hulking crib dam to Spruce Grove Trail Camp (3.5 miles), named for the big-cone Douglas-fir (a.k.a. bigcone spruce) trees that attain truly inspiring proportions hereabouts.

A little higher, at a fork, the Gabrielino Trail forks right to climb toward Newcomb Pass (see Trip 13). You go left on the signed Sturtevant Trail. Go left again, 0.1 mile on, at the entrance to Sturtevant Camp. Cross above a crib dam to the opposite side of the creek from the camp, continue another 0.1 mile, and look for stone steps rising on the left—the beginning of the Mt. Zion Trail (3.9 miles). This restored version of Sturtevant's original trail (reconstructed in the late '70s and early '80s) winds delightfully upward across a ravine and then along timber-shaded, north-facing slopes.

When you reach the trail crest in a notch just northwest of Mt. Zion, take the side path up through manzanita and ceanothus to the summit, where a broad if somewhat unremarkable view can be had of surrounding ridges and a small slice of the San Gabriel Valley.

Return to the main trail and begin a long, switchback descent (1000 feet of elevation loss in about 1.5 miles) down the dry, north canyon wall of Winter Creek—a sweaty affair if the day is sunny and warm. At the foot of this stretch you reach the cool canyon bottom and a T-intersection with the Winter Creek Trail (6.7 miles), lying just above Hoegees Trail Camp. Turn right, going upstream momentarily, follow the trail across the creek, and climb to the next trail junction. Bear left on the Upper Winter Creek Trail and complete the remaining 2.6 miles, cool and semi-shaded most of the way.

Area A-6, Trip 5
Mount Wilson Loop

Distance	13.8 miles
Total Elevation Gain/Loss	3300'/3300'
Hiking Time	8 hours
Optional Map	USGS 7.5-min *Mount Wilson*
Best Times	October through June
Agency	ANF/ASD
Difficulty	★★★★

Basically an extension of Trip 4 above, this loop hike from Chantry Flat will take you all the way to Mt. Wilson, where a host of roads and trails converge. Completion of the entire loop is a respectable achievement, even for those in excellent physical condition. Of course, those with a penchant for downhill walking only, and the wherewithal to arrange the necessary transportation, can utilize either the uphill or the downhill segments described here as a strictly one-way downhill route. (If you plan to start topside and go down through Big Santa Anita Canyon, note that you must pass through a gate at Skyline Park, open daily only from 10 A.M. to 5 P.M., in order to reach the top end of the Sturtevant Trail.)

As in Trip 4's description, start from Chantry Flat's lower parking area and proceed to Sturtevant Camp (3.8 miles) using the Gabrielino Trail route up Big Santa Anita Canyon. Beyond the camp, continue up the left side of the main canyon on the Sturtevant Trail, in deep shade most of the while. A series of switchbacks begins at about 4.6 miles as the trail tackles a steep slope consisting of crumbling outcrops and decomposed granite soil. Usually there's some kind of trail maintenance going on—or at least badly needed—here. (Take care not to hasten erosion yourself by breaking off the edge of the trail. Hard-packed snow on this stretch would call for the use of an ice axe for safety.)

"Halfway Rest," at 5.2 miles, features a log bench in a restful, sylvan setting overlooking the uppermost reaches of Big Santa Anita Canyon. You're now exactly halfway between Sturtevant Camp, 1.4 miles below, and the top of the trail at Echo Rock on Mt. Wilson's east shoulder. Switchbacks continue on the upper 1.4-mile segment, now mostly through sunny chaparral.

Echo Rock (6.6 miles) features a grandstand view of ridges marching east toward Mt. San Antonio and south into the usual haze or smog blanket over the San Gabriel Valley. Continue west about 100 yards to a paved service road, and follow it west past the domes of the historic 60-inch and 100-inch reflector telescopes (each having held the distinction of being the world's largest telescope for a long period), the 150-foot-high solar telescope, and assorted smaller instruments. It was here that astronomer Edwin Hubble, using the great 100-inch Hooker Reflector in the '20s and '30s, gathered evidence that supported the notion of an expanding universe populated by billions of galaxies—the accepted modern view. Today, operations at the observatory have slowed to a crawl—light pollution has seriously hampered its effectiveness—but the observatory still maintains a small museum (on your right, open 10 A.M. to 4 P.M.) for the convenience of visitors and travelers like yourself.

At 7.0 miles you'll come to the "Pavilion," centerpiece of Skyline Park, a small picnic-and-sightseeing facility run by Metromedia, Inc. in the '60s and '70s, but now under Forest Service jurisdiction. A snackbar concession operates in the Pavilion today. To the west lies a string of towering radio and TV antennas. Virtually every major broadcasting station in the L.A. area transmits its signal from here.

After a bite to eat, exit through a gate to the west (one-way, westbound only for pedestrians from 5 P.M. to 10 A.M.) into a large, circular parking area. Two paths depart from the south side of this lot—a gated fire road (the old Mt. Wilson Toll Road from Altadena) and a foot trail (signed MT. WILSON TRAIL) that switchbacks downward to join the toll road on the saddle between Mt. Wilson and Mt. Harvard. Take the trail—it's shorter and more interesting.

On the saddle (7.8 miles), you'll find a cluster of Monterey pines and stone foundations, all that remains of Camp Wilson (a.k.a. Martin's Camp) a popular resort for hikers and sportsmen in the late 1800s and early 1900s. Continue downward on the old toll road 0.5 mile to the intersection of the Mt. Wilson Trail on the left, just as the toll road begins curving west. You follow a fire break down about 100 yards, then pick up a narrow trail to the right offering a gentler descent. It follows the sunny ridgeline between Winter Creek and Little Santa Anita Canyon, known variously as Manzanita Ridge and Santa Anita Ridge. At 8.8 miles, stay left atop the ridge as the Mt. Wilson Trail forks right and descends into Little Santa Anita Canyon. You're now on the Winter Creek Trail. At 9.6 miles, this trail veers left off the ridge and starts a long, crooked descent down Winter Creek's canyon wall. Hearty growths of live oak and bigcone Douglas-fir make this a cool and agreeable stretch, even though there's no relief from the jarring descent. Bigleaf maples near the bottom of the canyon herald your arrival at the junction (11.2 miles) with the trail to Hoegees on the left. Keep straight at this intersection and finish up the easy way—on the Upper Winter Creek Trail.

Area A-6, Trip 6
Mount Harvard

Distance	2.5 miles round trip
Total Elevation Gain/Loss	800'/800'
Hiking Time	1½ hours (round trip)
Recommended Map	USGS 7.5-min *Mount Wilson*
Best Times	All year
Agency	ANF/ASD
Difficulty	★★

Few tourists who drive up to Mt. Wilson for a view of the city, by day or by night, are aware that a more panoramic vantage point exists a short hike away. Mt. Harvard, a prominent bump on the ridge south of Mt. Wilson (named in the hopes that a Harvard University telescope would be located there) remains undeveloped, much as it was a century ago when tourists visiting nearby Martin's Camp climbed its summit for awe-inspiring vistas.

For a special treat, walk out to Harvard's summit at dusk on a clear winter evening. The carpet-like spread of lights down below is unforgettable.

The hike begins at the end of Mt. Wilson Road, about 4½ miles from Red Box, where there's a large, circular parking lot (always open) below Skyline Park. From the south edge of the lot, find and follow either the Mt. Wilson Trail (a footpath) or the former Mt. Wilson Toll Road (now a gated fire road). The latter route offers easier walking at night. At a point 0.7 mile below by way of the trail, or 0.9 mile below by way of the road, you arrive at the Wilson-Harvard saddle, where Martin's Camp stood. Some old foundations, a cluster of Monterey pines, and a newer concrete shed are there now. From the saddle, either of two routes can be used to reach Harvard's summit. You can go more easily by way of an old road slanting up the east slope. Or you can ferret out the unmaintained pathway—mostly west of the ridgeline—used a century ago by Martin's Camp guests.

Area A-6, Trip 7
Mount Wilson to Sierra Madre

Distance	7.4 miles
Total Elevation Gain/Loss	100'/4800'
Hiking Time	3½ hours
Optional Map	USGS 7.5-min *Mount Wilson*
Best Times	December through May
Agency	SMPD
Difficulty	★★★

On the Mt. Wilson Trail you can almost feel the weight of history. This is the oldest and most direct route connecting Mt. Wilson's summit and the San Gabriel Valley floor, and the first of many trails that were built to something resembling modern standards in the San Gabriel Mountains. In 1864, Benjamin Wilson widened and improved this former Indian path in order to exploit timber resources near the summit. Very little timber was actually cut, but the precipitous trail soon became popular among hikers and horsemen. By 1889, the first instrument placed on the mountaintop that would someday host the world's foremost observatory was hauled up in pieces on the same trail—a journey that took a month to accomplish.

By 1891, a "new" Mt. Wilson trail from the mouth of Eaton Canyon (Mt. Wilson Toll Road) was constructed, largely preempting the shorter but steeper older trail. Still in use today, the old trail remains a viable route only by virtue of the care of volunteers who maintain it.

The lower two thirds of the trail lies outside Angeles National Forest, but within a wilderness area administered by the City of Sierra Madre. The trail is open for day use without permit from about June 1 to December 15 each year, and closed during the summer and fall fire season except by special permit on certain low-fire-hazard days. The Sierra Madre Police Department (818-355-1414) issues the permits; closure fine is $50.

From the south edge of the parking lot at the end of Mt. Wilson Road, take the signed Mt. Wilson Trail, which immediately starts zigzagging down a steep slope. After 0.7 mile you join Mt. Wilson Toll Road. Continue on the old toll road 0.5 mile to the intersection of the Mt. Wilson Trail on the left, just as the toll road begins curving west. Follow a fire break down about 100 yards, then pick up a narrow trail to the right offering a gentler descent. At 1.7 miles, the Mt. Wilson Trail forks right and starts descending through chaparral into the headwaters of Little Santa Anita Canyon. Live oaks, sycamores, bigleaf maples, alders, and bigcone Douglas-firs cluster about the canyon bottom below. You cross the canyon bottom and descend along a shady, westside slope for a while. Next, a set of tight switchbacks takes you down to a wooded glen along the canyon stream at 3.5 miles.

There you'll find the foundation ruins of Orchard Camp (a resort), earlier known as Halfway House because it was located almost exactly half way between Mt. Wilson and the foot of the trail in Sierra Madre.

After a more-or-less level stretch under oaks, look for a side path to the left (4.3 miles) leading to an open spot—a sometime heliport—on the shoulder of a ridge overlooking the canyon. Thereafter, you begin an almost constant, steep descent across dry, chaparral slopes. In spring, sweet alyssum (a non-native escapee from foothill gardens) blooms along the path. The trail splits at 5.1 miles. An older, obscure branch goes down the canyon bottom to a spot called "First Water" and then up to the main trail again, while the newer branch stays high on the west slope. Below the reconvergence, retaining screens anchored to the canyon side have so far managed to keep the trail from slipping completely away.

The trail becomes a dirt road at 7.0 miles. Just beyond this point, take the path to the right, because the road ahead is private. You end up on a paved drive, and after 0.1 more mile reach the lower trailhead on Mira Monte Avenue. This trailhead is easily reached from Interstate 210 by following Baldwin Avenue north to Mira Monte.

Area A-6, Trip 8
Bailey Canyon

	Distance	1.2 miles round trip
	Total Elevation Gain/Loss	350'/350'
	Hiking Time	1 hour (round trip)
	Optional Map	USGS 7.5-min *Mount Wilson*
	Best Times	All year
	Agency	SMPD
	Difficulty	★

Sierra Madre's impeccably maintained Bailey Canyon Wilderness Park (at Carter Avenue and Oak Crest Drive) includes a small, shady picnic area, and the lower end of an unfinished trail that will one day tie into the Mt. Wilson Trail above Orchard Camp. As with the previous trip, permits (from the police department) are required for summer and fall use of the trail.

From the fenced parking lot and picnic area, walk through a gate to the west. Go up a paved service road past a Passionist Fathers monastery on the left, and a debris basin on the right. The road plays out, but you continue on trail up Bailey Canyon's usually dry bottom. You can bypass the unfinished trail on the right (which goes up the slope for about a mile) and follow the sandy stream bottom ahead to reach, 0.6 mile from the start, a dead end. Further travel is blocked by a 15' ledge—a dike of black gabbro rock wedged between lighter-colored granite. After a wet storm you could possibly wade this last stretch and behold an impressive waterfall here.

Area A-6, Trip 9
Eaton Canyon Falls

	Distance	3.4 miles round trip
	Total Elevation Gain/Loss	400'/400'
	Hiking Time	1½ hours (round trip)
	Optional Map	USGS 7.5-min *Mount Wilson*
	Best Times	All year
	Agency	ECCP
	Difficulty	★★

Dependably impressive during the wetter half of the year, Eaton Canyon Falls possesses, as John Muir once put it, "a low sweet voice, singing like a bird." Unfortunately, this all-too-easily-reached grotto has suffered from years of vandalism. The graffiti sprayed on the rock walls and broken glass strewn about are hard to ignore. One can only wish for a massive gully-washing storm to clear the mess out. Still, the falls are worth visiting, especially in the aftermath of a larger winter storm, if only to witness the power of large volumes of falling water. (Don't do this if the stream level rises to the point where it becomes dangerous to ford.)

Although it's not the shortest way in, you might as well enjoy a mile-long stroll down Eaton Wash before you enter the portals of the canyon. To do so, park in the lot beyond the nature center at Eaton Canyon County Park (entrance on Altadena Drive just north of New York Drive in Altadena).

The park's Eaton Canyon Trail crosses the cobbled flood plain (there's water here in the wet season), then sticks to an east-side stream terrace for a mile, passing some live-oak woods. At 0.5 mile you pass a horse trail going up a draw to the right, and at 1.1 miles, you rise to meet the Mt. Wilson Toll Road bridge over Eaton Canyon. Cross to the west end of the bridge, descend on the upstream side, and then make your way up the trailless canyon. You'll skip across rocks in the stream several times, or resort to wading. Except for a line of alders along part of the stream and some live oaks on benches just above the reach of floods, the canyon bottom and the precipitous walls are desert-like.

After ½ mile of canyon-bottom travel, you reach the base of the falls, where the water slides and then free-falls a total of about 35 vertical feet down a narrow chute in the bedrock.

If you prefer, you can shorten the walk to the falls by starting from the lower gate of Mt. Wilson Toll Road on Pinecrest Drive; or

Eaton Canyon Falls

by parking in a dirt lot just east of Altadena Drive across from Roosevelt Avenue, and descending a path leading to Eaton Canyon's floor, 0.5 mile south of the toll-road bridge.

Area A-6, Trip 10
Henninger Flats

	Distance	5.4 miles round trip
	Total Elevation Gain/Loss	1400'/1400'
	Hiking Time	3 hours (round trip)
	Optional Map	USGS 7.5-min *Mount Wilson*
	Best Times	October through June
	Agency	HFFS
	Difficulty	★★★

Park-like Henninger Flats is a pleasant surprise to come upon after the sunny, often sweaty climb up the lower end of Mt. Wilson Toll Road. The flats and slopes hereabouts have been the site of an experimental forest for more than 60 years now, with seedlings of pine, cypress, cedar, and other trees raised for reforestation projects. Run by the Los Angeles County Fire Department, the area encompasses four delightful camp and picnic areas, a visitor center, a pioneer museum, a short nature trail, and a seedling nursery. The visitor center features a large relief model of the Mt. Wilson/Front Range area, and outside there's a diminutive lookout structure that stood on Castro Peak in the Santa Monica Mountains during 1925–71. Henninger Flats' half-mile-high elevation perched directly over the edge of the city gives it a commanding view—by day and especially by night. Backpackers register with the ranger on duty. Campfire permits and wood are usually available.

The old toll road—now a fire road used by fire-department or forestry trucks, and plenty of self-propelled travelers of all sorts—starts at 2260 Pinecrest Drive (0.5 mile east of Allen Avenue and Altadena

Drive. Walk through a gate (open between sunrise and one hour after sunset) and down across a bridge over Eaton Canyon. Dogged determination, and hopefully the inspiration of fabulous views over the big city below, will get you up the moderately steep and steady grade ahead. This well-engineered road/former trail was built and improved (among other reasons) to haul telescope parts to the summit of Mt. Wilson, including those of the 100-inch Hooker Reflector—the world's largest telescope for 31 years.

You can easily use up a couple of extra hours at Henninger Flats poking around the museum and the visitor center and taking short side trips to check out the groves of trees. For the best view of the surroundings, I'd recommend climbing a little higher to Henninger Ridge: continue upward on Mt. Wilson Toll Road another 0.6 mile, and turn left on the dirt road that loops around to a heliport. This puts you on the shoulder of a ridge perched 400 feet above the groves of Henninger Flats, where the view of the city below stretches 180°. From the north side of the ridge, Mt. Wilson rears up starkly, 2½ miles away. After a winter storm, the spike-shaped antennas on its crest look exactly like upside-down icicles.

Mt. Wilson from Henninger Ridge

Area A-6, Trip 11
Idlehour Descent

	Distance	10.8 miles
	Total Elevation Gain/Loss	1200'/5300'
	Hiking Time	5 hours
	Optional Map	USGS 7.5-min *Mount Wilson*
	Best Times	October through June
	Agency	ANF/ASD
	Difficulty	★★★★

Not an idle descent at all, this one-way hike passes through some of the most varied and interesting terrain in the Front Range. From shady canyon to mountainside view, the landscape is ever changing along the way. Over a distance of almost 11 miles on roads and trails, you journey 4 air-line miles from the crest of the Front Range at Eaton Saddle all the way down to the edge of the L.A. Basin at Eaton Canyon County Park. The name "Idlehour" comes from Idlehour Trail Camp, formerly a trail resort, passed at the midway point of the hike. (Note: area map A-5 in this book shows the first part of this route at a more generous scale than map A-6.)

You start at the parking lot at unmarked Eaton Saddle, mile 2.4 on Mt. Wilson Road (2.4 miles up the road from Red Box). You'll end at Eaton Canyon County Park (entrance on Altadena Drive just north of New York Drive in Altadena).

From Eaton Saddle, follow Mt. Lowe Fire Road 0.5 mile west to Markham Saddle, where trails intersect left and right. Bear left on the Mt. Lowe Trail.

At a trail junction (1.3 miles) the Mt. Lowe west trail comes in acutely from the right. Keep straight to remain on the shorter, better-maintained east-side route down along the flank of the mountain. (See Area A-5, Trips 5 and 11 for more on this area.) At 2.1 miles you can either drop to the fire road on your right or stay on the trail another 0.2 mile to meet the same fire road farther south. Continue walking south on the fire road, curving left toward Inspiration Point as the road on the right descends to Mt. Lowe Trail Camp. About 100 feet farther, turn left on the Idlehour Trail (2.4 miles).

Descend through scattered north-slope groves of live oak and bigcone Douglas-firs to a crossing of a west fork of Eaton Canyon, 3.7 miles. You then climb a bit to cross a chaparral-covered divide to the east, and begin a switchback descent into Eaton Canyon. Look for the fault-like discontinuity in the igneous rock exposed on Eaton Canyon's sheer east wall.

At the bottom (4.8 miles) the trail goes down-canyon and becomes intermittently lost in a refreshingly chilly wonderland of crystal-clear cascades, overarching oaks and maples, and crispy carpets of orange and brown leaf-litter. Cabin foundation ruins can be found under the trees, a reminder that even in this inviting hideaway, no construction is spared for long the ravages of fire and flood—or in this case removal by the Pasadena Water Department. After some easy boulder-hopping, you come to Idlehour Trail Camp (5.4 miles), nestled on an oak-shaded flat lying next to a rock fin, with vertical striations, dividing Eaton Canyon from its aforementioned west fork. Naturally, this is the best place for a picnic if you're day-hiking, or home for the night if you're backpacking the route.

The narrow, wild section of Eaton Canyon below the camp was eschewed by trail builders in favor of a route up the east canyon wall to Mt. Wilson Toll Road. (Some people have followed the dangerous lower canyon route, including John Muir, who later described the front face of the San Gabriels as "rigidly inaccessible.") The safe and easy Idlehour Trail goes east up a tributary (Harvard Branch) momentarily, then climbs up and over a ridge to meet Mt. Wilson Toll Road (6.9 miles).

Descend on the old toll road past Henninger Flats (8.1 miles) to a hairpin turn (9.8 miles), where an equestrian trail (sign says EATON CANYON TRAIL) takes off down the slope to the left. Switchbacks, steep at times, take you down 0.5 mile to the wide Eaton Canyon Trail following Eaton Canyon wash. Turn left and complete the remaining 0.5 mile to the nature center at Eaton Canyon County Park.

Area A-6, Trip 12
Rattlesnake-Valley Forge Trail

Distance	7.6 miles
Total Elevation Gain/Loss	1750'/2300'
Hiking Time	4 hours
Optional Maps	USGS 7.5-min *Mount Wilson, Chilao Flat*
Best Times	October through June
Agency	ANF/ASD
Difficulty	★★★

The proposed Falls Canyon Research Natural Area on the north slope of Mt. Wilson would help protect, primarily for research and education, a steeply sloping, 1,030-acre block of land covered by magnificent stands of bigcone Douglas-fir and canyon live oak. Today, you can travel the perimeter of this delightfully cool and shady area without restriction. Our route follows the Rattlesnake, Gabrielino, and Valley Forge trails, completing about four fifths of a circle. (You can make this a full-circle hike if you close the loop by walking 2 miles along the narrow shoulders of Mt. Wilson Road. If you start early, you can walk Mt. Wilson Road first, before traffic picks up.)

The Rattlesnake Trail begins on the north side of Mt. Wilson Road, 4.4 miles from Red Box, where Mt. Wilson Road splits and becomes a one-way loop around an antenna-spiked ridgeline. Parking space is available in a roadside turnout to the west. On long and sometimes poorly maintained

switchbacks, you descend the drainage of Strayns Canyon, crossing the stream of the main canyon or tributaries at least four times. (The canyon's name is apparently a corruption of the the the name of A.G. Strain, who operated a tourist camp on Mt. Wilson's north slope in the 1890s.) Deeply shaded by alders and bigleaf maples down along the stream, this is a thoroughly enjoyable stretch.

At 3.0 miles there's an easy-to-miss junction. The combined Rattlesnake/Gabrielino Trail continues down-canyon, on the right-hand side of the stream, to Rincon-Red Box Road. You go left, across the stream, westbound on the Gabrielino Trail. On it you contour, more or less, through shady glens or through sunny thickets of chaparral highlighted by big, gorgeous manzanitas.

At 4.9 miles you come to an intersection with the Valley Forge Trail, which is your route back up to Mt. Wilson Road. On the Gabrielino Trail, just beyond this junction, there's a side path to Valley Forge Campground down along the bank of West Fork San Gabriel River. This makes a good overnight campsite for trail travelers, as the road from Red Box is now gated year round. Under consideration as an officially sanctioned off-road vehicle route some years ago, the Rincon-Red Box Road instead was closed in 1989 to motor use by the public as a cost-cutting measure. This closure, which may be permanent, has instantly transformed the upper West Fork country into a *de facto* primitive area, much to the benefit

of wilderness-loving hikers, horsemen, and mountain bikers. The two former drive-in campgrounds along the upper West Fork are now quiet (check with the Forest Service to find out what facilities, such as drinking water, are available).

On the Valley Forge Trail you go up through the semi-shade of oaks, bays, and tall chaparral—first on switchbacks, then on a straighter course high on the west wall of Falls Canyon. At 7.6 miles you reach the Eaton Saddle parking lot on Mt. Wilson Road, 2.4 miles up from Red Box and 2 miles west of your starting point.

Area A-6, Trip 13
Angeles Crest to Chantry Flat

	Distance	11.0 miles
	Total Elevation Gain/Loss	1800'/4400'
	Hiking Time	7 hours
	Recommended Maps	USGS 7.5-min *Chilao Flat,* *Mt. Wilson*
	Best Times	October through June
	Agency	ANF/ASD
	Difficulty	★★★★

This wide-ranging traverse takes you from Shortcut Saddle to Chantry Flat, through wooded and fern-draped canyons, and over a major divide. The closure of the Rincon-Red Box Road to motor vehicles has made this area effectively more remote from civilization (and any form of help in an emergency) than it has been for decades.

The drive between start and end points takes well over an hour at best, so a good arrangement would be to line up someone to drop you off on Angeles Crest Highway and later pick you up at Chantry Flat.

Shortcut Saddle is considered to be on the nebulous dividing line between the "Front Range" of the San Gabriels, south and west, and the "High Country," of which Charlton-Chilao Recreation Area (see Area A-7), just north, is a part.

You'll find Shortcut Saddle at the point where the Silver Moccasin Trail crosses Angeles Crest Highway, mile 43.3 according to the mile-markers. The Silver Moccasin Trail, in theory given special attention by its classification as a National Recreation Trail, dates from 1942, when Boy Scouts mapped out what is now a 52-mile route from Chantry Flat to Vincent Gap near Mt. Baden-Powell. Today it combines with parts of the Pacific Crest and Gabrielino trails. The part of the Silver Moccasin Trail you'll be traveling on was originally Newcomb's Trail, a turn-of-the-century short-cut route for hikers and sportsmen between Big Santa Anita Canyon and the High Country.

From the south side of Angeles Crest Highway at Shortcut Saddle, the trail zigzags down 120 vertical feet to a dirt road. Turn right, go 0.1 mile along the road, and then turn left on the continuation of the trail. You now descend hot, south-facing, chaparral-covered slopes, finally settling into the aptly named Shortcut Canyon (1.5 miles). There's only a trickle here winter through spring, but more and more water ahead. At one point, the trail passes directly beneath the exposed root system of a bigleaf maple that will surely tumble in the next great flood. Manmade improvements in the form of gabions (rock-filled, wire-mesh structures used to stabilize the banks) are seen not long before you reach Shortcut Canyon's confluence with the West Fork San Gabriel River.

Cross West Fork to reach West Fork Campground (3.2 miles) and the site of a historic ranger station built in 1900, now removed to Chilao. Either this camp or Devore Camp ahead is good for overnight stays.

From West Fork Campground, go east (downstream), fording the river again almost immediately. Your sometimes-obscure trail meanders down one of the most beautiful riparian stretches in the county. The stream slides over and around smooth boulders, while sunlight filtering though the tall alders and maples glances off lens-like convexities and concavities on the water surface.

At Devore Camp (4.2 miles), you turn away from the river and head south—very steeply at first—up along a shady draw to the south. Soon the upgrade eases. Endless switchbacks take you 1300 vertical feet up past a crossing of Rincon-Red Box Road to Newcomb Pass (5.7 miles), where a couple of picnic tables have been thoughtfully placed. Ignoring both the Rim Trail to Mt. Wilson to the right, and the spur of a fire road to the left, continue south into the watershed of Big Santa Anita Canyon.

The gradual descent across a sun-baked chaparral slope (great views from here on a clear day), then through oak and bay woods, leads to a trail junction (7.6 miles), deep in the shaded bowels of Big Santa Anita. Turning downstream on a now-well-traveled stretch of the Gabrielino Trail, you pass Spruce Grove Trail Camp, Cascade Picnic Area, and Sturtevant Falls. From the Winter Creek confluence, follow the crowds up the paved road to Chantry Flat.

Big Santa Anita Canyon below Spruce Grove

Area A-7: Charlton-Chilao Recreation Area

Gateway to the High Country of the San Gabriel Mountains, the Charlton-Chilao Recreation Area draws a good fraction of the travelers headed east on Angeles Crest Highway from Los Angeles. On the way up there are scattered trees aplenty along the highway, but at Charlton Flats the traveler first comes upon what looks like true forest—stately pines, firs and cedars. It's plain to see the Forest Service has gone all-out to accommodate large numbers of visitors. Charlton Flats Picnic Area (entrance at mile 47.5 on Angeles Crest Highway, 24 miles east of I-210 at La Canada) has over 100 tables and stoves.

Three miles beyond Charlton Flats is a turnoff (mile 50.6) for the new Chilao Visitor Center. This is *the* major interpretive facility in the Angeles National Forest, with exhibits, lots of free printed information, books for sale, scheduled summer activities, and knowledgeable rangers on duty. Three short interpretive trails start from here and loop outward into the forest. The center is open daily, admission free. Groups may arrange for special tours. Phone (818) 796-5541 for more information.

The blacktop road to the visitor center continues past spacious camp and picnic grounds, and returns to the highway. Newcomb's Ranch Cafe, the first commercial establishment on Angeles Crest Highway up from La Canada, is around the corner from the visitor center. (Important note: your car should be gassed up before driving to the High Country; there are no service stations on the 60-mile stretch between La Canada and Wrightwood.)

Winter snows block access (by car) from the highway to Charlton Flats and part of the Chilao complex, but that's no reason not to come. Both areas, with their meandering, gently graded access roads, are perfect for cross-country skiing after the bigger winter storms. Unplowed Santa Clara Divide Road from Three Points is another good bet. (Hint: go on weekdays or arrive early in the morning on weekends and holidays.) Restrooms and plowed parking areas are maintained at the entrance to Charlton Flat Picnic Area, at Chilao Visitor Center, and at Three Points. A snow-play area suitable for kids is located at Upper Chilao Picnic Area, just beyond the visitor center.

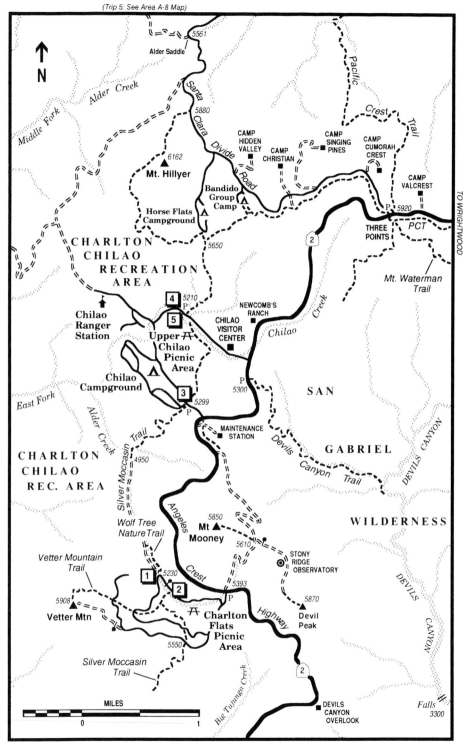

(Trip 5: See Area A-8 Map)

Area A-7: Charlton-Chilao Recreation Area

Area A-7, Trip 1
Wolf Tree Nature Trail

Distance	0.5 mile
Total Elevation Gain/Loss	50'/50'
Hiking Time	½ hour
Optional Map	USGS 7.5-min *Chilao Flat*
Best Times	All year
Agency	ANF/ASD
Difficulty	★

Tucked away in a far corner of the sprawling Charlton Flats Picnic Area is the Wolf Tree Nature Trail, one of the more interesting self-guiding trails in the National Forest. After turning into the picnic area from Angeles Crest Highway, swing right at the first intersection and continue on pavement 0.6 mile to a gate. The trail starts beyond the gate, on the right. (During the off-season, part or all of the picnic area may be closed to auto traffic; you may have to walk a little to reach the trailhead.)

The trail runs along a conifer-shaded draw, wet only during times of snowmelt.

Among other features, the interpretive plaques point out clear evidence of a fire in 1878. While other woods have long since rotted away, fallen logs and standing snags of durable incense cedar are still in evidence.

The "wolf tree"—the dominant tree of the forest—is in this case an outsized (roughly 100 feet tall) Coulter pine. Since Coulter pine cones are the largest and heaviest of the native conifers (up to 14 inches in length and 5 pounds), you would not want to spend much time beneath that wolf tree.

Area A-7, Trip 2
Vetter Mountain

Distance	3.3 miles
Total Elevation Gain/Loss	700'/700'
Hiking Time	1½ hours
Optional Map	USGS 7.5-min *Chilao Flat*
Best Times	All year
Agency	ANF/ASD
Difficulty	★★

Vetter Mountain's pint-sized fire-lookout building, perched on a rounded summit nearly devoid of vegetation, takes advantage of a 360° view over the midsection of the San Gabriels. But fire watchers no longer spend lonely vigils here in cramped quarters. Instead, the lookout may be moved down to the Chilao Visitor Center for use as an interpretive exhibit.

Aside from visiting Vetter's summit, this loop-hike also includes pleasant passages through Charlton Flats' heterogeneous forest of live oak, Coulter pine, Jeffrey pine, sugar pine, incense cedar, and bigcone

Douglas-fir. With binoculars, a bird book, and a wildflower guide, you and your kids can take your sweet time, stopping as you please to admire a soaring hawk or raven, a noisy acorn woodpecker or Steller's jay, or an unfamiliar plant in bloom.

As in Trip 1 above, drive (or walk) to the start of the Wolf Tree Nature Trail. Across the road to the west, starting up the south side of a ravine, is a signed path to Vetter Mountain, uphill all the way. About 200 yards up the path, the Silver Moccasin Trail swings left—don't take it; this is your return route. Keeping straight, you ascend through mixed forest and then scattered pines, crossing paved service roads twice. A final switchbacking stretch through chaparral leads to the lookout, 1.3 miles from the start.

Looking north and east from the lookout perch, you'll spot Pacifico Mountain, Mt. Williamson, Waterman Mountain, Twin Peaks, Old Baldy, and other High Country summits. The Front Range sprawls west and south, blocking from view most of the city.

When it's time to descend, follow the dirt road downhill instead of the trail. After 0.7 mile you'll meet a paved service road. Continue straight (east) on the pavement for another 0.6 mile and look carefully for the crossing of the Silver Moccasin Trail. Turn left on the trail, cross pavement again in a short while, and complete the final, mostly level stretch across a forested slope.

Area A-7, Trip 3
Chilao-Charlton Loop

Distance	5.4 miles
Total Elevation Gain/Loss	800'/800'
Hiking Time	3 hours
Optional Maps	USGS 7.5-min *Chilao Flat, Waterman Mtn.*
Best Times	October through June
Agency	ANF/ASD
Difficulty	★★★

This trip makes use of a variety of dirt roads, paved roads, and trails to accomplish a circumnavigation of Mt. Mooney, one of several small summits rising above the flats of Charlton-Chilao. If the air is crystal-clear, an optional side trip to either Mt. Mooney or Devil Peak (involving extra mileage) is highly recommended as well.

Let's assume you start the hike along the entrance road to Chilao Campground: turn west off Angeles Crest Highway at mile 49.7, and drive 0.2 mile to a small parking area where the signed Silver Moccasin Trail crosses the entrance road.

On foot, go south up along a brushy hill overlooking some campsites (the trail is easy to lose at first) and then crookedly down along a brushy ravine. At 0.9 mile, you reach an attractive pine-fringed valley—East Fork Alder Creek. Here you pick up a dirt road and continue south up along the East Fork to join a hairpin curve on a paved service road (1.9 miles) just below the edge of Charlton Flats Picnic Area. Bear left and continue uphill on pavement to the restroom building at the entrance to the picnic area (2.8 miles). From there, walk across Angeles Crest Highway and pick up a dirt road (not directly across the highway, but a little to the left) going north. This road takes you up to a saddle (3.5 miles) on the ridge between Mt. Mooney and Devil Peak.

Both peaks are dotted with Jeffrey and Coulter pines, making them good sites for a picnic, but the view from Devil is far superior as it includes more of the rugged San Gabriel Wilderness and also (when the smog is lying low) Santa Catalina Island. Both peaks have climbers' registers, although few people sign in at Devil Peak. The side trip to Devil is 0.8 mile each way, first on a dirt road and then on a steep fire break. Mooney's ascent from the saddle is just 0.4 mile by way of a steep trail.

From the saddle, your circle route continues north on the fire road down a sparsely wooded slope. After two hairpin turns and a stretch through chaparral, the road swings back to Angeles Crest Highway (4.8 miles). Just short of where the road reaches the highway, turn right onto the old trail that contours through chaparral alongside the highway. This is really a piece of the original highway (dirt road) that preceded the present paved highway. Follow this to an access road leading to a Caltrans maintenance station. Jog left on the access road, right on Angeles Crest Highway, and left on the entrance road to Chilao Campground.

Area A-7, Trip 4
Mount Hillyer

	Distance	5.8 miles
	Total Elevation Gain/Loss	1100'/1100'
	Hiking Time	3 hours
	Optional Map	USGS 7.5-min *Chilao Flat*
	Best Times	All year
	Agency	ANF/ASD
	Difficulty	★★★

Lovers of the high Sierra Nevada may get some sense of deja vu atop the rounded ridge known as Mt. Hillyer. The breeze sings in the branches of sugar pines, Jeffrey pines, Coulter pines and bigcone Douglas-firs. Angular outcrops and large boulder piles lie on the slopes. The granite here is not so fractured and pulverized as it is in other parts of the San Gabriels. The view is only fair; the main attractions are the peace and quiet, and the pine-scented air.

For small kids the complete loop route described here is long, steep in parts, and challenging, but you can customize the hike to suit your needs. Horse Flats Campground can be reached by car in the warmer part of the year from Three Points. You could start the Hillyer climb from the campground, or end a trip there by making use of a car shuttle.

Our loop route starts near Upper Chilao Picnic Area, at a small parking lot for users of the Silver Moccasin Trail. To reach it, drive 0.7 mile up the side road that passes Chilao Visitor Center.

Start hiking north on the Silver Moccasin Trail, using switchbacks to gain a slope covered by scattered pines and dense, sweet-smelling chaparral. From just south of Horse Flats Campground (1.1 mile), the Silver Moccasin Trail continues over a low ridge to the east, but you veer left (west) toward Mt. Hillyer's south ridge. Well-beaten, sometimes steep switchbacks take you to a rounded summit area, where two high points (6200+ feet) lie. Continue down the ridge to the northeast, passing a 6162' knoll labelled Mt. Hillyer on the topo map.

Due north of the 6162' knoll, an old road bed goes sharply downhill. Follow it to paved Santa Clara Divide Road (3.5 miles), which carries no traffic during the off-season, and light traffic otherwise. Turn right, walk south on the road 0.5 mile to the Horse Flats Campground turnoff, then go 0.7 mile to the south end of the campground. There you can pick up the Silver Moccasin Trail and retrace your steps back to Chilao.

Granite boulders
on Mt. Hillyer

Area A-7, Trip 5
Pacifico Mountain Traverse

👞	**Distance**	11.3 miles
	Total Elevation Gain/Loss	2600'/2900'
	Hiking Time	7 hours
🧭	**Recommended Maps**	7.5-min *Pacifico Mountain, Chilao Flat*
	Best Times	March through November
🏔️↗🚶	**Agency**	ANF/ASD
	Difficulty	★★★

This rambling, one-way hike from the crest of Angeles Forest Highway (Mill Creek Summit) to Upper Chilao Picnic Area takes you over the top of Pacifico Mountain, a pine-fringed rampart overlooking the Mojave Desert from a commanding 7124' elevation. There are several ways to accomplish this goal; the route described here is rather direct and includes some passages over steep, trailless terrain—difficult with a heavy pack.

Spring and fall are usually the best seasons to do the trip. Parts of the route can be snowbound for weeks in winter, while summer temperatures often hit the 90s. Summer's good if you're going to camp overnight along the way: you can avoid most of the heat by leaving in late afternoon and concluding your hike early the next morning.

Refer to maps A-7 and A-8 in this book when reading the text below. Neither of the recommended topo maps shows any part of the Pacific Crest Trail, but they're useful for navigation if you lose your way. The car shuttle between start and end points is 24 miles (about 35 minutes) by way of Angeles Forest Highway, Upper Big Tujunga Road, and Angeles Crest Highway.

The starting point, Mill Creek Summit, is 24 miles from La Canada by way of Angeles Crest and Angeles Forest highways, or 23 miles from Sunland via Big Tujunga Canyon and Angeles Forest Highway. When you approach the summit, you'll see a picnic area (with water fountain) on the south side. Turn south on a paved side-road here and drive 0.3 mile to a PCT trailhead parking area.

From the parking area, an often-gated dirt road—Pacifico Mountain Road (an unadventurous route to Chilao)—takes off up a slope to the south. You go east, across the pavement and down-slope a few yards to pick up the PCT. Turn right and commence a gentle, coiling ascent across generally north-facing slopes. The mostly chaparral-covered slopes (scrub oak, manzanita, and ceanothus) are relieved occasionally by groves of mixed-conifer forest (bigcone Douglas-fir, incense cedar, white fir, and Jeffrey pine) clinging to the sides of the north-flowing ravines.

At 3.2 miles, the PCT rounds the nose of a ridge overlooking Santiago Canyon, and turns abruptly south on a old road bed going up a ridgeline dotted by Jeffrey pines. After another 0.5 mile, you bear left on the narrower PCT; the road bed continues south to meet Pacifico Mountain Road. A rather level stretch, and then a climb, takes you around the headwaters of Santiago Canyon to a saddle (5.4 miles) west of Pacifico Mountain's summit, where you nearly touch a road going up the mountain's south flank. There are several alternatives here: you could circle the mountain's north flank on the PCT, or pick up one of the dirt roads to the south that either climbs or bypasses the summit. To get right down to the task at hand, however, leave the PCT at this point and scramble straight up to Pacifico's summit on the loose-dirt slope to the east (450 vertical feet in 0.3 mile).

On top, the panoramic view encompasses the Antelope Valley, much of the San Gabriels, and even a slice of Pacific Ocean. Small, waterless and often underused Mt. Pacifico Campground (labelled Upper Pacifico Campground on the topo map), just east of the summit boulder pile, is a great place to camp overnight.

When it's time to move on, follow the campground's access road down the ridge to the southeast. Where the road swings abruptly right, continue southeast down a spur road that soon plays out. Continue southeast (not south) down an old fire break, more or less parallel to a now-overgrown foot trail plotted on the topo maps. You should end up rejoining the PCT on a saddle 0.1 mile north of, and 180 feet higher than, a bend in Pacifico Mountain Road. Take the steep path (not much more than a game trail) that leads down to the road. You've now come 7.1 miles from Mill Creek Summit.

Follow Pacifico Mountain Road east to a seasonal gate at Alder Saddle (8.0 miles), where you meet paved Santa Clara Divide Road. You could have planned to finish the hike here (assuming the vehicle gate at Three Points is open), but we'll presume you're continuing south to Chilao. Follow Santa Clara Divide Road uphill to a 5880' summit, then downhill to the Horse Flats Campground turnoff. Go to the south end of the campground, and on down the Silver Moccasin Trail to Upper Chilao Picnic Area—pleasant and easy walking all the way.

Area A-8: Little Rock

Popular on holidays and weekends among sightseers, off-road-vehicle drivers and fishermen, Littlerock Canyon (as it's referred to by the Forest Service) offers hikers plenty of wide-open hiking space as well. Your visits will be rewarding (as mine were) if you avoid the weekends and instead explore the area on the weekdays.

This is pinyon-juniper and chaparral country, with a touch of high desert—a few Joshua trees at the edge of their range eke out an existence along the margins of Little Rock Reservoir. It's hot in summer, chilly (even snow-dusted) in winter, but delightfully warm in spring and fall.

Littlerock Recreation Area—the developed area adjacent to the reservoir—has four Forest Service campgrounds and a small store, along with 125 acres of reservoir flood plain reserved for off-road vehicle free-play. Official "green-sticker" ORV trails climb east up Alimony Ridge and southwest up Santiago Canyon. The Forest Service has erected numerous barriers to curb illegal ORV use off these designated routes.

Littlerock Canyon can be approached either by way of an all-weather route from the north or a seasonal route from the south. From south of Palmdale in the north, exit Antelope Valley Freeway (Highway 14) on Pearblossom Highway. After 5.5 miles, bear right at the traffic light, staying on Pearblossom Highway. One block farther, turn right (south) on Cheseboro Road. Continue south past the Little Rock Ranger Station to the reservoir.

From the south, use Santa Clara Divide Road (see maps A-7 and A-8) to reach the poor dirt road that goes north past Pinyon Flats Shooting Area and then down into Littlerock Canyon. Check first with the Forest Service to see if this route is open. Camping is not permitted along this dirt road.

Area A-8, Trip 1
Little Rock Creek

Distance	2 miles round trip
Total Elevation Gain/Loss	400'/400'
Hiking Time	1½ hours (round trip)
Optional Map	USGS 7.5-min *Juniper Hills*
Best Times	All year
Agency	ANF/VD
Difficulty	★★

Whenever accessible by road, the small pools and riffles at the confluence of Little Rock Creek's main and south forks draw plenty of fishermen and motoring sightseers. The main stream comes tumbling out of the mountains to the east year round, delivering

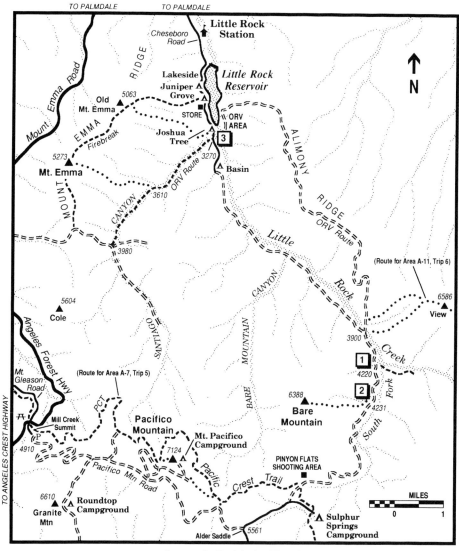

Area A-8: Little Rock

cold, clean water from the slopes of Mt. Williamson, Kratka Ridge, and Waterman Mountain. Hikers and fishermen have worn trails upstream from the confluence, both along the main branch of the creek itself and along a sloping terrace that parallels it to the south. The former, poison-oak-lined route is only for the very determined; we describe the latter route here.

The starting point is a roadside turnout 9.0 miles north of Little Rock Ranger Station, and 5.9 miles north of Alder Saddle. Scramble down the stream bank and ford South Fork just above its confluence with the main Little Rock Creek. Climb up the far slope, where you'll find a well-beaten trail going east along a chaparral-covered terrace. This "river terrace," much like others you can see for miles down the

canyon of Little Rock Creek, represents a former level of the stream. Subsequent geologic uplift caused the creek to cut a new and deeper channel.

The path works its way into a narrower part of the canyon, climbing about 200 feet above the alder-, cottonwood-, and sycamore-lined stream. Hidden fishing holes are glimpsed below. About 1 mile from the start, the trail starts to peter out along a progressively steepening slope. Don't be tempted to push too far, as the slopes are unstable ahead.

Intrepid hikers have descended Little Rock Creek's stream bottom down from its confluence with Cooper Canyon up in the High Country, taking about three days to negotiate some of the roughest territory in the San Gabriels.

Little Rock Creek's rocky gorge above South Fork confluence

Area A-8, Trip 2
Bare Mountain

	Distance	3.0 miles round trip
	Total Elevation Gain/Loss	2300'/2300'
	Hiking Time	1 hour (round trip)
	Recommended Map	USGS 7.5-min *Juniper Hills*
	Best Times	October through May
	Agency	ANF/VD
	Difficulty	★★★

Because it's on the Sierra Club's Hundred Peaks list, Bare Mountain's scrubby summit manages to draw dozens of people every year despite its remoteness and apparent unfriendliness. Most people seem to go up the traditional way, which is along a fire break up the south ridge; but that route passes uncomfortably close to Pinyon Flats Shooting Area. A safer way is to go straight up the mountain's east flank. This is a tough scramble on sparsely vegetated slopes, mostly over loose dirt and small rocks—challenging for experienced hikers, and fun if done on a cool, clear day.

You begin at the former Little Cedars Campground, 5.2 miles north of Alder Saddle, and 9.7 miles south of Little Rock Ranger Station. Park by a stone-walled culvert, west of the road. Go up the ridge to the left of the culvert. The route, partly threaded by a deer trail, stays south of a small canyon heading west. It leads, with only a few slight bends and a couple of flat stretches, directly to the summit. Toward the top you'll be wading through some thickets of scratchy chaparral—scrub oak, ceanothus, mountain mahogany, and yucca—so don't forget to wear long pants. The panoramic view at the top includes the High Country peaks of Pacifico and Waterman to the south and the long ramp of Pleasant View Ridge to the east. Antelope Valley's flat floor stretches interminably north.

On the way down, check your bearings. It's quite easy to turn down the wrong ridge or get side-tracked into one of the steep ravines plunging down Bare Mountain's east slope.

Area A-8, Trip 3
Mount Emma Ridge

	Distance	8 miles
	Total Elevation Gain/Loss	2600'/2600'
	Hiking Time	6 hours
	Recommended Map	USGS 7.5-min *Pacifico Mountain*
	Best Times	November through April
	Agency	ANF/VD
	Difficulty	★★★

Mt. Emma Ridge, a northern rampart of the San Gabriel Mountains, stands tall over the great, flat basin of Antelope Valley. On its flanks, three plant communities—pinyon-juniper woodland, chaparral, and Joshua tree woodland—intermix. More than any other trip in this book, this one gives a taste of hiking cross-country in the high desert. Do it on a clear, crisp autumn or winter day, or during the peak of the wildflower season in late March and April. Weekdays are strongly recommended; weekends can be noisy.

A good starting point is the large, dirt parking area at the south end of Little Rock Reservoir, 2.6 miles south of Little Rock Ranger Station. Park your car and then head up the shallow canyon to the southwest—Santiago Canyon—following a ORV trail (classified "most difficult") that goes directly up the rocky stream bed. Scattered cottonwoods, willows, and sycamores grow beside the usually dry bottom, while pinyon pines, junipers, yuccas, manzanitas, and scrub oaks cling to the slopes a little higher up.

When you come to the third major right-branching tributary canyon (1.8 miles), leave Santiago Canyon and follow a trailless route up the sharply defined ridge just south of and parallel to the third tributary. This ridge leads generally west, then a little northwest to meet a fire break on Mt. Emma Ridge just north of Mt. Emma's high point (3.8 miles). Soft soil and sparse vegetation on all but the last part make the ascent a straightforward affair. Before you reach the top, the pinyons, junipers, and chaparral thicken, and you'll have to dodge a few limbs and bushes. There's not much of a view from Mt. Emma's flattish summit, but good, flat campsites abound amid the stunted trees. You'll find climbers' registers both here and on Old Mt. Emma ahead. Two designated shooting areas lie well below to the west, one along Mt. Emma Road and another along Angeles Forest Highway. They are seldom used on weekdays.

The fire-break route to Old Mt. Emma is strictly an up-and-down affair, very steep in a couple of places. We sledded down one snow-covered stretch on our backsides. Old Mt. Emma's summit (5.3 miles) is barren, but it features an almost aerial view of the desert floor. Palmdale, one of the fastest-growing cities in the nation, sprawls below, its arrow-straight streets mostly aligned with the cardinal directions. Beyond Palmdale is the smaller city of Lancaster and the large hangar where the space shuttles were assembled. Close against the north spurs of the San Gabriels, the blue ribbon of the California Aqueduct curves along an imperceptibly gradual downhill gradient to the east.

On the return to Little Rock Reservoir, you can either continue east on the fire break, descending to meet Cheseboro Road near Juniper Grove Campground; or you can work your way cross-country down a ridge to the east-southeast, passing over a 4274' bump and later a 3693' bump. Either way, the return to the starting point involves about the same distance. On the way down you'll pass mormon tea shrubs, cholla cactus, stunted junipers, and Joshua trees—vegetation very typical of the Mojave Desert's higher elevations.

Area A-9: Crystal Lake Recreation Area

Historian/author John Robinson compares the form of the San Gabriel River's mountain watershed to a "colossal live oak, standing squat on a stout trunk, with an erect center limb and long horizontal branches extending outward in both directions." The West and East forks form the horizontal branches, while the center branch, the North Fork, drains the top of the tree—Crystal Lake Recreation Area. Highway 39 goes north from Interstate 210 at Azusa and travels up the "trunk" and the center limb—the main San Gabriel Canyon—and then dead-ends just beyond the Crystal Lake turnoff.

The spacious, oak- and conifer-dotted flats that make up Crystal Lake Recreation Area are quite a rarity in the tectonically active San Gabriels. Here, too, is found bantam-sized Crystal Lake, the only permanent natural lake on the south slopes of the San Gabriels. The area was first opened to visitors as a county park in 1932; after World War II it reverted to Forest Service administration. Now, as then, it caters mostly to day trippers and campers seeking a quick escape from the big city.

As you drive up San Gabriel Canyon toward the Crystal Lake basin, it may be interesting to recall some of the canyon's tortured history. John Robinson's book *The San Gabriels II* covers in fascinating detail the efforts to exploit and tame the canyon for mineral riches, water resources, flood control, electrical power, transportation, and recreation. Many of these attempts ended in monumental failures that could easily be blamed entirely on "acts of God"—fire, flood and landslide—were it not for human arrogance and stupidity.

Perhaps the biggest fiasco was the abortive and costly attempt in the late 1920s to erect below the West and East forks what would have been (for a time) the world's largest dam. A massive landslide during construction put that project to rest. (Later, the much smaller San Gabriel and Morris dams were successfully completed downstream).

The history of California Highway 39, the only road link between Crystal Lake and the outside world, is a story of dashed hopes as well. It took 1½ years to rebuild this highway after torrential flooding in 1938. About 20 years ago, an ambitious effort to realign a narrow, cliff-hanging section of the highway south of Crystal Lake was aborted when road crews bored through 200 feet of canyon wall without finding solid bedrock suitable for anchoring a bridge. You can see the ugly scars of this experiment below the recreation area near Coldbrook Campground.

A dubious scheme to extend Highway 39 northward to Angeles Crest Highway by way of the sheer, unstable upper slopes of Bear Creek canyon actually came to fruition in 1961. The road remained in service intermittently until 1978, when a landslide swept away a 500'-long section. As of 1990 about 500 slides had been reported in the area, and estimated repair costs had soared to $20 million—a dollar amount five times larger than the original construction cost. The northernmost 6 miles of the highway will probably never be reconstructed, yet the scarred canyonside will continue to be an eyesore for centuries.

None of these misfortunes has in any way rolled back the demand for recreation in the canyon. In fact, things got a bit out of hand in the late '80s as evidenced by mounds of trash at nearly all the roadside turnouts along Highway 39, vandalized restrooms, and spray-painted walls and boulders all the way up to and including the campgrounds at Crystal Lake Recreation Area. In 1988, Los Angeles County and the Forest Service initiated a parking-fee program to raise funds to clean up the canyon and provide better security. The result has been a much cleaner looking and friendlier canyon.

Weekend and holiday visitors must now purchase a daily pass ($3 per car per day) for parking on any National Forest lands in the San Gabriel Canyon area, with certain exceptions—most notably Crystal Lake Recreation Area and all private lands. The parking fee can be paid at the San Gabriel Information Station (open 8 A.M. to 5 P.M.) near the mouth of the canyon just north of Azusa, and at certain 24-hour businesses in the Azusa area. Call (818) 335-1251 or (818) 334-1065 for more information. For the hikes listed below, the parking-permit program applies only to Trips 1 and 2.

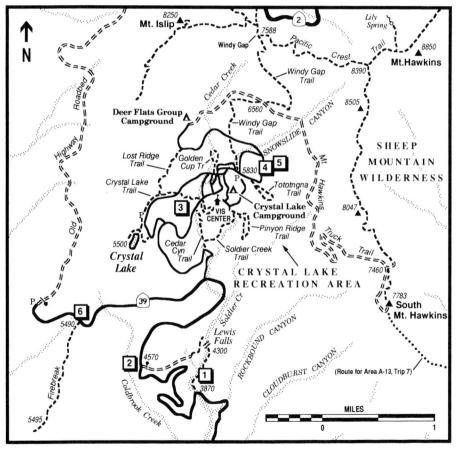

Area A-9: Crystal Lake Recreation Area

Area A-9, Trip 1
Lewis Falls

	Distance	0.8 mile round trip
	Total Elevation Gain/Loss	300'/300'
	Hiking Time	½ hour (round trip)
	Optional Map	USGS 7.5-min *Crystal Lake*
	Best Times	All year
	Agency	ANF/MBD
	Difficulty	★

On the precipice called Lewis Falls, Soldier Creek shoots (or cascades, or merely dribbles) some 50 feet down a two-tiered rock face. The volume of water splattering on rocks and sand below is seldom dramatic; but the cool spray and the sounds of falling water are refreshing. The hike to the base of the falls is short—only about 15 minutes, a manageable adventure (with some assistance) for small children.

Drive 2.3 miles north of Coldbrook Campground on Highway 39 to reach a small, shaded turnout on the right (mile 34.8), where Soldier Creek tumbles through a culvert under the highway. This is your starting point. Make your way up a well-beaten trail on the east side of the creek, under shade-giving oaks, bays, and bigcone Douglas-firs. Near the last cabin upstream, the trail virtually disappears in the flood-scoured bed of Soldier Creek. A final, 200-yard scramble along the stream takes you to the base of the falls.

Most of the year Soldier Creek is a tame brook, easily jumped by the average adult. But a major storm, or a rapid thaw in the snowpack above, could produce runoff deep and swift enough to be hazardous—at least for kids.

Lewis Falls

Area A-9, Trip 2
Upper Soldier Creek

Distance	1.4 miles round trip
Total Elevation Gain/Loss	250'/250'
Hiking Time	1 hour (round trip)
Optional Map	USGS 7.5-min *Crystal Lake*
Best Times	All year
Agency	ANF/MBD
Difficulty	★★

Just above Lewis Falls, but not accessible by way of Trip 1 above, is a beautiful stretch of Soldier Creek featuring half a dozen small cascades. Deeply shaded by oaks and conifers, and adorned with ferns, this rugged little hideaway is, again, just a short walk away from Highway 39.

Drive to mile 36.8 on Highway 39, where a wide, gated road goes east. Park on the shoulder of Highway 39 so as not to block the gate. On foot, follow the road 0.5 mile east to its end. This stub of a road was part of a projected realignment of Highway 39 that would have been in place sometime in the 1970s if it hadn't been for insurmountable construction difficulties.

From the road end, find the narrow trail, on the left, that contours through manzanita brush. It leads about 300 yards to the creek bottom upstream from Lewis Falls. Parts of the narrow trail edge precariously along steep, erodible slopes, so watch your step.

Soldier Creek above Lewis Falls

Area A-9, Trip 3
Crystal Lake Nature Trails

	Distance	½–1 mile (per trail)
	Optional Map	USGS 7.5-min *Crystal Lake*
	Best Times	April through December
	Agency	ANF/MBD
	Difficulty	★ (each trail)

Briefly stated, the several short nature trails of Crystal Lake Recreation Area offer one of the best introductions to the high, forested country of the San Gabriel Mountains. You won't ever get very far away from the sounds of auto traffic or happy campers on these trails, but you can certainly learn quite a bit about the area's natural features.

Stop by the visitor center to obtained detailed maps of the trails and campground access roads of the Crystal Lake area, and self-guiding leaflets for some of the trails listed below.

The **Tototngna Trail**, a self-guiding, 0.7-mile walk, starts from the main trailhead parking area 0.5 mile beyond (northeast of) the visitor center. *Tototngna*, "place of the stones" in the Gabrielino tongue, refers to the boulder-filled gullies sweeping down toward the Crystal Lake basin from the steep mountain walls surrounding it. On this oak-shaded walk, you'll discover such minutiae as lichens, oak galls, and a small geologic fault.

The **Golden Cup Trail**, starting halfway between the visitor center and the main trailhead parking lot, loops for 0.3 mile through a grove of golden cup oaks, better known as canyon live oaks. The more colorful of the two names comes from the golden color of the shallow pod cup that holds the acorn. Other names for this tree are iron oak and maul oak, allusions to the great density and durability of its wood.

The **Pinyon Ridge Trail**, starting just southeast of the visitor center, travels one mile through habitats ranging from the lush oak-and-conifer forest to barren, sun-baked slopes. This 20-stop, self-guiding loop trail climbs to a high and dry ridge dominated by an isolated colony of pinyon pines. These stunted pines seem quite at home in their local microhabitat, but actually they're quite far from their normal range on the desert-facing slopes of the San Gabriel Mountains.

The **Soldier Creek Trail** diverges from the Pinyon Ridge Trail at a small footbridge just below the starting point. You can make a 1.5-mile loop by descending the Soldier Creek Trail to its junction with the **Cedar Canyon Trail**, climbing the Cedar Canyon Trail to meet the main entrance road into the recreation area, and following the entrance road east past the visitor center over to where you started. Both trails are deeply shaded by live oaks, incense cedars, and other trees. "Soldier Creek Trail" is a bit of a misnomer because the trail actually follows a tributary of Soldier Creek. Both this creek and Cedar Creek turn into delightful, tumbling brooks during times of snowmelt—typically winter through early spring.

Just east of the starting point for the Pinyon Ridge Trail, on the lower entrance road to campground loop C, is a 100-yard-long side trail to the Goliath Oak. Set amid a thicket of lesser oaks, this giant canyon live oak measures 20 feet in trunk circumference and 82 feet in height.

The **Half Knob Trail** starts on the south side of the entrance road, just west of the visitor center. It loops halfway around and then back (0.6 mile total) along the side of a wooded knoll—or "knob" if you prefer.

The **Lake Trail** allows you to hike from

the visitor center to Crystal Lake, 1.0 mile one-way. On the way you'll pass the **Lost Ridge Trail,** which climbs along a sharply defined ridgeline and joins the paved access road to Deer Flats Group Campground. If you follow the Lost Ridge Trail, you could loop back to the visitor center by way of the access road and the **Windy Gap Trail** (See Trips 4 and 5 for more on the Windy Gap Trail).

Crystal Lake

Area A-9, Trip 4
Mount Islip—South Approach

Distance	7.0 miles round trip
Total Elevation Gain/Loss	2400'/2400'
Hiking Time	4 hours (round trip)
Optional Map	USGS 7.5-min *Crystal Lake*
Best Times	May through November
Agency	ANF/MBD
Difficulty	★★★

The south approach of Mt. Islip feels a bit like real mountain climbing, despite the rather straightforward ascent by way of marked trails. You begin amid spreading oaks and tall conifers in Crystal Lake basin, rise through progressively smaller and sparser timber, and finally reach the nearly bald and often windblown summit. There, a comprehensive view both north over the Mojave Desert and south over the metropolis is offered on clear days. For the slight effort of an extra ¾ mile on the way up or down, you can spend the night at Little Jimmy Campground (see Area A-11, Trip 5), one of the nicest trail camps in the San Gabriels.

You start on the marked Windy Gap Trail, which begins at the main hikers' parking lot, 0.5 mile beyond the Crystal Lake Recreation Area visitor center. On the way to Windy Gap (2.5 miles), you cross Mt. Hawkins Truck Trail twice, and then tackle the steep, upper slopes of the cirque-like rim overlooking Crystal Lake basin. Windy Gap is the lowest spot on the north side of that rim.

At Windy Gap you meet the Pacific Crest Trail, which joins from the right (east). Continue north on the PCT to the next junction. From here the left branch takes you more directly to the summit of Mt. Islip,

while the right branch leads to Little Jimmy Campground and a more roundabout ascent of the mountain. In either case, you'll end up on the trail that follows the sunny east ridge of Mt. Islip to its summit. (Note: Hard snow or ice can linger on the steep, north-facing slopes north of Windy Gap until sometime in May. You can avoid that stretch if need be by going straight up the east shoulder of Mt. Islip from Windy Gap; that route becomes snow-free earlier in the season.)

On the summit you'll see footings of a fire lookout tower that stood on the summit from 1927 until it was removed to South Mt. Hawkins in 1937. The shell of a stone cabin stands just east of the summit.

Two switchbacks below the summit of Mt. Islip, you'll probably spot a new trail heading southwest down the slope. As of this writing this trail ends 1 mile down Mt. Islip's south ridge. A future extension of this trail will either loop east back to Windy Gap Trail or follow the south ridge down to Crystal Lake.

Area A-9, Trip 5
Mount Hawkins Loop

	Distance	11.5 miles
	Total Elevation Gain/Loss	3400'/3400'
	Hiking Time	7 hours
	Optional Map	USGS 7.5-min *Crystal Lake*
	Best Times	May through November
	Agency	ANF/MBD
	Difficulty	★★★

The recent completion of a well-graded pathway along the high, east rim of Crystal Lake basin has made the popular traverse between Mts. Hawkins and South Hawkins considerably easier than before. On this trip you'll start at the main Windy Gap trailhead down in the basin, climb to South Mt. Hawkins and its historic lookout tower, climb north to the higher Mt. Hawkins, and

return by looping back on the Pacific Crest and Windy Gap trails.

Most years, the route becomes snow-free sometime in May. Don't be fooled if the slopes visible from Crystal Lake basin appear to be clear of snow in April or early May; icy passages with seemingly bottomless runouts could still await you on the high, north end of the Hawkins ridge. Check first at the visitor center, or with a ranger.

Start, as in Trip 4 above, by taking the Windy Gap Trail north to the second crossing of the Mt. Hawkins Truck Trail, 1.0 mile. Turn right and follow the dirt road as it climbs steadily and moderately across the steep slopes east of Crystal Lake Basin. It's best if you can cover these 3 miles of somewhat tedious road-walking before the morning sun breaks over the high crest to the east.

On a sparsely forested saddle at 3.9 miles, you'll get your first glimpse east into some of the rugged canyons of Sheep Mountain Wilderness. From the saddle, it's better to take the foot trail going south along the ridge to the South Hawkins summit, rather than staying on the road. The freshly whitewashed lookout tower on top, now being renovated for interpretive use, presides over a wrinkled landscape of dry, sinuous ridges and steeply plunging canyons. One way or another, nearly all the mountainous terrain in your field of view sheds water into the San Gabriel River.

After your visit to South Hawkins, retrace your steps back to the saddle (4.7

miles). Take the spur road curving north to the site of an old heliport, and continue north on the new footpath cut high along the east-facing slope of the Hawkins ridge. Jeffrey pines, sugar pines, and white firs cling to the slopes, serving as picturesque frames for the wraith-like profiles of lower ridges engulfed in fog or smog.

At 6.9 miles, you reach a junction with the Pacific Crest Trail. A second side trip is necessary if you want to reach Mt. Hawkins, one of several rounded summits defining the crest of what's known as the middle High Country—Mt. Islip to Mt. Baden-Powell. Turn east and head for the obvious promontory ½ mile away. You'll scramble up the last 300 yards or so through scattered pines. To the east, the rounded summits of Troop Peak, Mt. Burnham, and Mt. Baden-Powell can be seen curving to the right. In the north, beyond lesser summits, spreads the flat Mojave Desert floor.

You return to Crystal Lake by way of the shortest route—west on the Pacific Crest Trail to the trail junction at Windy Gap, then left down the Windy Gap Trail.

Ridge north of South Mt. Hawkins

Looking into Iron Fork from Hawkins Ridge

Area A-9, Trip 6
Bear Creek Overlook

👟	**Distance**	2.2 miles round trip
	Total Elevation Gain/Loss	400'/400'
🏔	**Hiking Time**	1 hour (round trip)
	Optional Map	USGS 7.5-min *Crystal Lake*
	Best Times	All year
↗	**Agency**	ANF/MBD
	Difficulty	★★

From Highway 39's road closure west of Crystal Lake's entrance, there's a dramatic view across the V-shaped gorge of Bear Creek and deep into the heartland of San Gabriel Wilderness. If you want to stretch your legs a bit, and enjoy an even better view to boot, then try this short hike along the top of a nearby ridge.

Drive to a gated road (fire break) on the south side of Highway 39, mile 39.4, or 0.6 mile east of the road closure. Walk around the gate and follow the wide fire break south along the top of an undulating ridge. You'll pass a few weather-beaten white firs and

Coulter pines along the ridgeline, and dark thickets of bigcone Douglas-fir down below in protected hollows. Just over a mile out, the ridge starts descending quickly to the south. Stop here and enjoy the panoramic view. Between 5111' Smith Mountain (1 mile south) and the 7761' east shoulder of Twin Peaks (4 miles west), Bear Creek and its tributaries carve their way through some of the most rugged territory in Southern California. This is prime bighorn-sheep habitat—steep, rocky, almost inaccessible to humans.

Area A-10: San Gabriel Wilderness

San Gabriel Wilderness was first set aside as a protected area in 1932—well before the advent of the National Wilderness Preservation System in 1964. Its 36,137 acres encompass some extremely rugged terrain, with elevations ranging from under 2000 feet to over 8000 feet. Many areas in this wilderness are characterized by slopes steeper than 100 percent, that is, steeper than a 45° incline.

Green ribbons of riparian vegetation cling to the narrow bottoms of the two principal drainages—Bear Creek and Devils Canyon—while dense chaparral forms an almost impenetrable cover on the lower canyon walls. Scattered bigcone Douglas-firs at lower elevations gradually give way to statuesque ponderosa, Jeffrey, Coulter, lodgepole and sugar pines; incense cedars; and white firs on the higher slopes of Waterman Mountain and Twin Peaks.

This varied, rough, and remote habitat harbors mule deer, Nelson bighorn sheep, black bear, and mountain lions. You're most likely to see the former two, least likely to encounter the latter. Grizzly bears, once a common hazard, were hunted to extinction here by about the turn of the century.

Although a trans-mountain Indian trail once followed the length of Bear Creek, no such trails cross San Gabriel Wilderness today. The currently maintained hiking trails only graze the edges of the Wilderness, leaving the interior (especially south of Twin Peaks) virtually unexplored in modern times.

You can easily enter San Gabriel Wilderness at least six ways, as described in the trips listed below. Once inside the boundary the trails tend to fade, but the possibilities for further exploration (mostly of a very rugged kind) are almost endless. At present, you may enter San Gabriel Wilderness without having the usual wilderness permit that is required for most other wilderness areas around the state. This does not absolve you from obtaining a fire permit, if applicable. If you do plan to venture well off the beaten track, then for your own safety it would be wise to consult with a ranger first.

Fire-singed pine on Mt. Waterman Trail

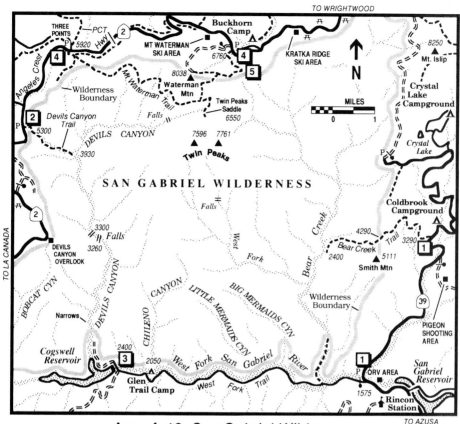

Area A-10: San Gabriel Wilderness

Area A-10, Trip 1
Bear Creek Trail

	Distance	9.7 miles
	Total Elevation Gain/Loss	1100'/2800'
	Hiking Time	7 hours
	Optional Map	USGS 7.5-min *Crystal Lake*
	Best Times	October through June
	Agency	ANF/MBD
	Difficulty	★★★

Bear Creek and its myriad tributaries drain about half of San Gabriel Wilderness—roughly 25 square miles of steeply plunging ravines and canyons. Virtually none of this convoluted landscape ever experiences the tread of hiking boots except for the lower stretch of Bear Creek, reached by way of the Bear Creek Trail from Highway 39. The one-way route described here takes you into the heart of this wild area and includes almost four miles of boulder-hopping along perennially flowing Bear Creek.

A short car-shuttle along Highway 39 is needed to connect the two ends of the hike. Leave one vehicle at the West Fork (San Gabriel River) Bridge parking area, just north of Rincon Station and the San Gabriel Canyon off-road-vehicle staging area. Take the other vehicle 5½ miles farther north to the start of the Bear Creek Trail at the edge of a large roadside turnout, mile 32.2. The San Gabriel Canyon parking-fee program applies at both of these parking lots (see Area A-9 introduction for details).

Wide and easy at first, the Bear Creek Trail twists and turns up through sun-struck chaparral, gaining 1000 feet in a moderately easy 2.5 miles. On weekends, traffic noise from the highway below, as well as the annoying popping sounds emanating from the popular Pigeon Shooting Area across the highway, will make you want to travel this stretch quickly.

The 4290' saddle at the top of that grade marks the high point on the hike as well as the wilderness boundary. Down the other side you descend quickly on a narrower and rougher trail, and all vestiges of civilization (save an occasional passing aircraft) instantly disappear from view. Tall, nearly impenetrable chaparral on the steep north slopes keeps most of the sunlight away during the fall and winter months. To the northwest, the Twin Peaks ridge soars impressively over the far wall of Bear Creek canyon. Caution is in order in a couple of spots where the trail crosses perpetually eroding ravines.

The descent concludes with a zigzag passage down along a ridge between two steep ravines. You arrive at Bear Creek's east bank, where blackened boulders indicate a small trail camp, 4.7 miles. (A spectacular narrow section of Bear Creek, with vertical granite walls, begins 0.3 mile upstream from this point—worth a look if you have time for the side trip.)

Little hint of any trail can be found in the next 4 miles as you follow the stream to its confluence with West Fork San Gabriel River. Narrow and vegetation-choked at first, the canyon becomes wider, flatter, and talus-filled as you press on ahead. Once the stream has room to meander across the canyon floor, it curves from wall to wall, forcing you to plunge into the streamside alders and boulder-hop or wade across the water. You'll repeat that process about 25 times.

Atop low, oak-shaded terraces at 5.7 miles (at the West Fork Bear Creek confluence) and at 7.5 miles (next to the remains of a stone cabin), you'll find plenty of room to set up a tent in a picturesque, shady setting. Below the lower campsite, a well-beaten but intermittent path helps improve your speed for the last mile or so. At 8.7 miles, you cross West Fork San Gabriel River and join the paved West Fork National Recreation Trail, which is the main access road to Cogswell Reservoir, doubling as a bike and hike trail. Turn left and walk a mile out to Highway 39 and your waiting car.

Area A-10, Trip 2
Upper Devils Canyon

	Distance	9.8 miles round trip (to falls)
	Total Elevation Gain/Loss	2100'/2100'
	Hiking Time	6½ hours (round trip)
	Optional Maps	USGS 7.5-min *Chilao Flat,*
		Waterman Mtn.
	Best Times	October through June
	Agency	ANF/ASD
	Difficulty	★★★

If you stand at Devils Canyon Overlook (just below Charlton Flat on Angeles Crest Highway) on a warm spring day, a withering updraft fans your face like the hot breath of a furnace. There's no hint of the clear, cascading stream and the cool, shady micro-environment hidden in the deep crease of the canyon 2000 feet below.

Getting down there isn't bad at all; most of the effort comes in getting back up. I'd recommend spending a full day (or parts of two days) exploring the canyon. You can splash around in some of the shallow pools (in May or June, when the water warms), watch ducks and water ouzels at work or play, fish for trout (you'll need a state license) and/or trek down to the upper of two waterfalls in the canyon. If the weather's warm, you should plan to wait until the sun sinks to the west before making the long climb back up the afternoon-shaded west canyon wall.

There's plenty of parking space at the Devils Canyon trailhead on the west side of Angeles Crest Highway—mile 50.4, just south of the Chilao Visitor Center turnoff. The zigzagging descent on the trail takes you across slopes clothed alternately in chaparral and mixed conifer forest. By 1.5 miles you reach a branch of what will soon become a trickling stream—one of the several tributaries that contribute to Devils Canyon's ample springtime flow. The deeply shaded trail leads to the main canyon (mark this spot or take note of surrounding

landmarks so you can recognize this place when it's time to head back up the trail), 2.6 miles, and then downstream a bit farther to the site of a former trail camp on a flat bench west of the Devils Canyon stream. In accordance with the philosophy of returning designated wilderness areas to as natural a condition as possible, this former trail camp, as well as all others within the wilderness borders, have had their stoves and tables removed.

Downstream, you follow a fairly distinct path in places; otherwise you boulder-hop and wade. Mini-cascades feed pools 3–4 feet deep harboring elusive brook trout. Water-loving alders and sycamores cluster along the stream, while patriarchal live oaks and bigcone Douglas-firs stand on higher and dryer benches and slopes, waiting in the wings, as it were, for the next big flood to sweep the upstarts away. Watch for poison oak as the canyon walls narrow; and keep an eye out for a silvery, two-tier waterfall at the mouth of a side canyon coming in from the east, mile 4.5.

Beyond the two-tier fall, 0.4 mile of rock scrambling and wading takes you to a constriction in the canyon where water slides down a sheer incline some 20 vertical feet. Avoiding the slippery lip of these falls, you can climb the rock wall to the right for an airy view of the cascade and shallow pool below. Without rappelling gear, this is basically the end of the line (a second waterfall just below this one can be reached from

Cogswell Reservoir below—see Trip 3). You'll have to return by the same route.

If you're interested in exploring more of the area and don't mind some rough-and-tumble scrambling, try visiting an enigmatic basin, located in a saddle high above the canyon bottom, 1 mile northeast of the foot of the Devils Canyon Trail. This is depicted as a topographical depression (4680') on the *Waterman Mtn.* topo map. To reach it, follow Devils Canyon 1.5 miles upstream

from the foot of the trail, then turn south and climb up a steep ravine. Some careful map work is required. The basin's flat, silty floor is a rarity in the generally vertically inclined San Gabriel Wilderness. A very secluded if dry camp could be made near (but not directly under the pendulous cones of) some large Coulter pines at the basin's west rim. The basin's floor is soggy in the early spring; presumably a shallow lake forms here after sufficient rainfall.

Top of upper fall in Devil's Canyon

Area A-10, Trip 3
Lower Devils Canyon

	Distance	9.4 miles round trip (Cogswell Reservoir to falls)
	Total Elevation Gain/Loss	1200'/1200'
	Hiking Time	7 hours (round trip)
	Optional Maps	USGS 7.5-min *Azusa, Waterman Mtn.*
	Best Times	November through May
	Agency	ANF/ASD
	Difficulty	★★★★

In the lower reaches of Devils Canyon, a vociferous little stream darts over an obstacle course of rounded boulders perpetually shaded by thickets of alder and sycamore. Now and again the water slackens in transparent pools of Zen-like simplicity, cupped in naked granite. Skittish trout lurk in the watery depths, while a great blue heron stalks the shallows. Hawks wheel through the sky overhead, ever-watchful of the movements of small, furry creatures below. This is quintessential wilderness—remote, pristine, and in this case devilishly difficult to reach.

The journey into lower Devils Canyon begins with . . . a bike ride! If you don't have bike wheels, then you necessarily face 15 miles of round-trip walking on pavement in addition to the 9.4 miles of hiking described here. You should allow more than an extra hour for the pedaling part.

Park your car next to the Highway 39 bridge over West Fork San Gabriel River (use the paved lot north of the bridge, or the large dirt turnout south of the bridge). On weekends and holidays you'll have to pay a parking fee at the San Gabriel Canyon entrance (see Area A-9 introduction for details).

From the south end of the bridge, wheel your bike around the vehicle gate onto the West Fork National Recreation Trail. This paved service road/bike path meanders up the beautiful West Fork canyon to the top of Cogswell Dam 7.5 miles away. Once you get past the first graffiti-scarred half-mile, the remainder of the ride is a refreshing prelude to the Devils Canyon hike. (The epilogue for the hike is even nicer—you hardly have to pedal at all when coasting back to your car.)

After 6.3 miles of riding—nearly 500 feet of elevation gain—you reach Glen Campground (hike-in or bike-in; first-come, first served). You then continue another 1.2 miles (350 feet gain) to Cogswell Dam. You're allowed to walk or ride your bike across the dam to gain access to the dirt road along the far (north) side. If you have a road bike, secure it at the dam (or somehow conceal it) and continue on foot—Cogswell Dam is our assumed starting point for the hike. If you have a mountain bike, you can continue riding on dirt for another 1.5 miles.

Either way, the rapidly deteriorating road at 1.5 miles will force you to scramble, one way or another, down about 80 feet to the wide, sand- and boulder-filled floor of Devils Canyon. This barren, often-bone-dry stretch bears no resemblance to what you'll find only a mile up-canyon. The first small pools, where water sinks below the surface and percolates into the porous substratum, will probably be found a short distance ahead.

At 2.3 miles, the canyon floor suddenly narrows and you must somehow get past a moat-like pool, about 10 feet deep, squeezed between nearly vertical rock walls. Beyond lies a veritable Shangri-La of crystalline pools and miniature cascades. A half-rotten log helped me get across the moat and into the narrows ahead. You, however, should count on the possibility of having to swim; take along a water-proof plastic bag you can use to package your clothes and other gear you can't afford to get wet.

The barest hint of an animal trail threads through the canyon ahead. Mostly you'll scramble, boulder-hop, and wade. This part of the canyon is much like upper Devils Canyon (Trip 2), except the pools are more grand. The best one (at 2.8 miles), about 10 feet deep and bounded by water-polished granite and banded metamorphic rock, is a sensational swimming hole. There are lots

of alder trees and some sycamores down along the stream; oaks, incense cedars, and scattered poison oak a little higher above the stream; and hardy bigcone Douglas-firs clinging to the slopes.

At about 3.5 miles the canyon floor widens considerably. High and dry campsites can be found in the next mile. At 4.5 miles the canyon narrows again, and just ahead of that, progress comes to a halt because of an unclimbable waterfall. This is the lower of two closely spaced falls that rock climbers have been able to descend by means of rappelling. Here, the waters of Devils Canyon funnel though a sheer-walled constriction in the canyon floor and drop about 20 vertical feet into a pool about 40 feet wide and 4 feet deep.

Lower falls in Devil's Canyon

Area A-10, Trip 4
Mount Waterman Trail

	Distance	7.8 miles
	Total Elevation Gain/Loss	1400'/2250'
	Hiking Time	4½ hours
	Optional Map	USGS 7.5-min *Waterman Mtn.*
	Best Times	May through November
	Agency	ANF/ASD
	Difficulty	★★★

The Mt. Waterman Trail traverse across the north rim of San Gabriel Wilderness provides almost constant views of statuesque pines, yawning chasms, and distant, hazy ridges. You start near the entrance to Buckhorn Campground and you end up half-circling broad-shouldered Waterman Mountain by the time you arrive at Three Points, 5 miles away by car. Snow can linger on the easternmost mile of the trail until May, but it tends to disappear much earlier on the remaining (mostly south-facing) parts of the trail. This is one of the most popular High Country summer hikes—one that I can heartily recommend for all but the warmest days.

(If you prefer, you can shave some time, distance, and elevation gain from this hike—as well as Trip 5 below—by making use of the Mt. Waterman Ski Lift, which is open on summer weekends to cater to hikers. The lift carries you 900 feet up from Angeles Crest Highway to a point about ¾ mile north of Waterman Mountain's summit. Because of the maze of dirt roads and ski trails at the top of the lift, you may find a topo map is handy for navigation there.)

The Mt. Waterman Trail starts on the south side of Angeles Crest Highway, opposite the Buckhorn trailhead, where there are a parking lot and restrooms at mile 58.0 on Angeles Crest Highway. Three Points trailhead, at the far end of the hike, is located at the intersection of Santa Clara Divide Road, mile 52.8 on Angeles Crest Highway.

From the Buckhorn end, follow the well-graded foot trail—not the old road bed that parallels the trail at first—along a shady slope. After 1.0 mile of easy ascent through gorgeous mixed-conifer forest, you come to a saddle overlooking Bear Creek. The trail turns west, follows a viewful ridge, and then ascends on six long switchbacks to a trail junction, 2.1 miles. The trail to Waterman Mountain's summit goes right; you stay left and contour west about ½ mile, then zigzag south down to a second junction, 3.5 miles. Twin Peaks saddle, a spacious camping spot, lies below to the left. If you're simply day-hiking this stretch, then stay right (west).

The remaining 4+ miles take you gradually downhill (more steep at the very end) along Mt. Waterman's south flank. You wind in and out of broad ravines, either shaded by huge incense cedars and vanilla-scented Jeffrey pines, or exposed to the warm sunshine on chaparral-covered slopes. The older cedar trees are gnarled veterans of past fires.

Near the end, you hook up briefly with the Pacific Crest Trail. On it you swing down to cross Angeles Crest Highway, and climb up to Three Points trailhead.

Area A-10, Trip 5
Waterman Mountain—Twin Peaks

	Distance	11.8 miles round trip
	Total Elevation Gain/Loss	4000'/4000'
	Hiking Time	7 hours (round trip)
	Recommended Map	USGS 7.5-min *Waterman Mtn.*
	Best Times	May through November
	Agency	ANF/ASD
	Difficulty	★★★★

The "top of the world" views from Waterman Mountain and especially Twin Peaks ridge are among the best in the San Gabriel Mountains. This peak-bagging extravaganza visits both Waterman Mountain's summit and the east summit of Twin Peaks (11.8 miles out-and-back for the whole trip). You can, however, easily customize this hike to include more or include less, to suit your ability and desire.

Start, as in Trip 4 above, by hiking up the Mt. Waterman Trail to the first trail junction, 2.1 miles. A right turn here starts you on the way to the summit of Waterman Mountain, 0.7 mile west. The trail itself swings around the north side of a lesser summit, crosses a saddle, and then bypasses, on the north, the true 8038' summit. You leave the trail and walk about 200 yards up a sparsely treed slope to the summit plateau. A summit register has been in place here since 1924.

When you arrive back at the first trail junction, turn west and continue following the Mt. Waterman Trail. You contour west for about ½ mile, then start zigzagging down a forested south slope to a second trail junction. Make a hard left here and continue descending a more primitive trail to Twin Peak Saddle (6550'), the lowest point on the divide separating upper Devil Canyon from upper Bear Creek. You could pitch a tent here, but there's much more room—and a better view—atop a 6816' knob 0.3 mile southeast.

From Twin Peaks Saddle, the now-sketchy trail contours south to reach a second saddle (6580') at the north base of Twin Peaks ridge. From there, you simply go straight up the slope, dodging boulders and trees, until you arrive on the ridgeline between the two peaks. Climb a short distance east to bag the 7761' eastern peak. If you drop a short way down to rock outcrops south and east, just below the summit, you'll have a dizzying view of the secret, upper reaches of Bear Creek's West Fork. Serrated ridges of shattered diorite, a rock-climber's nightmare, seem to tumble into the pit below. Quite often you can look out over a low-lying blanket of smog in the L.A. Basin and see Santa Catalina Island floating out at sea beyond the hazy dome of Palos Verdes. The Santa Anas, Palomar Mountain, the Santa Rosas, San Jacinto Peak and Old Baldy arc around the horizon from south to east. Also clearly in view is the east wall of upper Bear Creek canyon, ripped apart during the grading for the now-closed section of Highway 39.

Before returning to Buckhorn, consider visiting the 7596' west summit of Twin Peaks. From there, the view south is even more vertiginous, and the ugly scars of Highway 39 are hidden by the slightly higher eastern peak. Just west of the west summit is a superbly situated small campsite—a flat, sandy hollow amid boulders and scattered pines. According to the summit registers on both peaks, more than 100 people climb the east peak every year, while only about a dozen make the west peak. Hikers signing in frequently report sightings of bighorn sheep.

Area A-11: High Country/North Slope

North of Angeles Crest Highway and down the slopes toward Devil's Punchbowl country, the San Gabriel Mountains meld into desert in a most pleasant way. Timbered slopes dominate the cool crest, while on the warmer desert flats below, Joshua trees and high-desert scrub vegetation clearly hold sway. In between these two extremes there thrives an enigmatic mixture of oak and conifer forest, pinyon-juniper woodland, chaparral, and (in the bigger watercourses) riparian vegetation.

The trail system through these parts is quite well-maintained, although a bit under-utilized as compared to trails farther west which are closer to the metropolis. The Pacific Crest Trail skims the crest of the range here, never straying too far from Angeles Crest Highway, while the High Desert National Recreation Trail probes the wild ridges and canyons of the slopes to the north. Not really a single trail, the High Desert Trail consists of several connected trails: Burkhart Trail, Punchbowl Trail, South Fork Trail, and Manzanita Trail. I've described trips along each of the segments, as a day hiker would walk them to the best advantage, except for the Manzanita Trail,

which is the least interesting of the four. Serious backpackers could put together a marathon-length (26-mile) loop on the High Desert Trail by including the leg of the PCT that stretches from Islip Saddle to Little Rock Creek.

Roadside campgrounds in the area include the perennial favorite Buckhorn Campground, which was used as a high-country sportsman's camp long before Angeles Crest Highway permitted easy access to it. On the desert side, there are three campgrounds, Sycamore, South Fork, and Big Rock—all located in the Big Rock Creek drainage. These latter three are among the better sites for stargazing in the San Gabriels, as they're shielded by the mountains from much (but not all) of the L.A. Basin light pollution.

In winter, snow often closes the upper parts of Angeles Crest Highway (particularly east of Kratka Ridge Ski Area) and lesser roads in the area, so you'll want to check with the Forest Service before you head up there early in the season. If you're a cross-country skier, you'll want to take advantage of any and all unplowed roads while the snow is fresh.

Area A-11, Trip 1
Cooper Canyon Falls

Distance	3.0 miles round trip
Total Elevation Gain/Loss	800'/800'
Hiking Time	1½ hours (round trip)
Optional Map	USGS 7.5-min *Waterman Mtn.*
Best Times	April through November
Agency	ANF/ASD
Difficulty	★★

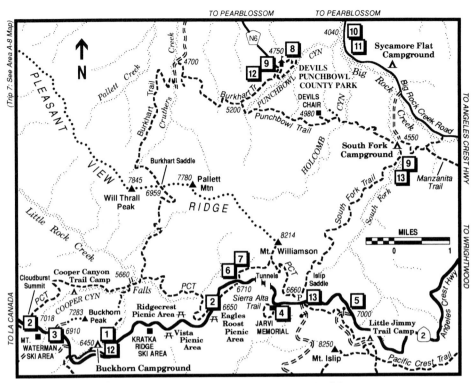

Area A-11: High Country/North Slope

Cooper Canyon Falls roars with the melting snows of early spring, then settles down to a quiet whisper by June or July. You can cool off in the spray of the 25′ cascade, or at least sit on a water-smoothed log and soak your feet in the chilly, alder-shaded pool just below the base of the falls. In the right season (April or May most years) these falls are one of the best unheralded attractions of the San Gabriel Mountains.

The Burkhart Trail takes you quickly to the falls, downhill all the way, and then uphill all the way back. The forest hereabouts is dense enough to give plenty of cool shade for most of the unrelenting climb back up.

To get to the start of the Burkhart Trail, turn off at the Buckhorn Campground entrance road, mile 58.3 on Angeles Crest Highway. Drive all the way through the campground to the far (northeast) end,

where a short stub of dirt road leads to a trailhead parking area.

The trail takes off down the west wall of an unnamed, usually wet canyon garnished by two waterfalls. The first, at 6220 feet in the canyon bottom, is easy to reach by descending from the trail—this little gem of a cascade drops 10 feet into a rock grotto. The second, 30′-high falls, at 6050 feet, is very hazardous to approach from above, but is reachable from below by scrambling up the canyon bottom from Cooper Canyon.

At 1.2 miles, the trail bends east to follow Cooper Canyon's south bank. Continue another 0.3 mile, down past the junction of the trail (Pacific Crest Trail) that doubles back to follow the north bank upstream. Look or listen for water plunging over the rocky declivity to the left. A rough pathway leads down off the trail to the alder-fringed pool below.

Cooper Canyon Falls

Area A-11, Trip 2
Cooper Canyon—Rattlesnake Trail

Distance	6.3 miles
Total Elevation Gain/Loss	1200'/1550'
Hiking Time	3 hours
Optional Map	USGS 7.5-min *Waterman Mtn.*
Best Times	April through November
Agency	ANF/ASD
Difficulty	★★

Snowmelt and spring waters flow into Little Rock Creek from hundreds of small rivulets and creases in the High Country, giving rise to the happy stream that tumbles, forthwith, toward the thirsty floor of the Mojave Desert. Here, amidst magnificent groves of pine, fir, cedar and oak, the Pacific Crest Trail deigns to descend from the high and dry ridgelines and, for a brief while, tracks Little Rock Creek and its main upper tributary—Cooper Canyon.

This delightful stretch of the PCT, one of the best in Southern California, is best hiked one-way. Leave one car at or outside Eagles Roost Picnic Area (mile 61.6 on Angeles Crest Highway), and take the other to Cloudburst Summit (mile 57.2), where the PCT begins as a disused fire road that starts contouring north.

Once on the trail, you soon start descending along sparsely wooded slopes. After a sharp hairpin turn at 1.2 miles, the trail settles alongside a moist ravine blanketed by bracken fern. Presently you arrive at Cooper Canyon Trail Camp (1.6 miles), which features a huge fire ring, and quiet campsites—if the Scouts aren't whooping it up around the campfire.

Your descent continues along the north bank of year-round Cooper Canyon. Colorful patches of lupine dot the sunny clearings, and columbines nod in the air set in motion by the flowing water. At 2.7 miles, you swing across the creek to meet the Burkhart Trail.

Bearing left, you continue down-canyon past Cooper Canyon Falls (see Trip 1) and reach the shady confluence of Little Rock Creek at 3.1 miles. This is the nadir of your trip—you mostly climb from now on. The Burkhart Trail splits to the north here; you go east on the PCT, a section formerly known as the Rattlesnake Trail. Setting a course well above trickling Little Rock Creek, the trail winds along the slope to the north, circuitously contouring around every ravine. You pass just below a seasonal spring in a ravine at 3.6 miles, and below even-less-dependable Rattlesnake Spring at 4.5 miles.

After a slight descent, you meet Little Rock Creek again (5.1 miles), and swing sharply right to commence the final uphill grind to Eagles Roost Picnic Area. To the north (mostly behind you as you climb) looms the white- and pink-tinted rock outcrop known as Eagles Roost.

Area A-11, Trip 3
Buckhorn Peak

	Distance	1.4 miles round trip
	Total Elevation Gain/Loss	400'/400'
	Hiking Time	1 hours (round trip)
	Optional Map	USGS 7.5-min *Waterman Mtn.*
	Best Times	April through November
	Agency	ANF/ASD
	Difficulty	★★

You won't find Buckhorn Peak labelled on most maps, but the summit register on this rounded peak high above Buckhorn Campground dutifully records its informal name. The pine-dotted summit is a great retreat for a picnic lunch, and is also suitable for an easy overnight backpack. There are no facilities, nor water, but a flat, sandy area just below the summit offers plenty of room for a couple of tents.

You begin hiking at a roadside turnout on the north side of Angeles Crest Highway, mile 57.7 (just east of Mt. Waterman Ski Area). Walk 0.3 mile northeast on an old logging road to reach a point just below a saddle, where old road beds diverge north and east. These old roads loop around most of Buckhorn Peak at the 7000' contour.

From the saddle, simply follow the main, sparsely treed ridge 0.4 mile east to the summit. There's only a faint trail along the ridgeline, so small children will probably need assistance. Watch carefully where you're going so you can retrace your steps on the return; there's only one easy way back down.

If you prefer, you can return by way of a rougher and more scenic route: Descend about 0.2 mile through dense woods to the north, where you'll cross the north lateral road following the 7000' contour. Follow this level road west and south around the mountain to reach the aforementioned saddle.

Area A-11, Trip 4
Sierra Alta Nature Trail

	Distance	0.3 mile
	Total Elevation Gain/Loss	100'/100'
	Hiking Time	¼ hour
	Optional Map	USGS 7.5-min *Crystal Lake*
	Best Times	April through November
	Agency	ANF/ASD
	Difficulty	★

Jarvi Memorial Vista (mile 63.6 on Angeles Crest Highway) offers motorists a great view of both the yawning gorges of Bear Creek to the south and a sheer, frac-tured slope to the north punctured by two closely spaced tunnels on the highway. The memorial honors Sim Jarvi, former Angeles National Forest supervisor, and also serves as a trailhead for the Sierra Alta Nature Trail.

The trail, strictly good for education, not exercise, feature plaques highlighting some examples of ponderosa pine, Jeffrey pine, and canyon live oaks, as well as views in various directions. Clear-day vistas can include the ocean, as well as Santa Catalina and San Clemente islands.

Area A-11, Trip 5
Mount Islip—North Approach

Distance	5.6 miles round trip
Total Elevation Gain/Loss	1250'/1250'
Hiking Time	3 hours (round trip)
Optional Map	USGS 7.5-min *Crystal Lake*
Best Times	May through November
Agency	ANF/ASD
Difficulty	★★

The ascent of Mt. Islip from Crystal Lake to the south has already been described (see Area A-9, Trip 4). The north approach—via an easier route—takes you through aromatic pine- and fir-forest most of the way. The gradual climb is well suited for children or anyone else who can handle moderate altitudes and hiking distances. If need be, you can shorten the hike by turning back at Little Jimmy Campground, 1.5 miles up the slope.

Drive to the gated fire road on the south side of Angeles Crest Highway, mile 65.5 (this is opposite the now-removed Pine Hollow Picnic Area shown on older maps). Walk up the pine-cone-strewn road to where the Pacific Crest Trail crosses it, 0.5 mile up and 350 feet higher. Both the road and the PCT go south and east to Little Jimmy Campground, but the trail is nicer.

Little Jimmy Campground, which honors early-century newspaper cartoonist Jimmy Swinnerton (creator of the "Little Jimmy" comic strip), who summered here in 1909, nestles comfortably in a little flat shaded by statuesque pines. Tables and stoves make this a convenient spot for a picnic or an

overnight layover. Down the trail contouring south toward Windy Gap (below the trail ¼ mile away) is year-round Little Jimmy Spring.

From the campground, the summit trail goes uphill (west at first), and continues looping upward to gain Mt. Islip's east shoulder (stay right where a trail slants left and descends to meet the PCT). You ascend along this shoulder, swing around two switchbacks just below the summit, and arrive at the old hut and lookout site on top.

Area A-11, Trip 6
Mount Williamson

	Distance	3.4 miles round trip
	Total Elevation Gain/Loss	1500'/1500'
	Hiking Time	2 hours (round trip)
	Optional Map	USGS 7.5-min *Crystal Lake*
	Best Times	April through November
	Agency	ANF/ASD
	Difficulty	★★

Mt. Williamson isn't the highest peak on the San Gabriels' crest, but it hovers more closely over the desert than Mts. Islip, Hawkins, Baden-Powell, and others south of Angeles Crest Highway. From the bare patch at the summit, you look down upon the obviously linear traces of the San Andreas and Punchbowl faults, and often over thousands of square miles of Mojave Desert. During the very best visibility, the southernmost Sierra Nevada can be seen, as well as Telescope Peak high on the west rim of Death Valley.

The hike to the top is short and sweet. Start at the large, north-side turnout on Angeles Crest Highway at mile 62.5—this is 0.3 mile west of the western tunnel entrance on the highway. You start by walking northwest on an old road bed, but soon veer right on the narrow Pacific Crest Trail. It wastes no time in switchbacking up the steep, sparsely forested southwest flank of Mt. Williamson. Behind you, from time to time,

you can catch a great view of Bear Creek's V-shaped chasm and Twin Peaks to the south.

After only 1.3 miles (but 1200 feet higher) you arrive at a trail junction on the south ridge of Mt. Williamson. The PCT continues straight ahead, descending to Islip Saddle in 1.6 miles—that PCT segment can be used as an alternative route to or from Williamson. You go left on the unmaintained but well-beaten path up the rocky ridge toward the summit.

In a cairn at the top you'll find a register, where you can dutifully add your name (and any comments) to the hundreds of other signatures recorded here annually. If you want to spend the night, there's plenty of room on the open summit to pitch a tent or lay out to watch the stars. If you do so, don't miss the spectacle of the sun rising as a fiery orange ball over the desert floor, May through August.

Mt. Williamson summit, looking east

Area A-11, Trip 7
Pleasant View Ridge

Distance	11.5 miles
Total Elevation Gain/Loss	2800'/7000'
Hiking Time	8 hours
Recommended Maps	USGS 7.5-min *Crystal Lake, Valyermo, Juniper Hills*
Best Times	April through May; September through November
Agency	ANF/VD
Difficulty	★★★★

From the conifer-clad heights of Pallett Mountain and Will Thrall Peak to the pinyon-dotted swells just above the desert's reach, Pleasant View Ridge delivers what it promises. When north or northeast winds sweep smog and humid air away from Southern California, the ever-changing panoramas on this hike take in everything from sail-flecked Santa Monica Bay and the Channel Islands to the mind-stretching sweep of the Mojave Desert floor.

The long, undulating traverse, generally downhill along the spine of Pleasant View Ridge, involves a rather extreme range of elevation change. You'll top out at 8248 feet rather early in the trip and finish at 3900 feet. An early-morning temperature hovering near freezing at the start can be followed by 90° heat on the desert's edge a few hours later; so plan accordingly. Bring lots of water—none is available along the route unless you come across snow patches. You'll run into some short but difficult passages through thick chaparral; so you'll need long pants as well. Before you undertake the trip, be sure to sketch the route (as described below) on the topo maps recommended above.

The hike begins, exactly as in Trip 6 above, with a climb to Mt. Williamson's summit. It ends, down along Little Rock Creek, at the site of the former Sycamore Campground, i.e., the intersection of Alimony Ridge ORV route and Little Rock

Creek road (see Area A-8 map and introductory text). This point is 8.0 miles south of Little Rock Ranger Station. Transportation logistics will be simplified immensely if the upper part of Little Rock Creek road, leading to Santa Clara Divide Road north of Three Points, is open. Check with the Forest Service first to find out what roads are open. If it's early in the season, be sure to ask about snow conditions as well. The lofty stretch of Pleasant View Ridge northwest of Mt. Williamson includes some steep, north-facing slopes that may harbor icy patches of snow until sometime in May.

After you've hiked up to 8214' Mt. Williamson (1.7 miles) and perhaps paused a while to sign the register and admire the view, you'll make your way northwest along the undulating spine of Pleasant View Ridge. You'll pass over two even higher but unnamed points—8244' and 8248'—at 2.0 and 2.3 miles respectively, then begin the first of the many very sharp, rocky descents that characterize much of this trip. Over sparse pines and firs to the north, you'll look down upon some upthrust sandstone slabs known as "Sandrocks"—a part of the same Punchbowl Formation that is abundantly exposed at Devil's Punchbowl County Park.

At around 2.7 miles, look for the glittering wreckage of an aircraft caught near the top of a ridge 0.5 mile north. At 3.0 miles the Pleasant View ridgeline turns abruptly left (west) at a high point. (The wreckage lies about 0.2 mile northeast of here). You descend, then climb again, to Pallett Mountain (4.0 miles), where you'll find another summit register.

You then descend a well-worn climber's path to Burkhart Saddle, cross the Burkhart Trail, and continue straight up the ridge west toward Will Thrall Peak (the old hiking trail shown on the topo map skirting the peak is gone). The peak (5.1 miles), offering the most pleasant view of all from atop the ridge, also features a plaque honoring Will H. Thrall, editor of the Depression-era *Trails Magazine*. Will was an inveterate hiker of the San Gabriels from the 1920s through the '50s.

After signing the register on Will Thrall Peak, continue northwest down to a saddle and then up to a 7983' survey peak (5.8 miles) labelled "Pallett" on the topo map. You now begin a net descent of more than 4000 feet, interrupted several times by short, uphill stretches. As you draw nearer to the desert, the thinning forest soon consists only of Jeffrey pines, which are more able than most trees to withstand the effects of heat and drought. You could make camp on some flats just northwest of "Pallett." On the steeply plunging ridgeline at about 7.0 miles, thick chaparral replaces the forest.

In about 8 miles, you meet an old fire break running along the ridge ahead, and progress improves for a while. Sparse groves of pinyon pines appear, providing the only shade you'll get during the rest of the hike. At the 6586' survey point "View" (9.3 miles), the main ridgeline turns west. Proceed along the broad top of the ridge for another 0.7 mile to the head of a small canyon draining toward old Sycamore Campground. You now have two choices of equal difficulty: descend either the ridge just north of that canyon or the ridge just south of the canyon. Both routes are steep and rocky; proceed with care.

A rare runnable stretch, on Pleasant View Ridge

Area A-11, Trip 8
Devil's Punchbowl Loop Trail

	Distance	1.0 mile
	Total Elevation Gain/Loss	300'/300'
	Hiking Time	½ hour
	Optional Map	USGS 7.5-min *Valyermo*
	Best Times	All year
	Agency	DPCP
	Difficulty	★

Tens of millions of years in the making, Devil's Punchbowl is without a doubt L.A. County's most spectacular geological show-place. An observer looking down into this 300'-deep chasm immediately senses the enormity of the forces that produced the tilted and tangled collection of beige sand-stone slabs.

The Punchbowl is caught between two active faults—the main San Andreas Fault and an offshoot, the Punchbowl Fault—along which old sedimentary formations have been pushed upward and crumpled downward, as well as transported hori-zontally. Erosion has put the final touches on the scene, roughing out the bowl-shaped gorge of Punchbowl Canyon and carving, in a host of unique ways, the rocks exposed at the surface.

Operated by the county as a special-use area under permit from Angeles National Forest, the 1310-acre park includes a superb nature center, a couple of short nature walks (including the loop trail described here), and the Punchbowl Trail—a part of the High Desert National Recreation Trail. Devil's Punchbowl is open 7 days a week from

sunrise to sunset, no admission charge. To get there, exit Antelope Valley Freeway at Pearblossom Highway, and follow it east through the town of Littlerock to Pearblos-som. At Pearblossom, turn right on Long-view Road (County N6) and follow signs for the park, 7 miles ahead.

The Loop Trail is a perfect introduction to the Punchbowl area. It begins just behind the nature center, zigzags down off the rim to touch the seasonal creek in Punchbowl Canyon, and then climbs back out of the canyon opposite some of the tallest upright formations in the park. Near the start of the trail is a side path—the 0.3-mile Pinon Pathway—a self-guiding nature trail that loops through the pinyon-juniper forest along the Punchbowl rim.

During winter, occasional snowfalls dust the 4000' elevation of the Punchbowl itself and leave a lingering mantle of white on the pine-dotted slopes of the San Gabriel Moun-tains right above. During these episodes the trail can become muddy and slippery, and therefore probably not suitable for small children.

**Devil's Punchbowl
in winter**

Area A-11, Trip 9
Devil's Chair

	Distance	5.5 miles
	Total Elevation Gain/Loss	1200'/1400'
	Hiking Time	3 hours
	Optional Map	USGS 7.5-min *Valyermo*
	Best Times	September through June
	Agency	DPCP
	Difficulty	★★

The fenced viewpoint at Devil's Chair presides over what looks like frozen chaos—a vast assemblage of sandstone chunks and slabs tipped at odd angles, bent, seemingly pulled apart here, compressed there. This is really not so surprising when you realize that the Devil's Chair sits practically astride the "crush zone" of the Punchbowl Fault.

Devil's Chair can be reached with equal ease by starting either from Devil's Punchbowl County Park on the west or from South Fork Campground on east. With a little help from a friend, you can do the whole traverse in a one-way direction, as we suggest here. The west-to-east direction has a slight downhill advantage. You'll need a permit, free from the ranger at the county park's nature center, if you'll be camping along the trail.

If snow is present, check at the nature center to see if the route is safe. You should be aware that snow closes South Fork Campground, and that South Fork Big Rock Creek (next to the campground) could be difficult to ford after a big storm.

The Trip 8 description above gives driving directions to the county park. After dropping you off, your friend with the car should circle around to South Fork Campground by way of Fort Tejon and Valyermo roads, a 13-mile drive.

From the south side of the parking lot, find and follow the signed Burkhart Trail as it climbs northwest along the rim of the punchbowl. You're actually following the upper (south) edge of a downward sloping terrace—part of an alluvial fan left high and dry when the Punchbowl creek began carving a new course northeast. You join an old road at 0.5 mile, pass a small reservoir at 0.7 mile, and arrive at a trail junction at 0.8 mile. Here, in a Coulter-pine grove, bear left on the Punchbowl Trail leading east. The delightful, contouring path takes you around several shady ravines, all draining into the Punchbowl. After some sharply descending switchbacks, you reach a trail junction (3.0 miles) from where a 0.1-mile spur goes west and then north over a narrow, rock-ribbed ridge to the high perch known as Devil's Chair. Protective fencing furnishes some psychological comfort for the nervous-making traverse.

East of the junction the trail keeps dropping, touches a saddle, descends crookedly past large manzanita shrubs, and crosses a small stream in the bottom of pine- and oak-shaded Holcomb Canyon (3.7 miles). Flat areas suitable for camping can be found hereabouts.

Continue east up chaparral-smothered slopes to a saddle, then down the other side for a crooked mile to South Fork Campground.

Area A-11, Trip 10
Lower Punchbowl Canyon

	Distance	2.0 miles round trip
	Total Elevation Gain/Loss	400'/400'
	Hiking Time	1½ hours (round trip)
	Optional Map	USGS 7.5-min *Valyermo*
	Best Times	October through June
	Agency	ANF/VD
	Difficulty	★★

On this trip you enter Devil's Punchbowl by a little-known back way—the mouth of Punchbowl Canyon. Once above the lower canyon portals, you'll find yourself in a maze-like wonderland reminiscent of the "slickrock" country of southern Utah, save for the reddish hues. The hike is best done in winter, when snowmelt courses down the canyon and its tributaries.

To get to the canyon mouth, drive 0.5 mile south from Pearblossom on Longview Road to Avenue W, where you turn east. Avenue W becomes Valyermo Road. Continue about 7 more miles to a fork, where you keep straight on Big Rock Creek Road (Big Pines Road goes left). After another 0.5 mile you pass the Angeles National Forest boundary (large sign). Go 0.2 mile farther to a parking turnout on the left.

On the west side of the road you'll see a gated, private footbridge spanning Big Rock Creek. Don't use it. Instead ford the creek where you can, and start boulder-hopping up the narrow gorge to the west—Punchbowl Canyon. The canyon divides at 0.3 mile; stay right, in the main fork. Soon the familiar Punchbowl Formation rocks are all around you. The slabs of pebbly sandstone rise dramatically to the south—if you're game for it, scramble up for a great view of the brooding San Gabriels. Caution is in order when the rock is wet; it tends to disintegrate grain by grain much as Utah's slickrock does.

A small waterfall about 1 mile up the meandering canyon blocks any further easy walking. You can head back at this point, or you can find a way to scramble around it and reach the Devil's Punchbowl Loop Trail a short distance above.

Inside the Punchbowl

Area A-11, Trip 11
Holcomb Canyon

	Distance	3.7 miles
	Total Elevation Gain/Loss	700'/700'
	Hiking Time	3½ hours
	Recommended Map	USGS 7.5-min *Valyermo*
	Best Times	October through June
	Agency	DPCP
	Difficulty	★★★

Much of the fascination of the Devil's Punchbowl area lies in its trailless canyons, where the erosive forces of water have carved deep furrows in the soft sandstone. This beautiful loop trip, off-trail almost the whole way, includes alder-shaded Holcomb Canyon as well as the large tributary of Punchbowl Canyon overlooked by the Devil's Chair.

As in Trip 10 above, park in the small turnout on Big Rock Creek Road, 0.2 mile south of the National Forest boundary. (Another, much larger turnout is 0.3 mile farther, west of the road). This stretch of the creek is popular with fishermen.

Walk down the shoulder of the road 0.3 mile to the larger turnout, cross Big Rock Creek wherever convenient, and start following the rocky banks of a tributary creek heading due south into Holcomb Canyon. A nice mountain-desert mix of vegetation pervades the area: alder, willow and sycamore along the creek banks; live-oak, incense cedar and mountain mahogany higher on the banks; pinyon pine dotting the dry slopes. The bedrock here is mostly the San Francisquito Formation—a marine sandstone formed about 60 million years ago. The Punchbowl Formation, which is a nonmarine sandstone only about 8 million years old, is seen briefly on the right (west) in the form of a blocky outcrop soaring over a pinched section of the canyon, 1.1 miles from the start. Soon you'll return to the Punchbowl Formation and stay in it for most the remainder of the trip.

At 1.6 miles, you'll notice a shallow draw on the left (east). Look for the crossing of the Punchbowl Trail a short distance ahead. Use it to climb 0.3 mile west via switchbacks to a saddle. You then leave the trail and descend cross-country, northwest through manzanita and scrub oak, into the head of a ravine. Proceed down the ravine to a 3-way junction of ravines in a small flat just below the stony gaze of the Devil's Chair, 2.1 miles. From there on, you simply continue down-canyon (north) and eventually hook up with the lower end of Punchbowl Canyon, 0.3 mile short of your car. Meanwhile, there are lots of interesting rock formations to explore along the way. Don't forget your camera!

Area A-11, Trip 12
Burkhart Trail

	Distance	12.2 miles
	Total Elevation Gain/Loss	2000'/3700'
	Hiking Time	6 hours
	Optional Maps	USGS 7.5-min *Waterman Mtn.,* *Juniper Hills, Valyermo*
	Best Times	April through November
	Agency	ANF/VD
	Difficulty	★ ★ ★

Far from sight and sound of the city, the Burkhart Trail blazes a lonely path over Pleasant View Ridge and down into the upper margins of the Mojave Desert. Here the natural landscape is not marred by canyon-carving highways and fire roads, not blemished by powerlines, and mercifully free, for the most part, from the noxious clouds of air pollution that drift across the county.

Although this is certainly one of the better hiking routes in the San Gabriels, relatively few hikers make the long climb, descent and traverse all the way to Devil's Punchbowl County Park. Of course, you'll need to solve some transportation problems first. At best, you can have someone drop you off at the start, Buckhorn Campground, and pick you up later at Devil's Punchbowl. The shortest way around to it is via Vincent Gap and Big Rock Creek Road (partly dirt) to the east. The second shortest way is via Big Pines and Big Pines Road (paved all the way).

Begin hiking, as in Trip 1, by descending to Cooper Canyon Falls, and descending farther to Little Rock Creek, 1.7 miles. After crossing the creek, bear left and commence a long climb to Burkhart Saddle—a gap on the high crest of Pleasant View Ridge. You wind steadily upward on sparsely forested slopes lacking underbrush, but resplendent (in springtime) with blue and white lupines, red and blue penstemons, sunflowers, and other wildflowers. Little Rock Creek lies below, its stream

coursing through a thirsty-looking gorge.

Around 2.8 miles the trail crosses a perpetually sliding slope of sheared metamorphic rock, then gains better footing as it angles over to and finally crosses a tributary of Little Rock Creek. A series of long switchbacks takes you up the slope to the west, across the tributary once more, then up to Burkhart Saddle, 5.0 miles. There, a cool, dry breeze chills your sweat-soaked skin and clothing as you contemplate whether it's worth it to climb either Pallett Mountain or Will Thrall Peak for a better view of what you can already see.

Down the other side, conifer forest grades into chaparral as you drop north down along a canyon wall overlooking the upper gorge of Cruthers Creek. After a couple of zigzags near the bottom you join a ranch road (8.3 miles). Its crooked course takes you down along the creek, then east onto a gently sloping hillside. Look for the signed trail veering right toward Devil's Punchbowl County Park (the road itself continues north into the private Lewis Ranch).

You climb about 500 feet, then contour for almost 2 miles across the northern spurs of the San Gabriels. When you reach a dirt road at 11.5 miles where Punchbowl Trail keeps contouring ahead, bear left (northeast) on the road and walk down to a narrow trail continuing northeast along the rim of Punchbowl Canyon. The trail leads to the parking lot at Devil's Punchbowl County Park.

Area A-11, Trip 13
South Fork Trail

	Distance	5.2 miles
	Total Elevation Gain/Loss	100'/2200'
	Hiking Time	2½ hours
	Optional Maps	USGS 7.5-min *Crystal Lake, Valyermo*
	Best Times	April through November
	Agency	ANF/VD
	Difficulty	★★

The easy-going descent of the South Fork Trail doesn't take much effort; you simply put one foot in front of the other and let gravity do the rest. The well-graded trail descends (or ascends if you'd rather get more exercise and reverse the directions given here) along the west wall of the V-shaped gorge cut by Big Rock Creek's South Fork. Narrow, but seldom steep, the trail follows a natural, swaying contour as it curves around more than a dozen ravines indenting the canyon wall. South Fork creek murmurs far below (at least when swollen by melting snows), accompanied by the doleful trills of canyon wrens.

By April or May, it's usually possible to drive around from one end of the trail to the other the easy way—via Angeles Crest Highway and Big Rock Creek Road. The latter road has a graded dirt surface for 2 miles northwest of where it touches Vincent Gap, at mile 74.8 on Angeles Crest Highway.

You begin walking at the Islip Saddle parking lot, mile 64.1 on Angeles Crest Highway. Take the trail contouring to the north, not the sharply ascending Pacific Crest Trail, which climbs northwest toward Mt. Williamson's summit. Traffic noises fade quickly as you begin descending through a heterogeneous forest of Jeffrey pine, sugar pine, incense cedar, live oak, and bigcone Douglas-fir. As you descend, the high-country forest thins; pinyon pine, manzanita, mountain mahogany, and blue-

and white-blossoming ceanothus clothe the dry and rocky slopes.

The trail loses elevation faster than the South Fork, so by 4.4 miles you'll be traversing a sheer slope only 200 feet above the stream. A couple of short switchbacks at 4.9 miles take you down to meet the alder- and sycamore-shaded creek. Cross over to the other side and continue walking through South Fork Campground until you reach the trailhead parking area just below (north of) the campsites.

South Fork Campground is one of Angeles National Forest's more pleasant and secluded drive-in campgrounds. During April and May, flannel bush, or fremontia, blooms on the broad, alluvial terraces along the creek, opposite and downstream from the campground. Considered one of the showiest of California native plants, the fremontias here stand up to 15 feet high and bear thousands of large, waxy, yellow flowers.

If you have time for further exploration, climb southeast from the campground on the Manzanita Trail about 0.5 mile to some sandstone (Punchbowl Formation) outcrops. You'll get a great view of both the South Fork canyon and the main Big Rock Creek wash.

Area A-12: San Antonio Canyon/ Old Baldy

San Antonio Canyon, a yawning gap in the fortress-like south front of the San Gabriels, also serves as the main gateway to the third highest mountain mass in Southern California—Mt. San Antonio, or Old Baldy. At 10,064 feet, Baldy's summit looms large over the eastern Los Angeles Basin, the Inland Empire communities of Riverside and San Bernardino, and the western Mojave Desert. It can be seen as far north as the southern Sierra Nevada, and as far south as the Mexican border adjoining San Diego County.

Both San Antonio Canyon and Old Baldy lie astride the Los Angeles-San Bernardino county line. Old Baldy's summit is a county-line bench mark, making it the highest point in Los Angeles County, but not in San Bernardino County. Our coverage of the trails in this area includes some that are outside the L.A. County boundary, but we don't include anything east of the divide defined by Cucamonga Peak, the "Three T's," and Mt. Baldy Notch, nor north of Old Baldy. You may refer to John Robinson's *Trails of the Angeles* for more on these areas, which are a part of San Bernardino County's share of the San Gabriel Mountains.

The opening of San Antonio Canyon to automobiles, starting in 1908, helped facilitate the rapid development of cabins and resorts in the area. Several hundred cabins dotted the main canyon and its tributaries by the mid '30s. Camp Baldy—the site of today's Mt. Baldy village—grew to become one of the most popular mountain retreats in Southern California. The great flood of 1938, which tore up the whole front face of

the San Gabriels, washed away most of Camp Baldy, as well as scores of other cabins that were sited too close to the streams.

The resort era is long-forgotten today, but Mt. Baldy (or Baldy Village, as it's known to most residents) remains a viable cabin community. The greater Mt. Baldy area, with a population of about 1000, is the second-largest community in the San Gabriels, after Wrightwood.

San Antonio Canyon gets a huge influx of skiers and snow seekers during the winter, while a less hectic crowd of hikers and sightseers makes use of the area during the warmer months. In Baldy Village you can stop by the Forest Service information station (Friday through Sunday, 8:30 A.M. to 4:30 P.M.) for the latest on trail conditions, and to obtain permits if needed.

The upper end of San Antonio Canyon includes the Forest Service's Manker Flats Campground and Glacier Picnic Area, as well as a large parking lot for the privately operated ski lift. Backpackers can hoof it to Cedar Glen Trail Camp, the only developed trail camp in the area, or camp just about anywhere on Forest Service land, subject to the regulations for remote camping.

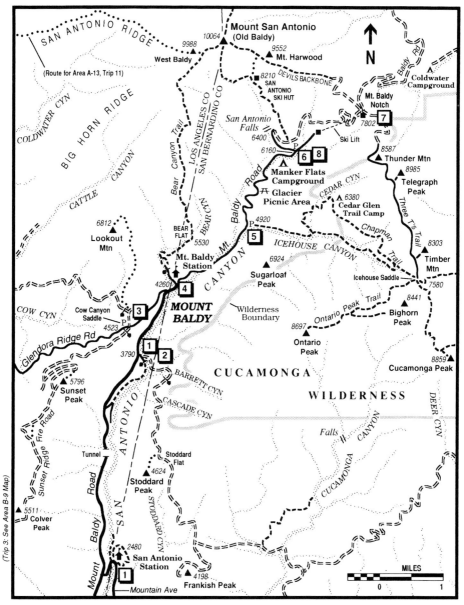

Area A-12: San Antonio Canyon/Old Baldy

Area A-12, Trip 1
San Antonio Canyon

👢	**Distance**	3.8 miles
	Total Elevation Gain/Loss	100'/1400'
🏴	**Hiking Time**	2½ hours
	Optional Map	USGS 7.5-min *Mt. Baldy*
	Best Times	October through May
🗻 ↗	**Agency**	ANF/MBD
	Difficulty	★★★

Over the past century and a half, lower San Antonio Canyon's flood-prone bed has seen the creation and the demise of many a trail, wagon road, and auto road. On this ramble down along the boulder-filled canyon bottom, you'll trace the route of an auto road (now about 75 percent obliterated) that, like so many of its predecessors, was built too close to the temperamental stream.

Today's road—Mt. Baldy Road—curves along the canyon's west slope, staying a comfortable 200 feet or so above the stream. You'll use it to get from one end of the hike to the other, a drive of about 4 miles. You could turn this into a loop trip by walking, running or biking Mt. Baldy Road, but fast traffic and two narrow tunnels make that a risky undertaking—at least under normal traffic conditions. On the canyon hike itself you must cross the stream several times, so don't go if the water level is too high.

You begin at the intersection of Mt. Baldy Road and the dead-end "Mountain Avenue," mile 1.1 on Mt. Baldy Road. (This Mountain Avenue was once connected to the Mountain Avenue near San Antonio Station). The intersection is 1.3 miles south of Mt. Baldy village. Park here and walk south on the old pavement. After you bypass a vehicle barrier, the badly deteriorated road bed swings low across the cliff-like face of a promontory called the Hogback. Until 1908 the Hogback, along with a picturesque waterfall in the canyon just below it, were formidable obstacles to

travel by man or beast. That year, a toll road suitable for automobiles was pushed through, destroying the falls in the process. The road was widened and paved in the early '20s, then badly washed out in the 1938 flood, and then rebuilt again. The final demise came during flooding in 1969; by that time, however, the old road had been rendered obsolete by the straighter and faster Mt. Baldy Road, completed in 1955.

At the beginning of the hike, and again 1.4 miles later, you'll pass small hydro-electric power plants, their turbines loudly humming whenever the stream flow allows. These are the descendants of the first power station installed below the Hogback in 1892. It proved to be an efficient but somewhat erratic (because of poor flows in years of drought) source of electric power for communities as distant as Pomona and San Bernardino.

At about 1.8 miles, just below the Mt. Baldy Road tunnels, the canyon narrows. Some boulder-hopping and bushwhacking are in order, along with some foot-wetting fords. But soon the canyon floor widens and becomes open and sunny, with willows and alders growing along the stream. You can either try to trace pieces of the old road, or stay closer to the stream and travel over the rock-strewn flood plain. During the last mile of the hike you may come upon scores, possibly hundreds, of people out enjoying the sun and the stream, especially if the weather's warm.

Just before the end (3.6 miles) you can

climb a bridge abutment to reach a piece of the old road on the east bank. This leads toward San Antonio Ranger Station—the end of the hike.

Behind the station, the Elfin Forest Nature Trail winds for a mile amid typical sage-scrub and chaparral vegetation. It's a worthwhile walk whenever the vegetation is in bloom during the springtime.

Area A-12, Trip 2
Stoddard Peak

	Distance	6.0 miles round trip
	Total Elevation Gain/Loss	1100'/1100'
	Hiking Time	3 hours (round trip)
	Optional Map	USGS 7.5-min *Mt. Baldy*
	Best Times	October through May
	Agency	ANF/MBD
	Difficulty	★★

Stoddard Peak's 4624' height places it above most of the shaggy, chaparral-covered foothill country, but well below the stony gaze of the western ramparts of the Cucamonga Wilderness. When dusted or spotted with snow, the peak becomes a dichotomous perch between the white-mantled world above and sun-warmed slopes and canyons below. The hike to the top involves mostly road-walking, with a short, rugged stretch near the peak itself.

Start hiking at the intersection of the dead-end Mountain Avenue, mile 1.1 on Mt. Baldy Road (1.3 miles south of Mt. Baldy village). Don't take the old, paved, canyon-bottom road to the south (Trip 1 route), but rather head east on the dirt road that descends past a small hydro-powerplant. Cross San Antonio Canyon's stream and continue curving south, then east on the dirt road as it contours into Barrett Canyon. After passing some picturesque cabins and yapping dogs, you arrive at a locked vehicle gate, 0.8 mile. Bypass it and keep following the road. You climb amid dense oak forest, contour along a sunny slope, curl around steep Cascade Canyon, and then climb gradually to a saddle (2.6 miles), where the road begins to descend into the Stoddard

Canyon drainage. The gently sloping area adjoining on the east, Stoddard Flat, is suitable for trail camping.

From the saddle, a faint path leads west up through tall brush, and then turns south along the top of a sunny ridge. Proceed 0.4 mile on this path, passing over two false summits, to the true summit of Stoddard Peak as marked on the Mt. Baldy topo map. The second false summit you pass over is actually slightly higher than Stoddard Peak (contrary to the contour lines as printed on the topo map).

The ridge falls sharply beyond Stoddard Peak, so there's no need to go on—the view is the best from here. Looking down into San Antonio Canyon, you can see disconnected segments of the old canyon-bottom road, pummelled by floods and slides. Old Baldy, its snow-cap gleaming in winter, dominates the view to the north. To the south, beyond San Antonio Dam (and its dry flood-control reservoir), spread the Pomona valley and the Chino Hills. If it's clear enough to see the ocean horizon, you can often see sprawling Santa Catalina Island, plus the low dome of San Clemente Island a little to the left.

Area A-12, Trip 3
Sunset Ridge

Distance	12.7 miles
Total Elevation Gain/Loss	1700'/4700'
Hiking Time	6 hours
Recommended Map	USGS 7.5-min *Mt. Baldy*
Best Times	October through May
Agency	ANF/MBD
Difficulty	★★★

The hike to Sunset Peak from Cow Canyon Saddle (just outside the village of Mt. Baldy) offers up fine views of the archipelago of high peaks stretching from San Gabriel Wilderness in the west to Cucamonga Wilderness in the east. Mt. San Antonio rises from center stage in the north, its bald summit often accented by a brilliant snow cap.

The climb of Sunset Peak is just the beginning of this one-way trek along Sunset Ridge, which takes you all the way down to the rim of the San Gabriel Valley at Marshall Canyon County Park (Area B-9, Trip 3). On rare, very clear days, you'll have spectacular, rim-of-the-world vistas throughout the entire trip. Quite often, an abrupt temperature inversion at about 3000–4000 feet puts a tight lid on the marine layer, with warm, clear air above, and cool, moist air below. In this case you may have (as I did) the interesting experience of descending into pillowy clouds.

Part of the route described here (Sunset Ridge Fire Road) briefly enters the San Dimas Experimental Forest, which is off-limits to hiking without a special permit. Contact the Mt. Baldy District rangers to inquire about the permit, which may be needed for walking the fire road.

From the large parking area at Cow Canyon Saddle on Glendora Ridge Road, start hiking up the gated fire road on the opposite (south) side of the road. You gain elevation steadily, accompanied by a mixture of tall chaparral, live oaks, bigcone Douglas-firs, and bigleaf maples. You reverse direction at 1.9 miles, and again at 2.5 miles. Just after the latter switchback, bear left on an old fire break and head southwest straight to the summit (2.9 miles). This worthwhile and fun shortcut, with some easy rock scrambling at the top, saves time and distance over the alternative—a mile of tedious road walking.

Sunset Peak's flat, barren summit makes a fine (but dry) campsite. A fire lookout stood here from the 1920s to the '70s; you'll notice the building's foundation and also the remains of a rainwater collection system.

When it's time to move on, head south down the ridge to rejoin Sunset Ridge Fire Road. Proceed south to a saddle (4.0 miles), marked with a "no entry" sign on the boundary of the San Dimas Experimental Forest. All slopes to the right of the ridgeline lie within the closed (except by permit) area. Much of our current knowledge about fire ecology and erosion in the chaparral plant community has been gained from carefully controlled experiments performed in this outdoor laboratory over the past six decades.

To make shorter but steeper work of the descent, leave the road at the saddle, skirt a small hill on the left, and descend south on a steep fire break to where you join the road again (4.3 miles). You've now lost sight of the high peaks behind, but you're gaining an almost aerial view of trench-like San Antonio Canyon on the left, and the flat San Gabriel Valley ahead.

At 5.5 miles, a signed side trail leads right to 5511' Colver Peak, named after Charles Colver, manager of the experimental forest. Just ahead lie several ridgetop antennas collectively known as the Sunset Ridge Electronic Site. Just below the antennas (about 6.0 miles), you swing southwest along the ridge, where a broad view of nearly the entire L.A. Basin is revealed.

Descending in earnest now on long S-curves, the road takes you down to a flat area on the ridge at 9.4 miles (point 3551 on the topo map). North of the road is a large tree plantation. Leave the fire road at this point and turn south down a wide, very steep fire break (the scar of this fire break is plainly visible from many miles away in the valley below). Sunset Ridge Fire Road itself continues several miles west and south, coming to an end within a private, gated community on the north fringe of La Verne.

On the fire break you lose 1100 feet of elevation in just 0.7 mile. Amazingly, mountain-bike tracks are revealed in the dirt. When you reach the bottom, turn right on the fire road there. Proceed 0.6 mile west to the Marshall Canyon Trail, which descends a ridge to the left (southwest). Two miles of descent (choose the downhill trail at each fork) will take you to the Marshall Canyon Trail equestrian parking lot on Golden Hills Road in La Verne. See Area B-9, Trip 3 for more details on Marshall Canyon County Park.

Mt. Baldy seen from Stoddard Ridge

Area A-12, Trip 4
Bear Flat

	Distance	3.5 miles round trip
	Total Elevation Gain/Loss	1300'/1300'
	Hiking Time	2 hours (round trip)
	Optional Map	USGS 7.5-min *Mt. Baldy*
	Best Times	All year
	Agency	ANF/MBD
	Difficulty	★★

Barely a mile's walk from the busy little community of Mt. Baldy, you can be sitting on a rock, communing with Nature, feet dangling in the sun-and-shade-dappled, crystalline stream of Bear Canyon. With a bit more time and energy, you can climb to Bear Flat, where a binocular sweep of the surrounding hillsides often nets sightings of bighorn sheep.

Begin at the intersection of Mt. Baldy Road and Bear Creek Road, in the center of Mt. Baldy village. (A small parking lot is located right at the foot of Bear Creek

Bear Canyon stream

Road.) Walk—don't drive—up the ungated paved road to its end (0.4 mile), then continue on a dirt trail that soon becomes narrow. Many cabins, in various stages of repair (or ruin), line the way. At one point, a rickety rope-and-plank footbridge serves as the only link between a cabin on one side of the creek and the trail on the other.

Like other inhabited canyons in the Front Range of the San Gabriels, lower Bear Canyon is overrun by non-native ground covers like ivy and vinca, but shaded by magnificent live oaks, bays, and bigcone Douglas-firs. After crossing the creek twice, the trail divides. Take either path: the right branch climbs up the right slope; the left branch stays low along the stream, passing more cabins, before curving right to join the other branch.

After the two paths rejoin, the main Bear Canyon Trail goes by a water tank (part of the town's water supply), switches back, curves around sun-struck slopes, and plunges into a shady oak grove high on the east slope of the canyon. At about 1.7 miles, the trail crosses the stream for the last time. Bear Flat is the bracken-fern-filled, sloping meadow just above this crossing. For casual hikers, this is the place to sniff a few spring wildflowers, look for bighorn sheep tracks, and then think about turning back. Beyond this, the Bear Canyon Trail switchbacks up to the south ridge of Mt. San Antonio and relentlessly continues all the way to the summit, almost 5 miles away, 4500 feet higher than Bear Flat.

Area A-12, Trip 5
Cucamonga Peak

	Distance	12.0 miles round trip
	Total Elevation Gain/Loss	4300'/4300'
	Hiking Time	7 hours (round trip)
	Optional Map	USGS 7.5-min *Mt. Baldy,*
		Cucamonga Peak
	Best Times	May through November
	Agency	ANF/MBD
	Difficulty	★★★★

Cucamonga Peak's south and east slopes feature some of the most dramatic relief in the San Gabriel range. At 8859 feet, the peak stands sentinel-like only 4 miles from the edge of the broad inland valley region known as the Inland Empire. Go all the way to the top for the view, but don't be too disappointed if there's nothing below but haze and smog. So much beautiful high country can be seen along the way that reaching the top is just icing on the cake.

Most of the hike lies within Cucamonga Wilderness, requiring a permit for both day and overnight use. Near Cucamonga's summit you'll tackle a steep, north-facing gully that can retain snow into May. Be sure to discuss with a ranger the possible hazards of snow and ice if it's early or late in the season.

Your trip begins at the Icehouse Canyon parking area, a short way down the spur road signed NO OUTLET, 1.5 miles up San Antonio Canyon from Mt. Baldy village. Walk past the ruins of the recently torched Ice House Canyon Lodge, and then up along the path that follows the alder-shaded stream. The first couple of miles along the canyon are a fitting introduction to a phase of Southern California scenery not familiar to a lot of visitors and newcomers. Huge bigcone Douglas-fir, incense cedar, and live oak trees cluster on the banks of the stream, which dances over boulder and fallen log. Moisture-loving, flowering plants like columbine sway in the breeze. Some of old cabins along the lower canyon still survive, while others, destroyed by flood or fire, have left evidence in the form of foundations or rock walls.

Old newspaper reports suggest that an ice-packing operation existed in or near Icehouse Canyon during the late 1850s. The ice was packed down San Antonio Canyon on mules to a point accessible to wagons (below the Hogback), whereupon it was carted, as quickly as possible, to Los Angeles for use in making ice cream and for chilling beverages. Whether ice was actually quarried in this canyon or in another, Icehouse Canyon's name is apt enough: cold-air drainage produces refrigerator-like temperatures on many a summer morning, and deep-freeze temperatures in winter.

The Chapman Trail intersects on the left at 1.0 mile. It goes up Icehouse Canyon's north wall, passes Cedar Glen Trail Camp, and contours over to meet the older, canyon-bottom trail. Stay on the latter (Icehouse Canyon) trail; it's about 1.7 miles shorter, it's cooler, and it offers better scenery. At Columbine Spring (2.4 miles, last water during the warmer months), the trail starts switchbacking up the north wall. After passing the upper intersection of the Chapman Trail at 2.9 miles, you continue to pine-shaded Icehouse Saddle, 3.5 miles, where trails converge from many directions. The trail to Cucamonga's summit contours southeast, descends moderately, and climbs to a 7654' saddle (4.4 miles) between Bighorn and Cucamonga peaks. Thereafter, it switchbacks up a steep slope dotted with lodgepole pines and white firs.

At 5.8 miles, the trail crosses a shady draw 200 feet below and northwest of the summit. A signed but indistinct side path goes straight up to the summit, 6.0 miles from your starting point in Icehouse Canyon. Return the same way, or take the alternate route, the Chapman Trail, if you'd like a longer but more gradual descent from Icehouse Saddle.

In Icehouse Canyon

Area A-12, Trip 6
San Antonio Falls

	Distance	1.2 miles round trip
	Total Elevation Gain/Loss	250'/250'
	Hiking Time	1 hour (round trip)
	Optional Map	USGS 7.5-min *Mount San Antonio*
	Best Times	April through July
	Agency	ANF/MBD
	Difficulty	★

At San Antonio Falls, San Antonio Canyon's fledgling stream shoots down a broken rock face, falling a total of about 100 feet in three tiers. With a drainage area of only a few hundred acres, the falls put on a decent show only after a rather big storm or when the snow above is melting at a rapid rate. Three springs in the headwaters of the canyon help keep the falls alive, at a greatly subdued level, after all the snow has melted.

The easy hike to the base of the falls begins on the gated fire road just above Manker Flats Campground and just below the parking area for the Mt. Baldy ski lift. The road, which is closed to all but ski-lift-maintenance vehicles, is paved for the first 0.6 mile. That's just enough to reach a hairpin curve with a good glimpse of the falls to the left.

From the curve, a short but slightly precarious trail contours to the base of the falls, where the plummeting water hits not a pool but a stream bed of broken rock and gravel. If you have small kids, watch them carefully on this trail and near the base of falls to ensure their safety.

Area A-12, Trip 7
Old Baldy—East Approach

Distance	6.4 miles round trip
Total Elevation Gain/Loss	2300'/2300'
Hiking Time	3½ hours (round trip)
Optional Map	USGS 7.5-min *Mount San Antonio, Telegraph Peak*
Best Times	May through November
Agency	ANF/MBD
Difficulty	★★★

No Southland hiker's repertoire of experiences is complete without at least one ascent of Mt. San Antonio—Old Baldy. The east approach is the least taxing of the several routes to the summit, but it's by no means a picnic. You start at 7800 feet, with virtually no altitude acclimatization, and climb expeditiously to over 10,000 feet. With easy access, it's beguilingly easy to come unprepared for high winds or bad weather, which although fairly rare, may come up suddenly. Ice, if present, can be a serious hazard as well.

By mechanical means (a car) you can get to the upper terminus of Mt. Baldy Road in less than half an hour from the valley flatlands below. Further mechanical means—the Mt. Baldy ski lift—carries you to an elevation of 7800 feet at Mt. Baldy Notch, where you begin hiking. Although the ski-lift caters mostly to skiers (7 days a week during the winter season), it remains open during the summer season on weekends (9 A.M. to 4:45 P.M.) for the benefit of sightseers and hikers. If it's a weekday, or you don't like being dangled over an abyss, you can always walk up the ski-lift-maintenance road starting from Manker Flats. That option adds 3.6 miles and an elevation change of about 1600 feet both on the way up and on the way down. A lodge at the upper terminus of the lift offers food and beverages.

From Mt. Baldy Notch (about 200 yards northeast of the top of the main ski lift), take the maintenance road to the northwest that climbs moderately, then more steeply through groves of Jeffrey pine and incense cedar. After a couple of bends, you come to the road's end (1.3 miles) and the beginning of the trail along the Devils Backbone ridge. Sign in at the register provided near the beginning of the trail. The stretch ahead, once a hair-raiser, lost most of its terror when the Civilian Conservation Corps constructed a wider and safer trail, complete with guard rails, in 1935–36. The guard rails are gone now, but there's plenty of room to maneuver, unless there are problems with strong winds and/or ice. Devils Backbone offers grand vistas of both the Lytle Creek drainage on the north and east and San Antonio Canyon on the south.

The backbone section ends at about 2.0 miles as you start traversing the broad, south flank of Mt. Harwood. Scattered lodgepole pines now predominate. At 2.6 miles you arrive at the saddle between Harwood and Old Baldy, where backpackers sometimes set up camp (no water, no facilities here). Continue climbing up the rocky ridge to the west, past stunted, wind-battered conifers barely clinging to survival in the face of yearly onslaughts by cold winter winds. You reach the summit after a total of 3.2 miles.

On the rocky summit, barren of trees, but not of a few inconspicuous alpine plants and lichens, you'll find a rock-walled enclosure and a register book that fills up with the names of hundreds of hikers on a fair-weather weekend. Most days you can easily make out the other two members of the triad of Southern California giants—San Gorgonio Mountain and San Jacinto Peak— about 50 miles east and southeast, respectively. On days of crystalline clarity, the panorama includes 90° of ocean horizon, a 120° slice of the brown desert floor, and far-off ramparts of the southern Sierra Nevada and Panamint ranges, as much as 160 miles away.

Area A-12, Trip 8
Old Baldy—South Approach

Distance	8.4 miles round trip
Total Elevation Gain/Loss	3900'/3900'
Hiking Time	6 hours (round trip)
Recommended Map	USGS 7.5-min *Mount San Antonio*
Best Times	May through November
Agency	ANF/MBD
Difficulty	★★★★

This route, which makes use of the "ski-hut trail" through upper San Antonio Canyon, is the most varied and interesting of the several ways to reach the top of Old Baldy. The approach is direct and satisfying. The higher you climb, the more rewarding the view, and the greater your sense of accomplishment.

From Manker Flats, walk up the ski-lift-maintenance road 0.9 mile to the unmarked ski-hut trail on the left. This junction is ⅓ mile past the sharp hairpin turn opposite San Antonio Falls. The trail climbs up a rocky slope, then maintains a steep but well-graded ascent high along the east wall of upper San Antonio Canyon. Bigcone Douglas-fir, Jeffrey pine, sugar pine, and white fir trees clothe the slopes, which are accented by blooms of Indian paintbrush, wallflower, and yucca during the late spring and early summer.

Near the last of the big trees, and just below the big, open bowl scooped out of Old Baldy's southeast flank, you arrive at the Sierra Club's San Antonio Ski Hut (2.5 miles). Still in excellent repair today, the hut was built in 1937 by Sierra Club ski mountaineers who pioneered the then-unfamiliar sport of snow skiing in Southern California. Use of the hut is by reservation only (call the Sierra Club, (213) 472-6768, for details). Trail campers without reservations are invited to camp in the so-called "Rock Garden" ⅛ mile southwest of the hut.

Just beyond the hut, the now-more-primitive trail swings west across a small creek, crosses the Rock Garden, and then switchbacks up the west wall of the canyon. At 3.2 miles, you reach the top of the south ridge of Old Baldy, where you have a fine view down San Antonio Canyon. Continue north along that ridge, following a rocky, primitive trail, 1 mile to the summit.

If you don't want to retrace your steps on the way back, you could return to your starting point by way of the Devils Backbone Trail, and then either ride the ski lift down or walk down the maintenance road to Manker Flats. With the use of a car shuttle, you could descend the spectacular but foot-punishing Bear Canyon Trail, which loses 5800 feet in 6.4 miles, ending at Mt. Baldy village. Or, if you like fast descents down talus and scree slopes, you could walk down to the saddle just west of Mt. Harwood, and then drop straight down to the ski lodge 1200 feet below. Sturdy, ankle-protecting footwear is essential for the latter route, which can be recommended only for hikers with an excellent sense of balance.

On the Ski Hut Trail

Area A-13: Sheep Mountain Wilderness

Sprawling over 44,000 acres, Sheep Mountain Wilderness is the largest and most recently (1984) designated federal wilderness in the San Gabriel Mountains. The name refers to the Nelson bighorn sheep, which are quite abundant throughout the area, and also to Iron Mountain—sometimes called Sheep Mountain—which lies near the geographic center of the Wilderness.

The Wilderness lies almost entirely in the grip of the many-branched, upper watershed of East Fork San Gabriel River. Rapid uplift and erosion have created relief on a prodigious scale here. Boulder-strewn ridges dotted with sturdy conifers and clothed in tough blankets of chaparral fall thousands of feet to streams that tumble down V-shaped gorges. Elevations within the wilderness area range from 2400 feet on the East Fork near Swan Rock to 10,064 feet at Old Baldy's summit, which lies on the east boundary.

From the 1850s until the early 1900s, gold mining was king on the East Fork, with important ore-producing prospects located high on the slopes of Mt. Baden-Powell and Old Baldy and on some of the steep slopes overlooking the East Fork. On the banks of the East Fork itself, mountains of gold-bearing alluvium were literally washed away during a spate of hydraulic mining activity in the 1870s. A fascinating history of East Fork's mining heyday can be read in John Robinson's slender book *Mines of the East Fork*. Mining for gold and tungsten continues today at a number of sites within the wilderness; this is because certain mining claims were legally "grandfathered" when the area was declared a wilderness.

Most trails of Sheep Mountain Wilderness don't penetrate very far into its interior; however, cross-country hiking through the canyons and along many of the high ridges is possible. Four of the routes detailed below (Trips 1, 5, 6, and 7) actually lie outside Sheep Mountain Wilderness, but are included here because of their proximity to it.

It is not necessary to obtain a wilderness permit for entry into Sheep Mountain Wilderness, except when you start from the end of East Fork Road. Permits can be obtained from the East Fork Ranger Station, or you can fill out a self-issuing permit at the entrance to the station, taking the permit with you and leaving a duplicate behind.

Even when a permit is not required, you should consult with a Mt. Baldy District ranger to check on the latest snow conditions, stream levels, or other possible hazards if you're planning a long trip to the interior of the wilderness. You should also be aware that the trailheads on Angeles Crest Highway (Vincent Gap and Dawson Saddle) can be unreachable by car for several months out of the year because of winter-season snow cover or rockslides.

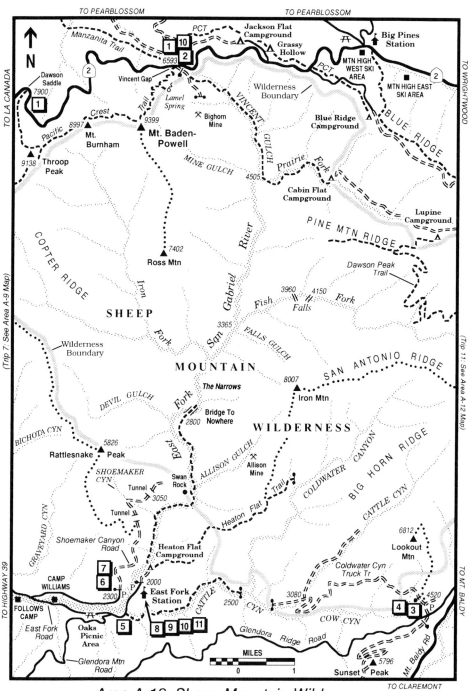

Area A-13: Sheep Mountain Wilderness

Area A-13, Trip 1
Mount Baden-Powell Traverse

	Distance	9.2 miles (includes Throop Peak and Mt. Burnham summits)
	Total Elevation Gain/Loss	2400'/3700'
	Hiking Time	5 hours
	Optional Map	USGS 7.5-min *Crystal Lake*
	Best Times	May through November
	Agency	ANF/VD
	Difficulty	★★★

Named in honor of Lord Baden-Powell, the British Army officer who started the Boy Scout movement in 1907, massive Mt. Baden-Powell stands higher than any other mountain in the San Gabriels—except the Mt. San Antonio complex to the east. Many thousands of hikers troop to Baden-Powell's summit yearly, mostly by way of Vincent Gap on Angeles Crest Highway.

Baden-Powell's summit is the last major milestone on the 52-mile trek from Chantry Flat to Vincent Gap known as the Silver Moccasin Trail (in this part of the range it coincides with the Pacific Crest Trail). The five-day-long Silver Moccasin backpack is a rite-of-passage for L.A.-area Scouts.

If you want to climb Mt. Baden-Powell in a most interesting way, try this one-way hike from Dawson Saddle to Vincent Gap. The effort involved is only little more than what's involved in the usual round trip from Vincent Gap, and you'll visit two other peaks as well. All three peaks offers their own unique and panoramic perspective of the rugged Sheep Mountain Wilderness below. The shuttle between ending and starting points is only 5 miles long.

You begin where the Dawson Saddle Trail meets Angeles Crest Highway, mile 69.6, just east of Dawson Saddle. There's parking space on the north side of the highway. On the trail you switchback up through pines and firs to gain the top of a long, gradually ascending ridge leading toward the main crest of the San Gabriels at Throop

Peak. An impressive 3540 hours of volunteer labor by Boy Scouts were required to build this trail, completed in 1982.

At 1.8 miles, near the bench mark 8789', you join the Pacific Crest Trail. Head southwest on the PCT, then climb cross-country about 300 yards to reach the summit of Throop Peak. Hiker's registers are found here, as well as on the other two peaks you'll be visiting.

Return to the Dawson Saddle Trail junction and continue northeast on the PCT, which follows the main ridgeline. You descend to a saddle, then ascend to Mt. Burnham's north flank, where switchbacks take you over to Burnham's east shoulder. You can make an easy side trip to Burnham's summit from the east shoulder.

After bagging Burnham, continue east, climbing a breathless 400 feet more, to reach the impressive Boy Scout monument on Baden-Powell's summit. Weather-beaten lodgepole and limber pines dot the summit area, one of the latter identified by an interpretive sign.

Return by way of the trail descending Baden-Powell's northeast ridge. After 40 switchbacks and 3.8 miles of descent you'll reach the large Vincent Gap parking area (mile 74.8 on Angeles Crest Highway). About halfway down the trail, on the 25th switchback corner, a side trail leads about 200 yards east to a dribbling pipe at Lamel Spring.

Area A-13, Trip 2
Ross Mountain

👢	**Distance**	13.4 miles round trip
	Total Elevation Gain/Loss	5500'/5500'
🧭	**Hiking Time**	8 hours (round trip)
	Recommended Map	USGS 7.5-min *Crystal Lake*
	Best Times	May through November
🏔️ ↗ 🥾	**Agency**	ANF/MBD
	Difficulty	★★★★

Isolated and difficult to reach, Ross Mountain stands tall on the divide between the trench-like East Fork San Gabriel River and a shallower but equally steep-walled tributary called Iron Fork. To get there you must first climb Mt. Baden-Powell, and then descend 2000 feet down a hardscrabble ridge. Weary peak-baggers have dubbed the mountain "Ross Pit"—you'll know why when it comes time to turn around and return the same way you came.

Starting from Vincent Gap (mile 74.8 on Angeles Crest Highway), hike the 40 switchbacks of the Pacific Crest Trail to Mt. Baden-Powell's summit (3.8 miles). Once you reach the top, you simply follow the rounded ridge leading south for another 2.9 miles to Ross Mountain's 7402' high point.

From the Baden-Powell summit, you swoop down along the eroding south rim of Mine Gulch and reach (one mile and 1000 feet below) a flat area shaded by stately Jeffrey pines, suitable for camping. Ahead, there are fewer trees, and more chaparral. Short climbs alternate with long, steep, rocky downhill stretches.

According to the register kept on Ross Mountain, only a dozen or so climbers come this way every year. Die-hards have set speed records from Vincent Gap, while others have ascended the mountain by bushwhacking up the south slope from Iron Fork, a very impressive feat indeed.

A panoramic view of the canyons below Ross Mountain may be had by walking 0.2 mile farther to the mountain's south brow. When it's time to return, breathe a long sigh of regret and then tackle the job. The climb back up to Baden-Powell is nearly always a sweaty affair, with a southern exposure all the way and little shade.

Area A-13, Trip 3
Lookout Mountain

👢	**Distance**	4.0 miles round trip
	Total Elevation Gain/Loss	2300'/2300'
🧭	**Hiking Time**	2½ hours (round trip)
	Recommended Map	USGS 7.5-min *Mt. Baldy*
	Best Times	October through June
🏔️ ↗	**Agency**	ANF/MBD
	Difficulty	★★★

Lookout Mountain, a prominent bump on the south ridge of Mt. San Antonio, was named after "Baldy Lookout," a wooden tower constructed there during 1915–16 and used every season until 1927. After being seriously damaged by a windstorm in 1927, the lookout was moved over to neighboring Sunset Peak, where it remained in place until the '70s.

In the mid '20s, Lookout Mountain was one of two sites used by Nobel-prize-winning physicist Albert Michelson during a several-year effort to obtain a precise value for the speed of light. Beams of light from a rapidly rotating octagonal prism at "Station Michelson" on Mt. Wilson were fired toward "Station Antonio" at Lookout Mountain, where they were reflected back to the prism on Mt. Wilson by means of a large concave mirror. The distance between the stations (approximately 22 miles) was obtained with unparalleled precision by triangulation from a carefully surveyed baseline down in the San Gabriel Valley. The travel time of the light was measured as a function of the rate at which the prism had to turn in order to properly intercept the reflected beam. The round-trip distance divided by the round-trip travel time of the light gave the speed, which as every student knows is close to 300,000 kilometers per second, or 186,000 miles per second (about 670 million miles per hour).

Today Lookout Mountain draws about 100 visitors yearly, many of whom are lucky enough to spot a bighorn sheep or two. The primitive path to the top, unmaintained since the days of the Baldy Lookout, is narrow but still followable.

From Cow Canyon Saddle on Glendora Ridge Road (1 mile southwest of Mt. Baldy village), drive 0.3 mile north on a dirt road to a large parking area. Notice the fire break going north up a steep ridgeline. Climb 50 feet up that fire break and look for the trail contouring to the left. The trail curves along a west-facing slope, and at 0.9 mile gains a saddle southeast of Lookout Mountain. It then turns northwest and zigzags up Lookout Mountain's southeast ridge until the ridge becomes too steep, at 1.4 miles. Barely recognizeable from now on, the trail traverses the shady northeast flank of the mountain, gains the north ridgeline, and turns south to reach the summit (2.0 miles).

Rusted metal and shards of plate glass are reminders of the old lookout. You'll also find the three in-line concrete pillars, pointing toward Mt. Wilson, that supported the large mirror used during the Michelson experiments.

The summit makes a fine spot for a picnic lunch, complete with a great view of Old Baldy looming above and parts of the metropolis below. Since bighorn sheep frequent this area, don't camp on the summit—just come for the day.

Old Baldy seen from Lookout Mountain

Area A-13, Trip 4
Coldwater Canyon Truck Trail

	Distance	10 miles round trip to Cattle Canyon
	Total Elevation Gain/Loss	1600'/1600'
	Hiking Time	5 hours (round trip)
	Optional Map	USGS 7.5-min *Mt. Baldy*
	Best Times	October through May
	Agency	ANF/MBD
	Difficulty	★★★

Although wilderness areas do not normally contain maintained dirt roads, Sheep Mountain Wilderness does. Several private inholdings and preexisting mining claims were necessarily included within the boundary of Sheep Mountain Wilderness when it was created in 1984. Coldwater Canyon Truck Trail guarantees access to several private ranches in the Coldwater Canyon area as well as an active tungsten-mining operation in Cattle Canyon. The road is open to hikers and equestrians, but not open to bicycles (mountain biking is prohibited in all wilderness areas).

Hiking down Coldwater Canyon Truck Trail is one of the easiest ways to maximize your chance of sighting a bighorn sheep in the San Gabriels. Cool or cloudy days are best; sunny days are scorchers most of the year, as you'll be on shadeless south-facing slopes most of the way.

From the large parking area 0.3 mile north of Cow Canyon Saddle, take the gated road that contours west, well above Cow Canyon's floor, and well below Lookout Mountain's summit. Take note of the fantastically jumbled and contorted exposures of granitic (quartz diorite) and metamorphic (gneiss) rock exposed in the road cuts. Ancient movements along the San Gabriel Fault are responsible. Cow Canyon Saddle marks the eastern terminus of the fault; from there the fault continues almost due west, paralleling Cow Canyon, lower Cattle Canyon, and the East and West forks of the San Gabriel River.

At 2.5 miles, you reach a saddle on the ridge between Cow and Cattle canyons. Bighorn sheep prints in the road dust reveal this to be a popular crossing point for the agile creatures. Ahead, the road continues crookedly down the falling ridgeline between the two canyons. At a sharp hairpin turn at 4.4 miles, there's a fine view up rubble-filled upper Cattle Canyon toward Bighorn Ridge.

You can keep going all the way to the wide floor of Cattle Canyon (5 miles), where a seasonal stream makes its way through a barren, boulder-filled wash. Less than a mile ahead (west) down Coldwater Canyon, there's a private ranch—no trespassing. You can, however, turn north on a dirt road going about 2 miles up Cattle Canyon. There's an active tungsten mine near the road's end.

Area A-13, Trip 5
Cattle Canyon

Distance	6.0 miles round trip
Total Elevation Gain/Loss	700'/700'
Hiking Time	3 hours (round trip)
Optional Maps	USGS 7.5-min *Glendora, Mt. Baldy*
Best Times	September through June
Agency	ANF/MBD
Difficulty	★★

From Coldwater Canyon to East Fork, Cattle Canyon carves a sinuous course through a gorge impressively flanked by walls abruptly soaring 1000 feet or more. An old jeep road—now a pleasant hiking path—follows the canyon bottom, crossing the alder-lined stream about two dozen times.

The trail starts from the west side of an old bridge on East Fork Road just east of the intersection of Glendora Mountain Road. Roadside parking space is available at several spots in the immediate area. On weekends and holidays, you'll need to post a parking permit on the dash of your car—see Area A-9 introduction for details.

You can follow the gradually ascending trail through Cattle Canyon as far as 3.0

miles to a locked gate, posted no-entry. The River Forks Ranch and other private properties in Cattle and Coldwater canyons lie beyond.

This is a great spring or early summer trip for families. You can go as far as you like, and turn back at any point. The stream flows clear and cool, but not normally so high as to create a hazard when crossing. Streamside vegetation flourishes, and wildflowers dot the sunny flats. The stream and its moist banks are a perfect habitat for a variety of snakes, including rattlesnakes. During the first couple of episodes of warm weather in April or May, you should be wary of the latter, as they are often irritable when they awaken from a long period of hibernation.

Area A-13, Trip 6
Shoemaker Canyon Road

Distance	5.5 miles round trip
Total Elevation Gain/Loss	900'/900'
Hiking Time	2½ hours (round trip)
Optional Maps	USGS 7.5-min *Glendora, Crystal Lake*
Best Times	October through May
Agency	ANF/MBD
Difficulty	★★

Known colloquially as the Convict Road, Shoemaker Canyon Road should really be called the Road to Nowhere. The

road was part of what was projected to be a 23-year effort to build a highway up along the East Fork canyon to Vincent Gap. (This project was not connected with an earlier road-building effort that included the construction of the famous, stranded "Bridge to Nowhere.")

During 1954–69, the county road department, utilizing prison labor, managed to carve out and grade 4½ miles of new roadway on the canyon wall opposite East Fork Station and Heaton Flat. The project was rendered moribund in 1969 in the face of budget cuts and opposition by conservationists. The creation of Sheep Mountain Wilderness in 1984 finally put to rest, probably once and for all, a project that would have irreparably scarred Southern California's deepest canyon—The Narrows of the East Fork. The enduring legacy of this misdirected road-building effort—massive cuts and fills—will probably be visible on the canyon walls for centuries to come.

Today you can drive the first 1.8 miles of Shoemaker Canyon Road on pavement, then walk the remaining graded-dirt section

to reach a pair of tunnels. Beyond the second tunnel there's a great view of the East Fork gorge and its mile-high east wall culminating at 8007' Iron Mountain.

Don't forget to pick up a parking permit (required weekends and holidays) at the San Gabriel Canyon entrance station—see Area A-9 introduction for details. From Highway 39, drive east on East Fork Road 3.3 miles to where you bear left on the paved Shoemaker Canyon Road. Continue 1.8 miles to a vehicle gate and parking area.

After 1.7 miles of walking, you reach the first tunnel, about 400 yards long, completed in 1961. Ahead lies a small abyss— Shoemaker Canyon. It was never bridged; a narrower road contours around it and continues northeast to a second tunnel, about 250 yards long, dated 1964. On the far side of that tunnel, you can veer right and backtrack, circumventing the tunnel by way of an old road bed. There you'll have the best view of the East Fork gorge.

Area A-13, Trip 7
Rattlesnake Peak Traverse

Distance	12.5 miles
Total Elevation Gain/Loss	4250'/8800'
Hiking Time	9 hours
Recommended Maps	USGS 7.5-min *Crystal Lake, Glendora*
Best Times	April through June; September through November
Agency	ANF/MBD
Difficulty	★★★★

After Big Bad Iron (Iron Mountain to the east), Rattlesnake Peak is probably the second most inaccessible peak in the San Gabriels. Hikers have reached its summit by way of Bichota Canyon on the west, by traversing the ridge southeast from South Mt. Hawkins, and from Shoemaker Canyon Road via routes up the south or east ridge. Only by way of the south ridge is there some

semblance of a trail; all other approaches involve some gut-busting scrambling and bushwhacking.

On the point-to-point route detailed here, you start out by walking up to South Mt. Hawkins from the Crystal Lake Recreation Area—see Area A-9, Trip 5 for details. You then follow a ridge down and then up over Rattlesnake Peak, and finish at the terminus of the paved Shoemaker Canyon Road—see Trip 6 above. An old fire break along the ridge makes things a little easier, but here and there you'll run into lots of chaparral that has knitted itself together into nearly impenetrable masses. An old, long-sleeve shirt, long pants (denim jeans or thick wool pants work well), gloves, and eye protection (such as sunglasses) are recommended. It's important to get an early start whenever the days are short, as in late fall. Most of the route is fully exposed to the sun, and there's not a drop of water along the way, except for snow patches early in springtime.

The car shuttle between start and end points, via Highway 39 and the lower East Fork, is about 18 miles long—a 30-minute drive. A parking permit (see Area A-9 introduction for details) is required on weekends and holidays for Shoemaker Canyon Road, but not for Crystal Lake.

The off-trail phase of the trip begins at South Mt. Hawkins (mile 4.3 as measured from the starting point) as you descend the southeast ridge. On the way down there are great views down the V-shaped tributaries of the East Fork to your left, and into the North Fork canyon, laced with the curling grey ribbon of Highway 39, on the right. The pines and firs so prevalent up around South Hawkins soon disappear from the ridgeline, yet they continue to blanket many of the north-facing hillsides lying just below you all the way to Rattlesnake Peak.

At 6.5 miles, you pass over a 6100' knob. Now the challenging part of the trip begins. The main ridge seems to continue southwest, but you must veer left (southeast) through the thick brush to stay on the ridge leading to Rattlesnake Peak—the imposing bump 1.5 miles to the southeast. After an abrupt loss of 1100 feet you reach the brush-covered saddle between Bichota Canyon and Devil Gulch, where a trail once joined from the west. No trace of that trail is visible today.

The crux of the trip lies ahead, 0.7 mile of horrendous bushwhacking up and over

peaklet 5346 to a saddle at the head of Graveyard Canyon. Somehow deer manage to traverse this section quite handily, as indicated by their tracks. A more open, but very steep ascent over rock outcrops takes you 800 feet higher to the crystalline-rock summit of Rattlesnake Peak (8.3 miles). A few conifers straggle up this way via the north slope, providing welcome shade. On top you'll discover how few climbers reach this peak—only about 5–10 hiking parties sign the register per year.

A faint climbers' path continues down the brush-covered south ridge of Rattlesnake Peak, passing over several bumps and over the top of a spectacular dropoff (9.2 miles) overlooking Graveyard Canyon on the right. The ridge becomes more level at 9.8 miles. You pass over one bump at 9.9 miles and a second bump at 10.0 miles (4050'). On the latter bump, the path leaves the main ridge, turning abruptly left. Stick close to the top of an east-dipping ridge for another 0.5 mile, then veer southeast and descend sharply to a huge cut on the hillside above the abandoned and unfinished East Fork highway (Shoemaker Canyon Road). Make your way down, left or right, to the graded surface of the road. You'll end up south of the tunnel marked "under construction" on the topo map. Turn south and walk the remaining 1½ miles down the unfinished highway to the vehicle gate and parking area.

Area A-13, Trip 8
East Fork to Bridge

	Distance	9.6 miles round trip
	Total Elevation Gain/Loss	1000'/1000'
	Hiking Time	4½ hours (round trip)
	Optional Map	USGS 7.5-min *Glendora, Crystal Lake, Mount San Antonio*
	Best Times	October through June
	Agency	ANF/MBD
	Difficulty	★★★

Born of snow-fed rivulets, the many tributaries of the East Fork gather together to form one of the liveliest mountain streams in the San Gabriels. At The Narrows of the East Fork, the water squeezes through the deepest gorge in Southern California. From the bottom of The Narrows, the east wall soars about 5200 feet to Iron Mountain, and the west wall rises about 4000 feet to the South Mt. Hawkins divide.

During the 1930s, road-builders managed to push a highway up through the East Fork to as far as the lower portals of The Narrows. There, an arched, concrete bridge was constructed, similar in style to those that were built in the same era along Angeles Crest Highway. The bridge was to be a key link in a route that would one day carry traffic between the San Gabriel Valley and the desert near Wrightwood. But fate intervened. The great 1938 flood thoroughly demolished most of the road, leaving the bridge stranded far upstream. The next and last attempt to construct a road through the East Fork gorge utilized a high-line approach instead (see Trip 6), but that effort was ultimately abandoned as well.

The trek to the old bridge is in the same league as the climb of Old Baldy—an obligatory experience for L.A.-area hikers. On warm summer weekends, hundreds of people walk the trail going up from East Fork Station. A fraction venture as far as the bridge, a leisurely half-day's round-trip hike.

Over the last century, gold mining in the East Fork has evolved from a serious business to more of a recreational pastime. Today, claims are being worked around The Narrows area, but mostly it's the fun of playing around in the stream and catching a bit of color that keeps recreational miners coming back year after year. Typical yields, for those who know what they're doing, are $3 or less worth of gold per hour of labor.

There are several creek crossings of ankle- to knee-depth, so wear shoes that you don't mind getting soaked. During parts of winter and spring, high water may render these crossings unsafe.

The hike starts from the parking area at the end of East Fork Road. Don't forget to fill out a wilderness permit at the self-issuing register near the drinking fountain at the foot of the ranger station entrance road. You'll also need a parking permit on the weekends and holidays (see Area A-9 introduction for details).

Follow the gated service road upstream, high along the right bank, to Heaton Flat Campground, 0.5 mile. Beyond Heaton Flat the road ends, but a well-traveled trail continues up the flood plain. At 2.5 miles, you pass Swan Rock, a cliff-exposure of metamorphic rock branded with the light-colored imprint of a swan. You can see it best under flat lighting conditions. You're now entering Sheep Mountain Wilderness.

At 3.5 miles, the trail swings abruptly right and climbs about 60 feet to meet a remnant of the old highway. The old road bed carves its way along the east canyon wall, high above what is now a wide, boulder-filled flood plain laced with the meandering, alder-lined stream. The Bridge to Nowhere appears at 4.8 miles, just as the canyon walls start to pinch in. The bridge appears remarkably undamaged after half a century of neglect, except for its crumbling concrete railings.

The bridge and the area just south of it lie within an island of posted private property. You're allowed passage across the bridge, but please don't stray from the road or the bridge when inside the posted area. From the north abutment of the bridge, a narrow trail contours above the stream, then drops into the lower part of The Narrows. See Trips 9 and 10 for more on the upper canyon.

The Bridge to Nowhere

Area A-13, Trip 9
Fish Fork Falls

Distance	17.6 miles round trip
Total Elevation Gain/Loss	2400'/2400'
Hiking Time	10 hours (round trip)
Recommended Maps	USGS 7.5-min *Glendora, Crystal Lake, Mount San Antonio*
Best Times	October through June
Agency	ANF/MBD
Difficulty	★★★★

The long trek up through The Narrows of the East Fork and lower Fish Fork reminds hikers that the grandeur of the San Gabriels lies more in its soaring canyon walls and rushing streams than in its non-dramatic summits. The trip can be done either as an exhausting day hike or a more leisurely weekend backpack. Trout inhabit both streams, so take a fishing rod (and fishing license) if you're so inclined.

As in Trip 8 above, walk up to the Bridge to Nowhere, 4.8 miles, and then into The Narrows. An informal trail, worn in by hikers, traverses this one-mile-plus section of fast-moving water. You'll pass swimmable (if very chilly) pools cupped in the granite and schist bedrock, crossing the stream when necessary. Listen and watch for water ouzels (dippers) by the edges of the pools. The summit of Iron Mountain stands high above you on the right, unseen just over the top of the steeply rising walls—almost one vertical mile higher and only 1.7 horizontal miles away. Old mining trails once threaded the canyon walls here and to the north (they're still shown on the Mount San Antonio topo map), but all are virtually obliterated now.

Iron Fork comes in from the left at 6.2 miles. Be sure to stay right at the confluence (not hard to do, as the hiker's trail goes that way). At 7.0 miles, as the canyon bends sharply right, you'll pass under some wet travertine formations overhanging the west wall that look like dripping tongues. Just ahead, 7.1 miles, Falls Gulch comes in from the right—the namesake falls a 50'-high dribble of water just above the East Fork stream.

Fish Fork Canyon is the next tributary, 7.3 miles. To the left, the canyon-bottom trail proceeds past a flat area good for camping (the former Fish Fork Camp), and on up the East Fork toward Prairie Fork and Vincent Gulch. You stay right and continue up the trailless Fish Fork stream.

Chock full of alder and bay, narrow with soaring walls, its clear stream tumbling over boulders, Fish Fork is one of the wildest and most beautiful settings in the San Gabriels. You'll either be in the stream itself, or scrambling over boulders, brush, and fallen trees on the banks. Be watchful of both poison oak and stinging nettles (long, thick pants are recommended for both). As you're scrambling along the stream, don't miss the left turn 0.8 mile up from the East Fork confluence. A lesser, often-wet tributary enters from the southeast at this point.

At 1.5 miles from the confluence, you'll pass a shaded bench on the north bank suitable as a campsite for perhaps 10 people. From there you can go only another 0.1 mile. There's an impasse where the waters of Fish Fork drop 12 feet into an emerald-green pool set amid sheer rock walls. Don't attempt to climb the canyon walls; they're too steep and slippery, or unstable. A bigger waterfall lies about 0.2 mile upstream, accessible only by way of a long, steep descent from Pine Mountain Ridge.

Fish Fork Falls

Area A-13, Trip 10
Down the East Fork

	Distance	14.5 miles
	Total Elevation Gain/Loss	200'/4800'
	Hiking Time	9 hours
	Recommended Maps	USGS 7.5-min *Crystal Lake, Mount San Antonio, Glendora*
	Best Times	April through November
	Agency	ANF/MBD
	Difficulty	★★★★

On the epic journey down the East Fork from Vincent Gap to the East Fork roadhead, you'll descend nearly a mile in elevation, travel from high-country pines and firs to sun-scorched chaparral, and cross three important geologic faults—the Punchbowl, Vincent Thrust, and San Gabriel faults. In a single day you could experience a temperature increase of as much as 60°F.

You can do this trip in one long day with an early start at Vincent Gap, or plan to camp overnight on one of the shaded streamside terraces near the mid-point of the trek. The better camping sites include former trail camps at Fish and Iron forks, and the lower part of The Narrows. Navigation is easy throughout—you simply head in the down-canyon direction the whole way. Consult a map often if you want to confirm exactly where you are. Heavy runoff can create hazardous stream crossings after a storm or major snowmelt, so check with the rangers first.

It's best to have someone drop you off at Vincent Gap and later pick you up at East Fork Station, an 85-mile drive around by way of Interstate 15 to the east. After the winter season, Angeles Crest Highway usually opens to traffic from the east (Wrightwood) side sometime in April.

From the parking area on the south side of Vincent Gap walk down the gated road to the southeast. After only about 200 yards, a footpath veers left, into Sheep Mountain Wilderness. Take it; the road itself con-

tinues toward the posted, privately owned Bighorn Mine, an inholding in the Wilderness. Intermittently shaded by bigcone Douglas-firs, white firs, Jeffrey pines, and live oaks, the path descends along the south slope of Vincent Gulch. The gulch itself follows the Punchbowl Fault, a splinter of the San Andreas. At 0.7 mile, on a flat ridge spur, look for an indistinct path intersecting on the right. This leads about 100 yards to an old cabin believed to have been the home of Charles Vincent. Vincent led the life of a hermit, prospector, and big-game hunter in the Baden-Powell/Old Baldy area from 1870 until his death in 1926.

After a few switchbacks, the trail crosses Vincent Gulch (usually dry at this point, wet a short distance below) at 1.6 miles. Thereafter it stays on or above the east bank as far as the confluence of Prairie Fork, 3.8 miles. At Prairie Fork a sign on the left points the way east to Cabin Flat. You veer right (west) down a gravelly wash, good for setting up a camp. Shortly after, at the Mine Gulch confluence, you bend left (south) into the wide bed of upper East Fork.

Proceed down the rock-strewn flood plain, crossing the creek (and battling alder thickets) several times over the next mile. Old trails (still shown on the topo map) thread the canyon walls left or right over the next few miles, but they're now overgrown or eroded away. The canyon becomes narrow for a while starting at about 5.0

miles, and you must wade or hop from one slippery rock to another. Fish Fork, on the left at 7.3 miles, is the first large stream below Prairie Fork.

The remainder of the route is included in the descriptions of Trips 8 and 9 above. You reach Iron Fork at 8.4 miles, the Bridge to Nowhere at 9.7 miles, Heaton Flat at 14.0 miles, and the East Fork parking area at 14.5 miles.

Area A-13, Trip 11
San Antonio Ridge

	Distance	14.0 miles
	Total Elevation Gain/Loss	4400'/10200'
	Hiking Time	10 hours
	Recommended Maps	USGS 7.5-min *Telegraph Peak, Mount San Antonio, Mt. Baldy, Glendora*
	Best Times	May through November
	Agency	ANF/MBD
	Difficulty	★★★★★

Get set for a spectacular and very challenging traverse along the spine of the San Gabriel Mountains. From the top of Old Baldy, you descend a net elevation of 8000 feet to East Fork San Gabriel River by way of San Antonio Ridge and Iron Mountain. Done in the manner described here (net downhill), the trip is probably the most tortuous hike of all those listed in this book.

My companion and I did the trip in reverse, from East Fork to Baldy, an option open to you if you're a real glutton for punishment. One of our rewards, besides the aerial-like views, was the sighting of a large herd of bighorn sheep. Some 25 sheep scooted over a rocky saddle on San Antonio Ridge as we watched in amazement from a hundred yards away.

You begin with the standard approach to Old Baldy's summit by way of the Mt. Baldy ski lift and the Devils Backbone Trail (see Area A-12, Trip 7 for the details). Remember that during the non-snow-skiing season the lift operates on weekends and holidays only, starting at 9 A.M. If you're making this a one-day hike (practical only around the summer solstice when the days

are long) be sure you're at the lower station of the lift by 9 A.M. If you're backpacking the route, an internal-frame pack with a compact and narrow profile will save you much grief. External-frame packs tend to get entangled in the brush.

From the 10,064' summit of Old Baldy (3.2 miles), proceed west to the 9988' summit of West Baldy (3.7 miles). From there you can visually trace the rounded San Antonio Ridge in the distance as it curves gradually left and finally becomes a serrated spine leading to Iron Mountain's summit. Based on what you can see, estimate how long it will take you to walk over to Iron Mountain—then multiply that figure by at least two.

From West Baldy, you descend through talus and timberline *krummholz* and then through taller and straighter trees to the first saddle in the ridge at 5.2 miles (7772'). On the undulating ridge ahead, you travel through sparse groves of timber and thickets of snowbrush, a low-growing but very thorny variety of ceanothus. The topo map shows old trails connecting several old mines in the upper Coldwater Canyon drainage to the south, but mines and trails alike have been unused for decades. The Forest Service has long-range plans to build a trail up past the old mines to San Antonio Ridge, but at current levels of funding that may not happen until well into the 21st century.

At a low point in the ridge west of peak 7758 (7.0 miles) some hand-and-toe rock climbing begins on a savage-looking arete to the west. This is your last chance to reconsider and turn back. Consider that only about 40 percent of your total effort has been expended so far. The mile-long traverse to Iron Mountain ahead is by far the most taxing stretch on the whole trip.

Work your way over and around pinnacles of upthrust rock on the arete, mostly a slow process of stepping over or bashing through low chaparral. Bighorn sheep tracks may guide you. Take great care not to pull on or otherwise dislodge blocks of rock; many seem to be delicately balanced and poised to tumble. Also make sure that no two climbers are in the same "fall line." Ropes are of practically no value here as much of the rock is too crumbly to be used as an anchor. While you're on this tense stretch, try to relax occasionally and enjoy the dizzying vistas into the precipitous Fish Fork canyon on the north and the more gentle Coldwater Canyon drainage on the south.

At the top (7.9 miles) you'll find a register in a red can appropriately labelled BIG BAD IRON. In it, a scribe has written "Through bad chaparral and stinging nettle; to do Big Iron you need pants of metal . . ."

Most climbers do Iron by way of the south ridge, easier than the way you came, but tortuous (and torturing) all the same. Take a long breather on top and revel in the view. Some nice camp or picnic sites can be found amid the scattered pines just below the summit.

When it's time to leave, head down the south ridge on a rather-well-beaten but occasionally very steep climbers' path. Huge yuccas, some with a thousand slender

daggers, grow uncomfortably close to the path. Keep your speed down lest you slide into one of them. A couple of pine- and-fir dotted flat areas on the way down offer a chance to rest and cool off. At a 4582' saddle (10.3 miles) you come upon the newly refurbished Heaton Flat Trail (the Allison Trail, west of the saddle, is all but gone now). The Heaton Flat Trail zigzags southeast up a hill, gaining about 150 feet, then descends, more or less steadily over the next 3 miles, to Heaton Flat. From there, walk out the service road to the East Fork roadhead.

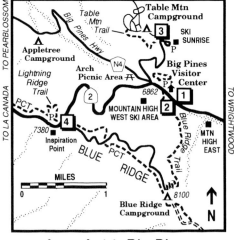

Area A-14: Big Pines

Area A-14: Big Pines

On the eastern extremity of the Angeles Crest, far from L.A.'s smoggy blanket of air, lies the Big Pines Recreation Area, an area set aside by the Forest Service specifically for year-round recreation. Blanketed by a heterogeneous mixture of pines, firs, and oaks, and perched high above the desert, Big Pines boasts the clean, dry, evergreen-scented air and crystalline blue skies characteristic of the melding of mountain and desert environments.

During the winter months, Big Pines' three downhill ski areas draw crowds of snow-starved city-dwellers who would rather not drive an extra 250 miles or more to reach the major-league ski resorts in the Sierra. In summer, several campgrounds (including the big, 115-space Table Mountain Campground), picnic areas, and interpretive trails serve the needs of visitors escaping the lowland heat. Ironically, relatively few people come up during the seasons that the area is really most beautiful—spring and fall. Daytime temperatures are most pleasant then, and the colors of the foliage are bold and vibrant.

From central Los Angeles, the fastest way to get to the Big Pines area is by way of Interstates 10 and 15, then by way of Angeles Crest Highway through the mountain community of Wrightwood. The entire trip should take less than 90 minutes, assuming light traffic. During winter, this may be the only way to go, as snow blocks other highways, including Angeles Crest Highway west of Big Pines.

Big Pines and Wrightwood share the distinction of lying smack dab on the San Andreas Fault. The crossroads of Big Pines itself (4 miles west of Wrightwood) marks the highest surface trace of the entire fault—

6862 feet. Jackson Lake, a "sag pond," fills a small, natural depression along the fault 2 miles northwest of Big Pines. Wrightwood, one of the most attractive communities in Los Angeles County and the largest settlement in the San Gabriel Mountains, sprawls across another, much larger fault-caused depression called Swarthout Valley. Unfortunately for its roughly 5000 (summer) residents, Wrightwood is acutely susceptible to destruction not only by Southern California's incipient Great Quake, expected to occur on this stretch of the San Andreas within 20–30 years, but also by fire, flooding, and mudslides.

At Big Pines, where Big Pines Highway (County N4), and the road to Table Mountain meet Angeles Crest Highway, you'll find the Big Pines Visitor Center, housed in a corner of the former Swarthout Lodge. Now being refurbished, the lodge once served as headquarters for Big Pines County Park, which was open from 1923 to 1940. Unable to afford the cost of administering the park, the County deeded the property to the Forest Service in 1940. The County had spent about $4 million creating a first-class recreational complex consisting of campgrounds, cabins, picnic areas, organizational camps, a swimming pool, an ice-skating rink, tennis courts, toboggan and ski runs, and more. An arched pedestrian overpass, built of native stone, was built over the access road, its twin towers containing barred holding cells for drunks and troublemakers. Only the north tower stands today near the visitor center.

After falling into disuse during and after World War II, Big Pines experienced a resurgence of attention in the 1950s. New facilities for campers and day-users were

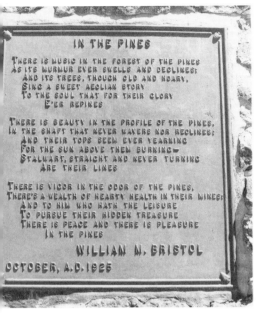

IN THE PINES

There is music in the forest of the pines
As its murmur ever swells and declines;
And its trees, though old and hoary,
Sing a sweet Aeolian story
To the soul that for their glory
        E'er repines

There is beauty in the profile of the pines,
In the shaft that never wavers nor declines;
And their tops seem ever yearning
For the sun above them burning—
Stalwart, straight and never turning
        Are their lines

There is vigor in the odor of the pines,
There's a wealth of hearty health in their mines;
And to him who hath the leisure
To pursue their hidden treasure
There is peace and there is pleasure
        In the pines

        WILLIAM M. BRISTOL

OCTOBER, A.D. 1926

Plaque at Big Pines

constructed, and winter-sports areas were expanded and modernized. The use of snow-making machines today ensures that some of the ski slopes stay usable from November into April.

The visitor center, open year round Wednesday though Sunday, offers printed leaflets, maps, interpretive brochures for some of the area trails, and reference materials such as a wildflower identification guide. Eleven campgrounds and four picnic grounds are located within a 5-mile radius of the center. Interpretive programs— guided walks, campfire talks, and children's activities—are offered during the summer months.

Below, we profile four short trails in the Big Pines area, all of them fine for family use. Trips 3 and 4, the Table Mountain and Lightning Ridge trails, feature numbered posts keyed to interpretive leaflets available at the visitor center.

Area A-14, Trip 1
Big Pines Nature Trail

Distance	0.5 mile
Total Elevation Gain/Loss	200'/200'
Hiking Time	½ hour
Optional Map	USGS 7.5-min *Mescal Creek*
Best Times	All year
Agency	ANF/VD
Difficulty	★

The short and easy, self-guiding Big Pines Nature Trail highlights many of the native trees and shrubs of the Big Pines area. The trail originates behind the visitor center and starts by winding up through a sparse grove of centuries-old Jeffrey pines. If you aren't, as yet, very familiar with the local flora, this is a good trail to further your education.

Along the way, you'll be introduced to the canyon live oak and black oak, four kinds of pines, and shrubs such as ceanothus (mountain lilac), manzanita, yerba santa, flannel bush, service berry, and mountain mahogany. Interpretive plaques cover some of the uses of these native plants by the Gabrielino, Serrano, and Cahuilla Indians.

Area A-14, Trip 2
Blue Ridge Trail

	Distance	4.6 miles round trip (to Baldy view)
	Total Elevation Gain/Loss	1300'/1300'
	Hiking Time	2½ hours (round trip)
	Optional Maps	USGS 7.5-min *Mescal Creek,*
		Mount San Antonio
	Best Times	May through November
	Agency	ANF/VD
	Difficulty	★★

Tall, aromatic pines and firs, and thin air (elevation averages 7500 feet) lend a High-Sierra-feel to the north slope of Blue Ridge. The nicely maintained Blue Ridge Trail climbs about 1000 feet up this slope to meet the Pacific Crest Trail just outside Blue Ridge Campground. From there you can climb a bit farther for a panoramic view of Mts. San Antonio, Baden-Powell, and other giants on the roofline of the Angeles Forest.

You have a lot of flexibility on this hike: From the campground you can return the way you came, walk down the PCT to Angeles Crest Highway, or arrange to get a ride down the Blue Ridge road (assuming the road is snow-free and open to traffic).

The Blue Ridge Trail starts near the restrooms opposite Big Pines Visitor Center. About half-way up the slope (1.0 mile), the trail crosses an old road bed and continues climbing. To the north, on Table Mountain, you'll spot the white domes of the Table Mountain and Smithsonian observatories. After several switchbacks, you meet the Blue Ridge road at Blue Ridge Campground. The PCT swings around the far side of the campground; you can join it by walking southeast about 0.1 mile on the road. Head southeast on the PCT, uphill along a ski run for another ¼ mile. Then veer right to the top of a sage-covered rise dotted in spring and early summer with paintbrush and wallflower blossoms. There you'll have a panoramic view of Old Baldy's north slope—streaked with snow and often wreathed in cottony clouds in springtime.

Return the way you came.

Area A-14, Trip 3
Table Mountain Nature Trail

	Distance	1.0 mile
	Total Elevation Gain/Loss	200'/200'
	Hiking Time	½ hour
	Optional Map	USGS 7.5-min *Mescal Creek*
	Best Times	April through November
	Agency	ANF/VD
	Difficulty	★

This interpretive trail swings down a hillside below the entrance of Table Mountain Campground and later climbs back up to the campground's edge. You'll be introduced to Jeffrey pines, canyon live oaks, black oaks, and several other plants and trees that grow in the immediate area. Numbered posts correspond to the entries on the self-guiding leaflet available at the Big Pines Visitor Center.

As you're traversing the south-facing slope traveled by the trail, you'll spot Mt. Baden-Powell rising impressively in the west, and Blue Ridge, complete with the scars of ski runs, in the southeast. Blue Ridge was logged several decades ago, accounting for the even-aged appearance of the trees on its slopes.

Watch out for false paths that take off from some of the switchback corners of the trail; it's easy to lose the main trail. At trail's end, make a right on the paved campground road and walk back to the entrance.

Area A-14, Trip 4
Lightning Ridge Nature Trail

	Distance	0.8 mile
	Total Elevation Gain/Loss	250'/250'
	Hiking Time	½ hour
	Optional Map	USGS 7.5-min *Mount San Antonio*
	Best Times	April through November
	Agency	ANF/VD
	Difficulty	★

The Lightning Ridge Trail (opposite Inspiration Point 2 miles west of Big Pines by way of Angeles Crest Highway) contours through the cool precincts of a wooded northeast-facing slope, then switchbacks upward to meet the Pacific Crest Trail on a windblown crest. You'll see Jeffrey pines, sugar pines, and white firs, and pass right through a beautiful glade of black oaks called Oak Dell—very nice in October when the leaves turn crispy gold and acorns fall. Near the crest are a number of stunted and distorted trees battered by winds and flattened by snow drifts that can pile up 10 feet high.

When you reach the PCT junction, try stepping off the trail and walking a short distance over to the top of the ridgecrest. The view from there is similar to that from Inspiration Point below, only a bit more panoramic. Old Baldy and Mt. Baden-Powell rise like massive sentinels, bracketing the rugged slopes and canyons of Sheep Mountain Wilderness. To the south you look straight down the V-shaped, linear gorge of East Fork San Gabriel River.

Oak Dell on the Lightning Ridge Trail

SANTA CATALINA ISLAND

Area I-1: Avalon

From high points on the mainland, Santa Catalina Island is often seen either floating over a blanket of fog like a mirage, or rising boldly from the surface of the sea. The island, third largest of the several Channel Islands strung along the Southern California coast, lies only 19 miles at its closest point from the Palos Verdes peninsula. It's the only Channel Island with a town of any real size, and the only one catering to large numbers of tourists.

"Catalina" stretches 21 miles in length and up to 8 miles at maximum width. A half-mile-wide isthmus called Two Harbors separates the 6-mile-long northwestern end of the island (called the West End) from the larger southeastern part. The town of Avalon and Avalon Bay snuggle into an eastern corner of the island, protected from the prevailing winds which come out of the west and northwest. Avalon experiences the same almost-frost-free climate as the most even-tempered areas of the Southern California coastline, and enjoys what is probably the cleanest air of any populated area near the Southern California coastline.

For most of this century, Catalina was owned by the Wrigley family (of chewing-gum and Chicago Cubs fame), whose interest in developing the island as a vacation destination was mostly limited to the Avalon area. Catalina's interior remained largely off-limits to tourists until the creation of the Santa Catalina Island Conservancy in 1972, whose function is to preserve and protect the wild lands of the island. Today 86 percent of the island is owned by the Conservancy, and is open to light recreational use. The Los Angeles County Department of Parks and Recreation has entered into an agreement with the Conservancy whereby it manages certain recreational activities such as hiking.

The languid pace of life on Santa Catalina Island reflects its aloofness from the increasingly frantic business of living on the Southern California mainland. A weekend visit there is truly relaxing, whether you choose to lodge in Avalon or prefer to rough it at one of the several campgrounds spread around the island's coast and interior.

Ferries to Catalina depart from terminals at San Pedro, Long Beach, Newport, and San Diego (summer only). Air service is also available from Long Beach. Lodging in Avalon ranges from $50-per-night cottages to $100-plus Bed and Breakfasts. For more information, contact the Catalina Visitor's Bureau, Box 217, Avalon, CA 90704; (800) 428-2566. You may also contact Avalon's Visitor Information and Services Center, 423 Crescent Avenue, Avalon, CA 90704; (213) 510-2000.

Planning a trip to the island involves much more than we have room to include in this book. A good, overall source of information is Chicki Mallan's *Guide to Catalina and California's Channel Islands*.

Hikers wishing to walk the many roads and trails of the "interior" of the island (outside Avalon and its immediate environs), must first obtain a free hiking permit from the L.A. County Department of Parks and Recreation office, 213 Catalina Street,

Avalon, CA 90704; (213) 510-0688. Campground reservations for Hermit Gulch Campground (one mile outside Avalon) and for campgrounds in the central portion of the island (not covered in this book) are also handled by that office. Camping reservations for the island's western end (see Area I-2) are handled by another agency. Note: Camp stoves are not allowed on the island ferries, nor are they available for rent in Avalon. If you're going to cook your meals at a campground, one solution is to buy charcoal at the supermarket in Avalon.

Limited use of the island's interior is allowed for mountain biking as well as

hiking, although biking is more stringently regulated. Riders pay a fee of $50 (good for a year), whereas hiking is free. Bikers are excluded from many of the trails that are really better suited for hiking.

In this section and the next, we profile four of the best hikes on Catalina, each readily accessible to the two island hubs— Avalon and Two Harbors. For all backcountry exploring on Catalina, you should obtain a copy of the *Catalina Conservancy Visitor Map & Guide* (a map/brochure), available from the County Parks office, indicating all routes open to travel by foot.

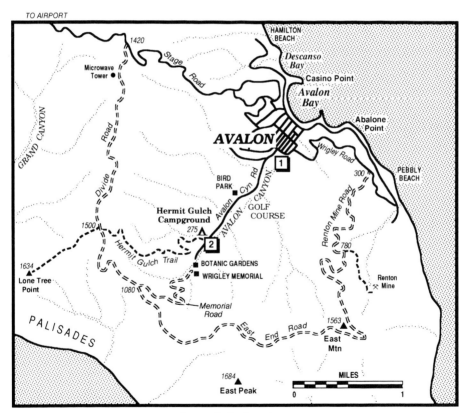

Area I-1: Avalon

Area I-1, Trip 1
East Mountain

Distance	8.5 miles
Total Elevation Gain/Loss	2000'/2000'
Hiking Time	5 hours
Optional Map	USGS 7.5-min *Santa Catalina East*
Best Times	October through June
Agency	SC/LACP
Difficulty	★★★

On certain crystal-clear days (most common between November and March) this "grand tour" of the eastern end of the island affords an ever-changing panorama of the blue ocean, San Clemente Island to the south, and the snow-capped summits of the San Gabriel Mountains on the mainland.

The route takes you up along gently graded paved and dirt roads to East Mountain, a broad summit area marking the last gasp of the island spine before it falls eastward into the ocean. No matter what the time of year, beware of the sun. You'll be climbing along the lee side of the island, fully exposed to morning and midday temperatures easily 20° higher than along the immediate coastline. Bring lots of water and don't forget your shade hat either.

We'll assume you start from Clemente Avenue and Wrigley Road (a.k.a. Mt. Ada Road) on Avalon's south edge, about 4 blocks from the County Parks office. On paved Wrigley Road you swing around the high ridge overlooking Avalon Bay, enjoying picture-postcard-perfect views of boats at anchor and of the famous round Casino building on the bay's far side. The distinguished edifice on the right at 0.5 mile is The Inn on Mt. Ada, now a bed-and-breakfast, but formerly the Wrigley family home. The home was designed to take advantage of the sunrises and sunsets visible from its commanding perch.

Go right at 1.3 miles on Renton Mine Road; the paved road descends left toward a power plant at Pebbly Beach. A gradual ascent takes you to another junction, 2.7 miles, where you make another right on East End Road. On the slopes hereabouts, notice the St. Catherine's lace, a type of buckwheat endemic to the dry slopes of the island. The flower clusters on this large (up to several feet high) shrub can spread as wide as a foot, with a creamy white color fading to rust in the fall.

After curling around East Mountain, East End Road proceeds due west along the ridgecrest, with spectacular views north down to Avalon Bay and south over the sparkling waters to San Clemente Island. You'll notice that thick accumulations of chaparral coat the north-facing slopes, while the sunnier, south-facing slopes are much more parched and brown. Drought-resistant prickly-pear cacti grow abundantly on the ridgecrest and down along the drier slopes. Detracting from the scene is the devastation wrought by herds of feral goats that have overrun and overgrazed Catalina's steeper and drier slopes. These ornery but somewhat shy creatures were introduced to the island sometime prior to a century ago. Lacking no natural enemies, they multiplied quickly and have been hard to control ever since.

At 6.8 miles, you'll veer sharply right on Memorial Road. Some easy walking down this dirt road takes you along a cool, north-facing slope covered by tall and luxuriant (by mainland standards) growths of scrub oak, manzanita, and toyon. At the bottom of the hill you come upon Wrigley Memorial, a

130'-tall edifice built as a memorial to chewing-gum magnate William Wrigley, Jr., who purchased the island in 1918.

The famed botanic gardens started by Wrigley's wife (Ada Wrigley) in the 1920s lie just below the monument. Distinguished by a virtually frost-free climate, the gardens are home to an extensive array of native Southern California plants, as well as exotics from distant corners of the world. Once beyond the garden gates, 1.4 miles of road-walking down Avalon Canyon will take you back to the center of Avalon.

Area I-1, Trip 2
Lone Tree Point

Distance	5.5 miles
Total Elevation Gain/Loss	1500'/1500'
Hiking Time	2½ hours
Optional Map	USGS 7.5-min *Santa Catalina East*
Best Times	October through June
Agency	SC/LACP
Difficulty	★★

This popular springtime hike starts from Hermit Gulch Campground and loops over the main divide of the island overlooking Avalon. The highlight is a side trip over to Lone Tree Point, which commands an unparalleled view of the cliff-like Palisades falling sheer to the ocean. You'll encounter a couple of very steep grades on the old fire break leading to Lone Tree Point, so be sure to wear running shoes or boots with a studs or lugs to ensure plenty of traction. Small children would need some assistance on that stretch.

Buffalo, boar, deer, and goats—all introduced to the island at one time or another—are commonly seen on various parts of the island. On this particular trip you're most likely to spot feral goats.

From the campground, follow the narrow but distinct trail up the ravine to the west (Hermit Gulch). Before long you leave the trickling stream in the canyon bottom and begin a twisting ascent up along a shaggy slope. Red monkey flower, shooting star, and lupine dot the trailside and adorn small clearings amid the tangles of chaparral. After a 1200' gain (1.5 miles) you meet Divide Road, a fire road following the eastern spine of the island. Most of the elevation gain for the hike is now behind you.

Turn right, walk a few paces, and then climb the steep embankment to the left. Ahead you'll see an old fire break heading southwest, up and over several rounded, barren summits. Continue for 0.7 mile or more, passing over the peaklet designated Lone Tree on most maps. That's where you'll find the best view of the ocean and shoreline. Sometimes you can gaze south over the shore-hugging fog and spy the low dome of San Clemente Island, some 40 miles across the glistening Pacific.

After taking in the visual feast, backtrack to Divide Road. From there you can loop back to the starting point via a somewhat longer but more gradually descending route. Head south down Divide Road for 0.8 mile, then veer left on Memorial Road. Easy walking down this dirt road takes you down to Wrigley Memorial, through the botanic gardens, and finally to Hermit Gulch Campground, a short distance down Avalon Canyon Road.

Area I-2: Two Harbors

If the popular Avalon area seems a bit crowded for you, try Two Harbors, a quintessential "sleepy village." Camping, hiking, backpacking, water sports, and wild-life-watching are the norms here (even though much of the local wildlife consists of wild goats, deer, pigs, and bison—all imported to the island at one time or another).

In addition to a small lodge and cabins in tiny Two Harbors itself, hillside campsites abound at Little Fishermans Cove Campground just east of town. The more remote Parsons Landing Campground is accessible by way of a 7-mile road (see Trip 1 below).

Two Harbors is served by ferries from San Pedro (year round) and also from Long Beach and Avalon (summer only). For information on transportation and lodging, and to make reservations for either campground, call (213) 510-2800 or 510-0303. If you're camping and plan to cook your own meals, be sure to ask about the availability of firewood, charcoal, or stoves at either campground.

Area I-2, Trip 1
Parsons Landing

Distance	14.0 miles round trip
Total Elevation Gain/Loss	900'/900'
Hiking Time	6 hours (round trip)
Optional Map	USGS 7.5-min *Santa Catalina North, Santa Catalina West*
Best Times	All year
Agency	SC/CC
Difficulty	★★★

Parsons Landing is not only the site of a small beach and a spacious camping area; it is also the home of one of the best examples of native Southern California grassland. Grey-green after winter rains, bleached grey during drought, the perennial grasses here have found the right combination of fine-grained soil, soaking winter rains, desiccating summer drought, and the absence of heavy grazing by domestic animals in the past.

The native grasslands of Parsons Landing are only one example of the botanical richness and diversity of the north slope of Catalina's West End. This side is not so overrun by the hordes of feral animals that flourish elsewhere, and therefore is developing healthy-looking chaparral and oak-woodland habitats. On the sheltered, north-facing slopes (especially at Cherry Valley) you'll find plenty of the native Catalina cherry, a large shrub or tree (up to 45 feet tall) displaying spike-shaped clusters of white flowers during the spring. Its dark, red fruits resemble large black cherries.

The hiking route from Two Harbors to

Parsons Landing sacrifices economy of travel for ever-changing scenic delights. Covering an air-line distance of only 3½ miles in 7 walking miles, the gently graded road hugs the shoreline, swinging around every ravine and canyon along the way.

The trip is most rewarding, and not at all exhausting, if you can spend a night at Parsons Landing Campground. From there, if you're ambitious, you can loop around the island's west end—see Trip 2 below. Some people like to use mountain bikes to get to Parsons Landing, then travel farther on foot into areas where bikes are prohibited.

From Two Harbors, head for the road clearly etched onto the steep, dry slope west of Isthmus Cove. At 1.5 miles, the sinuous course of the road takes you on a long detour into Cherry Valley. Over the next few miles you'll pass several Scout or organizational camps and private marinas.

At about 6.2 miles, past Emerald Bay, you come to an intersection: the Boushay Trail goes left; you stay right. After another 0.5 mile, where the road bends left (southwest) you continue going straight (west) on a trail through grassland to the scattered camp and picnic sites of Parsons Landing. Try the boulder-backed picnic area close to the water's edge.

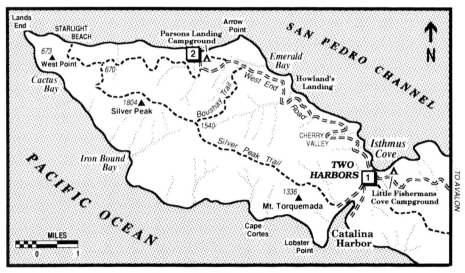

Area I-2: Two Harbors

Area I-2, Trip 2
Silver Peak—Starlight Beach

	Distance	10.5 miles
	Total Elevation Gain/Loss	1700'/1700'
	Hiking Time	5 hours
	Optional Map	USGS 7.5-min *Santa Catalina West*
	Best Times	October through June
	Agency	SC/CC
	Difficulty	★★★

This hike to the highest point on the west end of Catalina, 1804' Silver Peak, introduces you to the wild and often windswept windward edge of the island. Spectacular views are the norm most of the way.

Assuming you're starting the hike at Parsons Landing Campground, go back toward Two Harbors to the point where the Boushay Trail (an old fire road) takes off, up-slope to the south. The old road's winding course takes you 2 miles along chaparral-coated slopes and a ridgeline to a junction with the Silver Peak Trail—a fire road traversing the spine of the island's west end. Here, amid brick-red soils and rock outcrops, you get your first glimpses of the west end's dry and heavily eroded south-facing slopes falling precipitously to the blue and emerald ocean below. You'll probably hear and see many of the hundreds—possibly thousands—of feral goats that roam these desolate environs. In some areas, nearly all the vegetation is gone except for scattered prickly-pear cacti.

Just over a mile west of the Boushay Trail, Silver Peak Road passes about 100 feet below Silver Peak's nearly barren summit. You can scramble up through a sparse grove of Catalina ironwood trees and reach the top for an all-inclusive panorama. San Nicolas and Santa Barbara islands can be seen to the west on many days. Very rarely, Anacapa, Santa Cruz, and Santa Rosa islands off the coast of Santa Barbara, as well as the mainland shoreline west of Ventura, can be seen in the northwest. Quite often, especially in spring and summer, there's nothing to see at all, as you may be wreathed in low clouds scudding over the island's spine.

Past Silver Peak, the fire road (now nothing more than a wide 'dozer track) swings sharply downhill, beginning a sometimes very sheer descent down the wind-buffeted ridgeline to the west. After descending a total of about 1100 feet, you reach a T-intersection. You'll return to Parson's Landing on the road to the right. But first make the side trip left down to Star-light Beach, one of the most isolated and wild stretches of Catalina's coastline. You'll have to scramble a bit in the end to reach the rocky shore, where the ebb and flow of the waves dance over rock-dimpled sand. On clear days you can clearly see the low dome of the Palos Verdes peninsula some 20 miles across the San Pedro Channel, and it's hard to believe such a serene and beautiful place as Catalina's northwest shore can exist so close to the L.A. metropolis.

Climb back up to the T-intersection and return to Parsons Landing on the road that contours and lazily drops across steep, north-facing slopes. Each ravine you cross harbors a mini-forest of tangled oaks and chaparral. By the late afternoon, the often-misty atmosphere of the morning may have turned transparent, rendering the waters of the San Pedro Channel down below a deep azure.

Starlight Beach

APPENDIX 1: BEST HIKES

BEST BEACH HIKE
Point Dume to Paradise Cove (Area C-1, Trip 1). During low low tides, the Point Dume coastline offers up the finest array of tidepool life in the county.

BEST SUBURBAN HIKES
Placerita Canyon (Area B-2, Trip 1). A quiet, woodsy retreat only a few minutes away from San Fernando Valley.

Walnut Creek Trail (Area B-9, Trip 2). Explore one of the last remaining examples of oak and riparian woodland habitat on the L.A. Basin floor.

Marshall Canyon Trail (Area B-9, Trip 3). Hike through two of the best-preserved canyons of the San Gabriel foothills.

Will Rogers Park (Area S-1, Trip 1). Ocean and city lie at your feet on this island of open space on L.A.'s west side.

Millard Canyon (Area A-5, Trips 7, & 8). A deep, shady cleft graced by a small stream and a 50' waterfall, barely 10 minutes drive from the edge of the Pasadena suburbs.

BEST MOUNTAIN HIKES
The Grotto (Area S-4, Trip 8). Here, the primeval mountain and canyon country of the Santa Monica Mountains survives intact.

The Pothole (Area A-1, Trip 1). An intriguing introduction to the Sespe condor country bordering L.A. County on the northwest.

Hoegees Loop (Area A-6, Trip 2). The riparian splendor of the Front Range (San Gabriel Mountains) at its best.

Old Baldy (Area A-12, Trips 7 & 8). An obligatory climb, 10,064' Old Baldy is the highest point in the San Gabriel Mountains as well as in Los Angeles County.

BEST CANYON HIKES
Lower Solstice Canyon (Area S-2, Trip 8). Alongside a trickling stream, enjoy some of the county's finest oak woodlands.

Zuma Canyon (Area S-3, Trip 2). Big-scale canyon country within a small-scale mountain range.

Big Santa Anita Canyon (Area A-6, Trips 4 & 5). A shady wonderland of cascades, pools, and streamside greenery.

Icehouse Canyon (part of Area A-12, Trip 5). An easy mile or two up the tumbling Icehouse stream takes you to tall-timbered canyon recesses.

East Fork San Gabriel River (Area A-13, Trips 8, 9 &10). The East Fork has carved out the granddaddy of Southern California canyons, a mile deep as measured from the top of the east wall.

BEST WATERFALLS AND SWIMMING HOLES
Trail Canyon Falls (Area A-4, Trip 2). A beautiful and unexpected find tucked amid the chaparral country of lower Big Tujunga Canyon.

Royal Gorge (Area A-5, Trip 3). Features a deep, chilly pool fed by a small waterfall.

Sturtevant Falls (Area A-6, Trip 3). A scenic attraction for more than a century. Popular and easy to reach.

Devils Canyon (Area A-10, Trips 2 & 3). Two waterfalls in the middle canyon present a impassable barrier for hikers. Deep pools in the lower canyon are accessible (with difficulty) from canyon mouth.

Cooper Canyon Falls (Area A-11, Trip 1). A small but beautiful cascade in a sublime, High Country setting.

San Antonio Falls (Area A-12, Trip 6). Dependably impressive when swollen with snowmelt during spring and early summer. A very easy walk to the base.

BEST VIEW HIKES
Top of the Peninsula (Area C-2, Trip 1). Features a stunning panorama of ocean and islands on clear, winter days.

North End Traverse (Area B-5, Trip 3). Spectacular vistas of San Fernando Valley and all the basin-bordering mountain ranges.

Mount Hollywood (Area B-6, Trips 1 & 3). A top-of-the-city view from the top of Griffith Park.

Topanga Overlook (Area S-1, Trip 6). Unbelievably spacious views of Santa Monica Bay and the ocean.

Sandstone Peak (Area S-4, Trip 9). This volcanic outcrop crowning the Santa Monica Mountains overlooks the ocean, Channel Islands, and much of Los Angeles and Ventura counties.

Inspiration Point (Area A-5, Trip 11). Summon up the energy to go an extra mile to Panorama Point, where there's an even better perspective of the L.A. megalopolis below.

Twin Peaks (Area A-10, Trip 5). Some of Southern California's most wild and inaccessible terrain lies directly below these crags.

Cucamonga Peak (Area A-12, Trip 5). The peak's prominent southern exposure offers an unparalleled, panoramic view of both the L.A. Basin region and the Inland Empire.

Mount Baden-Powell (Area A-13, Trip 1). Its 360° view encompasses mountains, deserts, and the ocean.

Lone Tree Point (Area I-1, Trip 2). The pseudo-Hawaiian vista atop Catalina's east end includes eroded palisades and the green- and blue-tinted ocean.

BEST HISTORICAL WALKS

Old Stagecoach Road (Area B-3, Trip 1). Trace the notorious "Devil's Slide" segment of a 19th-century stage road linking Northern California with Southern California.

Mount Lowe Railway (Area A-5, Trip 10). Follow the path of more than 3 million passengers who rode rails into the sky on the Mt. Lowe Railway.

BEST WILDFLOWERS

Vasquez Rocks County Park (Area B-1, Trip 1). A convergence of three plant communities here yields a plethora of blooms during wet years.

Eagle Rock Loop (Area S-1, Trip 7). A broad range of wildflowers characteristic of the Santa Monica Mountains is represented here.

Lookout Loop (Area S-2, Trip 3). Good displays of meadow wildflowers.

Charmlee Regional Park (Area S-4, Trip 6). Wildflowers characteristic of grassland, chaparral, and oak woodland habitats.

La Jolla Valley-Mugu Peak (Area S-5, Trip 4). The giant coreopsis in La Jolla Canyon is especially noteworthy.

Devil's Punchbowl (Area A-11, Trips 8 & 9). Flora from both mountain and high desert areas are represented here.

BEST AUTUMN COLORS

Placerita Canyon (Area B-2, all trips). Willow, sycamore, cottonwood, bigleaf maple, and California walnut trees contribute various shades of yellow and rust.

Serrano-Big Sycamore Loop (Area S-5, Trip 2). Big Sycamore Canyon, in particular, is touted as the finest example of sycamore savanna in the California State Park system.

Liebre Mountain/Sawmill Mountain (Area A-2, Trips 1 & 2). The golden leaves of the black oak, a common tree in these northern reaches of L.A. County, put on a fine autumnal show.

Down the Arroyo Seco (Area A-5, Trip 2). Brightly colored sycamores and maples contrast with the somber browns and greens of the oaks and the chaparral.

Bear Canyon (Area A-5, Trip 6). Alders, sycamores, and maples line the narrow floor of this canyon.

BEST BIRD AND WILDLIFE WATCHING

Cheeseboro Canyon (Area B-4, Trip 2). At dawn and at dusk, deer, bobcats, and coyotes roam the oak-dotted hills and canyon floor. Birds of prey patrol the skies.

Lost Cabin Trail (Area S-2, Trip 2). The trail probes an area set aside for special protection within Malibu Creek State Park.

Vetter Mountain (Area A-7, Trip 2). Birds and animals typical of yellow-pine forests are found here.

Cow Canyon Ridge (Area A-13, Trip 4). Bighorn sheep are often seen crossing the fire road that serves as the trail.

Blue Ridge Trail (Area A-14, Trip 2). Birds and animals typical of lodgepole-pine forests are found here.

Santa Catalina Island (Areas I-1 and I-2). "Wildlife" on the island includes hard-to-control populations of feral goats and boar, as well as bison.

APPENDIX 2: RECOMMENDED READING

Los Angeles Area Outdoor Guidebooks

California Coastal Commission, *California Coastal Access Guide,* University of California Press, 1983.

Gagnon, Dennis R., *Hike Los Angeles, Volumes 1 and 2,* Western Tanager Press, 1985.

Immler, Robert, *Mountain Bicycling in the San Gabriels,* Wilderness Press, 1987.

Immler, Robert, *Mountain Bicycling Around Los Angeles,* Wilderness Press, 1990.

Levy, Lou, ed., *Day Walks in the Santa Monica Mountains,* Santa Monica Mountains Task Force (Angeles Chapter of the Sierra Club), 1986.

McAuley, Milt, *Hiking Trails of the Santa Monica Mountains,* Canyon Publishing Company, 1987.

McAuley, Milt, *Hiking Trails of Malibu Creek State Park,* Canyon Publishing Company, 1983.

McAuley, Milt, *Hiking in Topanga State Park,* Canyon Publishing Company, 1984.

McAuley, Milt, *Hiking Trails of Point Mugu,* Canyon Publishing Company, 1982.

Robinson, John W., *Trails of the Angeles,* Wilderness Press, 1990.

Schaffer, Jeffrey P.; et al. *The Pacific Crest Trail, Volume 1: California,* Wilderness Press, 1989. (Includes log and maps of the Pacific Crest Trail in Los Angeles County.)

Wheelock, Walt, *Southern California Peaks,* La Siesta Press, 1973.

History and Natural History

Bakker, Elna S., *An Island Called California,* University of California Press, 1984.

Bailey, H.P., *The Climate of Southern California,* University of California Press, 1966.

Belzer, Thomas J., *Roadside Plants of Southern California,* Mountain Press Publishing Company, 1984.

California Coastal Commission, *California Coastal Resource Guide,* University of California Press, 1987.

Dale, Nancy, *Flowering Plants, The Santa Monica Mountains, Coastal & Chaparral Regions of Southern California,* Capra Press, 1986.

Jaeger, Edmond C. and Smith, Arthur C., *Introduction to the Natural History of Southern California,* University of California Press, 1971.

Mallan, Chicki, *Guide to Catalina and California's Channel Islands,* Moon Publications, 1988.

McPhee, John, "The Control of Nature, Los Angeles Against the Mountains" (parts I and II), *The New Yorker,* September 26 and October 3, 1988.

Munz, Philip A., *California Spring Wildflowers,* University of California Press, 1961.

Munz, Philip A., *California Mountain Wildflowers,* University of California Press, 1963.

Peterson, P. Victor, *Native Trees of Southern California,* University of California Press, 1966.

Raven, Peter H., *Native Shrubs of Southern California,* University of California Press, 1966.

Robinson, John W., *The San Gabriels, Southern California Mountain Country,* Golden West Books, 1977.

Robinson, John W., *The San Gabriels II, The Mountains from Monrovia Canyon to Lytle Creek,* Big Santa Anita Historical Society, 1983.

Robinson, John W., *Mines of the San Gabriels,* La Siesta Press, 1973.

Robinson, John W., *Mines of the East Fork,* La Siesta Press, 1980.

Saunders, Charles F., *The Southern Sierras of California* (abridged edition), Big Santa Anita Historical Society, 1984.

Sharp, Robert P., *Coastal Southern California* (geology guide), Kendall/Hunt Publishing Company, 1978.

Sharp, Robert P., *Geology Field Guide to Southern California,* William C. Brown Company, 1972.

Thrall, Will, ed., *Trails Magazine,* L.A. County Dept. of Recreation, Camps & Playgrounds, 1934–39; 1941.

Nature Study Guides published by the Nature Study Guild: *Pacific Coast Tree Finder, Pacific Coast Bird Finder, Pacific Coast Fern Finder, Mammal Finder.*

Maps and Map/Brochures

U.S. Geological Survey 7.5-minute topographic quadrangles (complete coverage of Los Angeles County).

Los Angeles Sheet, Bouguer Gravity Map, 1974, California Division of Mines and Geology. (This map supersedes the 1:250,000 scale Los Angeles geologic map on which it is based.)

Geologic Map of the San Bernardino Quadrangle, 1:250,000 scale, California Division of Mines and Geology, 1986.

Santa Monica Mountains and Rim of the Valley Corridor Park Lands, Santa Monica Mountains Conservancy. (A map and guide to public recreation and open space lands.)

Trail Map of the Santa Monica Mountains National Recreation Area, Western Section, Tom Harrison, 1987 (covers Point Mugu State Park, Leo Carrillo State Beach, and vicinity).

Hileman's Recreational and Geologic Map of Griffith Park, 1986

Trail Map of the Angeles High Country, Tom Harrison, 1990. (A topographic map covering an eastern portion of the Angeles National Forest.)

Trail Map of the Santa Monica Mountains National Recreation Area, Eastern Section, Tom Harrison, 1989 (a topographic map covering Topanga State Park and vicinity).

Angeles National Forest recreation map/brochure, 1985.

Trail Map for *Trails of the Angeles,* Wilderness Press, 1989. (This topographic trail map, included with the book Trails of the Angeles, is also sold separately.)

Six Hiking Trails to Mt. Wilson, Big Santa Anita Historical Society, 1983.

Hiking Trails of Mt. Baldy, Big Santa Anita Historical Society, 1986.

Catalina Conservancy Visitor Map & Guide

APPENDIX 3: LOCAL ORGANIZATIONS

The following is a partial list of outdoor and conservation organizations in Los Angeles County:

Sierra Club, Angeles Chapter
3550 West 6th Street, Suite 321
Los Angeles, CA 90020
(213) 387-4287

(The Angeles Chapter, with more than 50,000 members, has 13 regional "groups," numerous standing committees, and several special activities sections. Its outings program offers 200–300 hikes and backpack trips monthly, the majority of them in Los Angeles County. All outings are published in a three-times-yearly schedule distributed free to members and also available for purchase at outdoor equipment stores.)

Audubon Society, San Fernando Valley
P.O. Box 2504
Van Nuys, CA 91404
(818) 347-3205

Audubon Society, Los Angeles
7377 Santa Monica Blvd.
Los Angeles, CA 90046
(213) 876-0202

La Canada Flintridge Trails Council
P.O. Box 852
La Canada, CA 91011

California Native Plant Society
(818) 348-5910

Santa Monica Mountains Conservancy
(213) 456-5046

TreePeople
(818) 753-4600

William O. Douglas Outdoor Classroom
(213) 858-3834

APPENDIX 4: AGENCIES AND INFORMATION SOURCES

Angeles National Forest
(Supervisor's Office)
701 N. Santa Anita Ave.
Arcadia, CA 91006
(818) 577-0050

Angeles National Forest,
Arroyo Seco District (**ANF/ASD**)
Oak Grove Park
Flintridge, CA 91011
(818) 790-1151

Angeles National Forest,
Mt. Baldy District (**ANF/MBD**)
110 N. Wabash Ave.
Glendora, CA 91740
(818) 335-1251

Angeles National Forest,
Saugus District (**ANF/SD**)
30800 Bouquet Canyon Rd.
Saugus, CA 91350
(805) 252-9710

Angeles National Forest,
Tujunga District (**ANF/TD**)
12371 N. Little Tujunga Canyon Rd
San Fernando, CA 91342
(818) 899-1900

Angeles National Forest,
Valyermo District (**ANF/VD**)
29835 Valyermo Road
Valyermo, CA 93563
(805) 944-2187

Note: The above offices are open weekdays only. On weekends you can call or visit the following Forest Service visitor facilities:

Big Pines Visitor Center (619) 249-3504

Chantry Flats Information Station (818) 335-0712

Chilao Visitor Center (818) 796-5541

Clear Creek Information Station (818) 797-9959

Crystal Lake Visitor Center (818) 910-1149

Littlerock Entrance Station (805) 944-2424

Mt. Baldy Information Station (714) 982-2829

San Gabriel Canyon Information Station (818) 969-1012

Brand Park (**BP**)
(818) 956-2000

Charmlee Regional Park (**CRP**)
(213) 457-7247

Chilao Visitor Center (**CVC**)
(818) 796-5541

Cold Creek Canyon Preserve
(Mountains Restoration Trust)
(213) 456-5625

Department of Fish and Game (**DFG**)
(213) 620-4341

Devil's Punchbowl County Park (**DPCP**)
(805) 944-2743 or 944-9151

Eaton Canyon County Park (**ECCP**)
(818) 794-1866

Griffith Park (**GP**)
(213) 665-5188

Henninger Flats Fire Station (**HFFS**)
(818) 794-0675

Los Angeles City Recreation & Parks Dept.
(**LACRPD**)
(213) 485-5555

Los Angeles County Dept. of Parks and
Recreation (**LADPR**)
(213) 738-2961

Leo Carrillo State Beach (**LCSB**)
(818) 706-1310

Los Padres National Forest
Ojai District (**LPNF/OD**)
(805) 646-4348

Malibu Creek State Park (**MCSP**)
(818) 706-1310

National Park Service (**NPS**)
(Santa Monica Mountains National Recreation Area)
30401 Agoura Road, Suite 100
Agoura Hills, CA 91301
(818) 597-9192
(*Note:* ask about their free, quarterly publication that lists guided hikes and other
events held in the Recreation Area)

O'Melveny Park (**OP**)
(818) 368-5019

Placerita Canyon County Park (**PCCP**)
(805) 259-7721

Point Mugu State Park (**PMSP**)
(805) 499-2112

Palos Verdes Estates Shoreline Preserve
(**PVESP**)
(213) 378-0383

Royal Palms State Beach (**RPSB**)
(213) 372-2166

Santa Catalina Island/Cove and Camp
Agency (**SC/CC**)
(213) 510-0303

Santa Catalina Island office,
Los Angeles County Dept. of Parks and
Recreation (**SC/LACP**)
(213) 510-0688

Santa Monica Mountains Conservancy
(**SMMC**)
(213) 620-2021

Santa Monica Mountains National Recreation Area
(see "National Park Service")

Sierra Madre Police Department (**SMPD**)
(818) 355-1414

Santa Susana Mountain Park (**SSMP**)
(818) 884-9610

Topanga State Park (**TSP**)
(213) 454-8212

Vasquez Rocks County Park (**VRCP**)
(805) 268-0991

Will Rogers State Historic Park (**WRSHP**)
(213) 454-8212

INDEX